PROFESSIONAL ACCOUNTING

IN 25 COUNTRIES

Title:- # PROFESSIONAL ACCOUNTING

IN 25 COUNTRIES

*American Institute of Certified
Public Accountants.*

AICPA COMMITTEE ON INTERNATIONAL RELATIONS.

This book represents the individual views of many authors. Its publication by the American Institute of CPAs does not constitute official endorsement or approval of the opinions expressed.

TABLE OF CONTENTS

Country	*Chapter*

(continued on page vi)

APPENDIX

Illustrative Financial Statements

INTRODUCTION

The mounting volume of international investment, credit and trade has led to increasing demands for improvement and greater uniformity in international accounting and professional standards. These demands were voiced by many participants in the Eighth International Congress held in New York in September 1962.

The need for improved and more uniform international accounting and professional standards has also been expressed by representatives of international financing and lending institutions such as the World Bank, the International Finance Corporation, the Inter-American Bank, and various individual and corporate investors.

What Is Needed

"Uniformity" has been suggested as the desired objective by many of the proponents of improved international standards. Uniformity suggests that a single body of accounting principles, auditing standards and reporting practices be first defined and then adopted by agreement among members of an international committee comprised of the representatives of the profession from various countries—and eventually become generally accepted for use throughout the Free World. As a practical matter, it is most unlikely that even the most enthusiastic proponent of uniformity would, within the near future, agree to the voluntary relinquishment of the principles, standards and practices prevailing in his country in favor of a body of international principles. Even within each country there is a lack of uniformity, and, in some cases, there is considerable feeling that complete uniformity is not a desirable objective. However, it is reasonable to expect that over the ensuing years, in some respects and to some degree, uniformity will be attained.

In the meantime, what is needed to facilitate international trade and investment are financial statements that are reasonable, dependable, informative, meaningful and understandable, and upon which investors of one country can base reliable judgments of the financial position and earning capacity of an enterprise in another country.

This does not require a uniform code of international accounting principles and auditing standards—nor does it require the wholesale adoption by all nations of the principles, standards and practices that presently exist in any one country. Rather, it requires a greater understanding by the business community in every country of the accounting principles, auditing standards and reporting practices that prevail in the various countries of the world. With such understanding, investors in any country should be better able to analyze and understand financial statements originating in other countries and form reasonably reliable judgments from them.

A logical starting point would be the adoption of more informative disclosure practices, so that whatever the principles of accounting or the reporting practices used, they can be reconciled by the foreign reader with those with which he is the most familiar.

Furthermore, if the practice of using professional accountants of investing or lending countries is ever to be replaced by full reliance on the accounting professions of the borrowing countries, these latter countries must develop both stronger professions adhering to higher standards and a general public acceptance of the need for such development.

The Initial Approach

The Committee on International Relations believes that a prerequisite to constructive action in this direction is to assemble authoritative information concerning professional requirements, accounting principles, auditing standards and reporting practices in various countries. Such information will enable the determination of the main areas of differences between countries. In turn, consideration of these differences may indicate the matters to which study of international principles of disclosure should be directed.

Since the files of the several international firms of accountants represented on this Committee contain a great deal of the basic material, it seemed appropriate that this Committee initiate the assembling and the classification of the available data. This has been done by Gilbert R. Byrne, CPA, a member of the AICPA, assisted by a staff, and with the cooperation of many other interested persons.

Drafts of the sections relating to each country have been reviewed by the representatives of United States firms abroad and have also been submitted for review to the professional accounting organizations in these countries.

The sections on the various countries include descriptions of the accounting profession, auditing and reporting standards, and accounting principles. They also include brief descriptions of the several forms of business organizations and requirements for stock exchange listing and security offerings. These latter descriptions are neither exhaustive nor legally complete, since they are only intended to indicate the auditing, financial reporting and disclosure implications, which exist in the various corporate laws or commercial codes.

Finally, United States principles, standards and practices have been adopted as a frame of reference—not because they are necessarily more proper or correct than any other, but simply because one set of criteria is needed for purposes of comparison. Information pertaining to all other countries, therefore, is presented in comparison to that prevailing in the United States.

Observations on World Accounting

A precise summary comparison of professional standards and the reliability of financial statements among the twenty-five countries reported on here is obviously impractical, because the factors upon which judgment might be based are both voluminous and diverse.

Moreover, as indicated in the succeeding paragraphs, a nation's business, political and fiscal practices, and public attitudes toward them, are undoubtedly more influential in determining the stage of development of the accounting profession in each of such areas than are the formal requirements of Companies Acts or professional society pronouncements.

A highly developed, competent and respected public accounting profession cannot exist in a vacuum. There must first be a business and financial climate which creates a demand for its services on a higher level than mere bookkeeping or detection of errors or fraud. Such a climate is usually present in an advanced industrial society where demands for large-scale financing of operations and expansion are met through short-term banking operations or longer-term financing by public sale of securities. Under these conditions, it becomes imperative that lenders and shareholders have dependable financial information available. The professional opinions of trained and experienced independent public accountants supply this credibility upon which the public relies when furnished with financial statements of corporations. Public reliance is in direct relation to the reputation of the public accounting profession for integrity, competence and independence in the performance of its work.

Such a reputation comes through the practice of the local members of the profession and not by laws alone. It must also be said that in some countries the standards expressed through legal or professional channels represent more of a statement of goals than achievements, and the reader must consider whether practice conforms to precept. He should be aware that such conformity does not always exist.

This study, intended to identify the main areas of difference in professional requirements, accounting principles, auditing standards and reporting practices among the countries included, is only a beginning. It is the Committee's hope that this report will contribute to a greater understanding on the part of public accountants everywhere of the problems faced by members throughout the world.

COMMITTEE ON INTERNATIONAL RELATIONS
AMERICAN INSTITUTE OF
CERTIFIED PUBLIC ACCOUNTANTS

DONALD J. BEVIS	ANDREW PETERSEN
JOSEPH P. CUMMINGS	J. S. SEIDMAN
WILLIAM S. KANAGA	HARRY SONKIN
ROBERT L. LUTZ	THEODORE L. WILKINSON
ROBERT L. MAY	J. HARRY WILLIAMS

JAMES J. MAHON, *Chairman*

November, 1964

UNITED STATES OF AMERICA

1

2

UNITED STATES OF AMERICA

The chapter on the United States is presented first in the text because its principles, standards, and practices have been adopted as a frame of reference—not because they are necessarily more proper or correct than any other, but simply because one set of criteria is needed for purposes of comparison. Information pertaining to all other countries, therefore, is presented in comparison with that prevailing in the United States.

FORMS OF BUSINESS ORGANIZATION

The most common forms of business organization in the United States are the corporation, the partnership and the sole proprietorship. The rules governing each form of organization are embodied in the statutes of the several states. The legal profession has been instrumental in formulating several important uniform statutes which have been adopted by many of the states such as: the Uniform Partnership Act, the Uniform Limited Partnership Act, the Uniform Commercial Code and many others. A uniform corporation law has not as yet been adopted. Nevertheless, the corporation laws of most of the states are quite similar in many respects.

Corporations may be organized for profit or for charitable, educational or religious purposes. The comments in this section, however, are applicable to those corporations organized for profit. Many large United States companies of this type were incorporated in the state of Delaware; consequently, except where otherwise indicated, the statutes referred to are those of that state as being representative of those in most states. Ordinarily, however, a corporation organized under the laws of one state may do business in another state if it registers in the other state and meets certain other requirements.

The Corporation

Under the Delaware Corporation Law, a corporation may be formed by three or more persons for purposes of transacting any lawful business. A certificate of incorporation must be filed with the Secretary of the State of Delaware setting forth various particulars including the name of the corporation (which must include a reference to "incorporated, corporation, association, etc." or an abbreviation thereof, such as "Inc."), nature of the business, classes and numbers of shares of authorized stock, par value per share (if applicable), and dates of corporate existence.

According to the Delaware Corporation Law, the business of every corporation will be managed by a Board of Directors, the number of directors to be provided in the corporate by-laws but not less than three (unless the number of stockholders is less than three). Directors need not be stockholders unless so specified in the certificate of incorporation or in the by-laws. Every corporation will have a president, a secretary and a treasurer.

The liability of the stockholders of a corporation is generally limited to the amount of their subscribed capital, whether paid for or not. In general, stockholders can freely transfer their paid-up shares unless specifically prohibited from doing so by the corporate by-laws. The minimum required amount of capital with which a corporation can commence business is $1,000 in the State of Delaware.

State laws generally do not require a corporation to appoint auditors to furnish stockholders with periodic financial statements. A corporation, intending to raise capital by offering securities for sale to the public in more than one state for an aggregate sales price in excess of a prescribed minimum must meet the requirements of the Federal Securities Act of 1933. These requirements include the filing of appropriate financial statements, which in most cases are audited by an independent certified public accountant or an independent public accountant (see later section).

Audited financial statements are also required, both with the original listing application (Form 10) and with the annual reports (Form 10-K), by the Federal Securities Exchange Act of 1934 which regulates securities exchanges and trading in securities listed for trading on such exchanges. Under the 1964 Amendments to the Act, audited financial statements are required for certain unlisted companies (see later sections of this chapter). In addition to the above statutes, the New York Stock Exchange, in general, requires all listing applications for securities of corporations to contain financial statements certified by independent public accountants who are qualified under the laws of some state or country and requires all future annual reports published or sent to stockholders to contain similar certified financial statements. Other major stock exchanges have similar requirements.

It is customary for publicly held companies, whether listed on an exchange or not, and most other companies of any substance to include in the published annual report a report of an independent public accountant, containing an opinion as to the fairness of presentation of the financial statements (with a few important exceptions, such as many railroads, banks, and insurance companies).

The Partnership

The Uniform Partnership Act defines a partnership as "an association of two or more persons to carry on as co-owners a business for profit." The Uniform Partnership Act has been adopted by many of the states and most of the remaining states have adopted laws similar in many ways to the Act. Delaware has adopted the Uniform Partnership Act but not the Uniform Limited Partnership Act. The former applies to a general partnership in which all of the partners are jointly and severally liable for partnership debts. The latter applies to a limited partnership which consists of both general partners who have the same liability as partners in a general partnership, and limited partners whose liability is limited to the amount of capital contributed. All partnerships must register in the state, giving names of partners, their respective interests, whether general or limited and other information.

The Sole Proprietorship

Any person may engage in business on his own account in any of the states or the District of Columbia, but he should first ascertain whether a license is necessary to conduct the particular type of business and whether a fee or tax must be paid before commencing business. The liability of such a sole proprietorship is not limited to the assets of the business but extends to all the personal assets of the owner.

Other Forms of Business Organization

The joint-stock company is an association of persons who have been issued shares in the association but, unlike corporate stockholders, they are personally liable for debts of the association. In the case of business trusts, the trustees are similar to the Board of Directors of a corporation, except that they can be held personally liable to third parties for their actions. Both joint-stock companies and business trusts must file a certificate of incorporation with the appropriate state official.

Business Records

The representative Delaware Corporation Law, contains no specific requirement that books of account (e.g., general ledger and journal) must be maintained by a corporation. But certain other records must be maintained such as: a stock ledger book which lists stockholders' names, addresses, number of shares held, etc., and a stock transfer book.

The New York State Business Corporation Law specifically provides that each corporation will keep correct and complete books and records of account and minutes of the proceedings of its shareholders, board and executive committee. It must also maintain a stock ledger book and stock transfer book.

The United States Internal Revenue Code and regulations thereunder provide that every person (including business entities) subject to United States income taxes must keep such permanent books of account or records, including inventories, as are sufficient to establish the amount of gross income, deductions, etc., required to be shown in an income tax return.

THE ACCOUNTING PROFESSION

The Certified Public Accountant

The designation "Certified Public Accountant" (CPA) is conferred in the United States by each of the fifty states, the District of Columbia, the Virgin Islands, and Puerto Rico. In these jurisdictions, individual regulations govern the practice of accountancy and the issuance of CPA certificates. CPAs in all jurisdictions of the United States were estimated to number over 80,000 in 1964. New York state enacted the first CPA law in the United States in 1896, and that state has issued more certificates than any other. The regulations and requirements of New York state are among the most stringent of the fifty-three jurisdictions and are summarized in this section as illustrative of professional qualifications. Some significant variations in other jurisdictions are explained.

Professional Requirements. The Education Department of New York State administers the New York Education Law governing the accounting profession. This includes issuing New York certificates of certified public accountant. In summary, an individual is eligible for a New York CPA certificate if he:

Is a citizen of the United States or has declared an intention to become a citizen

Is at least twenty-one years of age and of good moral character

Is a resident of the state or has a place for regular transaction of business in the state (except an individual applying for indorsement of a certificate received from another state)

Has satisfactorily completed a four-year high school course approved by the Education Department of the State of New York or the equivalent

Has graduated from a college after completing a curriculum in accounting which has been registered by the State Education Department (such curriculum to include at least 24 semester hours in accounting, six in law, six in finance, and six in economics, unless fewer hours at the graduate level are approved by the Department), or has graduated from college and has the equivalent of college training in accountancy as determined by the New York State Commissioner of Education, or has at least fifteen years' experience in the practice of public accounting satisfactory to the Board of Examiners

Has passed the examination required by the Department of Education

Has completed three years of experience involving the diversified application of accounting principles and the diversified application of auditing procedures in the practice of public accountancy either on his own account, as a member of a copartnership or as an employee on the professional staff of one engaged in the practice of public accountancy.

Anyone receiving the certificate of certified public accountant from the State of New York is entitled to use the designation "certified public accountant" or the letters "CPA" in connection with his name.

Each state and territory of the United States and the District of Columbia administers a uniform CPA examination prepared and graded under the supervision of a nine-member board of examiners of the American Institute of CPAs. The examination consists of four subjects: theory of accounts, commercial law, accounting problems, and auditing.

The CPA requirements vary by states as to education and experience. Several jurisdictions require a high school education only. Some states waive educational requirements if certain experience requirements are met and the converse is true in other states. Nearly all states require some form of accounting experience for various periods of time, generally from two to four years. Many states require public accounting experience while other states may accept, in lieu thereof, either private or government experience or both.

The (Noncertified) Public Accountant

Accountancy may also be practiced in the United States by individuals licensed as "public accountants" (PAs), a second public accountancy group. In most of the fifty-three accountancy jurisdictions in the United States, a public accountant's license is or was issued based on an application for such a license and certain broad requirements as to the extent of an applicant's practice in accountancy. These licenses are not dependent on the successful completion of a professional examination or specified education.

In 1963, thirty-six of the fifty-three jurisdictions had laws dealing with public accountants. Several United States jurisdictions no longer issue licenses for public accountants. Only nine of the thirty-six jurisdictions with provisions for public accountants permit new registrations, while the other twenty-seven stipulate dates after which no new public accountants' licenses are to be issued. For example, 1961 was the terminal year for public accountants' licenses issued by the State of New York. Jurisdictions without public accountant legislation permit accountants to practice without registration.

Practice by Accountants from Other Countries

The American Institute of Certified Public Accountants recommended, in 1956, a form of regulatory public accountancy bill for adoption by the several states. Section 4, which deals with the registration of foreign accountants, together with the Institute's comment is:

> *Registration of Foreign Accountants.* The Board may, in its discretion, permit the registration of any person of good moral character who is the holder of a certificate, license, or degree in a foreign country constituting a recognized qualification for the practice of public accounting in such country. A person so registered shall use only the title under which he is generally known in his country, followed by the name of the country from which he received his certificate, license, or degree.

> #### Comment

> It is proposed by this section to give effect to a recommendation of the Executive Committee of the American Institute of Accountants made many years ago that a qualified professional accountant of a foreign country in possession of a certificate, license, or degree in his country constituting a recognized qualification for the practice of public accountancy and which is issued under acceptable professional standards be permitted to practice in this country subject

to such requirements as to registration or payment of fees as may be required and be permitted to use the title under which he is registered in his own country provided the country of its origin is indicated.

The laws of about half of the jurisdictions include this provision.

Organizations of Accountants

American Institute of Certified Public Accountants. The American Institute of Certified Public Accountants and its predecessors have a history dating back to 1887, when the American Association of Public Accountants was formed. In 1916, the American Association was succeeded by the Institute of Public Accountants, at which time there was a membership of 1,150. The name was changed to the American Institute of Accountants in 1917 and remained so until 1957 when the name was again changed to the American Institute of Certified Public Accountants. The American Society of Certified Public Accountants was formed in 1921 and acted as a federation of state societies. The Society was merged into the Institute in 1936, and, at that time, the Institute agreed to restrict its future members to CPAs. As of January 31, 1964, the Institute's membership totaled about 48,700, of which 33,300 were in public practice.

The Institute currently has 54 principal committees and boards which, among other duties, issue Institute pronouncements on accounting principles, auditing standards and procedures, and professional ethics.

The official publication of the Institute is *The Journal of Accountancy* which is published monthly and currently has a circulation of 105,000. It contains technical articles and general comments discussing matters of current interest to accountants, as well as pronouncements and actions of the important committees and the Council of the Institute.

State Societies of Certified Public Accountants. State societies of certified public accountants exist in each of the states and territories of the United States and the District of Columbia. Each society develops its own policies and conducts its own programs. Even though the American Institute exerts no control over the state societies, their policies are usually influenced by the Institute which maintains a committee on relations with state societies. Many state societies publish periodicals dealing with subjects of interest to their members and have committee structures resembling those of the Institute.

Other Organizations of Accountants. Other organizations in various fields of accounting in the United States are:

The National Society of Public Accountants. Members are primarily noncertified public accountants, who are licensed or registered accountants. The Society was formed in 1945, at which time it had 3,800 members. It currently has 11,000 members, 98 per cent of whom are engaged in public practice, either on a full- or part-time basis.

American Accounting Association. Members include accounting educators at the college or university level as well as many professional accountants.

The Institute of Internal Auditors. Members are typically employed by industrial and commercial companies and perform administrative or supervisory internal auditing functions.

Financial Executives Institute. Members are corporate management executives with accounting and financial responsibilities, including financial vice presidents, treasurers, and controllers.

National Association of Accountants. Members are largely accountants with industrial and commercial companies.

Federal Government Accountants Association

Ethics (American Institute of Certified Public Accountants)

The reliance of the public and the business community on sound financial reporting and advice on business affairs imposes an obligation to maintain high standards of technical competence, morality, and integrity on the public accounting profession. To this end, a member or associate of the American Institute of Certified Public Accountants must maintain independence of thought and action, hold the affairs of his clients in strict confidence, strive continuously to improve his professional skills, observe generally accepted auditing standards, promote sound and informative financial reporting, uphold the dignity and honor of the accounting profession, and maintain high standards of personal conduct.

Each member of the Institute is bound by the following AICPA Code of Professional Ethics, as amended March 3, 1964, and is subject to disciplinary actions for any violations:

ARTICLE 1: *Relations with Clients and Public*

1.01   Neither a member or associate, nor a firm of which he is a partner, shall express an opinion on financial statements of any enterprise unless he and his firm are in fact independent with respect to such enterprise.

Independence is not susceptible of precise definition, but is an expression of the professional integrity of the individual. A member or associate, before expressing his opinion on financial statements, has the responsibility of assessing his relationships with an enterprise to determine whether, in the circumstances, he might expect his opinion to be considered independent, objective and unbiased by one who had knowledge of all the facts.

A member or associate will be considered not independent, for example, with respect to any enterprise if he, or one of his partners, (a) during the period of his professional engagement or at the time of expressing his opinion, had, or was committed to acquire, any direct financial interest or material indirect financial interest in the enterprise, or (b) during the period of his professional engagement, at the time of expressing his opinion or during the period covered by the financial statements, was connected with the enterprise as a promotor, underwriter, voting trustee, director, officer or key employee. In cases where a member or associate ceases to be the independent accountant for an enterprise and is subsequently called upon to re-express a previously expressed opinion on financial statements, the phrase "at the time of expressing his opinion" refers only to the time at which the member or associate first expressed his opinion on the financial statements in question. The word "director" is not intended to apply to a connection in such a capacity with a charitable, religious, civic or other similar type of nonprofit organization when the duties performed in such a capacity are such as to make it clear that the member or associate can express an independent opinion on the financial statements. The example cited in this paragraph, of circumstances under which a member or associate will be considered not independent, is not intended to be all-inclusive.

1.02   A member or associate shall not commit an act discreditable to the profession.

1.03   A member or associate shall not violate the confidential relationship between himself and his client.

1.04   Professional service shall not be rendered or offered for a fee which shall be contingent upon the findings or results of such service. This rule does not apply to cases involving federal, state, or other taxes, in which the findings are those of the tax authorities and not those of the accountant. Fees to be fixed by courts or other public authorities, which are therefore of an indeterminate amount at the time when an engagement is undertaken, are not regarded as contingent fees within the meaning of this rule.

ARTICLE 2: *Technical Standards*

2.01   A member or associate shall not sign a report purporting to express his opinion as the result of examination of financial statements unless they have been examined by him, a member or an employee of his firm, a member or associate of the Institute, a member of a similar association in a foreign country, or a certified public accountant of a state or territory of the United States or the District of Columbia. (See paragraph following enumeration of these articles.)

2.02   In expressing an opinion on representations in financial statements which he has examined, a member or associate may be held guilty of an act discreditable to the profession if:

(a) he fails to disclose a material fact known to him which is not disclosed in the financial statements but disclosure of which is necessary to make the financial statements not misleading; or

(b) he fails to report any material misstatement known to him to appear in the financial statement; or

(c) he is materially negligent in the conduct of his examination or in making his report thereon; or

(d) he fails to acquire sufficient information to warrant expression of an opinion, or his exceptions are sufficiently material to negative the expression of an opinion; or

(e) he fails to direct attention to any material departure from generally accepted accounting principles or to disclose any material omission of generally accepted auditing procedure applicable in the circumstances.

2.03   A member or associate shall not permit his name to be associated with statements purporting to show financial position or results of operations in such a manner as to imply that he is acting as an independent public accountant unless he shall:

(a) express an unqualified opinion; or

(b) express a qualified opinion; or

(c) disclaim an opinion on the statements taken as a whole and indicate clearly his reasons therefor; or

(d) when unaudited financial statements are presented on his stationery without his comments, disclose prominently on each page of the financial statements that they were not audited.

2.04   A member or associate shall not permit his name to be used in conjunction with any forecast of the results of future transactions in a manner which may lead to the belief that the member or associate vouches for the accuracy of the forecast.

ARTICLE 3: *Promotional Practices*

3.01   A member or associate shall not advertise his professional attainments or services.

Publication in a newspaper, magazine or similar medium of an announcement or what is technically known as a card is prohibited.

A listing in a directory is restricted to the name, title, address and telephone number of the person or firm, and it shall not appear in a box, or other form of display or in a type or style which differentiates it from other listings in the same directory. Listing of the same name in more than one place in a classified directory is prohibited.

3.02   A member or associate shall not endeavor, directly or indirectly, to obtain clients by solicitation.

3.03   A member or associate shall not make a competitive bid for a professional engagement. Competitive bidding for public accounting services is not in the public interest, is a form of solicitation, and is unprofessional.

3.04   Commissions, brokerage, or other participation in the fees or profits of professional work shall not be allowed directly or indirectly to the laity by a member or associate.

Commissions, brokerage, or other participation in the fees, charges or profits of work recommended or turned over to the laity as incident to services for clients shall not be accepted directly or indirectly by a member or associate.

ARTICLE 4: *Operating Practices*

4.01   A firm or partnership, all the individual members of which are members of the Institute, may describe itself as "Members of the American Institute of Certified Public Accountants," but a firm or partnership, not all the individual members of which are members of the Institute, or an individual practicing under a style denoting a partnership when in fact there be no partner or partners, or a corporation, or an individual or individuals practicing under a style denoting a corporate organization shall not use the designation "Members of the American Institute of Certified Public Accountants."

4.02   A member or associate shall not allow any person to practice in his name who is not in partnership with him or in his employ.

4.03   A member or associate in his practice of public accounting shall not permit an employee to perform for the member's or associate's clients any services which the member or associate himself or his firm is not permitted to perform.

4.04   A member or associate shall not engage in any business or occupation conjointly with that of a public accountant, which is incompatible or inconsistent therewith.

4.05   A member or associate engaged in an occupation in which he renders services of a type performed by public accountants, or renders other professional services, must observe the by-laws and Code of Professional Ethics of the Institute in the conduct of that occupation.

4.06   A member or associate shall not be an officer, director, stockholder, representative, or agent of any corporation engaged in the practice of public accounting in any state or territory of the United States or the District of Columbia.

ARTICLE 5: *Relations with Fellow Members*

5.01   A member or associate shall not encroach upon the practice of another public accountant. A member or associate may furnish service to those who request it.

5.02   A member or associate who receives an engagement for services by referral from another member or associate shall not discuss or accept an extension of his services beyond the specific engagement without first consulting with the referring member or associate.

5.03   Direct or indirect offer of employment shall not be made by a member or associate to an employee of another public accountant without first informing such accountant. This rule shall not be construed so as to inhibit negotiations with anyone who of his own initiative or in response to public advertisement shall apply to a member or associate for employment.

As this book goes to press, a number of amendments to the Code of Professional Ethics were approved by appropriate committees and the Council of the AICPA and will be presented for full membership ballot. The most important of the proposed amendments, internationally, is the revision of Article 2.01, which reads *in its proposed form*:

A member or associate shall not express his opinion on financial statements unless they have been examined by him, or by a member or employee of his firm, on a basis consistent with the requirements of Rule 2.02.

In obtaining sufficient information to warrant expression of an opinion he may utilize, in part, to the extent appropriate in the circumstances, the reports or other evidence of auditing work performed by another certified public accountant, or firm of public accountants at least one of whom is a certified public accountant, who is authorized to practice in a state or territory of the United States or the District of Columbia, and whose independence and professional reputation he has ascertained to his satisfaction.

A member or associate may also utilize, in part, to the extent appropriate in the circumstances, the work of public accountants in other countries, but the member or associate so doing must satisfy himself that the person or firm is qualified and independent, that such work is performed in accordance with generally accepted auditing standards, as prevailing in the United States, and that financial statements are prepared in accordance with generally accepted accounting principles, as prevailing in the United States, or are accompanied by the information necessary to bring the statements into accord with such principles.

The committee on ethics of the AICPA has issued various numbered opinions on questions involving ethical conduct of members.

A member of the Institute is bound by the ethical rules under the Institute's by-laws which state that a member (or associate) renders himself liable to expulsion or suspension by the Institute's Trial Board if he infringes on any of the by-laws or any provision of the Code of Professional Ethics. The Trial Board consists of twenty-one members, none of whom may be a member of the committee on professional ethics.

The New York State Society of Certified Public Accountants has its own rules of professional ethics which are, with minor exceptions, similar to those of the American Institute. The other fifty-two societies also have codes of professional ethics which are generally similar to that of the American Institute.

Thirty-six of the fifty-three legal jurisdictions have statutes or regulations governing professional conduct of public accountants which, for the most part, are similar to the American Institute Code.

AUDITING STANDARDS

The AICPA's committee on auditing procedure issued "Statements on Auditing Procedure No. 33" in 1963. This statement codifies all of the earlier pronouncements of this committee, eliminating duplicate material. A substantial portion of this section is quoted or summarized from Statement No. 33.

Generally Accepted Auditing Standards

The "Statements on Auditing Procedure No. 33" defines auditing standards as differing from auditing procedures in that "procedures" relate to acts to be performed, whereas "standards" deal with measures of the quality of the performance of those acts and the objectives to be attained by the use of the procedures undertaken. Therefore, auditing standards concern themselves not only with the auditor's professional qualities, but also with the judgment exercised by him in the performance of his examination and in his report.

The generally accepted auditing standards as approved and adopted by the membership of the American Institute of Certified Public Accountants are:

General Standards

1. The examination is to be performed by a person or persons having adequate technical training and proficiency as an auditor.
2. In all matters relating to the assignment an independence in mental attitude is to be maintained by the auditor or auditors.
3. Due professional care is to be exercised in the performance of the examination and the preparation of the report.

Standards of Field Work

1. The work is to be adequately planned and assistants, if any, are to be properly supervised.
2. There is to be a proper study and evaluation of the existing internal control as a basis for reliance thereon and for the determination of the resultant extent of the tests to which auditing procedures are to be restricted.
3. Sufficient competent evidential matter is to be obtained through inspection, observation, inquiries and confirmations to afford a reasonable basis for an opinion regarding the financial statements under examination.

Standards of Reporting

1. The report shall state whether the financial statements are presented in accordance with generally accepted principles of accounting.
2. The report shall state whether such principles have been consistently observed in the current period in relation to the preceding period.
3. Informative disclosures in the financial statements are to be regarded as reasonably adequate unless otherwise stated in the report.
4. The report shall either contain an expression of opinion regarding the financial statements, taken as a whole, or an assertion to the effect that an opinion cannot be expressed. When an over-all opinion cannot be expressed, the reasons therefor should be stated. In all cases where an auditor's name

> is associated with financial statements the report should contain a clear-cut indication of the character of the auditor's examination, if any, and the degree of responsibility he is taking.

All members of the American Institute of Certified Public Accountants agree to observe these standards. Most by-laws or codes of professional ethics of state societies and state statutes dealing with professional conduct include similar standards.

Materiality. Statement No. 33 (AICPA) deals with the concept of materiality which is inherent in the work of the auditor. In considering a question of audit procedure or of application of accounting principles, the effect of the resulting decision on the fairness of presentation of the related financial statements must be taken into consideration. If it is determined that the result of such decision is not material, the auditing procedures followed may be modified, and the strict application of a preferred accounting principle may be waived.

No criteria have been set by the American Institute as to what constitutes materiality. This is left to the judgment of the independent auditor in the particular case after he has considered all contributing factors.

Independence. The second general standard requires that the auditor be "independent"; that is, he must maintain an attitude of impartiality and be without bias with respect to the client under audit. To be recognized as independent, he is expected to be free from any obligation to or interest in the client, its management, or its owners. The auditor must not only be independent; in fact, he must avoid situations that may lead outsiders to doubt his independence.

The profession has established through the Institute's Code of Professional Ethics precepts to guard against the presumption of loss of independence. The Securities and Exchange Commission has likewise emphasized the importance of independence by adopting similar rules.

To emphasize independence from management, many corporations follow the practice of having the independent auditor appointed by the Board of Directors or elected by the stockholders.

Evaluation of Internal Control. In the United States, great stress is placed on evaluation of the client's internal control. Internal control comprises the plan of organization and all of the coordinate methods and measures adopted within a business to safeguard its assets, check the accuracy and reliability of its accounting data, promote operational efficiency, and encourage adherence to prescribed managerial policies. The reliance which may be placed on existing internal control determines the extent of the tests to which auditing procedures may be restricted.

17

Evidential Matter—Confirmation and Observation. The Institute members voted in 1939 to establish confirmation of receivables by correspondence with debtors and observation of the taking of physical inventories as generally accepted auditing procedures, where they are practicable and reasonable and the assets concerned are material to financial position or results of operations.

When the auditing procedures of confirmation of receivables or the observation of the taking of inventories are not practicable or reasonable, the independent auditor may be able to satisfy himself by the application of other auditing procedures and so state in the scope section of his report. If, however, the independent auditor has not satisfied himself by the application of other auditing procedures, he discloses in his report the limitations of the scope of his examination and the reason for the omission of an essential procedure and qualifies his opinion or disclaims an opinion on the financial statements taken as a whole.

Timing of Audit Work. Many audit tests can be conducted at almost any time during the year. The independent auditor makes tests of the client's records, procedures and representations at interim dates, and the practice of carrying out a significant part of an examination during the year is acceptable. When internal control is effective at interim and examination dates, audit procedures as of the examination date may consist mainly of comparisons of year-end balances with those at prior dates, and review and investigation of unusual transactions and significant fluctuations.

Consistency. The independent auditor is required to state in his report whether the accounting principles applied in the period under examination are consistent with those applied in the preceding period. When a change has been made in the accounting principles employed during the year or years the independent auditor is reporting upon and the change has a material effect upon financial position or results of operations, he should refer in his opinion paragraph to a note to the financial statements which adequately describes the change and its effect, or describe adequately in his report the nature of the change and its effect. If the comparability of the statements is affected by changes in business or other conditions, fair presentation of the financial statements may require disclosure of these changes in notes to the statements.

Disclosure of Subsequent Events. The auditor is charged with considering subsequent events and requiring, as appropriate, adjustment of the accounts or disclosure of those matters essential to proper interpretation of the financial statements being presented. If subsequent information is acquired which would have been utilized had it been available at the balance-sheet date, appropriate adjustments should be made in the financial statement. Examples are collection of receivables, or settlement or determination of liabilities on a substantially different basis from that previously anticipated.

Subsequent events which have no direct effect on the financial statements of the prior year but have a material effect on how such statements should currently be interpreted do not require retroactive adjustment, but do call for disclosure. Examples are the sale of a capital stock issue or large bond issue with restrictive covenants, purchases of businesses, or serious damage from fire, flood or other casualty.

Subsequent events such as war, legislation, management changes, product changes, strikes, unionization, marketing agreements, and loss of important customers do not, of course, call for any adjustment of past financial statements and, more often than not, do not even require disclosure in current financial statements in footnotes. However, in some cases, their effect may be so significant as to require disclosure.

Short-form Report. The short-form report of the auditor is customarily used in connection with the basic financial statements (see page 23). It is also often included as part of a long-form report. The usual short-form report consists of a representation as to the work performed, expressed in an opening or "scope" paragraph, and a representation as to the independent auditor's conclusions usually in a closing or "opinion" paragraph.

The short-form report cited in the AICPA Statements on Auditing Procedure No. 33 as the form which "the profession in general has adopted" is:

> We have examined the balance sheet of X Company as of June 30, 19. . . ., and the related statement(s) of income and retained earnings for the year then ended. Our examination was made in accordance with generally accepted auditing standards, and accordingly included such tests of the accounting records and such other auditing procedures as we considered necessary in the circumstances.
>
> In our opinion, the accompanying balance sheet and statement(s) of income and retained earnings present fairly the financial position of X Company at June 30, 19. . . ., and the results of its operations for the year then ended, in conformity with generally accepted accounting principles applied on a basis consistent with that of the preceding year.

The independent auditor may be required to deviate from the standard short-form report because:

A. The scope of his examination is limited or affected:

1. By conditions which preclude the application of auditing procedures considered necessary in the circumstances
2. By restrictions imposed by clients
3. Because part of the examination has been made by other independent auditors.

B. The financial statements do not present fairly the financial position or results of operations because of:
   1. Lack of conformity with generally accepted accounting principles
   2. Inadequate disclosure.

C. Accounting principles are not consistently applied.

D. Unusual uncertainties exist concerning future developments, the effects of which cannot be reasonably estimated or otherwise resolved satisfactorily.

Where the independent auditor is unable to satisfy himself by the application of customary auditing procedures, he indicates clearly in the scope paragraph of his report the limitations on his work and, depending on the materiality of the amounts involved, he either qualifies his opinion or disclaims an opinion on the financial statements taken as a whole.

When an independent auditor believes that the presentation of a material item is at variance with generally accepted accounting principles, he qualifies his opinion or, if he regards the effect of such variance as sufficiently material, expresses an adverse opinion. An adverse opinion states specifically that the financial statements *"do not* present fairly" the financial position and results of operations in conformity with generally accepted accounting principles.

Long-form Report. While the accounting profession has generally adopted the short-form report in connection with financial statements intended for publication, auditors also issue a substantial number of so-called long-form reports. In addition to the basic financial statements, these reports ordinarily include details of the items in these statements, statistical data, explanatory comments, other informative material, some of which may be of a nonaccounting nature, and sometimes a description of the scope of the auditor's examination more detailed than the description in the usual short-form reports. In some cases both a long-form report and a short-form report are issued on the same engagement, but in many cases the long-form report constitutes the only report issued.

In issuing a long-form report, the auditor is expected to state whether or not the data other than the basic financial statements included in the long-form report have been subjected to the same examination as the information contained in the basic financial statements.

ACCOUNTING PRINCIPLES AND PRACTICES

Development of Accounting Principles

Generally accepted accounting principles, which are required by generally accepted auditing standards to be referred to in the independent auditor's report, have evolved over many years of professional accountancy practice in the United States. These principles are generally accepted because the business and financial communities, as well as members of the accounting profession, recognize and use them in financial statements of business enterprises. They have not been codified by a professional organization or a government agency.

Committees and boards of the AICPA lead in developing accounting principles through issuing bulletins, statements, opinions and recommendations. In addition to the AICPA, three other organizations have a major influence on the development and adoption of accounting principles in the United States: (1) United States Securities and Exchange Commission, (2) New York Stock Exchange, and (3) Internal Revenue Service of the United States Treasury Department.

American Institute of Certified Public Accountants. From 1939 to 1959, the Institute's committee on accounting procedure issued bulletins on various accounting matters. These bulletins, known as Accounting Research Bulletins or "ARBs," are the most widely accepted pronouncements on recommended accounting principles.

The Institute reorganized and expanded its research efforts in 1959, with the aim to specifically state the nature of generally accepted accounting principles and to determine appropriate practices. The Accounting Principles Board replaced the committee on accounting procedure. The status of opinions issued by the Board depends on general acceptance, the same as Accounting Research Bulletins. Operations of the Board include an expanded accounting research division of the AICPA to carry out and publish research studies authorized by the Board. The results of this formal accounting research are published as individual Accounting Research Studies for consideration by the Board, the profession as a whole, and the public. The Board may issue formal opinions on the subjects of these research studies and may issue additional opinions on current problems or accounting practices of general interest. The Council of the AICPA in May 1964 adopted a resolution to the effect that members of the AICPA should disclose in their reports material departures from an opinion of the Accounting Principles Board. This is subject to approval by the general membership of the Institute.

Securities and Exchange Commission. The SEC was created by the Securities Exchange Act of 1934, and administers a number of securities acts and regulates the sale of corporate securities to the public and the trading of securities. The SEC is empowered to prescribe the form and content of the financial statements included in prospectuses and in the annual reports filed with it. The Commission has sweeping authority to require the application of certain accounting principles, but it has not used this authority fully or issued detailed rules on accounting methods. A series of SEC accounting releases generally endorse the accounting principles accepted by the accounting profession. The policy of the SEC is to cooperate with the professional accounting organizations, including the AICPA, and support the development of accounting principles by the profession.

New York Stock Exchange. The New York Stock Exchange also has significantly influenced the acceptance of accounting principles through its control over the financial reports issued by corporations whose shares are listed on the Exchange. Special cooperating committees between the Exchange and the Institute laid the groundwork for the development of accounting principles in the United States. Like the SEC, the New York Stock Exchange maintains a close liaison with the accounting profession and with the AICPA.

The Internal Revenue Service. The Internal Revenue Code and regulations, rulings, and court decisions interpreting it influence accounting principles adopted in the United States. The "Lifo" method of pricing inventories is the only accounting method which must be used for financial accounting purposes if it is employed for income tax purposes. Tax allowable accounting procedures and methods for other items need not be recorded in the books and thus affect financial reports to stockholders only indirectly. Many taxpayers desire to minimize differences between tax accounting and accounting underlying financial statements and consequently use an advantageous tax method for both purposes.

Accounting Practices

Financial statements represent reporting based on accounting principles, practices, and methods adopted by an individual enterprise. No attempt is made here to distinguish between principles, practices, and methods. The term "practices" is generally used to include all three. It is also used with regard to presentation, classification, and disclosure of items in financial statements.

The purpose of this section is to briefly describe the usual financial statements presented in the United States and those generally accepted accounting practices which often differ from those accepted in one or more of the other countries in this study. Part of the discussion includes recommendations of the Committee on Accounting Procedure and the Accounting Principles Board of the AICPA.

Form and Content of Financial Statements

The form and content of financial statements have been developed and clarified over the years by the appropriate committees of the Institute, by writings of professional accountants and educators, and, significantly, by requirements of the SEC in its Regulation S-X, which deals with the financial statements required to be filed with the Commission. The New York Stock Exchange also has particular requirements applicable to financial statements of companies whose securities are listed on this Exchange.

Management has the primary responsibility for the fairness of representations made through financial statements. The independent auditor's responsibility for the statements he has examined is confined to the expression of his opinion on them. However, the independent auditor is expected to suggest form and content of presentation of financial statements.

Presentation of Statements. The basic financial statements presented in the United States are the balance sheet, the income statement, and a statement of retained earnings (earned surplus) which is combined with the income statement or presented separately. In addition, supplementary information is often furnished to meet special reporting requirements or circumstances. Recent developments indicate that a statement of source and application of funds will be included.

Customary forms of basic United States financial statements are described briefly in this section and illustrated in the appendix to this book.

Balance Sheet. The general balance sheet form used by commercial and industrial companies in the United States is the "statement" form, in which assets are listed on the left in order of liquidity, beginning with current assets and descending to properties, deferred charges and intangibles. The right side begins with current liabilities, continues with long-term liabilities and deferred credits, and concludes with the stockholders equity—capital stock, capital surplus items and retained earnings (earned surplus).

Some specific industries vary this format. As an example, regulated utilities show properties as the first assets on the left side of their balance sheets and capital accounts are presented as the first sections on the right side of their balance sheets.

Statement of Financial Position. An alternative acceptable form of balance sheet is the financial position form. In this form net assets are generally shown equal to stockholders equity. Accordingly, net assets represent current assets less current liabilities, plus other assets less other liabilities, less long-term indebtedness. A balance sheet of this format is usually titled statement of financial position or statement of financial condition.

Income Statement. Income statements are presented in either "single-step" or "multiple-step" form. The difference between the two forms is that the multiple-step arrangement shows a number of intermediate balances such as gross profit on sales, income from operations and income before federal income taxes, whereas the single-step form consists of one grouping for revenues less a total of the expense groupings. All income statements normally show sales, cost of products sold, depreciation, selling, general and administrative expenses, other income, other deductions, federal income taxes and net income for the period. Substantial income or expense items are segregated in the income statement.

Statements of retained earnings, whether combined with income statements or not, are essentially reconciliations of retained earnings at the beginning and end of the period. A statement of changes in capital surplus may be given, or the information may be disclosed by footnote.

Notes to Financial Statements (Footnotes). Common practice in the United States is to disclose certain essential information in notes to financial statements. These notes are an integral part of the financial statements but cannot be a substitute for proper accounting treatment in the statements.

Notes to financial statements may be classified into the following types:

Financial and accounting data—information needed by the reader to obtain a fair understanding of the statements, such as the bases on which assets are stated, principles of consolidation, and descriptions of accounting methods for depreciation and amortization, tax accounting, or pension plans.

Restrictions and liens—provisions of debt or preferred stock agreements restricting the payment of dividends or requiring the maintenance of specified working capital; assets pledged against loans; foreign currency not realizable in United States currency

Commitments of an unusual nature—description of long-term leases; extraordinary commitments for plant or other expansion; compensation and stock option plans

Contingencies—descriptions of status of lawsuits, tax controversies, and assets and liabilities of uncertain amount

Changes in application of accounting principles—while disclosure of a change in the application of accounting principles having a material effect on the financial statements is required in the opinion of the independent auditor, the nature and effect of the change are ordinarily described in a note referred to in the opinion or, if necessary, described in the opinion itself

Events subsequent to the balance-sheet date, other than those recognized in the accounts.

The SEC emphasizes the importance of notes to financial statements, and in its own reporting requirements makes clarification by footnotes mandatory in certain instances.

Funds Statement. A statement of source and application of funds shows how financial resources were employed during the period covered by the financial statements. The form of the fund statements varies with the relative importance of respective financial events. Significant changes in individual current assets and current liabilities are shown separately whenever they are not disclosed adequately in the financial statements.

Comparative Financial Statements. It has become common practice that published financial statements included in reports to stockholders be shown in comparison with those of the preceding year. In many cases several years' summaries of earnings are given. The New York Stock Exchange for many years has required comparative financial statements in listing applications.

Consolidated Financial Statements. A corporation which owns or controls one or more other corporations customarily prepares consolidated financial statements. This procedure is adopted to present the financial position and results of operations of an entire enterprise. Institute pronouncements recommend presenting consolidated statements, and both the New York Stock Exchange and SEC generally require this practice.

In general, consolidated financial statements combine the parent company and all majority-owned subsidiaries, except in special circumstances. Intercompany balances and transactions are eliminated in preparing consolidated statements. Minority interests in subsidiary companies are presented on the credit side of the consolidated balance sheet between the liabilities and stockholders' equity sections; the amounts represent proportionate shares in the subsidiaries' net assets. Minority interests in earnings are shown as a separate deduction in the consolidated income statement.

Current Assets

Current assets designate cash and other assets or resources which are expected to be realized in cash or sold or consumed during one year or within the normal operating cycle of the business if this is longer than one year. The operating cycle of a business is considered to be the average time intervening between the acquisition of materials or services and the realization of cash from the sale of products or services.

Marketable Securities. Marketable securities classified as current assets exclude investments in securities or advances made for purposes of control, affiliation or other continuing business advantage and also exclude those held for special purposes. Marketable securities are usually stated at cost with current market value disclosed. The carrying amount is generally reduced to a lower market value only when a decline in the market price seems permanent.

Receivables. Receivables not collectible within one year from the date of the balance sheet are excluded from current assets, except that long-term installment notes and accounts may be classified as current assets if they conform generally to normal trade practices and terms within the industry. Unearned carrying and interest charges on installment accounts are shown in the balance sheet as a deduction from the related receivables.

Receivables from affiliated and subsidiary companies, employees, officers, directors, stockholders, and those arising from transactions outside the ordinary course of business are separately designated. Also shown separately are deposits, advances, interest and amounts receivable for returned purchases and claims. When receivables from other than trade debtors are not significant, they are usually grouped in one amount described as "accounts receivable—other."

Allowance for Doubtful Receivables. An allowance for doubtful receivables is an appropriate expense of the period and accumulated allowances are deducted from the related receivables in the balance sheet. The amount of a current allowance is determined on the basis of collection experience and the status of outstanding receivables in order to state total receivables at the estimated realizable amount.

Inventories. The components of inventory—finished goods, work in process, and raw materials and supplies—are generally shown separately in the balance sheet or a note to the financial statements. The basis of determining the amounts is disclosed and, to the extent practicable, the method of determining cost is indicated.

Chapter 4 of Accounting Research Bulletin No. 43 sets forth and discusses the various general principles applicable to accounting for inventories in the United States. The more important of ten summary statements are:

> The term *inventory* is used herein to designate the aggregate of those items of tangible personal property which (1) are held for sale in the ordinary course of business, (2) are in process of production for such sale, or (3) are to be currently consumed in the production of goods or services to be available for sale.

> The primary basis of accounting for inventories is cost, which has been defined generally as the price paid or consideration given to acquire an asset. As applied to inventories, cost means in principle the sum of the applicable expenditures and charges directly or indirectly incurred in bringing an article to its existing condition and location.

> Cost for inventory purposes may be determined under any one of several assumptions as to the flow of cost factors (such as first-in first-out, average, and last-in first-out); the major objective in selecting a method should be to choose the one which, under the circumstances, most clearly reflects periodic income.

> A departure from the cost basis of pricing the inventory is required when the utility of the goods is no longer as great as its cost. Where there is evidence that the utility of goods, in their disposal in the ordinary course of business, will be less than cost, whether due to physical deterioration, obsolescence, changes in price levels, or other causes, the difference should be recognized as a loss of the current period. This is generally accomplished by stating such goods at a lower level commonly designated as *market*.

> As used in the phrase *lower of cost or market* [or equally acceptable *cost or market, whichever is lower*] the term *market* means current replacement cost (by purchase or by reproduction, as the case may be) except that:
> (1) Market should not exceed the net realizable value (i.e., estimated selling price in the ordinary course of business less reasonably predictable costs of completion and disposal); and
> (2) Market should not be less than net realizable value reduced by an allowance for an approximately normal profit margin.

> Accrued net losses on firm purchase commitments for goods for inventory, measured in the same way as are inventory losses, should, if material, be recognized in the accounts and the amounts thereof separately disclosed in the income statement.

Prepaid Expenses. Expenses such as insurance, interest, and taxes that are paid in advance may be included in current assets, except that any material portion of such prepaid expenses that will not be used or absorbed within one year or within the operating cycle of the business is classified as a noncurrent asset.

Intercorporate Investments

Accounting Research Bulletin No. 51 states that the preferable method of accounting for investments in unconsolidated subsidiaries and in consolidated financial statements is to include the controlling company's share of net income or loss of the subsidiaries in consolidated income. This method is used except when one or more subsidiaries were excluded from consolidation because of exchange restrictions or other reasons which create doubt that an increase in equity has accrued to the controlling company.

A common alternative acceptable practice is to carry investments in subsidiaries at cost and to include in income dividends received. However, provision should be made for any material impairment of these investments, such as losses sustained by the subsidiaries, unless the impairment is deemed to be temporary. When the cost method is followed, the consolidated statements should disclose, in addition to the cost of investments in unconsolidated subsidiaries, the equity in their net assets, the dividends received from them in the current period, and the equity in their earnings for the current period.

Property, Plant and Equipment

Property, plant and equipment is generally recorded at cost. Cost includes all direct expenditures necessary to purchase or construct the property and make it usable: the invoice or contract amount, materials, supplies, labor, and related overhead employed in construction or installation, preliminary engineering studies, and title costs. The inclusion in costs of interest on funds used for construction during the construction period is acceptable but not a general practice except by certain industries, principally regulated utilities.

Nondepreciable property, such as land and idle property, is usually segregated in financial statements. The costs of all other property, plant, and equipment are assigned systematically to operations over their estimated useful lives using specific methods of depreciation and depletion. The accumulated allowances for depreciation and depletion are deducted from the cost of properties in the balance sheet.

Depreciation. Three principal methods of depreciation are used currently in the United States: (1) straight-line, (2) declining-balance, and (3) sum-of-the-years-digits. Another depreciation method used primarily in extractive industries is unit-of-production. All four are permissible for income tax purposes. Depending on individual circumstances, a company may use one method for some of its assets and another method for other assets. An appropriate method is selected based on factors such as industry, type of property, and useful life of property.

Lump sum write-offs may be appropriate in special situations, such as sudden obsolescence or changes in business operations or policies.

Depletion. Depletion, as an accounting term, is amortization of the cost of investment in natural resources by charges to operations over the period during which the quantities or units of such resources are extracted or exhausted. Generally, any one of several methods of computation is acceptable if the depletable base (cost plus certain development expense) is periodically charged to income on a systematic basis. Percentage depletion, a specific method allowed for income tax purposes, is not a generally accepted accounting practice because the amount of depletion under this method is computed as a percentage of income (as defined) from the depletable property and is not related to its cost.

Intangibles and Deferred Charges

Cost is ordinarily the initial amount assigned to all types of intangibles. The cost of some intangibles, such as those acquired in exchange for securities, may be either the fair value of the consideration given or the fair value of the property or right acquired, whichever is the more clearly evident.

Intangibles with limited life (such as patents, copyrights, and franchises) are amortized by systematic charges to income over the period benefited. Intangibles with unlimited life (such as goodwill and trade names) are carried in the balance sheet at cost until their lives are determined to be limited or are amortized by systematic charges to income. When reasonably evident that the life of unamortized intangibles becomes limited, their cost is amortized by systematic charges to income. It is not acceptable to make lump sum write-offs of intangibles to retained earnings immediately after acquisition or to charge the cost or amortization of intangibles to capital surplus.

Deferred charges include unamortized debt discount and expense, deferred research and development costs, organization costs, and prepaid expenses which will not be used or absorbed within one year of the operating cycle of the business.

Current Liabilities

Current liabilities include obligations for items entering into the operating cycle which result in accounts payable for materials purchased, accruals of wages, rentals, taxes and like items. There are also included estimated or accrued amounts for known obligations payable within the year, even though the amounts can be determined only approximately or the payee is unknown at the balance-sheet date.

Loans and Debt. The portion of long-term debt payable within one year is classified as a current liability unless it is clear that the amount is to be refinanced through other long-term debt. Obligations to banks, demand loans and notes payable to others are either shown separately in the balance sheet or are combined with details disclosed in a note.

Severance Pay. Neither federal nor state statutes provide for mandatory severance pay. Many companies adopt a policy to pay extra compensation to salaried employees on severance and account for the amounts as expense when paid. Union contracts frequently provide that "supplemental employment benefits" computed on various bases be paid to separated employees; many companies provide currently for an estimated related liability.

Unearned Revenues. Unearned revenues collected in advance, such as rents, royalties, and subscriptions, are allocated to income as earned, usually based on time or performance. That portion of unearned revenues which is applicable to the next year or relates to current assets is usually included in current liabilities. The remaining portions are commonly classified as noncurrent items.

Contingency Provisions

Under United States accounting principles, it is deemed desirable to provide, by charges in the current income statement, properly classified, for all forseeable costs and losses applicable against current revenues, to the extent that they can be measured and allocated to fiscal periods with reasonable approximation. But it is not considered proper to permit income to be affected by reserve transactions not related to current operations.

The AICPA committee on accounting procedure was of the opinion that reserves such as those created: (a) for general undetermined contingencies, or (b) for any indefinite possible future losses, such as, for example, losses on inventories not on hand or contracted for, or (c) for the purpose of reducing inventories other than to a basis which is in accordance with generally accepted accounting principles, or (d) without regard to any specific loss reasonably related to the operations of the current period, or (e) in amounts not determined on the basis of any reasonable estimates of costs or losses are of such a nature that charges or credits relating to such reserves should not enter into the determination of net income.

However, reserves of this nature or for general corporate purposes may be appropriated from retained earnings. This action, of course, has no effect on current results of operations, but merely segregates retained earnings as appropriated and unappropriated in the stockholders' equity section of the balance sheet.

Accordingly, it was the opinion of the committee that if a reserve of the type described above is set up:

1. It should be created by a segregation or appropriation of earned surplus.
2. No costs or losses should be charged to it and no part of it should be transferred to income or in any way used to affect the determination of net income for any year.
3. It should be restored to earned surplus directly when such a reserve or any part thereof is no longer considered necessary.
4. It should preferably be classified in the balance sheet as a part of shareholders' equity.

Capital Surplus

The term "capital surplus" is frequently used to describe capital in excess of par or stated value of capital stock. More precise terminology describing sources and avoiding the word surplus is recommended by the AICPA. Typical appropriate designations are:

Additional paid-in capital

Excess of proceeds of sale over cost of treasury stock

Capital in excess of par or stated values

Excess of market value of stock dividend over par or stated value of shares issued

Capital arising from reduction in par or stated value of capital stock.

Treasury Stock

Treasury stock is generally recorded at cost and shown separately as a reduction of total capital stock, capital surplus and retained earnings. Treasury stock may be classified as an asset if held for a specific corporate purpose, such as stock option, stock purchase, or profit-sharing plans.

Stock Options

Options to purchase shares of common stock of companies are often granted to directors, officers, or certain key employees of such companies. Option prices are generally set to realize maximum tax benefits to the grantees, which means that the option prices are usually at or near the market price at the date options are granted. Any element of compensation is generally not recorded in the accounts. Usual practice is to record as capital the amount of cash received when options are exercised and respective shares of stock issued.

The AICPA recommends that financial statements disclose the status of options or option plans at the end of the period stating the number of shares under option, the option prices, and the number of shares for which options were exercisable. The number and option prices of shares issued for options exercised during the period covered by the financial statements should also be disclosed. The New York Stock Exchange and SEC require still further disclosure.

Stock Dividends

Under United States definitions, stock distributions to existing stockholders are considered "stock dividends" when the newly issued shares are less than about 20 to 25 per cent of the number of shares previously outstanding. If a distribution exceeds these percentages, it is considered a "stock split-up" and usually capital stock amounts are unchanged because any par or stated value may be reduced proportionately.

A *publicly* held company in the United States issuing a stock dividend, transfers from retained earnings to capital stock and capital surplus, an amount equal to the fair value of the additional shares issued. This accounting practice recognizes that many recipients regard stock dividends as distributions of corporate earnings usually in an amount equal to the fair market value of the distributed shares. A stock split-up requires transfer from retained of only the amount necessary to meet legal requirements for par or stated value of total shares of stock.

Receipt of a stock dividend is not considered income in the United States. The recipient's investment is representd by an increased number of shares and the carrying amount is unchanged.

Retained Earnings

Retained earnings (earned surplus) are accumulated, undistributed earnings. Unappropriated retained earnings are normally available as a source of dividends. Negative retained earnings are called "deficit."

Capital surplus, however created, is not used to relieve the income account of charges from operations, and capital stock and capital surplus, whatever their nature, are not used to increase retained earnings.

Hidden Reserves

The term "hidden reserves" implies the existence of ownership equity concealed through the understatement or omission of assets, the overstatement of liabilities or inclusion of fictitious liabilities. In the United States, it is not considered acceptable to establish hidden reserves by charges to current income with possible restoration to income in a later year or with a view to leveling out reported income over the years.

Net Income

Income statements in the United States conclude with an amount of net income (or loss) for the period. The term "income" is used to describe a conventional general concept. Amounts reported as net income are based on the concept that an enterprise is a going concern and that unrealized gains are not recorded but all losses are recorded when foreseeable.

The question of what constitutes the most practically useful concept of net income for a period has been dealt with in Chapter 8 of the Accounting Research Bulletin No. 43 as follows:

> ... there should be a general presumption that all items of profit and loss recognized during the period are to be used in determining the figure reported as net income. The only possible exception to this presumption relates to items which in the aggregate are material in relation to the company's net income and are clearly not identifiable

with or do not result from the usual or typical business operations of the period. Thus, only extraordinary items such as the following may be excluded from the determination of net income for the year, and they should be excluded when their inclusion would impair the significance of net income so that misleading inferences might be drawn therefrom:

(a) Material charges or credits (other than ordinary adjustments of a recurring nature) specifically related to operations of prior years, such as the elimination of unused reserves provided in prior years and adjustments of income taxes for prior years;

(b) Material charges or credits resulting from unusual sales of assets not acquired for resale and not of the type in which the company generally deals;

(c) Material losses of a type not usually insured against, such as those resulting from wars, riots, earthquakes, and similar calamities or catastrophes except where such losses are a recurrent hazard of the business;

(d) The write-off of a material amount of intangibles;

(e) The write-off of material amounts of unamortized bond discount or premium and bond issue expenses at the time of the retirement or refunding of the debt before maturity.

The following, however, should be excluded from the determination of net income under all circumstances:

1. Adjustments resulting from transactions in the company's own capital stock;

2. Amounts transferred to and from accounts properly designated as surplus appropriations, such as charges and credits with respect to general purpose contingency reserves;

3. Amounts deemed to represent excessive costs of fixed assets, and annual appropriations in contemplation of replacement of productive facilities at higher price levels; and

4. Adjustments made pursuant to a quasi-reorganization.

Pension Costs

Accounting methods for costs and liabilities under pension plans in the United States are varied because the provisions and financing arrangements for the plans are diverse. Accounting Research Bulletin No. 47 expresses a preference for the accrual method of accounting for pension costs, which recognizes that costs of current and future services begín to accrue from the moment of the adoption of a plan and continue to accrue so long as the plan is in effect. In recognition of varying practices, the committee recommended that as a minimum the liability in the balance sheet together with the fund held by trustees or annuity contracts purchased should be sufficient to meet the liabilities for pensions already vested.

Pension costs based on past service (services rendered prior to adoption of the pension plan) are generally charged to income in periods subsequent to the adoption of a plan. AICPA statements recommend that costs based on past service should be amortized over the current and future service lives of employees. Generally, the minimum period permitted for federal income tax purposes is ten years and many corporations desire to avoid wide differences between book and tax treatments. Two bases of accounting for these costs have evolved: (1) a period of ten years and (2) a period representing an average of the remaining service lives of employees.

When a plan involving material costs is adopted or amended, it is necessary to disclose in a note to financial statements the important features of the plan or amendment, including the proposed method of funding or paying, the estimated annual charge to operations, and basis on which such annual charge is determined. Financial statements also disclose any changes in accounting procedures and any material costs based on past or current services for which no provision was made.

Tax-effect Accounting

Taxes are allocated when the difference between income for federal tax purposes and income for financial reporting purposes is material, thus producing a difference between the current tax obligation and the amount obtained by applying the current tax rate to accounting net income.

In general, the AICPA recommendations on tax allocation are:

1. Eliminate from income and allocate to retained earnings the tax effect of items credited or charged to retained earnings. For example, when substantial gains or losses on dispositions of property are recorded directly in retained earnings, the related increase or decrease in income tax for the period is recorded directly in retained earnings.

2. Recognize the tax effect of transactions included in taxable income but not includable in accounting income until a later period by adjusting accounting income and deferring the tax effect in

the balance sheet. For example, if a material item, such as accelerated depreciation, is deducted for tax purposes and not recorded in the accounts, the tax benefit is deferred. Also, advance rent is taxed when collected and the tax effect is deferred until respective rent revenue is recognized in the income statement.

3. Recognize the future tax effect of transactions included in accounting income but not includable in taxable income until a later period by adjusting accounting income and deferring the future tax effect in the balance sheet. For example, certain costs and expenses, such as deferred compensation and product warranties, are deductible for tax purposes when paid rather than when provided in the accounts and the future tax reduction may be included in income in the same period as the provision for the cost.

Investment Credit

The Revenue Act of 1962 (as amended by the 1964 Act), provides for an "investment credit" as an offset to income tax liability. In general, the credit equals a specified percentage of the cost of certain newly acquired depreciable assets. APB Opinion No. 4 recognizes two methods of accounting for the investment credit: (a) the credit may be reflected in net income over the productive life of the acquired property, or (b) the credit may be treated as a reduction of federal income taxes for the year in which the credit arises. The Board expressed a preference for method (a). The SEC also recognizes both methods but considers the (b) method preferable.

Long-term Construction Contracts

Two generally accepted accounting methods commonly followed by contractors in recognizing long-term construction contract revenue are:

1. The percentage-of-completion method, which recognizes as revenue the portion of estimated total revenue equal to the ratio of costs incurred to date to total estimated costs. This method recognizes revenue currently and reflects the status of uncompleted contracts, but is necessarily dependent on estimates.

2. The completed contract method, which recognizes revenue when the contract is completed. This method recognizes final results only and results of operations are not recognized currently.

When estimates of costs to complete a contract and the extent of progress toward completion are reasonably dependable, the percentage-of-completion method is preferred. Under either method, provision should be made for any anticipated losses.

International Operations and Foreign Exchange

Earnings of United States companies from international sources are includable in income to the extent to which they are received in the United States or represent unrestricted funds available for remittance. International earnings in excess of such amounts are included in income only after careful consideration of all the facts, and the amount is disclosed, if significant.

Whether or not foreign subsidiaries are included in consolidated statements, adequate information must be furnished concerning their assets and liabilities, income and losses, and the parent's equity therein.

Realized gain or loss from translating accounts expressed in foreign currencies should be recognized in income statements. Any unrealized losses, such as may arise from translating foreign net current assets, are charged to income. However, unrealized gains are deferred to the extent that they exceed prior provisions for unrealized losses.

Price-level Accounting

It is not customary in the United States to record the effects of price-level changes in the accounts or in the formal published financial statements of business enterprises. The importance of the effect of price-level changes, especially on the statement of income, has long been recognized, and numerous articles and studies on the subject have been published, including bulletins of the AICPA and an AICPA research study. The Institute supports the publication, as supplementary statistical data, of financial schedules, explanations, or notes by which management may explain and illustrate the need to retain earnings because of price-level changes. This procedure is not yet common, but a few corporations have experimented with some form of reporting on price-level changes.

Bases of Accountability for Enterprises

Business Combinations. Groups of stockholders may decide to combine their respective corporations. Two accounting bases are recognized for combinations—pooling of interests among the constituent corporations and purchase of one or more corporations by another.

In a pooling of interests, corporations are combined by an agreed upon exchange of shares. No new basis of accountability arises and the book values of each corporation are carried forward to the combined enterprise. Generally, retained earnings of the constituent companies continue as the retained earnings of the combined enterprise. The requisites to a pooling of interests specified by the AICPA are, among others, the combination and continuity of existing ownership interests.

A combination of businesses may also be effected through purchase of one corporation's assets by another corporation for cash or other consideration. In a purchase, some existing stockholders interests are eliminated or other factors requisite to a pooling of interests are not present. Under these circumstances, a new basis of accountability is created based on the consideration paid. Assets acquired in a purchase are recorded at the consideration directly or indirectly paid to achieve the business combination. Ordinarily, such consideration is allocated to the assets acquired on the basis of their relative fair values. This accounting frequently results in recording an intangible asset called goodwill.

REQUIREMENTS FOR PUBLIC ISSUE OF SECURITIES

With certain exceptions, companies offering securities for sale to the public must file a Registration Statement with the Securities and Exchange Commission under the Securities Act of 1933. The exceptions include offerings of which the aggregate offering price does not exceed $300,000, securities of governmental units, and those of certain common carriers, such as interstate railroads.

The Registration Statement consists of two parts—the Prospectus, which must be furnished to the buyer of the registered security, and a second part containing information not required in the Prospectus. The principal financial statements are contained in the Prospectus, whereas certain supporting schedules appear in Part II.

In general, a balance sheet is required as of a date within ninety days of the filing of the Registration Statement, or under certain conditions, within six months of such date. If this balance sheet is not certified by an independent public accountant, a certified balance sheet at the close of the fiscal year ending within one year prior to the filing date must be filed. Also, income and surplus statements must be filed for the three fiscal years preceding the date of the latest certified balance sheet and must be certified; in addition, uncertified income and surplus statements are required for the period from the close of the fiscal year to the date of the latest (uncertified) balance sheet filed and also for the corresponding interim period of the preceding fiscal year. In addition to certain other information, Part II of the Registration Statement includes schedules containing details of balance sheet and income statement items, some of which must also be certified.

If the company has subsidiaries, there must be filed consolidated financial statements and schedules at the same dates and for the same periods as those for the parent company, and similar reports of independent public accountants must accompany them. When consolidated financial statements are filed, unconsolidated financial statements of the parent company may be omitted under certain specified conditions.

In practically all cases, and for many years in the past, the sale of securities to the public has been underwritten by firms of investment bankers. Even before the passage of the Securities Act of 1933, it was general custom that prospectuses contain financial statements certified by independent certified public accountants. While the SEC requires a summary of earnings for at least five years to be included in the prospectus, such summary is not required to be certified. In practice, however, underwriters usually require that the summary of earnings be certified for at least that period (usually three years) for which the more detailed income statements required by the SEC must be certified.

In addition to the requirements of the Securities and Exchange Commission, and the matters included on advice of the underwriters and their counsel, prospectuses offering securities for sale in many states must comply with the respective state statutes, known as "Blue Sky" laws. These laws have been in effect in every state except Delaware and Nevada for many years; they vary among the states and often require information differing from that required by the SEC.

REQUIREMENTS FOR LISTING SECURITIES ON STOCK EXCHANGES

The Securities Exchange Act of 1934 governs the registration of national securities exchanges, securities listed on such exchanges, and brokers and dealers trading in the over-the-counter securities markets.

A corporation seeking to list its securities for trading on a national securities exchange must comply with two sets of requirements, those of the securities exchange and those of the SEC. In most respects, the information required is similar or identical. The SEC requires that a corporation prepare an application for registration of its securities under the 1934 Act which application is filed with the securities exchanges on which the corporation is to be listed, and also with the Commission. The SEC also requires the filing of annual reports by each listed company which are designed to give the public annual financial information about the company.

In addition, listed corporations must comply with listing and annual reporting requirements of the various exchanges on which they are listed, the most stringent of which are the requirements of the New York Stock Exchange.

Under the listing agreement of that Exchange, the company undertakes to publish annual reports, notify the Exchange of changes in the company's practices, and numerous other matters. It is also required that all financial statements submitted to stockholders be audited by independent accountants qualified under the laws of some state or country and be accompanied by the independent accountant's opinion. Exception has been made to this requirement in the case of railroads, banks and insurance companies, which are supervised by government agencies.

REPORTING REQUIREMENTS FOR UNLISTED COMPANIES

Under the Securities Acts Amendments of (August) 1964, many companies whose securities are not listed on a National Securities Exchange but are traded in "over-the-counter," are subject to reporting requirements similar to those applicable to listed companies. The companies which are required to register with the Securities and Exchange Commission are those with total assets of over $1,000,000 and having equity securities held of record by more than 750 stockholders, which latter requirement is reduced to 500 after July 1, 1966. Certain banks and insurance companies are exempt from these registration requirements, but must meet certain disclosure requirements of appropriate federal and state regulatory bodies.

While the form in which registration will take place has not yet been specified, it is expected to follow that required of listed companies, and accordingly will include financial statements at the close of the company's fiscal year, with statements of income and surplus covering the preceding three years, certified by independent public or certified public accountants. Subsequent to the original registration, annual reports in a form similar to that required of listed companies will also be required.

CANADA 2

1

FORMS OF BUSINESS ORGANIZATION

Canadians carry on business under much the same forms of organization as those prevalent in the United States. Foreign corporations wishing to do business in Canada may establish branches in any of the provinces, and are subject to the laws of that province in the same way as Canadian corporations incorporated in another province. The foreign corporation must register, establish an office address and be licensed as an extraprovincial corporation in accordance with the laws of the province.

The Corporation

Canadian law distinguishes between a public and a private limited-liability company. The latter differs from the public company in that it may have no more than fifty stockholders (excluding employees), its shares or other securities may not be offered to the public, and the right to transfer these securities must be restricted. It has greater latitude in permitted transactions with its stockholders and directors, and it is not required to make its financial statements public. The "private" company may be a useful vehicle for investment in Canada by an American corporation.

The "public" company corresponds quite closely to its United States counterpart. It may be formed by three or more persons, and may have an unlimited number of stockholders, who may freely transfer their shares if "calls" are fully paid. A company incorporated under the laws of most of the provinces must file a prospectus before offering its securities for sale to the public. The Securities law of Ontario is the most stringent, and when, as in most cases, it is expected that sales will be made in that province, the prospectus must comply with Ontario's requirements. If incorporated as a federal company, a prospectus which complies with the requirements of the Federal Companies Act must also be filed with the Federal Secretary of State.

A Canadian limited company (either public or private) can be created, as a legal entity distinct from the shareholders, in one of three ways:

1. By letters patent granted under the Federal Companies Act
2. By letters patent or by registration under the companies acts of one of the provinces
3. By special act of the Federal Parliament or of the legislature of one of the provinces. (Such corporations as banks, savings and loan corporations, trust companies, railways, etc., are invariably incorporated by special act).

The liability of a shareholder is limited to the amount unpaid on shares for which he has subscribed. The word "Limited" (or "Ltd.") must be included in the company's name, except for certain nonprofit organizations and certain companies incorporated under special acts, and in Quebec.

The "letters patent" system of incorporation used by five of the provincial companies acts is similar to that of the federal system. Under the "registration" system used by all of the other provinces, the Northwest Territories and the Yukon, there are two types of stockholder-liability companies in addition to the conventional limited-liability form; one in which the shareholder is limited to the amount which he has agreed to contribute in the event of insolvency or dissolution, and one in which, similar to a general partnership, the liability of the shareholder is not limited.

Under the Federal Companies Act, shareholders of companies must appoint auditors who, except in the case of private companies, may not be an officer or director, nor partner or employee of any director or officer. The auditors are to examine and report upon the financial statements of the company which are required to be submitted to the annual meeting of shareholders by the directors. A copy of the financial statements and reports of public companies must be filed with the Secretary of State. The provisions of the various Stock Exchange by-laws require similar filings if the company is listed on one of the exchanges. Provincial companies acts dealing with company meetings and appointment of auditors are similar to the Federal Act, and provincial legislation also requires the filing of certain statements and returns.

Although private companies are not restricted as to appointment of auditors as are public companies, the Ontario Corporations Act requires disclosure if the auditor is a director or officer, and this provision has been recommended for inclusion in the proposed Uniform Companies Act legislation.

Most public and private companies are required to file annual reports with the Dominion Statistician, unless their Canadian assets are less than $250,000 and their Canadian gross revenues are less than $500,000, or unless exempted under certain other provisions of the Corporations and Labour Unions Returns Act.

In addition to information about capitalization, stockholders and directors, financial statements together with the auditor's report thereon are required. Information must be given as to all amounts paid to nonresidents of Canada for dividends, interest, rents, royalties, insurance, advertising, research and development, management fees, payments to officers and directors, professional fees and the like. Information is classified as between Section A information and Section B information. The former is available for inspection. The latter, which includes audited financial statements, is treated as confidential.

Other Forms of Business Organization

The Sole Proprietor. Any person, resident or nonresident, may engage in business in Canada as a sole proprietor if he has the legal capacity to enter into a contract in Canada. If he wishes to do business under a style other than his own name or to use the words "and Company," he must file a statement in accordance with the laws of the province in which he does business in the same way as must general partnerships.

Partnerships. A group of persons may conduct business in the form of a partnership after provincial registration, and all Canadian partnerships can be classed as general or limited. General partnerships are those in which all partners are jointly and severally liable for partnership debts.

The limited partnership consists of general partners who manage the business and have the same liability as the partners of a general partnership, and of limited partners who contribute capital but who may not participate in the management, and whose liability is limited to the amount of their capital contributions. A few of the provinces limit the number of persons who may join in a partnership, but in general the differences in legislation affecting partnerships between the provinces are minor.

Partnerships are also required to register in the province of their domicile, and to furnish information which discloses the names of the partners, their respective interests, and whether general or limited, as well as other descriptive material.

In Quebec, however, general partnerships are divided between "commercial" and "civil" forms. The former are those carrying on a trade or business of a commercial nature; all others, including those of lawyers, accountants and other professional people, are civil partnerships. In the latter, the partners are equally liable to creditors regardless of the shares in the partnership held by the members.

Business Records

The Federal Companies Act and those of the several provinces contain similar provisions relating to books of account. In general, proper books of account are required to be kept at the company's head office or any other location in Canada specified by the Board of Directors. A federal company may keep its books of account outside of Canada provided the by-laws so authorize and the consent of the various taxing authorities is obtained, but they must be made available to the proper authorities on request. Generally speaking, the provincial companies acts require books of account to be kept in the province of incorporation, although, as a matter of fact, these provisions are not strictly enforced. A company must also maintain corporate records, such as letters patent, by-laws, capital stock records, etc., of which at least copies must be kept at the head office in Canada.

THE ACCOUNTING PROFESSION

The development of the accounting profession in Canada has been influenced in part by the tradition of the pioneering practitioners coming from the United Kingdom in the latter part of the nineteenth century, and in part by United States influences due to its proximity and to the economic ties with that country. The practice of accounting in Canada has reached a high level of standards and competence.

There is no federal act governing the use of the designation "chartered accountant" in Canada; the legislation involving accountants is a provincial, rather than a federal, responsibility. Accordingly, regulations governing the public practice of accountancy vary from province to province, as do the various state laws on this subject in the United States.

The Chartered Accountant

The designation of chartered accountant is issued by each provincial institute of chartered accountants, which prescribes the requirements for its issuance. While there are relatively minor differences in the various provinces, the candidate must either:

1. Qualify for university entrance (high school graduate) and com-

plete the prescribed course of training during a five-year period of service in the office of a chartered accountant. During this five-year period he must pass a primary examination (in most provinces) at the end of the first year of training, an intermediate examination at the end of the third year and a final examination at the end of the fifth year, or

2. Have a university degree and then complete a reduced term of service and course of studies. The B.A. or B.Sc. usually has the five-year term reduced by one year while a B.Com. or a Licentiate (in Quebec) might have his term of service reduced by two to four years and his course of study reduced substantially or, in Quebec, eliminated.

The provincial institutes either offer their own lecture courses during the training period or use the correspondence course of instruction developed by the Ontario Institute and administered by Queen's University. At present, the intermediate and final examinations are prepared and administered by the Canadian Institute of Chartered Accountants, a central authority representing all of the provincial institutes of chartered accountants. Some provincial institutes require their students to pass (or to have passed in a university) examinations for additional subjects such as English, mathematics, economics and law. A chartered accountant in one of the provinces may obtain admission to the institute of another province without examination, provided the latter institute recognizes the admission requirements of his prime institute.

The candidate (in Ontario) must not be under twenty-one years of age, be of good moral character, speak English, and be a resident.

Practice of the Chartered Accountant. The practice of the Canadian chartered accountant parallels that of his United States counterpart, including examinations of financial statements leading to his opinion thereon, preparation of and advice with respect to tax returns, and various types of services to management. The Federal Companies Act as well as the provincial companies acts require auditors to be appointed by the shareholders and to report to them upon the annual financial statements submitted by the directors. While there is no specific provision that the auditor must be a chartered accountant, the majority of companies, including practically all large publicly owned companies, appoint chartered accountants as auditors.

Under the Federal Bankruptcy Act, the Superintendent of Bankruptcy appoints licensed trustees with powers to act in bankruptcy matters in various provinces. Most of the larger firms of chartered accountants have at least one partner in each province so licensed, and the great majority of licensed trustees are chartered accountants.

7

The Certified Public Accountant

The Certified Public Accountants Association, which issues the corresponding certificate to its members, was organized in Ontario in 1926. There are organizations of certified public accountants in Manitoba, New Brunswick, Newfoundland and Saskatchewan. The requirements for the certificate of certified public accountant are basically similar to those of the chartered accountant, except that a thesis must be prepared as part of the final year's study and no experience in public accounting is required. Because of this latter factor, the designation CPA of Canada is not necessarily equivalent to the same designation in the United States.

In 1962, the Ontario Institute of Chartered Accountants and the Ontario Certified Public Accountants Association agreed to admit, on application, the members of the other body; the CPAs who were admitted to the Institute ceased to use the designation CPA. As a result, this latter designation has been almost entirely dropped in that province. Active steps are being taken to bring the two groups together in the remaining provinces in which the CPA Association is organized.

Licensing

Until after the Second World War there was no legislation restricting the practice of accounting in Canada. Three of the provinces now have legislation requiring a license to practice public accounting in their jurisdictions.

In 1946, Quebec licensed those who were then members of the Quebec Institute of Chartered Accountants; certain nonmembers in practice at the time who met certain conditions were admitted to membership and thus licensed. Others were granted licenses to continue in practice. In 1949, the province of Prince Edward Island passed similar legislation. An Ontario Act of 1950 imposed a licensing requirement upon the practice of accountancy, under which members of the Ontario Institute of Chartered Accountants and of the Certified Public Accountants Association of Ontario (since merged, see above) were entitled to registration upon application, and other accountants practicing at the time were also licensed without examination. The Act was amended in 1962, after the changes in the Ontario Institute outlined above, and now the eligible licensees are (1) chartered accountants, (2) those previously licensed under the old act, and (3) persons applying to and satisfying the Public Accountants Council that their qualifications and experience are such that they may be permitted to practice as a public accountant in that province. Comparatively few persons have been licensed under the latter provision. In the future, only chartered accountants will be granted licenses.

Organizations of Chartered and Other Accountants

At the national level there are four associations, each having been incorporated by a special federal act. The existence of these national associations is primarily to coordinate the activities of the various provincially incorporated bodies associated with the respective national organizations.

Canadian Institute of Chartered Accountants. The first Institute of Chartered Accountants in Canada was organized in Quebec in 1880, followed by Ontario in 1883, and Manitoba in 1886. Institutes have now been organized in all ten of the provinces and the Yukon Territory. In 1902, the (presently named) Canadian Institute of Chartered Accountants was organized, and in 1910, it was agreed by the provincial institutes that it should act as coordinator of national, as opposed to provincial, activities. Membership in a provincial institute automatically carries with it membership in the Canadian Institute. The latter publishes the monthly journal, *The Canadian Chartered Accountant,* administers uniform examinations, undertakes research and publishes bulletins on current questions, develops courses and programs of "continuing education" for CAs, maintains liaison with the federal legislature, and coordinates the work of the provincial institutes. There are over twelve thousand members, of whom a little less than half are in public practice.

Institute of Certified Public Accountants. In addition to the provincial associations, there was formed, in 1951, the Canadian Institute of Certified Public Accountants, which coordinates the work of the provincial associations. The membership in the various associations (after the Ontario amalgamation) totals about three hundred.

Other Organizations of Accountants. The Society of Industrial and Cost Accountants, incorporated in 1920, has about two thousand registered members, almost all of whom are employed in commerce and industry. This society is organized into provincial associations, with a national body to coordinate their activities.

There are a number of smaller organizations of accountants in Canada, the largest of which is the Certified General Accountants Association with about one thousand members functioning in most of the provinces.

Ethics

The Institutes of Chartered Accountants in Ontario and Quebec have adopted rules of conduct which are, for the most part, practically identical; other provincial institutes have also adopted such rules. The Canadian Institute of Chartered Accountants has proposed a uniform code of ethics, which is being circulated to the provincial institutes for their consideration.

The areas with which the rules of Ontario and Quebec are in accord are those covering the practice of accountancy, relations with clients, and relations with fellow members. Some of the more important provisions prohibit: the practice of public accounting by a corporation, soliciting clients through improper advertising, fees based on results of professional service, and fees paid to or received from the laity, and deal with the confidential character of information received in the course of work, competitive bidding and relations with retiring auditors.

Although the rules of the Quebec Institute deal with the subject in general terms, the Ontario rules specifically state that:

> In expressing an opinion on financial statements examined by him no member shall:
>
> (a) Fail to reveal a material fact known to him which is not disclosed in the financial statements but the omission of which renders the financial statements misleading; or
>
> (b) Fail to report any material misstatement known to him to appear in the financial statements.
>
> No member shall express an opinion on financial statements examined by him, if he fails to obtain sufficient information to warrant an expression of opinion, or if his exceptions are sufficiently material to nullify the expression of an opinion.
>
> No member or firm of which he is a partner shall express an opinion on the financial statements of any organization if the member, his partners, or his or their immediate families, have any direct or indirect financial interest (or such other interest as could influence the independence of the member or firm) in the organization unless the report discloses such interest.

AUDITING STANDARDS

While there has been no official pronouncement by the Canadian Institute of Chartered Accountants on the subject of auditing standards comparable to that of the AICPA Statements on Auditing Procedure No. 33, in practice Canadian Chartered Accountants adhere closely to the standards prevailing in the United States. The Bulletins of the Canadian Institute (Nos. 15 and 16) recommend the confirmation of receivables and observation of physical inventory-taking in much the same terms as the AICPA Statements.

Independence

As previously indicated, the Federal Companies Act and most of the provincial acts require that the auditor of a public company may not be a director or officer of the company, or a partner or employee of any director or officer of the company. There is no specific requirement that the auditor may not own securities of the company of which he has been appointed auditor, but this restriction is recognized by most chartered accountants. Certain of the provincial institutes (including Ontario) prohibit the holding of financial interests in client companies, unless disclosed in the auditor's report.

Standards of Reporting

The Federal Companies Act specifies the matters to be covered by the auditor's report, i.e:

(a) Whether or not he has obtained all the information and explanations required, and
(b) Whether, in his opinion, the balance sheet referred to in the report is properly drawn up so as to exhibit a true and correct view of the state of the company's affairs according to the best of his information and the explanations given to him, and as shown by the books of the company.

The form of the auditor's report also depends on the jurisdiction under which the company upon which he is reporting was incorporated. For example, in Ontario the auditor is required to state in his report: "Whether in his opinion the financial statements referred to therein present fairly the financial position of the company and the results of operations for the period under review." He is also required to make a statement of disclosure if he has not received all the information he has requested, if the statements are not drawn up in accordance with the requirements of the (companies) Act, and if certain other conditions exist. The Ontario Corporations Act requires indication by footnote, though not in the auditor's report, when there has been inconsistent application of accounting principles.

The balance sheet is required to be signed by two directors of the company. While the Acts in most provinces other than Ontario, and the Federal Act refer only to the balance sheet, it is customary that statements of profit and loss and surplus be presented to the stockholders and reported upon by the auditors.

The Canadian Institute of Chartered Accountants suggested a standard form of auditor's report in a bulletin which was first issued in 1951 and revised in 1954. Both of these pronouncements covered unqualified reports and took into account the applicable statutory requirements. These bulletins were superseded in 1959 by the issuance of Bulletin No. 17, which suggested the following form of Auditor's Report:

Auditor's Report

To the Shareholders of ABC Company Limited:

I have examined the balance sheet of ABC Company Limited as at.................... and the statements of profit and loss and surplus for the year ended on that date. My examination included a general review of the accounting procedures and such tests of accounting records and other supporting evidence as I considered necessary in the circumstances.

In my opinion the accompanying balance sheet and statements of profit and loss and surplus present fairly the financial position of the company as at .... and the results of operations for the year ended that date, in accordance with generally accepted accounting principles applied on a basis consistent with that of the preceding year.

Chartered Accountant

While this form suggests that the expression "presents fairly" be employed instead of the phrase " exhibits a true and correct view," the latter is required when the governing statute (for example, the Federal Companies Act) so specifies, and accordingly is frequently found in the auditor's report.

The Institute's bulletin recognized that the scope of the examination would be affected by the auditor's judgment of the effectiveness of the company's system of internal control, and that references to conformity with and consistency of application of generally accepted accounting principles should be made. Also, whether or not required by statute, statements of profit and loss and surplus should be included in the financial statements and covered by the auditor's report. When the auditor's report is to be used under the provisions of certain of the companies acts, special wording may be necessary to comply with the provisions of the specific act. When incorporated under the Federal Companies Act, the company's report to shareholders should incorporate the language specified in that act.

ACCOUNTING PRINCIPLES AND PRACTICES

Accounting principles applied in presentation of financial statements in Canada are generally similar to those current in the United States, although there are a few differences discussed later. They are enunciated in the bulletins of the Institute's Committee on Accounting and Auditing Research, and in articles published in the monthly magazine, and in textbooks.

Form and Content of Financial Statements

Statement Presentation. Financial statements, as presented in printed annual reports distributed to shareholders, are similar in form and content to those familiar in the United States, except that less detail is given in the Canadian statement of income, and sales, cost of sales, and selling and general expenses often are not shown.

The Institute's Committee on Accounting and Auditing Research published "Standards of Disclosure in Financial Statements" (Bulletin No. 14) in 1957, which indicated the nature and extent of information which the committee believed should be disclosed in balance sheets, profit and loss statements, and accompanying notes. These standards are practically the same as those incorporated in the Ontario Corporation Act as well as those proposed for the Uniform Companies Act now under consideration in Canada. They are also generally in harmony with those of the United States.

There are, however, some differences between current Canadian practice and United States practice, discussed below.

Financial Statements Required Under the Companies Acts. The requirements of the various provincial companies acts differ somewhat in detail, but, in general, compliance with the provisions of the Federal Companies Act will suffice for filing under the requirements of most provinces.

The requirements for the Province of Ontario, however, are generally more detailed than those of the other provinces, especially regarding notes to financial statements and adherence to generally accepted accounting principles. The requirements of this provincial act are similar to those specified in the Canadian Institute's Bulletin "Standards of Disclosure in Financial Statements."

Federal Companies Act. Section 116 of the Act requires the presentation of financial statements by the directors to the annual meeting of all companies consisting of a balance sheet, a general statement of income and expenditure, and statements of capital surplus, distributable surplus, and earned surplus showing the changes during the fiscal period together with the report of auditors and other supporting information. There is specified in some detail the various classes of assets and liabilities which must be shown in the balance sheet. Some of the items required to be shown which may be of special interest are:

Debts owing the company by directors, officers or shareholders

Expenditure made on account of future business

Loans to employees (other than directors) to enable them to purchase fully paid shares in the company

The amount of capital shares issued since the date of the last balance sheet for services rendered, for commissions or for assets acquired.

The unamortized amounts of:
Preliminary expenses of the company incurred since three years prior to the date of the Act
Any expenses incurred in connection with any issue of share capital or debentures.

The amount of any goodwill, franchises, patents, copyrights, trademarks, contracts or leases, and the amount, if any, by which the value of such assets has been written up within a period of three years prior to the date of the balance sheet.

Section 117 specifies that the statement of income and expenditure of a public company will show "net operating profit before depreciation, obsolescence and depletion and income taxes . . ." The reporting of sales and cost of sales is not required, but otherwise the items listed fit readily into the usual form of statement of income published in Canada and the United States. It is provided that if depreciation, obsolescence and depletion are charged to manufacturing or operating costs by the company, net operating profit may be shown after these items, with their amount disclosed in a note to the financial statements.

In addition, the total amounts paid to the directors as remuneration for their services as directors, to legal counsel of the company, and to executive officers, including directors who hold salary positions, must also be disclosed.

Section 118 provides for reporting on the basis of consolidated accounts where a parent company owns all or more than 50 per cent of the voting stock of another company or companies. This section also specifies the disclosure necessary where unconsolidated statements are prepared. These include a statement by the auditor of the holding company stating how the subsidiaries' profits and losses have been dealt with in the accounts of the holding company and to what extent losses, or provisions therefor, have been made in the parent's accounts. However, it is not necessary to give the actual amount of the profits and losses which have been dealt with in any particular manner.

Comparative Statements. The Canadian Institute's Bulletin No. 14, "Standards of Disclosures in Financial Statements" states that: "It is considered desirable that, under ordinary circumstances, annual statements should show comparable figures for the preceding year."

Consolidated Statements. Presentation of consolidated financial statements, recommended by Bulletin No. 14, is common in Canada, but an explanation of nonconsolidation of certain subsidiaries is not often found, although Bulletin No. 14 clearly states that such explanation should be given. The Ontario Corporations Act requires that a statement be given of the reasons why assets and liabilities and income and expense of nonconsolidated subsidiaries are not included in the financial statements of the parent company, and also information as to the parent company's equity in net assets, earnings and accumulated earnings.

Investments in nonconsolidated subsidiaries are usually stated at cost, in which case the basis is disclosed, and stating at underlying equity is uncommon. It is not a well-established practice to state the basis of valuation of such investments. The parent's equity in net assets and earnings is not always, shown, except in Ontario, as indicated above.

Excess or Deficiency of Cost of Subsidiary Over Its Book Amount at Acquisition. Under Bulletin No. 14, the difference between cost and equity at date of acquisition is merely required to be shown separately, "unless such difference has been disposed of" and such procedure disclosed in a prior year's statement. There are few such items disclosed in Canadian balance sheets. In practice, for statement presentation purposes, this difference is often "buried" in fixed assets or in surplus. This practice of disposing of the difference would be contrary to United States practice, which in general requires that such differences be identified as to their nature and so classified on the balance sheet.

Pooling of Interests

While there is no prohibition against the practice of accounting for certain types of merger or consolidation of companies on the basis of a "pooling of interest," this method of accounting is not common in Canada.

Current Assets

Inventories. The Lifo method of inventory valuation is not permitted in Canada for income tax purposes, and this discourages its use for financial reporting purposes. Except in the case of Lifo, it is not usual in Canada to disclose the method of determining "cost" or "market" in describing the basis of stating inventories.

Allowance for Bad Debts. Since Bulletin No. 14 does not require disclosure of the amount of any allowance for bad debts, in most cases the balance sheet does not indicate the amount of such allowance.

Fixed Assets and Appraisal Surplus

It is considered acceptable, but is ordinarily discouraged, to restate fixed assets on the basis of the report of an independent appraiser. When this is done, the fact is stated in the balance sheet description of the fixed asset item, or in a note to the balance sheet.

Bulletin No. 11 recommends that the excess of appraisal amount over cost should not be described as an appraisal surplus or reserve, but this suggestion is not always followed. It also states that once recorded the appraisal increase may remain indefinitely as a separate item in the shareholders' equity section of the balance sheet, or it may be transferred to earned surplus in amounts not exceeding the realization of appreciation through sale, or annual depreciation provisions. The publication, *Financial Reporting in Canada* (the Canadian Institute, fifth edition) indicates that about one-half of the companies reporting appraisal increases do extinguish this credit on some basis.

Leaseholds

The Ontario Corporations Act and Bulletin No. 14 of the Canadian Institute refer to disclosure of material contractual obligations in respect of long-term leases, and the bulletin states that disclosure should include in the year in which the transaction was effected, the principal details of any sale and lease transactions. However, the survey of Canadian companies by the Institute showed that only about 40 per cent of the companies that disclosed the existence of long-term leases gave the same details which are required by the United States Securities and Exchange Commission regulations and are often shown in published financial statements in the United States.

Reserves

While the Committee's Bulletin No. 9 suggests that reserves (such as for contingencies, inventories, insurance, replacements of fixed assets) representing appropriations of earned surplus should be classified as part of shareholders' equity, this recommendation has not been universally adopted. About one-third of the companies reviewed in the fifth edition of *Financial Reporting in Canada,* carried reserves either as deductions from assets or separate—apart from the shareholders' equity section.

The bulletin specifies that the term "reserve" should not be used to describe amounts which are required to be brought into account in the determination of net profit, and suggests, for example, "allowance for doubtful accounts," "accumulated allowance for depreciation," and "estimated damages payable," as preferable descriptions.

Stock Dividends

Stock dividends are not common in Canada, but, if issued, the distributor usually accounts for them at par value.

If the related investment is carried at cost, the recipient will usually record merely an increase in the number of shares held,without increasing the carrying value of his investment. If it is carried at market, the market value of the shares received as a dividend would be added.

Such dividends when received by a corporation are, in general, not taxable; when received by an individual, they may or may not be taxable, depending on circumstances.

Statement of Profit and Loss

In Canada there is still a slight preference for the title "Statement of Profit and Loss" rather than "Statement of Income" or other designation, but this preference has declined since 1957.

Sales and Cost of Sales. The disclosure of sales was encouraged in Bulletin No. 14, but such disclosure, although increasing, is considerably less common in Canada than in the United States. When the disclosure of sales is made in the directors' report or in a location other than the profit and loss statement, the amount of cost of sales is seldom given.

Pensions. There has been no pronouncement by the Canadian Institute regarding the kind and amount of information to be given in financial statements regarding pension plans. As a result, there is considerable divergence in Canadian practice in this area. The appropriate committee of the Canadian Institute has published a research study under the title "Accounting for Costs of Pension Plans."

Depreciation. When fixed assets have been restated upward as a result of an independent appraisal, depreciation for financial statement purposes should be computed and charged to income on the basis of the appraised amounts. For tax purposes, depreciation must be computed on cost, and some companies also follow the tax rule for book and financial reporting purposes.

The Canadian Income Tax Act allows deductions from income, for purposes of calculating taxable income, which are in lieu of depreciation and are called "capital cost allowances." These allowances are based initially on the cost of a particular fixed asset, and are determined by the application of specified rates on the diminishing-balance method. Some of these rates are somewhat higher than might be considered normal for business purposes. The maximum annual allowances applicable to each class of assets are set out in the regulations to the Income Tax Act, and a company may claim, at its discretion, a deduction of any amount up to these maxima. Also, the company may reduce or omit entirely the permissible deductions in any year. It is not necessary for depreciation recorded in the books of account to agree with that claimed for income tax purposes and accordingly differences frequently arise between the net book value as shown on the company's financial statements and that under the tax laws.

Although capital cost allowances and depreciation are distinctly different, in many cases the allowance would not be materially different from the depreciation which would be reflected in a taxpayer's regular books of account, and, accordingly, a number of companies provide depreciation in amounts equal to the corresponding capital cost allowances.

Depletion. Depletion of mining properties is rarely recorded.

Amortization. Amortization of various types of intangible assets is normally charged currently to income, but lump-sum writeoffs may be charged to surplus.

Tax-effect Accounting. The problem of allocating the amount of taxes "deferred" as a result of differences between "depreciation" and "capital cost allowances" was considered in Bulletin No. 10, "Depreciation, Capital Cost Allowances and Income Taxes." This bulletin discussed the methods of dealing with the differences between the tax which would otherwise be payable at current tax rates on "book income," and the actual tax payable according to the Income Tax Act. Two methods of dealing with the problem were suggested:

(a) To charge income with the amount of taxes actually payable, and to state in a note to the financial statements the effect on net income of the year of the reduction of taxes for that year, and also the accumulated amount of such reductions, or

(b) To charge income with tax expense equal to the cost resulting from the application of current tax rates against book income, but to defer the difference between this amount and the tax actually payable as being applicable to those future years in which book depreciation may exceed capital cost allowances.

While the effect of the latter procedure is the same as would be reached by methods usually followed in the United States, there is a slight difference in the concept. In the United States, the accumulated credit is regarded as a provision for future tax liability, whereas in Canada it is regarded as a deferred credit to tax expense.

The bulletin recommends that method (b) be followed in most circumstances; however, it appears that many companies in Canada utilize method (a).

The credit arising from method (b) is preferably captioned "Accumulated tax reductions applicable to future years," and the bulletin discourages the use of words such as "reserve," "liability," or "provision."

When there are other significant differences between book charges to income and tax-allowable deductions, it is not unusual to provide for the tax effect of such differences, except in the case of mining and oil companies.

Treasury Stock Transactions. Since transactions in a corporation's own common stock are not permitted in Canada, the problem of disposition of gains or losses does not arise. Except in Ontario there is no specific legislation to prevent a subsidiary corporation from acquiring the stock of its parent.

The Federal Companies Act requires that where a company is permitted under its letters patent to acquire its own preferred stock for cancellation or reissue, an amount equal to the par value of the stock acquired must be transferred from surplus to a capital reserve account. Any difference between cost and par value is adjusted through surplus.

REQUIREMENTS FOR PUBLIC SALE
OF SECURITIES

The Federal Companies Act describes the material required for prospectuses in connection with the public issue of securities incorporated under that Act. The Act requires that the prospectus be signed and filed with the Secretary of State. The filing is purely a formality and applies only to companies incorporated under the Federal Statute.

The provinces of Ontario, Alberta, Saskatchewan and Quebec have set up Securities Commissions to administer and enforce the regulations under which securities may be offered for sale in these provinces; the remaining provinces (except Prince Edward Island and Newfoundland), operate through Registrars of the securities acts.

The requirements of all provinces are not exactly uniform. However, because most public companies wish to sell at least some of their securities in Ontario, the majority of prospectuses conform to the requirements of that province's Securities Act. This Commission requires not only that the prospectus conform with the Securities Act under which the company was incorporated, but also with the standards of disclosure promulgated by the Commission itself. Such standards are identical with those contained in the Institute's Bulletin No. 14, "Standards of Disclosure in Financial Statements," and include the following:

> Where capital stock of the company was issued as consideration for property acquired, such consideration should be disclosed.

> If any fixed assets are valued on the basis of an appraisal, the date of the appraisal, the name of the appraisor, and basis of valuation should be shown. If the appraisal is recorded, subsequent charges against income for depreciation should be based on the new values.

> Reserves should, if important in amount, be set out separately in the balance sheet and in ordinary circumstances be shown as part of the shareholders' equity. Accruals in respect of liabilities, commitments or obligations often erroneously described as reserves should be described as accruals, provisions or by some other appropriate term, other than reserves, and should be treated as liabilities and the amounts disclosed, if material.

There must be presented a balance sheet (consolidated, if appropriate) and, where possible, a ten-year statement of profit and loss, on which the company's auditors have rendered an opinion.

Pro forma financial statements indicating the effect upon the balance sheet of the application of the proceeds of the proposed issue may be required.

As to the auditor's report, the Commission assumes:

(a) That the auditor is satisfied that the company's financial statements are in agreement with the accounting records (subject to such amendments as may be disclosed in the case of *pro forma* statements and to such adjustments between years as may be deemed necessary in the case of statements of earnings and surplus)

(b) That the company's financial statements are in accordance with the requirements of the Commission and those of the Companies Act to which the company is subject

(c) that proper accounting records have been maintained so far as appears from the auditor's examination.

If the auditor is reporting on a balance sheet of a company which does not consolidate one or more subsidiaries and such subsidiary or subsidiaries in the aggregate had an excess of net losses and dividends over net profits since the acquisition of the shares by the company and such excess has not been provided for in the accounts of the company, then the auditor's report will state such amount or additional amount as may be necessary to make provision for the company's portion of such excess.

REQUIREMENTS FOR LISTING OF SECURITIES ON THE STOCK EXCHANGE

For a company's shares to be listed on the Toronto Stock Exchange (the principal Exchange in Canada), a Listing Application must be filed with the Stock Exchange, which includes the following accounting information:

I   *Companies whose principal business is mining or the production of oil or natural gas*

The applicant company must furnish certain documents including the following:

(a) One copy of each of the annual reports for the past three years (if such were issued)

(b) Two copies of a statement of assets and liabilities and of profit and loss or revenue and expenditure or receipts and disbursements accounts covering, where possible, at least the last three yearly periods, duly certified by a chartered, public or certified accountant

(c) Two copies of an up-to-date financial statement (including a balance sheet and a profit and loss or revenue and expenditure account) in the customary form, reported on by a chartered, public or certified accountant and approved by the Board of Directors.

II *Industrial and investment companies*
The applicant company must furnish the following:

(a) The name, address and qualification of the company's auditors

(b) Two copies of each of the following:
    (i) financial statements, certified by a chartered, public or certified accountant as follows:
        (a) Balance sheet of a recent date and, unless permission is granted by the Exchange, not more than 90 days prior to the date of application

        (b) Detailed statement of profit and loss for each of the preceding five years, if possible, tabulated in comparative form.

    (ii) Annual reports of the last three years, if any were published, in the form in which such reports were distributed to shareholders.

III *General*
(a) By-Law No. 63 of the Toronto Stock Exchange requires that every company whose shares are posted for trading shall forward yearly to each of its shareholders and shall submit to the Exchange an annual report containing a financial statement (including a balance sheet and a statement of profit and loss) in the customary form, reported upon by a chartered, public or certified accountant and approved by the Board of Directors. This statement will also contain a record of its activities, if any, during the period covered, such report to be provided within six months from the close of the fiscal year or other period covered. The shares of a company which fails to forward and submit such report shall be removed from the trading list, provided, however, that the Board of Governors may, in its discretion, relieve any company or companies from this penalty.

In addition, the Board of Governors of the Toronto Stock Exchange may *at any time* require a company to submit to the Board a financial statement in the customary form and to submit such further particulars of its activities as the Board shall prescribe.

(b) By-Law No. 66 requires that companies whose shares are posted for trading shall file an annual questionnaire in the period and form prescribed by the Board of Governors. Failure to comply in providing up-to-date information about the activities of the company may result in its shares being removed from the trading list.

(c) Under ruling No. 49, prompt notice must be given by every company, whose shares are posted for trading, of each proposed material change in the business or affairs of the company. Considered material are: changes in the nature of the business of the company or the personnel on the Board of Directors; the acquisition or disposition by the company of any mining or oil property or interest, or shares of other securities in another company at a price in excess of $25,000, payable otherwise than in shares of the company; the entering into of any management contract; a change in the beneficial or registered share ownership of the company which is sufficient to materially affect control.

ARGENTINA

3

FORMS OF BUSINESS ORGANIZATION

The principal forms of limited liability organizations in Argentina are the corporation (Sociedad Anónima), the registered branch of a foreign corporation and the limited liability company (Sociedad de Responsabilidad Limitada or S.R.L.). Many organizations with local financing are formed as S.R.L. companies because of the limited liability feature, the speed of formation and the freedom from government supervision.

In addition, business may be carried on as one of several types of partnership or as a sole proprietorship. The majority of foreign corporations choose to operate in Argentina as corporations or branches.

Sociedad Anónima (S.A.)

The corporate form most closely resembling the typical United States corporation is the Sociedad Anónima. The corporate name must be followed by the words Sociedad Anónima as well as by an indication of the nature of the business in abbreviated form, i.e., Industrial y Comercial (Industrial and Commercial). Initials may be used, i.e., S.A.I. y C. Foreign corporations may be stockholders. There is no minimum capital required. The authorized capital is required to be divided into shares of equal par value. Twenty per cent of the capital must be fully subscribed and 10 per cent of the subscribed capital must be paid at the time of incorporation. The issuance of stock for less than par or nominal value is not permitted. Each province as well as the Federal District is empowered to approve the formation of a corporation.

The Argentine corporation may issue several different classes of shares. Shares may be nominative (registered) or bearer. Until the shares are fully paid, they must be registered; when fully paid, they may be issued as bearer shares. The latter are freely negotiable, while negotiability of registered shares may be restricted by the company's statutes.

Every Sociedad Anónima must have one or more statutory examiners

3

(Síndicos) who are appointed for a one-year term by the shareholders. Most companies have one statutory examiner and an alternate. (Síndico Suplente). Their principal function is to protect the interests of the shareholders. The qualifications and duties of the statutory examiners are discussed in a later section.

The financial statements of a corporation and the report of the Board of Directors, duly reported upon by the statutory examiner must be submitted to a stockholders' meeting and to the Inspección General de Justicia each year. All Sociedades Anónimas must have these financial statements reported upon by a National Public Accountant (C.P.N.), and all other businesses formed in the Federal District whose capital is in excess of 500,000 pesos or whose income is over one million pesos must also do so.

The several provinces have differing requirements. Condensed financial statements must be published in the *Official Gazette*. When complete statements are published, the report of the C.P.N. is also published.

Sociedad de Responsabilidad Limitada (S.R.L.)

The limited liability company is a partnership in which each partner's liability is limited to the capital subscribed by him. The number of partners may not exceed twenty plus an additional five employee-partners, who may be named subsequently. The capital must be at least p.5,000 and is divided into quotas of p.100 or multiples thereof. The capital of a S.R.L. may not be represented by bearer shares. A partnership or a corporation may be a partner in a S.R.L. Transfers of partnership interests require approval of all partners, if their number does not exceed five, otherwise a majority of three-fourths of the partners is required. The manager or managers of the limited liability company, who need not be partners, are jointly and severally liable for improper distributions in excess of realized profits.

Branch of a Foreign Corporation

A branch may perform all of the acts which its head office authorizes it to perform. Registration is a relatively simple matter and depending on the amount of assigned capital may be relatively inexpensive. In order to register a branch of a foreign corporation it is necessary to prove that the parent company's government extends reciprocity to Argentina, otherwise a special authorization of the executive power is necessary.

The certified financial statements of a branch must be submitted annually to the Inspección General de Justicia and must be published in the *Official Gazette* in the same manner as required for corporations.

Other Forms of Business Organization

Sociedad Colectiva. This type of organization is formed by two or more persons, jointly and severally liable, who combine to do business in common under a firm name. The death of a partner whose name is part of the firm name is cause for immediate dissolution of the partnership.

Sociedad en Comandita. In this type of partnership there are two classes of partners—general partners (socios solidarios), who have joint and several liability for partnership debts and management, and silent or limited partners (socios comanditarios), whose liability is limited to the amount which they contribute or promise to contribute. A limited partner who takes part in the management of the Sociedad en Comandita risks incurring unlimited liability.

Sociedad en Comandita por Acciones. This differs from the Socieded en Comandita only in that the interests of limited partners are represented by shares. In the event that there are ten or more silent partners, and their capital is more than 50 per cent of the total capital, the organization is treated as a Socieded Anónima and the general partners are considered as the Board of Directors.

Sociedad de Capital e Industria. This type of organization is formed when one or more persons supply funds for some business in general or for some specific commercial transaction, and where one or more others entering into the association contribute their personal services only.

Sociedad Cooperativa. These are companies organized for mutual benefit and to promote some common interest through an exchange of mutual services by the company for its members and by the members for the company. Profits are usually distributed to members in proportion to their usage of offered services.

Business Records

All businesses must maintain a daily journal and inventory book (or books kept in lieu of these) which must be bound and have prenumbered pages. At the commencement of operations they must be presented to the local commercial courts to be signed and dated on the initial page and to have all pages marked by the courts. Modern mechanized devises may supplement the registered books.

SÍNDICO (STATUTORY EXAMINER)

As stated previously, a statutory examiner is required to report upon the financial statements of a corporation and those of the "limited partnership with shares" when the number of silent partners exceeds nine and the capital of these partners exceeds that of the general partners. A statutory examiner is not required for a branch of a foreign corporation, a private company, or any of the remaining partnership companies.

The statutory examiner is responsible to the company and to third parties for improper performance of his duties. His first duty is to safeguard the interests of the shareholders. In addition to examining the books and records every three months, or more often if deemed necessary, his duties include the counting of cash and securities, attending meetings of the Board of Directors, and in general seeing that the directors comply with all laws, by-laws, regulations and statutes affecting the company.

There are no specific legal qualifications for the position of statutory examiner. He may be a shareholder but may not hold any other position in the firm. It is not necessary that he have any knowledge of or training in accounting. However, since the financial statements of larger corporations as submitted to the Inspección General de Justicia must be certified by a national public accountant (C.P.N.), it is customary for such a C.P.N. to also be appointed as statutory examiner (Síndico). In the opinion of most C.P.N.s such appointments do not violate their independent status, and the Council in Buenos Aires has also ruled to this effect. It is estimated that currently more than half of the statutory examiners are C.P.N.s.

It is apparent that the statutory examiner (Síndico) is not, either by education, training or objectives, necessarily equivalent to the United States CPA nor the United Kingdom C.A. Unless the Síndico also functions as a C.P.N., his approval of the financial statements of a corporation does not and is not intended to give the same assurance regarding financial statements as would that of a professional independent auditor.

INSPECCIÓN GENERAL DE JUSTICIA

In addition to the control exercised by the statutory examiners, the Argentine government exercises control over corporations by the use of government inspectors who are under the Department of Justice. These inspectors may attend shareholders' meetings and sign the minutes thereof. They also review the financial statements prior to presentation to the shareholders and have a right to inspect the books and accounts. They can require changes to be made in the financial statements if those statements are not prepared in accordance with existing regulations. Their responsibility is to see that the corporation is complying with Argentine law. Although these inspectors are considered to be qualified persons, their effectiveness is limited because of the small number of inspectors compared with the large number of companies to be examined.

Branches of foreign corporations are also controlled by the Inspección General de Justicia.

THE ACCOUNTING PROFESSION

Although the national public accountant degree (contador publico nacional—C.P.N.) has been established for almost fifty years, it was not until the year 1945, that Decree-Law No. 5103/45 was passed to regulate the economic sciences (economics, actuarial studies and accountancy). This was ratified by Law No. 12921/46. Professional practice is limited to those with degrees; however, persons in practice at the time the law was passed were permitted to register and continue with the same activities.

Requirements for Degree of C.P.N.

Matriculation in an Argentine national university follows twelve years of elementary and high school. The designation C.P.N. is a degree conferred by an Argentine national university upon completion of a five-year course. The prescribed curriculum is generally comparable to that required in United States universities. The candidate is also required to pass a final examination when he graduates from a private university. There is no specific experience requirement.

Up to 1960, graduates were trained in economics, accounting and actuarial work. After that date the courses were categorized into four specialized sections, the above three and general business administration. Most students now concentrate on two of these sections.

Duties of C.P.N.

Among the duties of the C.P.N. are the following which are prescribed under the law:

1. To act in legal matters when a public accountant is required
2. To advise businessmen on accounting matters
3. To certify financial statements and accounting entries when necessary
4. To certify financial statements for presentation to official entities.

Consejo Profesional de Ciencias Económicas

Decree-Law No. 5103/45 provided that each province and the federal capital be empowered to create a professional council (Consejo Profesional de Ciencias Económicas) which includes economists, actuaries and accountants. Among others, the duties of these councils are to:

1. Create and maintain a register of qualified professionals. An accountant must be registered before commencing practice
2. Prepare Codes of Ethics
3. Propose minimum fees
4. Advise the government on all questions pertaining to the profession
5. Take disciplinary action for violations of professional ethics or for charging fees lower than the minimum prescribed. Disciplinary action may include suspension or rescinding of registration.

In connection with Part 1 above, each council must also prepare and maintain a register of nongraduates (Registro Especial de Nograduados). This register includes those persons who at the time of passage of the decree-law were engaged in the practice of the profession without having graduated from the university. A registered nongraduate may not use the title Contador Público Nacional.

Professional Accounting Organizations

The accountants of each of the provinces and of the Federal District of Buenos Aires may organize their own accounting association or institute (Colegio de Graduados en Ciencias Ecónomicas). Some of these institutes have been in existence for more than fifty years. Committees of the Colegio in Buenos Aires have advised the government on commercial legislation. They are private, and membership is limited to legally qualified accountants. In the Federal District, there are close to eight thousand registered C.P.N.s; the Province of Buenos Aires has some forty-five hundred and the Province of Santa Fe about three thousand. These are the jurisdictions with the largest numbers.

Ethics

A Code of Ethics was prepared and approved by the Professional Council of Buenos Aires for application to economists, actuaries and accountants, and includes the following prohibitions (summarized):

The practitioner:

May not enter into an association for the purpose of carrying out professional activities with a person who is not a member of the profession.

Will maintain professional dignity

Will not slander another professional

May not serve both parties in a controversy

Will not try to influence legislation without the knowledge of the Council

Will not try to proselyte employees of other professionals

Must maintain independence

Must act in good faith

Must personally direct and review any work of his subordinates.

Similar codes have been approved in the provinces and all are policed by permanent committees of each Council, which normally act on complaint of a member or upon complaint of a third party. Penalties usually range from admonition to temporary suspension; permanent prohibition from practice is provided, but is seldom applied.

AUDITING STANDARDS

General Standards

There has been no official statement defining auditing standards in Argentina, although a study of this subject by a committee of the Institute of Buenos Aires is in the formative stages. The C.P.N. in Argentina has followed a course of study in accounting based on excellent textbooks which recommend the practices of confirmation procedures, observation of physical inventories and testing and sampling procedures. The international firms and several of the medium-sized national firms follow United States or British standards and practices.

The Fifth National Convention of Graduates in Economic Sciences, held in Rosario on September 29, 1960, approved a resolution recommending the following definition of "minimum auditing standards":

When a public accountant expresses that in the fulfillment of his work he has followed "minimum auditing standards," it will be interpreted that:

1. He has acted with independence and in accordance with norms of professional ethics.
2. He has performed his work with professional care and the technical knowledge proper to a specialist in a determined field of knowledge.
3. The work was duly planned in order to assure efficiency of the technical procedures applied.
4. In the case of using assistants, subordinated or not, their work was duly planned and controlled.
5. The procedures applied have had, apart from other purposes, the objective of evaluating the efficiency of the internal control being applied by the audited company.
6. The procedures applied included at least the following:

   a. Comparison of the amounts shown in the financial statements, or in the accounting document on which an opinion is given, with the balances in the books of accounts or other records
   b. Examination of the entries in the books of accounts or other records, with all supporting evidence he considers necessary and which are in the possession of the audited company (contracts, minutes, registers, documents, receipts, statements and other vouchers and business papers) to the extent that he has considered necessary in the circumstances
   c. Examination of balances with debtors and creditors, including banks and similar institutions by receiving directly from the debtors and creditors confirmations of said balances, to the extent to which it would be practical and reasonable to do so and to the extent he has considered necessary in the circumstances
   d. Observation of the physical counts of goods or tangible assets (wares, materials, products, productive equipment, livestock, etc.) to the extent to which it would be practical and reasonable to do so, including test-checks and comparison of the results with the records or books of accounts, to the extent he has considered necessary in the circumstances
   e. Obtaining written confirmation about explanations and in-

formation furnished by the client, where substantiation by other means would not be possible or reasonable.

There is some doubt whether the smaller firms and individual practitioners follow the recommendations above as to physical inspection of inventories and confirmation of accounts receivable.

Independence. The code of ethics in effect states that the C.P.N. must avoid situations which might compromise his independence, but these have yet to be defined.

Standards of Reporting

There is no standard form of auditor's report prescribed for the C.P.N. in Argentina, and a uniform opinion has not been developed, although the matter is under discussion by the profession. The C.P.N. who certifies the accounts of a corporation should assure himself as to the correct use of the official forms and compliance with the related instructions. The pertinent rule is stated in Section 75 of the regulations to the general law on accounting activities (Decree-Law No. 5103/45), which regulations were approved by Decree No. 4460/46 published in the *Official Gazette* of August 16, 1946. This section states:

> The certificate . . . shall be the consequence of an analytical study of the items forming the Balance Sheet and the Profit and Loss Account. It must reflect the clear, precise and objective opinion on the position being certified, and shall at the same time state the source from which the data has been obtained—books, vouchers, controls, etc.—, the samples taken for the analysis of the various items requiring such analysis and the other means employed for performing the job.

> The certificate shall guarantee (sic) that the figures in the statements of assets, liabilities and profit and loss accounts, agree with the amounts in the books of account, carried in accordance with legal requirements and supported by the corresponding vouchers; it shall also assure that in determining the values and operating results a technically correct criterion has been followed.

There is no specific requirement that the C.P.N. state his opinion that the financial statements have been prepared in accordance with generally accepted accounting principles.

Consistency. Both Decree No. 9795/54 and "Normas Mínimas" (subsequently referred to) require that changes in application of accounting principles in one year from those applied in the previous year be described in a note to the financial statements as well as their effect on the balance sheet and the statement of profit and loss.

Materiality. Decree No. 9795/54 does not include any pronouncement on the concept of materiality and its effect on the auditor's work and on his opinion on the financial statements. There is such a reference in "Normas Mínimas."

Disclosure of Subsequent Events. It is not common practice to disclose events subsequent to the balance-sheet date which might have a material effect on a proper evaluation of the financial statements, although "Normas Mínimas" provides for such disclosure and the Inspección General de Justicia usually requests information on the subject.

ACCOUNTING PRINCIPLES AND PRACTICES

The accounting rules and practices in Argentina do not differ materially from those in the United States since they are based predominantly on textbook materials, articles, etc., which utilize United States sources to some extent. There are some specific differences arising from the requirements of the commercial code and because tax law requirements are generally followed in company accounts. The more important of these differences are discussed later.

An academic group from the accounting faculty of the University of Buenos Aires prepared and recommended a set of standards for financial reporting (Normas Mínimas Para la Confección de Estados Contables) which was approved by the University Council of Buenos Aires in 1958, as a guide for the profession. These "Normas Mínimas" have no legal force; they may be used by the Councils to encourage and enforce minimum standards, and having been approved by the leading university teachers, are used as a teaching medium at the universities.

Form and Content of Financial Statements

The Argentine government, by Decree No. 9795/54, established the form to be used by domestic corporations and branches of foreign corporations in the preparation of financial statements. In addition to the forms prescribed, the law also contains general rules for the preparation of financial statements. These rules include the following:

1. The heading for the financial statements must include the following:
    a. Name of organization
    b. Legal domicile
    c. Principal object
    d. Date of permission to operate
    e. Date of registration with the Public Register of Commerce
    f. Changes in statutes
    g. Fiscal year number
    h. Date of beginning of year
    i. Date of year end.

2. Identification of Share Capital—

	Ordinary	Preferred	Deferred[1]	Privileged[2]	Total
Authorized					
Subscribed					
Paid up					

    Notes:

[1] Have right to capital or profits, or both, only after the holders of ordinary and preferred shares.

[2] Have additional benefits in profits or return of capital over other shares.

3. There should be footnote explanations of the accounting method used and methods of valuation of goods held for sale and securities.
4. Debts and receivables should be segregated between current and long-term portions.
5. Free reserves should be shown apart from earned surplus.
6. There should be three supporting schedules showing details of fixed assets, real estate and investments in other entities (supporting schedules must be signed by those who signed the balance sheet.)
7. Financial statements should reflect provisional dividends proposed by the directors but not approved by the stockholders.
8. Memorandum accounts must be used to reflect contingent liabilities, consignments and unpaid accumulated dividends.

Consolidated Financial Statements. Consolidated financial statements are infrequently prepared. There is no government requirement that consolidated statements be presented.

Inventories

Almost any inventory method which is consistently applied is acceptable in Argentina. The pricing of inventories at the lower of cost or market is widely used in practice. Law 9795/54 requires that disclosure be made as to method and valuation of inventories.

Securities

The same law also requires that disclosure be made of the basis of valuation of security investments.

Fixed Assets

Due to the severe devaluation of Argentine currency, a law was passed in 1960, which enabled business enterprises to revalue, in the years 1959 and 1960 only, their long-term tangible assets for both tax and accounting purposes. This revaluation could be partial or complete at the option of management. The procedure was to apply a published coefficient to the residual value of fixed assets. Residual value was considered to be tax-cost less depreciation computed on the basis of useful life. In the case of certain assets, useful life could be increased by 50 per cent. After revaluation the restated values became the base for computing gains or losses on disposal.

There are certain differences in the rules regarding revaluation for book purposes as compared with tax purposes. The two valuations are quite independent and either one could have been made without necessarily making the other.

For tax purposes, depreciation continues on the old basis until the asset is fully depreciated. The amount added to fixed assets resulting from revaluation, except that portion relating to land, is amortized at the rate of 10 per cent per year. The increment arising on revaluation was subject to a special tax.

Goodwill

Accounting authorities recommend that goodwill be recorded only if purchased. It should be amortized on a reasonable basis and should be written off immediately if found to have lost its value. The amortization of goodwill is not an allowable tax deduction.

Provision for Severance Liability

Under Law No. 11729, certain indemnities are payable in the event of an employee's death or in case of dismissal not justified by law. This may be insured against but would usually be rather expensive. There is no requirement in the law that a provision for this contingency be created. The company may elect to do so, in which case an annual provision equal to 2 per cent of salaries and wages is allowed as a deductible expense for tax purposes.

For book purposes, since the company is not liable when an employee resigns voluntarily or is pensioned, a reserve of from 35 to 50 per cent of the theoretical total liability at a balance sheet date is usually considered reasonable.

Reserves from Revaluation of Fixed Assets

The increase in fixed assets resulting from revaluation for book purposes is recorded in a restricted reserve account, which may be used for:

1. Absorbing past or future losses, provided such losses are the net result of the operations of one commercial year (or shorter period in certain exceptional cases), or
2. Increasing the capital of the company.

For corporations, either use must be approved by the shareholders; if a capital increase is approved, a stock dividend of an equivalent amount is distributed. For other than corporations, either use requires the decision of a partners' meeting.

Legal Reserve

A Sociedad Anónima must appropriate 2 per cent of annual net profits into a legal reserve until an amount equal to 10 per cent of the par value of subscribed capital stock has been accumulated.

In the partnership deed of a Sociedad de Responsabilidad Limitada provision must be made for a legal reserve appropriation of a minimum of 5 per cent of net profits annually until an amount equal to 10 per cent of subscribed capital has been accumulated.

These reserves may be used solely to absorb accumulated losses; no distribution of subsequent profits may be made until the reserves have been reinstated. Any balance remaining in these reserves is distributable to stockholders upon liquidation of the company.

Secret Reserves

It is not legally necessary to disclose secret reserves. Many C.P.N.s and foreign practitioners recommend such disclosure, if material, but there are others who do not.

Statement of Surplus

Since it is not required either by the Inspección General de Justicia or by Decree No. 9795/54, a statement of surplus is not usually included in financial statements.

Statement of Income

Stock Dividends. Stock dividends received are treated as income and recorded at the par value of stock by both the recipient and the issuer.

Depreciation. Any depreciation method is acceptable so long as it is consistently applied. The straight-line method is most prevalent.

Provision for Income Taxes. Income taxes are generally recorded as a charge against income on an accrual basis, often combined with other taxes in the administrative expense section. Some companies follow the older practices of reflecting taxes on income as a distribution of profits, or on a cash basis. Income tax may be shown separately as a final deduction before arriving at profit available for distribution. In some cases they are shown in the Board of Directors' report to shareholders (memoria) in the proposed profits distribution.

If a provision for taxes has not been deducted in arriving at net profit, it is customary to so state, giving an estimate of the amounts involved.

REQUIREMENTS FOR LISTING OF SECURITIES ON THE STOCK EXCHANGE (BOLSA DE VALORES) AND PUBLIC SALE OF SECURITIES

The Argentine Securities Commission (Comisión de Valores) approves applications for registration on the stock exchanges. Applicants must meet certain basic requirements, as follows:

1. Have a subscribed and paid-up capital of not less than p.50,000,000, with a par value for all shares of p.100 each
2. Have financial and management arrangements satisfactory to the Commission
3. Have statutes (i.e., charters, provisions, or by-laws) conforming to the requirements of the Commission.
   These include:
   a. Voting rights—no series or class of ordinary shares may be deprived of its voting rights
   b. Directors—qualification for the post of director may not be restricted to election by a certain class of stock. Any restriction as to remuneration must be specified
   c. Shareholders must have pre-emptive right to subscribe for subsequent issues.
4. There must be a commitment by shareholders to open quotations, within twelve months of acceptance for registration, with the offer of shares aggregating not less than p.5,000,000 par value.

Applicants must also furnish copies of their statutes and financial statements for five years. When an issue is to be offered publicly, a prospectus must be issued containing the following information:

1. Brief history of company
2. Composition of authorized and issued share capital and details relating to issues during previous ten years
3. Description of, and details relating to, forthcoming issues (within twelve months)
4. A list of board members and statutory examiners
5. Summary of royalties paid for previous three years
6. Balance sheets and profit and loss accounts for the previous three fiscal years; when the results shown in the latter statements are not strictly comparable, the pertinent additional information

must be shown in a specially prescribed form. All the statements and supplementary information must be certified by a C.P.N. in a form established by the Securities Commission

7. Details of distribution of profits during the last previous three years and of all fees and remunerations paid to directors during the same period, split between fees arising from distribution of profits and remunerations charged to expenses

8. Details, supported by financial statements, of investments in other enterprises where the holdings of the applicant are in excess of 20 per cent of the share capital of the issuing corporation

9. Details of real estate, and of any revaluations made thereof, and rates of amortization for these and other fixed assets

10. Details of any debentures, mortgages and compositions with creditors

11. Summarized analyses of payables and of all receivables

12. Information about acquired companies, if any, including a comparison of net book value and estimated market value of such assets acquired within the last five years with the price paid; if this comparison indicates an excess of price paid over book or market value, the reasons for this excess must be stated

13. Insurance coverage.

The prospectus also must state that the results of operations for the period have been stated in the same manner as those for the previous year.

When an issue is not to be offered publicly, a reseña (summary of information) of the information otherwise contained in a prospectus must be submitted to the Securities Commission and published in the Stock Exchange Bulletin for all issues of shares made by registered companies.

There are also additional rules to regulate investment corporations.

The specified form for the certificate mentioned under 6 above may be translated as follows:

We have verified that the figures contained in the preceding balance sheets and profit and loss accounts are in agreement with the corresponding entries in the principal books of account of the corporation and that the registrations in these books agree with those in the auxiliary books and supporting vouchers.

On the basis of the analysis referred to in the preceding paragraph and from the information and explanations which have been furnished to us at our request, we certify that the figures reflect faithfully the assets and liabilities of the enterprise in each of the financial periods included in the period under review.

We are also of the opinion that the adjustments made to the profit and loss accounts published in the company's annual reports and corresponding to the financial periods under consideration, establish figures which are homogeneous and representative of the net profits obtained by the enterprise in the exploitation of their usual business during said financial periods.

(In addition to the requirements of Decree No. 9795/54 a brief general explanation should be inserted regarding the basis used to make the adjustments to the profit and loss accounts, as well as the procedure followed to form the provision for staff dismissal indemnity.)

Registered companies are required to submit financial statements, quarterly and annually, duly certified by a C.P.N. and in the form prescribed by the regulations, to the Securities Commission and to the Stock Exchange.

The examinations made of the quarterly financial statements vary quite widely in scope, ranging from a mere comparison with the books to a review with procedures approaching an annual audit. The report accompanying such quarterly review would vary according to the type of examination made.

Subsequent issues of shares require similar registration, except that if shares are registered within two years of the original registration, a brief supplementary report may be filed.

BRAZIL

4

BRAZIL | 4

FORMS OF BUSINESS ORGANIZATION

Brazilian business laws are promulgated by the Federal Government and recognize the common forms of business enterprises found in other countries in which commercial legislation was originally derived from the Napoleonic Code. All business organizations are governed by the Commercial Code promulgated in 1850, as amended. Corporations are specifically regulated under the Corporation Law issued in 1940, and limited liability companies are governed by a law promulgated in 1919.

Foreign companies, depending on their requirements in each particular case, may adopt any of the following forms of doing business in Brazil:

Brazilian corporation (Sociedade Anonima)

Limited liability company (Sociedade por Quotas de Responsabilidade Limitada)

Branch of foreign corporation

Sociedade Anonima (S.A.)

"Sociedade Anonima" is the form that most closely resembles the United States corporation. It is designated by a corporate name that indicates its purpose, followed by the words "Sociedade Anonima," or its abbreviation "S. A.," i.e., Industria de Aluminio XYZ Brasileira, S. A., or the word "Companhia," or its abbreviation "Cia."

Every corporation must have a minimum of seven shareholders, but no minimum capital is required, although the entire authorized capital must be subscribed and at least 10 per cent of it paid at inception. Shares, both common or preferred, must have the same par value and may be issued only at or above par. Shares may be issued to "bearer" only when fully paid. A corporation may not deal in its own shares.

3

Participating shares (partes beneficiarias) are sometimes also issued to founders, stockholders, or third parties as remuneration for services rendered to the corporation, but are not permitted to be capitalized. These shares do not have par value and are independent of the corporation's recognized "capital," but they do participate in annual profits. Their annual participation, however, cannot exceed 10 per cent of the total amount of net profits for the year. These shares are always callable either for redemption or for conversion into stock, provided a special reserve has been created for this purpose. The corporation is free to determine the redemption price, but it must be established at the time they are issued; it does not have to be a fixed redemption price and is usually determined through a pre-established formula. In the case of liquidation, the claims of the holders of these shares rank ahead of other stockholders to the extent of the special reserve provided.

The shareholders of every corporation must annually elect a "Conselho Fiscais" (statutory examiners committee) composed of three or more members and an equal number of alternates, all of whom may be re-elected. The functions of the fiscal council are described hereafter.

An annual report of the directors accompanied by a balance sheet and profit and loss statement, together with the report of the statutory examiners committee, must be published in the *Diario Oficial* (Official Gazette) and in a local newspaper, not later than five days before the date of the annual shareholders' meeting. The requirements of Brazilian law with respect to the contents of financial statements are described in a later section. The practice of most companies is to publish only such information as is legally required.

Sociedade por Quotas de Responsabilidade Limitada

Formation of limited liability companies is regulated by Decree 3708 of January 10, 1919, and they may be organized by not less than two persons; foreign corporations or nonresidents may be partners (shareholders), provided a suitable power of attorney is held by a resident of Brazil to enable him to sign the deed of incorporation and to vote the "quotas" held by the nonresident. The partnership (shareholder) interests must be represented by "quotas," which are nominative shares, each with a fixed unit value. Certificates representing quotas are not issued. The company is designated by the names of one or more of its members or by the description of its purpose, adding in each case the word "Limitada" or its abbreviation "Ltda."

This type of company has many of the attributes of a corporation;

among which is that the liability of its members is limited to the amount of their respective capital subscriptions. It is similar to a partnership in respect to the absence of formalities and publicity attending its organization and operation. An attendant disadvantage, however, is that any changes in the partnership agreement, or any transfer of "quotas" by a partner requires the consent of all its members.

It need not appoint a conselho fiscal, provide a statutory reserve, or publish financial statements or minutes in the *Official Gazette* or a newspaper.

Branch of Foreign Corporation

Certain requisites must be complied with in order to obtain the approval of the Federal Government to establish a branch of a foreign corporation, and such approval also must be obtained in the event of any branch reorganization. As do Brazilian corporations, foreign branches must publish their annual statements in the *Official Gazette*. Generally, the branch operates under the name of its head office, adding the words "do Brasil" or "para o Brasil."

Other Forms of Business Organization

Sociedade em Nome Coletivo. General partnerships are known as "Sociedade em Nome Coletivo" and require the association of two or more partners all having unlimited liability.

Sociedade em Comandita. The "Sociedade em Comandita" is composed of one or more partners with unlimited liability, who manage the company, and one or more silent partners, whose liability is limited to their capital contributions. If the capital contributed by the silent partners is represented by shares, then its title is "Sociedade em Comandita por Acões" and it is governed by the law covering corporations. But this form is rarely seen in practice.

Sociedade de Capital e Industria. When one or more of the partners contribute only their personal services and are not personally liable with respect to the obligations of the partnership, the designation is "Sociedade de Capital e Industria."

5

Business Records

There is a very extensive list of books of account required by both Federal and state laws to be kept by commercial and industrial enterprises. The following books are the most common:

Journal (Diario)

Register of "Duplicatas" (Notes Covering Sales)

Inventory Register

Purchase Register

Cash Sales Register

In addition, corporations are required to keep minute books of stockholders' meetings and statutory examiners committee actions, also stock registers, stock transfer books, etc.

All the books mentioned above, except the inventory and purchase registers, must be bound, and, prior to being used, must be registered with the Department of Commerce and State Treasury. The first page of each must always contain a declaration of the name and registered number of the company, as well as a statement of the total number of pages and how they are numbered. An official signs a statement that the book has been correctly presented, and he or one of his authorized staff initials the top of each page.

During the last few years and because of the tremendous influence of mechanized accounting, some flexibility has been given to the above requirements.

CONSELHOS FISCAIS
(STATUTORY EXAMINERS COMMITTEE)

The members of the statutory examiners committees are elected annually at the general shareholders' meeting; they may be, but need not be, shareholders, and must be residents of the country. Their remuneration is fixed at the time of their election. Dissenting shareholders representing one-fifth or more of the corporation's capital, and holders of preferred stock are entitled to elect, separately, one of the members of the committee and the respective alternate. There are no specific educational or experience requirements, but employees of the corporation and relatives of directors up to the third degree cannot be elected to the committee.

Statutory examiners committees have duties specified in the Law of 1940, the most significant of which are to:

1. Examine at any time but at least quarterly the accounting records, cash and investments of the corporation. The directors are obliged to make all the required information available to them.
2. Record in the "Minute Book and Report of the Statutory Examiners Committee" the results of the periodic examinations.
3. Submit to the annual shareholders' meeting an opinion (parecer) on the operations of the corporation, based on the statements issued by its Board of Directors.
4. Report errors, frauds or criminal acts which they may discover and suggest the appropriate corrective measures to the corporation.

Since the members of the committee may not be professionally qualified to make the required examinations, the Corporation Law permits them to use the services of a legally qualified accountant in performing their duties. Corporations sometimes arrange for representatives of their auditors to serve on the statutory examiners committee. The question may arise as to whether acceptance of this appointment may compromise the independent position of the auditor and whether the report issued as a member of the committee (which may be in condensed form) is incompatible with that issued by his firm as auditors. There is also the fact that the legal responsibility of this statutory examiners committee exceeds the professional responsibility of the auditor. The policy of accounting firms as to accepting such appointments differs; some of them do so.

There is no fixed standard form of the report (parecer), which the statutory examiners committee issues, relating to the annual financial statements of a corporation. However, following is a typical example:

> The below signed members of the statutory examiners committee of the XYZ Corporation, having proceeded with the required examination of the balance sheet and the profit and loss account, as well as the other accounts and written accounting documents pertaining to the period ended December 31, 19.., declare that all is in perfect order, and are of the opinion that the statements are in full agree-

ment with the situation of the corporation and should thus be approved by the stockholders in general assembly.

It is evident that the report of the conselhos fiscais, who are not required to be competent in accounting and auditing, nor to be independent, does not, and is not intended to give the same degree of assurance as to the fairness of presentation of financial statements as would that of an independent certified public accountant.

THE ACCOUNTING PROFESSION

General

The designation "Contabilista" was first legally established in 1931 and 1932. It is a general one, embracing all those engaged in accounting and bookkeeping; it includes the "Tecnico em Contabilidade" (known previously as "Guarda-Livros"—bookkeeper) and the "Contador," who may offer his services as an independent accountant. The educational requirements and the areas of activity of each group were established by Decree-Law No. 9295 of 1946, which created the "Conselho Federal de Contabilidade" (Federal Council of Accountancy) and the Regional Councils where both "tecnicos" and "contadores" must be registered in the location where they practice.

There is no statutory or other governmental regulation which requires either a limited liability company or other form of corporation, or a partnership to have its financial statements examined and reported upon by an independent public accountant. However, financial statements and any other accounting documents must be signed by accountants or bookkeepers legally registered, and the respective registration numbers of the signers given.

Under recent income tax legislation, corporate income tax returns must be accompanied by a certificate issued by the competent Regional Council of Accountancy to the effect that the contador or the tecnico signing the financial statements is duly registered.

Tecnico em Contabilidade

The "tecnico" must be a graduate of a recognized "Escola Tecnica de Comercio," which is substantially the equivalent of the United States commercial high school. Because of the limited requirements of these schools, their graduates are numerous. At the end of a three-year accounting course, which does not include auditing, the "escolas" issue a diploma of "Tecnico em Contabilidade."

The duties of the tecnicos are limited to general bookkeeping and accounting services, and to the signing, in their capacity as company accountants but not as auditors, of the financial statements which corporations are required to publish annually. They are not allowed to perform judicial examinations, financial statement audits, or assist the statutory examiners committees of corporations. These latter functions, as well as those others specifically mentioned by law, are only to be performed by contadores.

Contador

The contador must now be a graduate of a recognized university offering an approved four-year curriculum. Entrance to the university requires the diploma either of a high school or that of tecnico em contabilidade (see above) and the passing of an examination before an examining board. No practical experience is required for one to be registered as a contador in the Regional Council of Accountancy.

A number of universities in Brazil offer business courses leading to a diploma of "Bacharel em Ciencias Contabeis." The accounting curriculum includes, in the first two years, subjects common to all students majoring in accounting, i.e., economics, actuarial science, and business administration; a two-year accounting specialization course follows, which includes financial mathematics, statistics, specialized accounting, advanced accounting, auditing, civil, business and fiscal legislation, finance, production administration, etc. The University of São Paulo has recently altered the curriculum to one year of general subjects, followed by three years of specialization. An elective two-year curriculum of post-graduate work leading to a doctorate degree includes advanced studies on finance, business administration, auditing and cost accounting. The candidate must submit and discuss his thesis at the end of the course.

University statistics show that out of 9,284 graduates in 1961, only 257 were accounting graduates, although recently the number of accounting students has been increasing.

The services provided to his clients by the contador are intended to be similar to those of the United States CPA. He may be selected by management, directors or stockholders to examine and report upon financial statements, act as a member of the statutory examiners committee or assist the members of the committee in their functions, give tax advice, prepare tax returns and do special accounting work in connection with lawsuits. To a limited extent, he may perform management services, although legally this area is reserved for the "economistas."

Brazilian public accounting firms are usually organized in the form of civil partnerships, although some operate as corporations or limited liability companies.

Organizations of the Accounting Profession in Brazil

Federal Council of Accountancy. The official bodies representing the accounting profession in Brazil are the Federal Council of Accountancy and the Regional Councils, which represent both the tecnicos em contabilidade and the contadores.

The Federal Council of Accountancy is composed of nine members, the president being appointed by the Federal Government; the rest of the membership is composed of two-thirds contadores and one-third tecnicos. The essential functions of the Regional Councils are: to register those qualified to act in either of the two mentioned capacities, and to impose sanctions on members in certain cases (see discussion under "Ethics"). The Federal Council annually publishes a list of registered accountants and hears appeals from sanctions imposed by Regional Councils.

Professional accounting firms formed for the purpose of rendering accounting and auditing services in Brazil must comply with the following:

1. The firm itself must be registered with the Federal Council of Accountancy, and such registration is evidenced by a fixed number given to the firm.
2. One of the partners of the firm must also be a registered accountant with his own registered number.

When the auditors' report is appended to the published financial statements of the client, both the firm's name and that of the "Contador

Responsavel" (registered accountant) must appear with their respective registered numbers and their respective names.

Instituto dos Contadores Publicos de São Paulo. This Institute, in the state of São Paulo, was the first Institute organized in Brazil. The title of "Contador Publico Certificado" (CPC) issued by the Institute is merely a certificate of membership and does not have official recognition. To be eligible for membership the applicant must:

1. Have at least five years of experience in public accounting
2. Be over twenty-five years of age
3. Be registered as "Contador" with the Regional Council of Accountancy
4. Have the technical and moral qualifications considered satisfactory by the "Conselho Tecnico e Administrativo" of the Institute.

Instituto dos Contadores Publicos do Rio Grande do Sul. This state Institute has somewhat less stringent membership qualifications than that of São Paulo, but few of its members are in public practice.

Sindicato dos Contabilistas. Nearly every state has its own "Sindicato," which is the association of both accountants and bookkeepers who practice in each state. It may be described as a union and is under the supervision of the Department of Labor. Any locally qualified professional must be registered with the respective Regional Council in order to practice, but he does not need to be a member of the Sindicato.

Ethics

The Code of Ethics approved at the Fifth Brazilian Congress of Accounting established the rules of ethics to which the professional accountants and bookkeepers should adhere. Among these, the following apply when the contador is reporting upon an examination of financial statements:

1. He should not fail to mention any comments regarding facts known to him, the omission of which would make misleading the financial statements he is examining.
2. He should only express opinions which are adequate and properly supported.
3. He should clearly explain any false interpretation or any deviation in the application of general accounting principles.

11

4. He should not express an opinion on the financial statements of any enterprise where he has a family relationship up to the third degree either with a member of its top management or with any other person who could have a decisive influence on it.

This last principle is the only one which deals with the concept of independence. The importance of an independent mental attitude on the part of public accountants as it is understood in the United States, however, is not believed to be generally recognized by most of the Brazilian accounting firms.

The law that created the Federal Council of Accountancy established sanctions applicable under specific circumstances, including:

1. Suspension of those professionals who, within the scope of their work and their technical capacity, are responsible for any falsification of documents signed by them and for irregularities in the accounting records committed for the purpose of evading taxes.
2. Suspension for a period of six months to one year of any professional who shows technical inability in performing his functions, at the discretion of the Regional Council of Accountancy to which he is subject.

The Federal or Regional Councils do not have the necessary organization or facilities to effectively police the Code except when complaints are made to them. There have been a few cases reported alleging professional incompetence, but no sanctions have as yet been imposed.

AUDITING STANDARDS

General Standards

Although the Brazilian practitioner does not have the support of pronouncements such as the AICPA's "Codification of Statements on Auditing Procedures" and other statements issued by the committee on auditing procedure, an effort is being made by the more prominent Brazilian accounting firms to adopt similar auditing standards. Local offices of foreign public accounting firms follow, in general, the standards of the countries of their origin. The matter of independence has been referred to under the section on "Ethics."

Standards of Field Work

With respect to auditing procedures of Brazilian local practitioners:

1. An annual investigation of internal control based on written questionnaires is not generally made.
2. A fairly extensive detailed check of individual transactions is customary.
3. Since banks do not return paid checks, disbursements are checked by inspecting the supporting documents and checking the information shown in bank statements (number of check and amount) to the client's records. Bank confirmations are not generally obtained.
4. A large portion of the audit time is devoted to the checking of *duplicatas,* which are the instruments representing amounts due from customers. Confirmation of *duplicatas* using mainly negative requests is sometimes practiced. Confirmations, when returned and signed by the debtor, are required to be revenue-stamped, which costs inhibit the use of such confirmation procedures.
5. The observation of physical inventories is accepted as a desirable technique, but has not become common practice.
6. Written representations of management are not generally obtained.
7. No consideration is given to a review of subsequent events.

Standards of Reporting

There is no standard report used in Brazil such as the standard short-form used in the United States and by the international firms practicing in Brazil. Brazilian accounting firms are beginning to apply the concept that the objective of the examinations of financial statements by the contador is to enable them to express an opinion as to whether the statements fairly present the financial position and the results of operations as of a certain date and for a specified period of time.

As previously indicated, the report is signed by the auditing firm's name and by a registered accountant, adding the respective registration numbers.

Consistency. The significance of consistency in accounting treatment from one year to another is not generally recognized by the majority of Brazilian practitioners.

Materiality. No pronouncements have been made in relation to this concept.

ACCOUNTING PRINCIPLES AND PRACTICES

The only authoritative source of accounting principles in Brazil is the Corporation Law of 1940, which laid down the rules with regard to the basis of valuation of assets and liabilities and the presentation of annual financial statements. The accounting profession, as such, has not established generally accepted accounting principles.

Form and Content of Financial Statements

Uniform systems of accounts have been prescribed for public utility companies, banks, insurance companies and certain other industries. The objective is to provide uniformity in presentation of financial statements and to some extent to establish certain accounting principles for these enterprises.

Statement Presentation—Balance Sheet. The Corporation Law of 1940, describes the contents of the balance sheet, as follows:

1. "Assets shall be classified into immobilized, available, realizable in short-term and in long-term, pending accounts and compensating (memorandum) accounts."
2. "Liabilities shall be classified as payable either at short or long-term, and nondemandable; the latter including capital as well as legal and statutory reserves; and shall also include pending accounts and compensating accounts."
3. The caption "sundry accounts" shown in the balance sheet either as an asset or as a liability should not amount to more than one-tenth of the corporation's capital.

4. Investments in and advances to affiliates and subsidiaries should be shown separately in the balance sheet.

Brazilian financial statements tend to show all accounts "broad"; that is, credit accounts such as valuation reserves are not deducted from the related assets. With the increasing number of foreign investments, financial statements are slowly evolving toward the presentation followed by American companies.

The structure of the balance sheet as required by law and as generally used and interpreted in conventional Brazilian published financial statements is shown below:

Available	Cash on hand and in banks.
Realizable in short term	Normally equivalent to current assets other than cash. However, accounts under this heading are generally stated gross, i.e., they do not have directly applied against them valuation reserves such as the reserve for bad debts, etc.
Realizable in long-term	Assets not due within one year; usually stated at gross amount.
Immobilized	Equivalent to fixed assets but usually not reduced by the reserves for depreciation. Intangibles such as patents and trademarks are also included under this caption; investments are sometimes shown in this group.
Pending	Since accounts like deferred charges are not available, realizable or immobilized, they are classified as pending.
Compensating accounts	See description below.
Payables	Equivalent to demandable. Represent liabilities segregated into current and long-term. However, since reserves are not "demandable," they are frequently excluded from this classification.
Nondemandable	This group covers all items of stockholders' equity.

Since Brazilian financial statements do not include notes or any explanatory comments (other than in the directors' report) and the structure of the balance sheet emphasizes only what is due and owned, a third group of accounts has evolved, i.e., the compensating accounts. These accounts show items not included above in the balance sheet which are not physically in the possession of the company and assets of third parties which are in the possession of the company. Listed below are explanations of the more usual compensating accounts:

1. *Deposits of the executive board.* This item represents the deposits required by the Corporation Law as a pledge of guarantee made by each director.
2. *Bank deposit account.* This account shows the amount of trade notes (*duplicatas*) held by banks as collateral.
3. *Bank collection account.* This balance represents the amount of trade notes (*duplicatas*) held by banks for collection.
4. *Portfolio account.* Trade notes still on hand at balance sheet date.

Statement Presentation—Profit and Loss and Surplus. The conventional Brazilian form of profit and loss statement combines the earned surplus and the income statements and follows the account form, i.e., gross profit, income from capital not employed in company's operations, other income and the beginning surplus balance are shown on the credit side; expenses and profit distribution are on the debit side. Since this form of presentation does not normally show net profit, there has been little development in the definition of net profit, and the distinction between earned surplus and income is not generally recognized.

A recent Profits Remittance Law and certain new income tax regulations (1963) require that companies which operate in Brazil and whose capital is partly or wholly owned by a foreign entity must show in its annual accounts the division of the following, as between Brazilian and foreign shareholders or partners:

Capital

.Undistributed profits and dividends paid

Income and expenses

This law also requires that "credits to persons domiciled or residing abroad" be shown separately in the balance sheet when such credits are registered with SUMOC (Superintendency of Currency and Credit).

Comparative Financial Statements. One of the most difficult aspects—and perhaps the most significant—in analyzing Brazilian comparative financial statements is the effect of inflation. Comparative statements can be very misleading if this feature is not properly considered.

Consolidated Financial Statements. It is not common for corporations to present consolidated financial statements, and they are not acceptable for income tax purposes.

Inventories

Inventories must be carried at the lower of cost or market and individual values adjusted accordingly—Lifo is not an acceptable method of pricing inventories for tax purposes.

Bad Debts

A reserve for bad debts up to a maximum of 10 per cent of the accounts receivable balance is generally acceptable for income tax purposes. For book purposes, the reserve actually needed may be provided, but the excess over 10 per cent is not tax deductible unless its necessity is proved to the satisfaction of the inspectors.

Fixed Assets

The Corporation Law states that property will be valued at cost. However, the pressing problems brought about by inflation have caused the Tax Department to permit upward restatements of property based on coefficients established by the government which are revised every year. For income tax purposes, depreciation in excess of that based on historical costs is not deductible; however, upon retirement of the asset, the amount corresponding to the restatement may be charged to income.

Since there is no obligation to restate property and a special 10 per cent income tax is charged on the increase of capital resulting from the net write-up of property and depreciation reserves, some enterprises have not restated these accounts, although generally the resulting increase in capital reduces the excess profits tax. Proposed changes in the law indicate that restatements of property will become obligatory in the future.

There is no requirement for disclosure of restatements in published financial statements, but the amounts must be carried in separate accounts on the books.

Disposition of Increase. The increase resulting from restatement of fixed assets within official coefficients may be used to absorb losses, but, if not, the amount is immediately capitalized with an accompanying issue of capital stock pro-rata to shareholders. Restatement of fixed assets and increase of capital on such basis take place simultaneously.

Organization Expenses

The law permits organization expenses to be carried as an asset up to a limit of 10 per cent of the corporation's capital, and they may be amortized annually or written off immediately.

Severance Payments

Brazilian law requires that employees discharged without just cause, legally proven, be paid an indemnity of one month's pay for each year of service. When an employee achieves ten years of service, he obtains a legal tenure. No indemnity is payable upon death or voluntary withdrawal or retirement.

Provisions for severance pay reserves are not deductible for tax purposes, unless the corresponding funds are invested in a special issue of public funds; however, amounts paid are deductible for tax purposes in the year of payment.

Most Brazilian companies do not make provision in their accounts for eventual severance compensation, and even when provision is made, the basis is usually arbitrary. Brazilian industry has grown so rapidly in recent years that many companies either have not yet determined their labor policy or do not have sufficient experience to provide accurate reserves.

Statement of Income

Sales and Cost of Sales. The Corporation Law does not require sales and cost of sales to be shown in the published profit and loss statement, and these figures are rarely given; gross profit is required to be shown separately for each of the various sources or groups of related activities, but generally only one figure of gross profit actually appears in published statements.

Depreciation. Depreciation on buildings is not allowed for income tax purposes, and is seldom provided for in the accounts. Depreciation on fixed asset valuations in excess of cost is rarely provided.

Depreciation on assets acquired at any time during the accounting period may be computed for the entire year at their applicable rates.

The new income tax law provides that the executive power may establish a coefficient for acceleration of depreciation, independent of actual physical wastage, with a view to stimulating renewal and renovation of plants.

Income Tax. It is not customary for Brazilian owned corporations to accrue income tax in the year the income is earned, but rather to charge the actual payment to operations in the year of payment. This is due to the fact that Brazil allows income tax as a deduction from taxable income in the year the tax is paid, if paid when due.

Exchange Losses. Reserves provided for exchange losses are not tax deductible until realized by remittance of foreign currency.

Legal Reserve

The Corporation Law provides that 5 per cent of the annual net profits of corporations (sociedades anonimas) should be set aside until the reserve equals 20 per cent of the issued capital. This statutory or legal reserve is classified as surplus. Although not described as restricted surplus, it is generally understood that it is not distributable.

Surplus

Any increase in reserves (excluding legal reserve) or earned surplus of a corporation which brings the total of such accounts to an amount in excess of paid-in capital is subject to a withholding tax of 30 per cent.

This effectively forces a distribution of earnings; however, a transfer from reserves or earned surplus to capital provides a means of accumulating earnings at the same time avoiding the full impact of this tax.

REQUIREMENTS FOR PUBLIC SALE OF SECURITIES

The Corporation Law of 1940, stated the requirements for public subscription of a corporation's securities. The principal requirement is the publication in the *Diário Oficial* (Official Gazette) and in local newspapers—at least three times—of the proposed by-laws together with a prospectus. The prospectus is defined as a precise and clear description of the corporation and the reasons why the founders expect the enterprise to be successful.

REQUIREMENTS FOR LISTING ON THE STOCK EXCHANGE

The two principal stock exchanges in Brazil are in Rio de Janeiro and São Paulo, and are privately owned, but are supervised by the Head of the Treasury. Corporations desiring to have their shares listed for trading on these exchanges must file an application addressed to the president of the Stock Exchange Association (Camara Sindical), giving full details of the securities intended to be listed. Listed companies must file with the stock exchange copies of their published annual or semi-annual reports to shareholders and their financial statements.

There are no state or Federal legal requirements, or any stock exchange requirement that the financial statements be examined and reported upon by independent public accountants.

CHILE

5

I

FORMS OF BUSINESS ORGANIZATION

The corporate form of business organization as well as that of the several forms of partnerships are similar to those of other South American countries, and are not unlike those of the United States. A United States corporation may obtain authorization by Presidential decree to engage in business in Chile by establishing a branch, or by organizing a Chilean subsidiary company to carry on its business in that country, after complying with specified formalities in each case.

A company in Chile may be either civil or commercial. A commercial company is one whose business consists of performing commercial acts; all others are civil companies. There are certain legal differences in their obligations. The discussion which follows deals only with commercial companies.

Sociedad Anónima (S. A.)

This closely resembles the corporate form existing in the United States. Shareholders are liable for the debts of the corporation only to the extent of their subscribed capital.

A Chilean government agency, namely Superintendencia de Sociedades Anónimas (Superintendency of Corporations), exercises the supervision and control of Sociedades Anónimas.

In order to organize a corporation, two or more persons must submit to the Superintendencia for approval the "estatutos" (charter and by-laws) in the form of a public instrument. The estatutos must fix the share capital and must define the rules for internal organization of the corporation. The share capital must be nominative shares, as the issue of bearer shares is no longer allowed. Dividends on existing bearer shares are now subject to a withholding tax of 40 per cent.

The Superintendencia also has the right to audit the operations of a

3

S.A., but this right is exercised only upon complaint or for some specific purpose, and is not a routine procedure.

Stockholders must approve the annual accounts and proposals for distribution of dividends at a general meeting called for that purpose. The annual accounts, together with the report to stockholders, must be presented to the Superintendencia and published in a newspaper; they must be signed by the company's general manager, its accountant, and two Inspectores de Cuentas (account inspectors [see below]).

Sociedad de Responsabilidad Limitada (S. R. L.)

The Sociedad de Responsabilidad Limitada has the characteristics of a partnership and a corporation; the right of management extends to all partners and their rights are neither negotiable nor represented by any transferable document. The liability of the members is limited, however, to the amount of their contribution to capital, or possibly to a larger amount if designated in the instrument of organization.

The firm name must contain the name of one or more partners followed by the word "Limitada" (Ltda.). There may be no more than fifty partners. A partner may not transfer his interest to an outsider without the unanimous consent of all other partners. An S.R.L. is constituted by a notarial instrument containing the same information as that required for the Sociedad Colectiva (see below), plus a statement as to the agreed liability of partners. An extract must be inscribed in the Commercial Register, (including a statement as to the limitation of liability of partners), and the extract must be published in the *Diario Oficial* (Official Gazette).

Other Forms of Business Organization

Sociedad Colectiva. The general commercial partnership is similar to its counterpart in the United States. The partners are jointly and severally liable for its debts. A partner may not transfer his interest in the partnership to an outsider without the unanimous consent of the other partners. A general partnership is organized by a notarial public instrument, which must contain certain information, among which are names and addresses of partners, name and domicile of firm, capital contributed, form in which contributed and basis of its valuation, basis of allocation of profits and losses among partners, and allowable drawing accounts.

4

The notarial instrument constituting both the Sociedad de Responsabilidad Limitada and the Sociedad Colectiva does not require the approval of the Superintendencia, but an extract must be inscribed in the Commercial Register and published in the *Diario Oficial.*

Sociedad en Comandita Simple. This type of partnership is comprised of both general partners (gestores) and limited partners (comanditarios). The general partners who supply capital or services or both, have the same liability as in a general partnership, and have exclusive right to management. Limited partners who supply capital have limited liability to the extent of their capital contribution to the enterprise, and may not participate in the management. The Sociedad en Comandita Simple is formed in the same manner as the Sociedad Colectiva, except that the names of the comanditarios are not allowed in the firm name nor are they stated in the extract of the constitutive document.

Sociedad en Comandita por Acciones. This form differs from the above only in that the interests of the comanditarios may be represented by shares. The capital of the S.C. por A., if less than 50,000 pesos, may not be divided into shares of a value less than 100 pesos each; if the capital is more than 50,000 pesos, each share may not be valued at less than 500 pesos.

Both forms of "Comandita" have fallen into disuse and are now seldom encountered.

Asociación o Cuentas en Participación (Joint Ventures). Two or more persons may enter into a contract to enter into one or several commercial operations to be performed by one of them under his own name and credit. Such a venture has no legal standing and does not have to comply with the formalities required of corporations or partnerships in connection with its organization. The managing partner's obligation is to render an accounting to his associates and to divide the profits and losses in the proportion agreed upon. He is also responsible for the tax obligations and should retain the income tax applicable to the other partners' participation in profits.

Business Records

The principal books required to be kept are the ledger, journal, cash book, and the "inventory and balance book," and these must be stamped by the local treasury (Tesorería Comunal) of the location where the entity is established. The Stamp Act Law requires that each page bears a fixed stamp of E 0.005. All official subsidiary records must also be stamped.

Special permission may be obtained to use loose-leaf or card records as part of the legal books.

INSPECTORES DE CUENTAS (ACCOUNT INSPECTORS)

Supreme Decree No. 4705 (1946), which contains regulations applicable to local and foreign corporations established in Chile, states in Article 5:

> Approval will not be granted for those estatutos (articles of incorporation) which fail to state that the General Annual Shareholders' Meeting must name yearly two account inspectors whose responsibility is to watch the company's operations and examine the accounting records and financial statements with the obligation of reporting to the next ordinary general shareholders' meeting that they have complied with their assignment.

There are no specified professional or other qualifications for the office of "account inspector," nor any description of the procedures he is expected to follow. In practice, the inspectors rarely do more than compare financial statements with ledger balances and append a one-line statement to that effect on the financial statements themselves. In a few cases, the company's independent auditor is named as an account inspector, and then a satisfactory independent examination may be made with a corresponding report upon it.

THE ACCOUNTING PROFESSION

The practice of public accounting in Chile dates from the latter part of the nineteenth century, when the first British Chartered Accountant opened an office in Valparaiso. Later other English and American firms established offices in the country. There are now about ten Chilean firms operating as auditors.

In addition, there are a number of individual practitioners whose practice consists mainly of serving small businesses by writing up books on a monthly basis and preparing financial statements and tax returns.

University Courses

There are four faculties of Economics and Business Administration in Chile:

Faculty of Economics of the University of Chile

Faculty of Economics and Business Administration of the Catholic University at Santiago

Faculty of Business Administration of the Catholic University at Valparaiso

Faculty of Economics and Business Administration at the University of Concepcion.

The curriculums include courses such as general accounting, specialized accounting, cost accounting and auditing. The degrees offered are Licenciado in Commerce (three and one-half year course), General Accountant (four and one-half year course), Public Accountant (four and one-half year course), and Commercial Engineer (major in accounting—five-year course).

Degrees in these subjects can also be obtained from certain commercial schools.

Colegio de Contadores

In 1958, an institution known as the "Colegio de Contadores" (College of Accountants) was created by law. This institution is the successor to the former Register of Accountants and its stated purpose is:

... to watch over the progress, prestige and prerogatives of the accounting profession and its regular and correct practice, to maintain professional discipline and to afford protection to accountants.

Its members consist of those persons holding the title of accountant issued by a commercial school, a university or a private educational institution recognized by the state. An accountant is considered to be in practice if he has registered his title in the Colegio de Contadores and has paid the required yearly dues.

The Colegio is governed by a General Council, domiciled in Santiago, with provincial councils in various cities. It has the duty to inscribe its members on its rolls; to collect an annual license fee; to establish and maintain publications of professional interest; to impose precepts of professional ethics; to dictate rules (standards) relative to professional practice; to establish, with the consent of two-thirds of its members, the scale of professional fees; to maintain contact with other bodies of accountants; and to organize conventions, studies or assemblies. Only those properly inscribed in the Colegio and the special register of their domicile may practice the profession of accountant. Persons practicing accountancy who are not entitled to do so are subject to fines and imprisonment.

The provincial councils may impose certain sanctions upon an accountant who, upon complaint, is adjudged to have acted unethically or not in accordance with professional dignity or standards. Appeal may be made to the General Council of the Colegio, and from that to the Supreme Court.

Instituto de Contadores Profesionales Auditores (INCPA)

This Institute was organized in 1962, and received legal recognition by government decree in April of that year. Its members are qualified accountants engaged in auditing. Its objectives are the development of the (public) accounting profession and of auditing standards and techniques to which its members agree to conform.

Ethics

The Colegio de Contadores has issued (1959) a Code of Ethics which, inasmuch as it is applicable to all of its members, is not specifically directed to those in the independent practice of public accountancy. The Code emphasizes the duty of the accountant to observe ethical and moral standards, to maintain the dignity of the profession, to observe proper relations with his colleagues and his employer, and similar matters.

It is stated that the accountant has the responsibility that his work, and his opinions and reports thereon, be clothed with complete independence and conform to the truth and to strict accounting technique.

The Instituto de Contadores Profesionales Auditores (see above) issued a Code of Professional Ethics in 1962, which was applicable to the independent public accounting profession, modeled on the "Code of Professional Ethics" of the American Institute of Certified Public Accountants and the "Members' Handbook" of the United Kingdom Institute of Chartered Accountants in England and Wales. The rules cover members' professional activities, relations among members, professional conduct, and solicitation of clients and advertising.

Other Organizations of Accountants

Sociedad Nacional de Contadores. The "Sociedad Nacional de Contadores" (National Society of Accountants), formed in 1935, through the merger of existing professional accounting associations, worked for and obtained legal recognition of the profession through the enactment of legislation which first created the Register of Accountants and later its successor, the Colegio de Contadores.

The Sociedad Nacional de Contadores is a member of the Interamerican Conferences on Accounting and in 1957, was the host to the Fourth Interamerican Conference on Accounting held in Santiago.

Other. There has also been organized the Asociacion de Contadores de la Universidad Catolica de Valparaiso (members qualified at this University) and the Asociación de Contadores Independientes.

These organizations' activities are limited to professional development and, in the case of the latter, are devoted mainly to social welfare.

AUDITING STANDARDS

The Sociedad Nacional de Contadores held a National Congress of Accountants in Chile in 1955. This Congress published a statement of Auditing Standards (Normas de Auditoria), which, in substance, was ratified at the Fourth Interamerican Conference held in Santiago in 1957. The Standards covered those of statement preparation, auditing procedures and the auditor's report. While summarized in form, it provided for most of the concepts laid down by the pronouncements of the American Institute of CPAs, such as basis of stating assets, presence at taking of physical inventories, confirmation of receivables, and, without prescribing the exact language, stated that the auditor's report should state his opinion upon the fairness of presentation of the financial statements examined, and that they were prepared on the basis of generally accepted principles, consistently applied, in accordance with generally accepted auditing standards and techniques.

The Colegio has not, however, actively enforced the standards recommended in this publication.

Auditors' Reports

The Chilean delegation to the Fourth Interamerican Conference on Accounting (1957) proposed a form of auditor's report generally similar to that in use in the United States. There is no present requirement in Chilean law or custom for a particular form of auditor's report.

Independence

While, as indicated previously, the Code of Ethics of the Colegio makes reference to the desirability of an independent attitude of the accountant toward his work, it does not specify the considerations which might promote such an attitude. While some firms of independent auditors in Chile generally adhere to the rules of independence as understood in the United States, ownership of a financial interest in a client's business by partners and staff is not always considered a detriment to independence.

Consistency

Some firms of independent accountants in Chile recognize the importance of consistency in the application of accounting principles, but such recognition is not common among all practitioners. However, taxing authorities consider consistency of treatment over a period of years a strong argument in favor of approval of a particular method.

ACCOUNTING PRINCIPLES AND PRACTICES

There has been no official statement of accounting principles by any of the organizations of accountants in Chile, but the teaching in the Universities and the practice of some firms is largely based on United States rules and procedures.

Form and Content of Financial Statements

Statement Presentation. The Superintendency of Corporations has prescribed a form of balance sheet and profit and loss statement for Sociedades Anónimas. The balance sheet includes:

Assets:
    Fixed assets

    Realizable assets (inventories and receivables)

    Cash assets

    Deferred assets

    Intangible assets.

Net worth:
    Capital and voluntary reserves

    Legal reserve.

Liabilities:
    Long-term

    Short-term.
Deferred liabilities and provisions

"Memo accounts", (cuentas de orden), for such items as contingent liabilities, guarantee and custodian deposits, and directors' guarantee deposits, etc., are also provided.

The profit and loss statement is in the "Account" form:

Debits:

Depreciation and amortization

General and administrative expenses

Interest, discounts, commissions and exchange losses

Building taxes, licenses, and social security

Income tax

Provision for legal bonuses, profit-sharing of management and staff, etc.

Directors' remuneration.

Credits:

Income of the business (generally, sales less cost of goods sold)

Income of nonbusiness operations (rent, dividends, commissions, interest, and exchange gains).

The Superintendencia de Sociedades Anónimas, in consultation with the Colegio de Contadores, the Instituto Nacional de Contadores Profesionales Auditores, and the Santiago Stock Exchange is actively engaged in a study of a new form of presentation of financial statements for Sociedades Anónimas, which is expected to be similar to the United States' form and to be published in the near future.

Consolidated Financial Statements. Consolidated financial statements are rare in Chile, because (1) the practice of operating through subsidiaries is uncommon, and (2) each individual company is obliged to publish and file its own individual statements. When subsidiaries are present, it is considered good practice to show any intercompany accounts separately on the balance sheet.

Inventories

The form of balance sheet prescribed by the Superintendency includes inventories under the "current assets" section, and requires them to be stated at purchase cost. However, many companies use the "lower of cost or market" method and, in a few instances, "base-cost" or "Lifo." The tax law formerly did not prescribe a particular basis for stating inventories, but under the new tax regulations, the Internal Revenue must establish bases. There is a tendency in some instances to write down inventories unduly or to establish undisclosed reserves against them, but the penalties now established for tax evasion are expected to discourage this practice.

Allowance for Bad and Doubtful Accounts

The tax authorities allow, as a deduction from taxable income, bad debts written off on the books, provided reasonable methods of collection have been exhausted. While some companies provide allowances for doubtful accounts based upon probable collectibility of the accounts receivable as a whole, many others do not.

Revaluations

Law 13305, modified by a tax law having effect from January 1, 1964, provides for the annual revaluation of owners' capital by a percentage equal to the increase in the cost-of-living index. Invested capital for this purpose is deemed to be, with certain modifications in respect of intangible assets, the paid-up capital, capital reserves and surplus. The amount of the revaluation so determined is applied to increase, by the same percentage as referred to above, the net book value of fixed assets; any excess is applied to revalue investments up to quoted market values and the remainder, if any, is a tax-deductible charge to operations, limited to 10 per cent of the taxable income.

In addition, real estate may also be revalued up to the amount at which it is assessed for property taxes, provided such amount exceeds its book value after incorporating the above mentioned revaluation of owners' capital.

Increase in capital computed in this manner is credited to a capital reserve; a corporation may issue free (bonus) shares against this reserve.

Previously, the revaluation was optional; under the new tax law it is now obligatory.

Investments

Investments in securities are required to be shown at quoted market, if any, at the balance sheet date; if, after taking up the re-

13

valuation of owner's capital referred to in the preceding paragraph, the resulting adjustment represents an increase, it is credited to a "Fluctuation Fund." If the revaluation represents a decrease, it may be written off immediately or carried as a deferred charge if the decline is considered temporary.

Statutory Reserve

Each Sociedad Anónima by law must provide a statutory reserve of 5 per cent of annual profits until the total equals 20 per cent of capital. This reserve is included in the capital section of the balance sheet.

Statement of Income

The form of income statement prescribed by the Superintendencia does not provide for the disclosure of sales or cost of sales, nor of operating profit or profit before taxes.

Depreciation. The tax authorities prescribe rates of depreciation which are generally followed in a company's accounts for the different groups of depreciable property. Special rates will usually be allowed, provided it is shown, in an application submitted for this purpose, that the prescribed rates are inadequate. Depreciation is calculated on the book amount of property, plant and equipment, which includes the revaluation increases previously discussed.

Amounts Paid to President and Directors. The regulations of the Superintendencia require that all amounts paid to the President and Directors of a Sociedad Anónima must be shown separately in the profit and loss statement.

Profits Distribution and Surplus. The law indicates that the balance of annual profits, after providing for the legal reserve and any special reserves of funds, be distributed pro-rata to the shareholders as a dividend. Accordingly, a balance sheet heading as "surplus" or "retained earnings" does not exist in Chile. If a corporation does not wish to distribute all of its distributable profits as a dividend, then such amount as exceeds the distributed portion is transferred to an account called "Fondo de Futuros Dividendos" (Future Dividend Fund). This can be distributed at some future date, but in practice is more frequently capitalized.

REQUIREMENTS FOR LISTING ON THE STOCK EXCHANGE

An application for listing on the Bolsa de Comercio (Stock Exchange) must include copies of the latest balance sheet and statement of income, and the company must agree to file copies of its balance sheet and report of its directors annually. These financial statements need not be examined or reported upon by independent public accountants.

COLOMBIA

6

FORMS OF BUSINESS ORGANIZATION

The form of business organization in Colombia which in general is similar to the United States corporation is the "Sociedad Anónima" (S.A.). In addition to the ordinary general partnership, there are special forms of partnership—the "Sociedad de Responsabilidad Limitada" (S.R.L.) and the "Sociedad en Comandita."

Foreign corporations may register to do business in Colombia by complying with the provisions of Colombian law, which include the assignment of a specific amount of capital. The more usual procedure is to organize a subsidiary under Colombian law.

Sociedad Anónima (S.A.)

The Sociedad Anónima must have at least five incorporators. The liability of the stockholders is limited to the amount of their respective stock subscriptions. The Sociedad Anónima is organized by means of a registered public instrument (estatutos), which must state among other items the number and value of the authorized and subscribed share capital of the corporation. Twenty per cent of the capital must be paid in at the time of incorporation. The public instrument must also state the powers and duties of the revisor fiscal (statutory examiner); the first statutory examiner and his alternate must be named and identified.

No minimum capital is required; the capital may be increased by approval of all of the stockholders or of a majority of stockholders if prescribed in the by-laws; authorization of the Superintendent of Corporations is necessary in either case. The capital may not be decreased during the life of the corporation.

At least once a year, every corporation must submit financial statements, signed by the statutory examiner, to the Superintendent of Corporations. Corporations with capital of P 150,000 or more must submit financial statements twice a year. Corporations that have issued bearer

3

shares or whose shares are traded on an exchange must publish financial statements in one of the major newspapers.

The Superintendent of Corporations supervises corporations and verifies that they are complying with the corporate purposes and other legal requirements.

Sociedad de Responsabilidad Limitada (S.R.L.)

This is a partnership in which the liability of the partners is limited to their contributions plus whatever additional amount may be agreed upon and stated. There may be no more than twenty partners. There must be a partnership agreement in the form of a public instrument executed before a notary and stating particulars of contributed capital, type of business, division of profits and losses, drawing accounts, etc.

The interest of any partner may be transferred to another partner by a notarial instrument; approval of partners representing 75 per cent of the capital is necessary to transfer an interest to someone outside the partnership.

The capital of a S.R.L. must be divided into equal parts, each partner having as many votes as he has parts in the company.

The firm name or designation of a S.R.L. must be followed by the word "Limitada"; if this is not done, the partners become jointly and severally liable for the firm's obligations.

The Superintendent of Corporations has jurisdiction over S.R.L. partnerships in which Colombian Sociedades Anónimas have an interest of 33 per cent or more.

Other Forms of Business Organization

Sociedad Colectiva. This is the common form of partnership composed of two or more partners who are jointly and severally liable for debts and obligations of the partnership. Initially, the organizational requirements are the same as for an S.R.L.

Sociedad en Comandita Simple. In this form there are two classes of partners, active (gestores) and limited (comanditarios). Active partners have unlimited liability and the exclusive right of administration. The liability of limited partners cannot exceed their capital contributons, and they may take no part in administration. It is formed and legalized in the same manner as a general partnership.

Sociedad en Comandita por Acciones. This partnership, which consists of active and limited partners as detailed above, has capital which is divided into shares or fractions of shares and in matters other than administration or partners' liability is subject to the same rules as general partnerships.

Business Records

All individual merchants, partnerships and corporations must maintain a book of inventories and balances, a journal, and a ledger. Each of the above books must be bound, must have numbered pages, and must be presented to the local chamber of commerce where each page is initialled and a certificate stating the number of pages is affixed. The journal and the ledger may be combined in one book.

Corporations must also maintain a stock transfer book and minute books, which must be initialled and certified in the same manner.

On proper application and approval, arrangements can be made so that modern mechanized records may be used.

REVISOR FISCAL (STATUTORY EXAMINER)

Colombian commercial law requires that the shareholders of each corporation elect a statutory examiner (revisor fiscal) and an alternate—both individuals must be public accountants. A person who is a public accountant (see later discussion) employed by the company may be appointed as its revisor fiscal. He may not be a shareholder of the company, nor may there be close family ties between him and the company's administrators, cashiers and accountants.

By law, he is required to inspect all the operations, inventories, minutes, books, correspondence and vouchers of the company. He must count securities and cash at least weekly and assure himself that the operations of the company are in accordance with its estatutos, with the resolutions of the board and of the general assembly, and with legal requirements. He is to report any irregularities to the shareholders, Board of Directors or the manager, and he is to report to the shareholders upon the balance sheet submitted to the annual meeting.

Upon signing a balance sheet the statutory examiner must state the following in his report:

1. Whether or not he has obtained all the information necessary for the performance of his duties

2. Whether or not he has carried out adequate auditing procedures
3. Whether or not he considers that the accounts are kept in accordance with legal requirements and sound standards of accounting and whether the operations recorded comply with the statutes and with the decisions of the shareholders and of the directors
4. Whether or not the financial statements have been properly taken from the books; whether or not, in his opinion, the balance sheet fairly presents, in accordance with generally accepted accounting practices, the state of the financial affairs of the company at the end of the period under examination; and whether or not the profit and loss statement reflects the results of operations for such period
5. Whether or not he has any reservations as to the fairness of presentation of the financial statements.

The statutory examiner is responsible to the shareholders, to the company, and to third parties for damage caused by negligence in carrying out his duties.

Statutory examiners who knowingly express an opinion on fraudulent financial statements may be prosecuted under the penal code for falsifying private documents.

An example of a report by a revisor fiscal follows:

Stockholders of
Company XXX S.A.
Location

Stockholders:

In accordance with statutory and legal requirements, I am pleased to inform you, as Revisor Fiscal, of said Company, that I have examined all operations of the Company for the year ended........., having obtained the necessary information to execute the duties of the Revisor Fiscal.

In the course of the examination, I followed recommended auditing techniques and procedures.

In my opinion, the accounting records are in accordance with legal standards and accounting practice, and the operations registered in the records are in accordance with the statutes and decisions of the General Assembly and the Board of Directors.

The balance sheet and statement of profit and loss mentioned above are in agreement with the books of the Company, and they present fairly the financial position of the Company and the results of its operation for the period ended .... and in accordance with generally accepted principles.

(signed by the appointed
Revisor Fiscal)

It is understood that, notwithstanding the law, some such reports are in greatly abbreviated form; often only the written signature of the revisor appears on the statements themselves.

The National Institute of Public Accountants and several groups of businessmen have been advocating changes in the section of the commercial code dealing with the duties of the statutory examiner. Many of these duties are more comparable to those of an internal auditor than to those of an independent public accountant. The Ministry of Justice has recently (1962) submitted to the legislature a proposal for a revision of the commercial code section dealing with the duties of statutory examiners.

Under present conditions, and especially since the revisor fiscal is normally expected to be a part- or full-time employee of the company, although not responsible to management, it may be said that the report of the statutory examiner, as such, does not give the same degree of assurance regarding the fairness of presentation of financial statements as would that of the independent professional auditor.

THE ACCOUNTING PROFESSION

As in many Latin American countries, public accounting is a new profession in Colombia; up to the year 1950, there were few accountants in public practice, and the demand for their services was small. Statutory examiners (revisores fiscales) were appointed to comply with legal requirements, and as a rule they were full-time employees carrying out routine internal audit functions. There were no regulations setting forth the personal requirements for this position.

The National Institute of Public Accountants (Instituto Nacional de Contadores Públicos) was formed in 1952, by a group of accounting students and professionals for the purpose of promoting their common aspirations, foremost of which was the promotion of regulatory legislation on professional practice. This group actively participated in drafting a public accounting bill which was channeled through lawyers and others to appropriate government officials. Legislative committees were appointed from time to time to study the draft and make modifications, but there were no open hearings or discussions. This process continued until Decree No. 2373 was promulgated in September 1956, which established the Central Board of Accountants (Junta Central de Contadores).

This decree was the first of two bills passed to regulate the accounting profession. It is important because it laid down the basic ground rules

7

for the profession and also because of the relatively large number of nonpublic accountants who were permitted to register as inscribed accountants (contadores inscritos) and public accountants (contadores públicos), and who, under a later law, were able to register as authorized public accountants. (See following.)

By August 1958, it was estimated that approximately 1,500 and 3,000 persons were registered as inscribed accountants and public accountants, respectively.

Junta Central de Contadores (The Central Board of Accountancy)

This Board, which was established in 1956, and continued under law No. 145 (1960), is composed of six persons representing the Minister of Education, the Superintendent of Corporations, the Association of Universities, the Dean of the National School of Economics and Accounting, and the Contadores Públicos Titulados and the Autorizados.

Its functions are to pass upon applications for registration of Contadores Públicos Titulados and Autorizados, to keep a register of those approved, to prepare and publish a Code of Ethics, and to impose penalties set forth in the law.

The law prohibits registration of persons who have been found guilty of breach of confidence, breach of ethics, or of a criminal act.

The Central Board of Accountancy is still processing applications for registration. Under its interpretation of Law No. 145, the Board requires re-registration of those who have previously registered under Decree No. 2373 (1956). These persons are allowed to practice while their applications are pending. The total number of applicants registered under the new law is approximately 2,000, with about 7,000 applications (both new and for re-registration) pending.

Contador Público (Public Accountant)

In December 1960, Law No. 145 was enacted to govern the practice of public accounting; all previous laws on the subject were automatically revoked. The Central Board of Accountancy continued as the body to pass upon and authorize the registration of public accountants.

Law No. 145 specifies that while there shall be only one class of public accountant, they shall be designated as either certified (titulado) or authorized (autorizado) as the case may be. Beginning February 1963, applications for registration as titulado only are being accepted.

The basic requirements for registration as a public accountant with either title are: (a) to be a Colombian citizen or a foreigner domiciled in Colombia for at least three years or who has passed an examination in Colombian legislation, (b) to be a person of good repute, and (c) not to have been subject to penalty resulting from violation of professional ethics.

Contador Público Titulado. In addition to the above stated basic requirements to be a certified public accountant (contador público titulado), the candidate for registration must have a diploma in accounting from a recognized Colombian university or from a foreign university in a country with which Colombia has reciprocity, or a university which has been approved by the Association of Colombian Universities. Failing this, he must pass an examination regulated by the Ministry of Education. A holder of a degree in economics issued prior to the passage of the Law may also be so registered. The candidate must also have one year's experience in practical accounting, gained either in public or private work. There are now about one hundred registered CPTs.

Contador Público Autorizado. To be registered as an authorized public accountant (contador público autorizado), in addition to the basic requirements, the candidate must either: (a) have received a license as an "inscribed" or "public" accountant under the 1956 decree, (b) hold a diploma or license issued under a 1931 law or by the Central Board of Accountancy prior to the enactment of the present law, or (c) apply for and obtain registration within two years of the passage of this law, based on four years' experience as accountant or bookkeeper in an organization of recognized importance. The number of registered "autorizados" is approximately 1,900.

Educational Requirements. As previously stated, it is specified that the applicant for registration as a "titulado" must possess a university degree in accounting, while such degree is not required of an autorizado.

There are five colleges in Colombia now giving courses leading to a degree in accountancy in that country; however, only one of them, the Facultad Nacional de Contaduria, has had graduating classes. There have been about two hundred graduates.

To enter the university, the candidate must have graduated from an elementary and a high school (eleven years), taken a "complementary" business course of one year for twenty-five hours per week, and then spent four years in university courses in accounting, auditing, cost accounting, business, labor and tax laws, economics, English, financial mathematics, etc. Textbooks are largely Spanish translations of United States texts. On completion of the University courses, the student must submit a thesis on an accounting subject.

9

Functions of the Public Accountant. A public accountant (who may be either "certified" or "authorized") is necessary in the following cases:

1. To act as statutory examiner
2. To certify annual financial statements for banks, insurance companies, general warehouses and listed corporations
3. To certify financial statements included in prospectuses of unlisted corporations
4. To act as an expert witness in technical accounting controversies
5. To act as goodwill evaluators in certain cases
6. To certify accounting information in insurance claims over P 300,000
7. To certify accounts of corporations or partnerships in liquidation where the capital is in excess of P 300,000
8. To certify statements of account and balance sheets presented by trustees in bankruptcy
9. To certify balance sheets and statements of account of decentralized public enterprises or establishments.

Professional Accounting Organizations

Instituto Nacional de Contadores Públicos (National Institute of Public Accountants). This organization was described in a previous section. At present it has approximately 320 members and the requirements for membership are as follows:

1. Prior to Decree 2373 of 1956, applicants had to prove five years' accounting experience and pass examinations in accounting theory and practice, Colombian labor law and Colombian tax law.
2. Current requirements state that applicants are to be registered as a contador público titulado or as a contador público autorizado with the Central Board of Accountancy and have five years' experience.

Academia Nacional de Contadores Públicos Juramentados (National Academy of Sworn Public Accountants). There are approximately seventy members of this organization whose membership is restricted to those who have a university degree. The Academy is understood to be relatively inactive.

Union Nacional de Contadores (National Union of Accountants). This organization is reported to have approximately 1,500 members; this number is changing constantly. The basic requirement for membership is apparently any document proving expectations of obtaining registration with the Central Board of Accountancy.

Federación de Contadores de Colombia (Colombian Federation of Accountants). It is reported that this organization has a membership of approximately 500, composed of members in about twenty-five regional organizations. Requirements for membership are similar to those for Union Nacional de Contadores.

Ethics

The present Code of Ethics was issued by the Central Board of Accountancy in 1959. Its coverage is limited as compared with similar codes in many other countries, but the Code does deal with the accountant's practice (must base his report on work done by himself or his employees, shall not prepare fictitious statements, must not omit material facts, must not divulge professional secrets), his relations with other practitioners (avoid personal opinions regarding them, may not solicit other practitioner's business), and includes a pronouncement on independence, discussed later.

Violation of the Code may be punished by the board by registration suspension of up to one year, or, in serious cases, by its cancellation. There have been a few sanctions applied under these or other disciplinary articles of the law.

There is a consensus of opinion among professional accountants that the present Code should be revised, and the board has appointed a committee to revise it. So far no recommendations have emanated.

AUDITING STANDARDS

General Standards

There has been no official statement defining auditing standards in Colombia, although the international firms and several of the medium-sized national firms follow United States or British standards and practices. Until quite recently, the educational opportunities in the field of accounting were very limited, and the best training available was practical experience with the international firms.

Independence. The Code of Ethics published by the Central Board of Accountancy states, in effect, that the public accountant may not act in a controversy if he is related by blood or marriage to either or any of the principals, or has a common interest in the business, or would be hampered by any other circumstances which might impair his judgment.

Standards of Reporting

The reporting standards of the contador público (titulado or autorizado), are governed mainly by the regulations concerning the duties of the revisor fiscal. The minimum contents of the statutory examiners' opinion have been described previously.

Consistency. There has been no official pronouncement by the professional organizations, the Central Board of Accountancy, or the Superintendent of Corporations on the consistent application of accounting principles.

Materiality. There has not been any pronouncement on the concept of materiality and its affect on the auditor's work and on his opinion on the financial statements.

Disclosure of Subsequent Events. It is not common practice for companies to disclose subsequent events which might have a material effect on a proper evaluation of the financial statements.

ACCOUNTING PRINCIPLES AND PRACTICES

The accounting rules and practices in Colombia do not differ materially from those in the United States. However, there are some specific differences arising from the requirements of the Superintendent of Corporations and the tax law. The more important of these differences are discussed below.

Form and Content of Financial Statements

The Superintendencia de Sociedades Anónimas (Superintendency of

Corporations) prescribes the forms to be used by corporations in the preparation of financial statements.

Statement Presentation. These forms consist of a balance sheet and a profit and loss statement, with supporting schedules for investments, fixed assets, depreciation, deferred and prepaid expenses, and reserves. Such statements are required to be presented annually or more frequently depending on the amount of capital of the company. Although statements are due within one month after the close of the period (see below), extensions for filing are usually granted.

For Colombian tax and regulatory requirements, only the calendar year is recognized no matter when a company may close its books for internal reporting purposes.

Consolidated Financial Statements. Consolidated financial statements are not frequently prepared. There is no government requirement that consolidated statements be presented.

Footnotes. Footnote disclosure is seldom used.

Allowance for Doubtful Accounts

Under a recent change in Colombian tax laws, an allowance for doubtful accounts may be created and maintained at up to 10 per cent of the outstanding receivables. The original provision and the annual addition to this allowance are deductible expenses. Credit adjustments to this allowance must be taken into income. These transactions must be recorded on the books in order for tax benefits to be allowable. In some cases the effect on income for the year, especially in the year when the allowance is first set up, may be so great as to have a material effect on the financial statements and, by United States standards, would require a qualification in the statutory examiner's report.

Inventories

Inventories must be stated at cost for Colombian tax purposes. Special permission must be obtained to determine cost on a basis other than specific, average, or first-in, first-out concepts.

Revaluation of Land, Buildings and Investments

A periodic reappraisal of land and buildings is required to be made for the purpose of computing the municipal tax assessment. (Annual registration fees to be paid to the Superintendent of Corporations are also affected by this reappraisal.) Companies must record on their books, the difference between cost and assessed value of land as well as between depreciated cost and assessed value of buildings. This revaluation is in memorandum form only, and although a resulting credit is included in the capital section of the balance sheet, it may not be capitalized or distributed.

Similarly, the market value of investments as of the date of the balance sheet is required to be compared with the net book amount; if the latter exceeds market, the difference is written off, and if market exceeds the net book amount, an appropriate entry is made in a valuation account.

The revalued balance of land and the market value of investments, regardless of the cost of these assets, are included in the base used in the computation of excess profits taxes; the higher the base, the lower the exposure to excess profits taxes.

Goodwill

Purchased goodwill is to be amortized on a reasonable basis. The amortization of this type of goodwill in five or more years is an allowable tax deduction.

In addition, the tax law provides for an official valuation of existing goodwill. In order to request this valuation, a company should have had abnormally high profits for at least five years caused by operating efficiency rather than by tariff protection or exploitation of labor. This goodwill is recorded as a memorandum account and is included in the capital base resulting in a reduction of excess profits taxes. After five years, application for revision of the original valuation must be made.

Interest Charges and Exchange Losses

In some instances, capitalization of interest charges and exchange losses have been accepted as appropriate by the Superintendent of Corporations.

Liability for Severance Pay

Under Colombian labor legislation, employers must pay a severance compensation of one month's salary for each year of service regardless of the reason for separation. Therefore, it is a normal practice to accrue the full amount of this liability. Such accruals are deductible for tax purposes if they have been recorded as accounts payable (rather than as a reserve), and full details of individual balances are submitted with the tax returns.

Liability for Pensions

Accounting for pensions payable under Colombian labor legislation is not too clearly defined. Companies with a net worth of over P 800,000 are liable for old age pensions. Such pensions ordinarily vest upon completion of twenty years' service and the receiver must be fifty-five years of age if male, or fifty years of age if female. The amount of monthly pension is 75 per cent of the average monthly salary earned during the last year of service, with a maximum of P 3,000 for those who have retired after December 29, 1961, and P 1,375 for those who have retired before that date. Employees dismissed without just cause after ten years of service and employees who resign after fifteen years are entitled to partial pensions. Accruals for pensions are not allowable tax deductions unless funded with the government or an approved insurance company. Actual pension payments are allowable expenses unless previously funded. There has not been any pronouncement on the proper accounting for past and present service pension costs. There seems to be a reluctance on the part of most corporations to face this problem.

A recent ruling of the Superintendency of Corporations requires that no reserves be provided for pensions payable under law. It is expected that the Superintendency will, in due course, change its position on this matter.

Statement of Income and Surplus

The combined statement of income and retained earnings is not generally used. However, one of the supporting schedules for the financial statements presented to the Superintendent of Corporations calls for an analysis of the movement on all the surplus (superávit) accounts including undistributed earnings from the end of the previous year.

Depreciation. Depreciation rates are prescribed for tax purposes (and usually adopted for book purposes), for each class of asset, on a straight-line basis. These rates are generally 5 per cent or less for buildings, 10 per cent for machinery and equipment, and 20 per cent for vehicles. It is possible to obtain permission to use special rates which are different from the above. Accelerated depreciation has been approved in certain cases. Depreciation is generally based on 90 per cent of cost, salvage value being considered as 10 per cent of cost. If there remains no salvage value after 90 per cent of the cost has been depreciated, the additional percentage may then also be depreciated.

Stock Dividends. For tax purposes, stock dividends received are treated as income based on the market value of the stock.

Reserve for Replacement of Fixed Assets

Under Colombian tax law, a surplus reserve may be created for replacement of machinery and equipment acquired prior to June 1, 1957. The yearly addition to the reserve is limited to 15 per cent of net profits for the preceding year and may not exceed, in any one year, 15 per cent of the cost of machinery and equipment held as of the qualifying date, until the total cost of the items is accumulated. This reserve must be appropriated by the shareholders in general meeting and must be reviewed by the statutory examiner. The annual addition to the reserve is an allowable tax deduction of the current year and will be taxed if distributed as dividends.

Legal Reserve

A Sociedad Anónima must create a legal reserve of 10 per cent of annual net profits to accumulate a minimum of 50 per cent of the par value of subscribed capital stock. Net losses must be offset against the legal reserve previously created. The legal reserve cannot otherwise be disposed of prior to liquidation of the company. The addition to the legal reserve is computed after net income for the period and is recorded in the following period after the stockholders' approval.

REQUIREMENTS FOR LISTING SECURITIES ON THE STOCK EXCHANGE (BOLSA DE VALORES)

Formal application and acceptance is required to trade a corporation's stock on the Bogota Stock Exchange (Bolsa de Bogota). As part of such application, the following documents must be submitted to the exchange:

1. Two copies of corporate by-laws and modifications
2. Copies of financial statements for the previous two years duly signed by manager, accountant and fiscal auditor
3. Copy of the resolution of the Superintendent of Corporations authorizing the company to do business
4. Number of shareholders and their shareholdings in order to prove that paid capital is at least P 500,000 and that it is more or less evenly distributed among at least fifty persons
5. The names of members of the Board of Directors and their alternates, manager, secretary, accountant, statutory examiner and his alternate. The statutory examiner must give proof that he is a Contador Público Titulado or a Contador Público Autorizado.
6. Sample of the stock certificate to be issued.

Upon acceptance certain minor fees are payable for registration and annual renewal.

There are no additional requirements for filing financial statements with the exchange. All listed companies must publish financial statements annually.

MEXICO 7

FORMS OF BUSINESS ORGANIZATION

The usual forms of sole proprietorship, partnership, and various corporate forms of business organization are found in Mexico, and may be organized with either fixed or variable capital. Foreigners, upon receiving permission from the Ministry of Foreign Relations, may organize a new corporation or acquire effective control of an existing one, but in either case their interest may not exceed 49 per cent. Such corporations are then subject to the laws regulating local companies in general, rather than to any special legislation limiting the operations of foreign corporations. A foreign corporation may, on approval of the Mexican Government, establish a branch office in Mexico. However, tax and other considerations usually lead to operating through a subsidiary rather than as a branch.

Ownership in petroleum, electrical utilities and railroads is reserved exclusively for government agencies; a number of other industries are required to be 100 per cent or majority-owned by Mexican citizens.

Sociedad Anónima (S.A.)

The corporate form most closely resembling the usual United States corporation is the Sociedad Anónima. The corporate name must be followed by the initials S.A. There must be at least five incorporators, and there must always be at least five shareholders. There must be fully subscribed capital stock of at least P (Mexican pesos) 25,000, and at least 20 per cent of the value of each share to be paid in cash must be paid in at the time of organization. The shares may be registered or bearer shares.

Every Sociedad Anónima (incorporated under the Mexican Companies Act) must have one or more statutory examiners (Comisarios) who are appointed by and represent the stockholders. Stockholders owning 25 per cent or more of the shares are entitled to elect a statutory examiner when there are three or more of the latter. The qualifications and duties of the statutory examiner are discussed in a later section.

Sociedad Anónima de Capital Variable (S.A. de C.V.)

This form of corporation under the Companies Act may be organized with a minimum fixed capital of P25,000. However, the variable capital may be increased as provided by the charter of incorporation. It may also be decreased down to the minimum of P25,000. Such capital changes may be made with fewer legal formalities than are required in the case of the Sociedad Anónima. All shares of the S.A. de C.V. must be in registered form.

Sociedad de Responsabilidad Limitada (S. de R.L.)

This entity includes some of the characteristics of both corporations and partnerships. It is formed by two (but not more than twenty-five) members who are liable only for the amount of capital subscribed by them. The capital of the S. de R.L. must be not less than P5,000 and cannot be subscribed publicly. At least 50 per cent of the subscription to capital must be paid in upon formation. The manager or managers need not be owners.

Incorporation fees are the same as those for the Sociedad Anónima, but filing and publication of financial statements are not required. Issuance of bearer shares or debentures is not permitted.

Other Forms of Business Organization

Sociedad en Nombre Colectivo. This is the general partnership operating under a firm name in which all partners are jointly and severally liable for partnership debts. A majority of existing partners is required to approve the admission of new partners, and the transfer of partnership interests is prohibited.

Sociedad en Comandita Simple. In this form of partnership there are two kinds of partners—the full partners, who are jointly and severally liable for partnership debts, and the special partners, who are liable only to the amount of their respective contributions. The firm name may contain the names of full partners only, and special partners may not take part in management.

Sociedad en Comandita por Acciónes. This partnership form differs from the above only in that the shares of full partners are in the form of registered stock, which may not be transferred without the consent of all full partners and two-thirds of the special partners.

Sociedad Cooperativa. This is a nonprofit membership organization, which may be formed by not less than ten members who are workers in or consumers of the products dealt with by the cooperative. The capital is variable, and the liability of the members is limited to the amount of their contributions to such capital.

Business Records

The Mexican Commercial Code requires that every business maintain certain books of account, including a general ledger, a general journal, and a book of inventories and balances. These books must be bound, have numbered pages and be stamped by the Federal Treasury Department before use. At the end of the year the inventory and the final trial balance must be entered in the inventory and balance book. The entries in the required books may be summarizations of details kept in loose-leaf or machine posted subsidiary records. There are also authorized procedures by means of which the general books may be mechanized and kept initially in loose-leaf form.

A corporation must keep minutes of the stockholders' and board's meetings, in books previously authorized by the Federal Treasury Department.

Mexican income tax law requires certain other records such as sales and purchase journals.

COMISARIO (STATUTORY EXAMINER)

The Mexican Companies Act provides that the shareholders of each Sociedad Anónima appoint one or more Comisarios (statutory examiners). The Comisario acts as the personal representative of shareholders, attends all meetings of the Board of Directors, and must report upon the financial statements of the company before they are submitted to the annual meeting of stockholders. He watches over the activities of the management, and reports to the shareholders upon any irregularities or unwise decisions noted. There are no specified qualifications for appointment—educational or professional—but there may not be appointed persons unfit to engage in business, employees of the company, nor relatives (of specified degree) of the directors. He may be, and often is, himself a shareholder. He is empowered to call a special meeting of shareholders if he deems it necessary; this power is seldom invoked in practice.

While the Comisario is required to "approve" financial statements presented to the stockholders' meeting by the directors, there is no requirement that he be qualified to, or that he should examine such statements in the sense as understood by a contador público (see following section). Nevertheless, the Comisario of a company often relies upon a report of its contador público as a basis for the Comisario's report to stockholders, and frequently a contador público is appointed Comisario of the company for which he or his firm makes annual audits. Most contadores públicos in Mexico feel that acceptance of appointment as Comisario of a company does not affect their status as independent auditors of the same company, and both the Instituto Mexicano de Contadores Públicos and the Colegio de Contadores have ruled that the duties of the Comisario and of the contador público are not incompatible.

There is, however, a difference in the responsibilities of the Comisario as compared with those of the contador público. Under the law, the Comisario oversees in general all company actions and is more concerned with the propriety and wisdom of its transactions than whether such transactions are recorded in accordance with generally accepted accounting principles; for the contador público, the emphasis would probably be reversed.

As a result, and because the Comisario is not, as previously stated, required to have competence in the accounting field nor to be independent, any report or opinion issued by him with respect to financial statements does not, nor is it intended to, give the same degree of assurance as to the fairness of financial statements as would that of an independent auditor.

THE ACCOUNTING PROFESSION

In Mexico there are two classes of accountants, similar to those in the United States, which serve the public. They are: the noncertified accountants (contadores privados) and the certified public accountants (contadores públicos).

Contador Privado

The contador privado is a person who, having some accounting education or experience, holds himself out to provide bookkeeping, tax and other accounting services to the public. He is not recognized by the government as a professional accountant (contador público) and is neither organized in a colegio nor in an institute. These persons may not perform those duties which by law are restricted to licensed contadores públicos (certified public accountants).

Contador Público

Requirements for the Title. The candidate for the degree of CP (whether a national or foreigner) must have met all related educational requirements in Mexico, and have passed the requisite examinations. The National Autonomous University of Mexico (Mexico City, D.F.), among others, requires two years of practical experience of the candidate, either in public accounting or in private industry, as well as a "social service" period of six months work if unpaid or one year if remunerated.

In order to be admitted to most institutions of higher learning leading to the degree of CP, the candidate must have completed his six years of elementary and three years of junior high school. He then must take a two-year (recently increased to three in certain universities) course to obtain the degree of "bachiller."

Having attained this degree, the holder is eligible to enter the National School of Commerce and Business Administration of the National Autonomous University of Mexico, the National Polytechnic Institute, certain private schools authorized by the Secretary of Education, or a state university which offers the degree of contador público. A five-year course of 125 hours is normally offered, covering subjects which compare favorably with those of typical United States universities. Having passed the required courses, the candidate must prepare a thesis and, after approval of the thesis by a board of five professors, he will then be subjected to a professional examination.

The professional examination consists of presentation of a thesis for approval of a board composed of five examiners. He is then given a problem to be solved within two days (four additional days are taken by the board to review the solution of the problem). There follows an oral examination before five examiners, whose questions usually concern his thesis and the theories supporting his solution of the practice problem. Upon satisfactorily completing these requirements, the certificate of CP is delivered to him by the university authorities, or by those other schools authorized to issue these certificates. The certificate, in turn, leads to the granting of a license to practice by the Dirección General de Profesiones (Directorate General of Professions).

School hours are usually from seven to nine or ten A.M. and four to nine P.M., and most higher grade accounting students work for public accountants or business concerns outside of school hours.

Legal Requirements for Practice. Article 25 of the Professional Law provides the following requisites for the practice of public accountancy or any other regulated profession by an individual in Mexico:

1. He must be Mexican by birth or naturalization, and enjoying and exercising his civil rights.

2. He must hold a legally issued and duly registered pertinent degree.

3. He must obtain a license from the Directorate General of Professions.

One peculiarity of the profession in Mexico is that firms arising from the association of two or more contadores públicos are no more than "de facto" partnerships with no formal recognition in the law, unless a form of partnership (Sociedad Civil) is organized under the Civil Code of the respective state. Very few contadores públicos adopt this form of partnership since, in any event, professional law places all responsibility on the individual signing the specific report and not on the partnership.

Functions of the Contador Público. The services provided to his clients by the Mexican CP are very similar to those of the CPA in the United States. He may be selected by management, directors or stockholders to examine and report upon financial statements of corporations or other business entities; prepare tax returns; represent taxpayers before the tax department, and give tax advice; and he may advise with respect to or supervise the installations of new or revised accounting systems.

Various laws of Mexico require that financial statements of certain companies be certified by a CP. For example, the Law of Titles and Credit Operations requires that when a company wishes to issue bonds or debentures, its financial statements must be certified by a public account- ant; the Mexican Companies Act requires that the financial statements of branches of foreign corporations operating in Mexico be examined and reported upon by a CP and be published; banking laws require banks to obtain similarly certified financial statements from credit applicants where the amount involved is material and the collateral offered is less than the minimum required to obtain exemption from the necessity for certified statements; banking laws require that corporations issuing bonds quoted on the market publish financial statements certified by a CP; the law establishing the Bank of Mexico states that the shareholders will appoint expert accountants (who must be CPs) to review the balance sheet.

In support of their income tax returns, taxpayers may file a report of a contador público(independent public accountant) registered in the Spe- cial Register of Auditors for Tax Purposes (see page 11). Such a report should contain an opinion on the financial statements under generally ac- cepted auditing standards, and the accountant's opinion as to the man- ner in which his client complied with all of the federal tax obligations applicable during the fiscal year. Reports filed for the first time must con- tain brief descriptions of the taxpayer's main legal, financial and ad- ministrative features as well as principal features of internal control as applied to cash and inventories; subsequent reports need only mention later changes. The public accountant's report is subject to review, in lieu of the taxpayer's records, as the basis for approval by taxing authorities of the corresponding tax returns. Authorities may, at their discretion, sup- plement their review with:

1. Oral and written explanations from the contador público

2. Examination of his working papers

3. Inspection of the taxpayer's records

Theoretically, the above procedure releases the taxpayer of *all* kinds of claims for *federal taxes* for the year. In practice, however, submittal of accountants' reports has caused taxpayers to receive a written release for *income tax* purposes *only,* which exempts the taxpayer from inspection by income tax authorities, except under "justified reasons" arising during the statute of limitations of five years.

9

Organizations of the Accounting Profession

The public accounting profession in Mexico has had a long history of gradual growth during the present century, based on steady improvement in educational opportunities and in the work of its professional societies. The present Instituto Mexicano de Contadores Públicos has its origin in the "Mexican Association of Public Accountants" (1917), which in 1923, became the Mexican Institute of Public Accountants.

Instituto Mexicano de Contadores Públicos. The Mexican Institute of Public Accountants, organized in 1923, functions in a manner similar to the American Institute of CPAs. It has an active Committee on Auditing Practice, which has issued seventeen bulletins to date, with several more in process at this time. These bulletins cover much of the same ground and do not differ in nature from similar bulletins of the American Institute of CPAs. The Instituto has a "Committee on Accounting Principles" comparable to similar organizations, past or present, of the American Institute, but it has not as yet issued any statements or bulletins. The Committee on Terminology has issued Bulletin No. 1 which, in the manner of the AICPAs' *Accounting Trends and Techniques,* covers for the period 1959-61, technical terms and examples of short-form reports of financial statements from eighty-five Mexican companies. Other committees are those on Management Services and Professional Ethics.

The Instituto has approximately four hundred members whose applications for membership include photostatic copies of their title and license to practice, as well as a copy of their professional thesis together with a statement of their educational curriculum and professional background. References are furnished by the applicant, and his application is sponsored by two Institute members. Names of applicants are listed in the Institute's weekly bulletin to enable other members to submit confidential objections to membership during a thirty-day period.

The Instituto Mexicano de Contadores Públicos pioneered in the establishment of the professional accounting profession in Mexico, and contributed greatly to its growth and stature. However, since the "Colegio" (discussed below) is the officially recognized body of professional public accountants in Mexico, and since its essential objectives coincide with those of the Institute, studies are being conducted to merge the two organizations, and to include the local colegios and institutos. This organization will then represent all public accountants in Mexico.

Colegio de Contadores Públicos, de Mexico, A.C. In 1946, a law was enacted to regulate the various professions in Mexico, which provided that only Mexican citizens may practice, except that those persons established in Mexico before that year may continue their practice. Under this law, members of professions, including that of public accounting, must associate themselves in organizations known as "colleges," in order to bring them under the provisions of the law. Thereupon, the Colegio de Contadores Públicos, de México, A.C. was organized, to which all holders of the certificate of contador público must belong. There are presently about one thousand members of the Colegio.

Other Organizations of Accountants in Mexico. Outside of the Mexico City area the following professional accountancy bodies are active:

Organizations affiliated with the Instituto Mexicano de Contadores Públicos:

Instituto y Colegio de Contadores Públicos de Chihuahua

Instituto de Contadores Públicos Titulados de La Laguna

Instituto Sonorense de Contadores Públicos

Instituto de Contadores Públicos de San Luis Potosí

There are a number of independent professional organizations (colegios or institutes) of public accountants located in the various states of Mexico, and there are also several organizations of noncertified public accountants, but the latter are not considered professional societies.

Special Register of Auditors for Tax Purposes

This Registry of Auditors is maintained by the Federal Treasury Department, and includes public accountants who apply and can meet the following requirements:

Must be a Mexican citizen

Must have a recognized degree as a public accountant that is registered in the Directorate General of Professions

Must be a member of a Colegio recognized by the Directorate General of Professions

Must not belong to a firm, office or association that has in its firm name or management the names of persons not having a recognized degree.

Public accountants who wish to file tax certificates must be enrolled in this special register.

11

Ethics

The Instituto Mexicano de Contadores Públicos has issued Rules of Professional Conduct (Ethics—1955), and a pamphlet, "The Independent Auditor's Report and his Responsibilities." The latter covers much the same ground as that of the American Institute's Committee on Auditing Procedure booklet entitled "Codification of Statements on Auditing Procedure."

In 1960, the Colegio also published a "Code of Professional Ethics," which is practically identical to that of the Mexican Institute.

The Code of Ethics states, inter alia, that the public accountant would not be considered independent or impartial if he has a financial interest in the firm under examination which is large enough to affect his opinion on the financial statements.

AUDITING STANDARDS

Auditing standards in Mexico for the contador público are practically identical with those prescribed in the United States. The pamphlet previously referred to—"The Independent Auditor's Report and his Responsibilities"—describes generally accepted auditing standards under the headings:

> General Standards
> Standards of Field Work, and
> Standards of Reporting

in much the same terms as those used in the comparable statement of the American Institute. The portion of the latter statement dealing with examinations of notes and accounts receivable by confirmation procedures, and with examinations of inventories by observation of physical inventory-taking, are covered in Bulletins Nos. 6 and 8, respectively, of the Instituto's Committee on Auditing Procedure.

The standard form of auditors' report in Mexico is a translation of the standard form used in the United States, with the same references to adherence to generally accepted auditing standards, the conformity of the financial statements with generally accepted accounting principles, and to the consistency of their application.

As discussed earlier, auditor's reports for tax purposes include a third paragraph containing the accountant's opinion as to compliance of his client with applicable federal tax legislation.

The bulletins issued by the Committee on Auditing Procedure are:

1. Introduction
2. General Concepts
3. Generally Accepted Auditing Standards
4. Planning the Audit
5. Examination of Internal Control
6. Examination of Accounts Receivable
7. Examination of Cash in Banks
8. Examination of Inventories
9. Examination of Sales and Cost of Sales
10. Examination of Operating Expenses
11. Examination of Plant, Machinery and Equipment
12. Sampling in Auditing
13. Examination of Accrued and Estimated Liabilities
14. Examination of Investments in Securities
15. Examination of Accounts and Notes Receivable
16. Examination of Long-term Debt
17. Examination of Contingent Liabilities.

There are a few areas in which Mexican law or custom dictates a somewhat different approach to auditing practice as compared with that in the United States. For example, Mexican law requires certain information to be shown on sales invoices in order that they may be tax-deductible. In order to evaluate income tax accruals, the auditor in Mexico usually feels it necessary to examine purchase invoices to determine whether they are proper tax deductions.

Since banks do not return canceled checks, accountants must do more extensive testing or sampling of the documentary support of disbursements.

In Mexico, sales invoices are considered to represent title to merchandise, and inspection of these documents is employed to a greater extent in Mexico than in the United States. Also, sales invoices still in the hands of the vendor are usually—when supported by strong internal control—good evidence of the existence of trade accounts receivable, so that Mexican auditors sometimes include in their work programs an inspection of sales invoices not delivered to customers as an alternative auditing procedure, especially when responses to confirmation requests are not very numerous, a situation which is likely in many audits.

In substantiating real property, contadores públicos sometimes request information from the Public Registry of Property, which would certify ownership of the property, freedom from encumbrances and, in installment sales, ownership under conditional contracts subject to the retention of the title. More often, as in the United States, representations are requested from company legal counsel or from the client.

It is rather common procedure to request direct confirmation of accounts payable.

ACCOUNTING PRINCIPLES AND PRACTICES

While, as indicated previously, the Mexican Institute of Public Accountants has not issued any bulletins or other pronouncements dealing specifically with accounting principles, those dealt with in university courses and discussed in the Institute's publication, *Finanzas y Contabilidad,* are in general similar to those followed in the United States. There are a few differences, discussed in the following pages.

Form and Content of Financial Statements

Statement Presentation. The general arrangement of financial statements in Mexico is similar to that customary in the United States—assets on the left side, liabilities and capital on the right. The statement of income and surplus is also similar, starting with sales, showing gross profit on sales, followed by general and selling expenses, other income and other deductions, and arriving at net profit after income taxes. Depreciation and amortization are sometimes shown separately below gross profit, or in a note to the financial statements.

Consolidated financial statements. It is not customary to prepare consolidated financial statements, nor to publish separate parent and subsidiary company statements.

Poolings of Interests

The accounting technique known in the United States as a "Pooling of Interests," applicable in certain circumstances when one company is acquired by or merged into another company, is not followed in Mexico.

Inventories

While, for accounting purposes, inventories are required to be and generally are stated on the basis of "lower of cost or market," there are some differences with United States practice resulting from the requirement of Mexican income tax law that inventories may not be valued below cost. Since most companies prefer to follow tax accounting in their books, there is some reluctance to write down inventories to salvage or market values, although many companies do provide non-deductible inventory reserves. It is possible to obtain permission for proper writedowns, and this is sometimes done.

There is no specific provision in tax law for "standard" or "direct" costing (there is for "Lifo" "Fifo," average and unit cost); again, in specific instances, permission may be given by the tax authorities for the use of these methods.

Fixed Assets and Their Revaluation

Fixed assets may not always be stated at cost, resulting from the permission given in 1954, to revalue certain assets reflecting the devaluation of the Mexican peso at that time. Such revalued assets are now fully or nearly fully depreciated.

The amount of the writeup was initially credited to "Surplus from Revaluation," and an amount equivalent to the "excess" depreciation must be transferred annually from the "revaluation" surplus, to a "Reserve for Reinvestment from Valuation." There are certain tax rules relating to these reserves principally affecting the computation of capital for excess-profits tax purposes.

"Surplus from Revaluation" may not be distributed but may be capitalized; but the "Reserve for Reinvestment from Valuation" may be capitalized, and the payment of "distributable tax" deferred until the date of liquidation of the company or reimbursement of any part of the capital to the shareholders.

Since 1962, Mexican income tax law has permitted revaluation of all of the fixed tangible assets, and the resulting depreciation is an accepted deduction, provided that the writeup is based on the findings of a recognized appraiser, and that a tax is paid on the amount of the writeup.

It is customary to indicate by footnote or otherwise the amount by which fixed assets are stated in excess of cost by reason of revaluation.

Liabilities

Liability for Severance Pay. Under Mexican law employees are entitled to severance pay based on length of service on involuntary termination of employment without just cause as defined by law. Such payments are tax-deductible, but provision for the accrued liability is not; unless, as in the case of mining companies, a deposit is made with the government of the amount of the accrual. It is generally accepted practice to make provision by charge to income for the accrued liability for severance payments.

Liability for Profit-sharing. Recent amendments to the Mexican Labor Law provide that employees will be entitled to share in the profits of their employers beginning with the 1963 year. The regulations for computation of the amount of profit-sharing, published in December 1963, provide for an amount of 20 per cent of net distributable profit, as defined in the regulations. The amount of profit-sharing is not deductible for income tax purposes.

Exchange Gains and Losses

Exchange gains and losses are recognized as realized for income tax purposes, only in the period in which devaluation occurs, and consequently reserves for exchange losses are not common.

The Mexican income tax law requires that all foreign currency assets and liabilities be translated into Mexican pesos at the closing rate of exchange at the end of each fiscal period.

Reserves

Reserves resulting from revaluation permitted in 1954, were discussed above. In addition, Sociedades Anónimas are required to set aside each year 5 per cent of book net income as a legal reserve until the total aggregates 20 per cent of the "capital." Companies engaged in manufacturing and commerce may apply for permission to set aside a part or all of net income (commerce up to 10 per cent) subject to distributable profits taxes as "Reserves for Reinvestment." Such reserves may be used to increase capital stock without incurring distributable tax liability, but if returned to unappropriated earned surplus, or utilized to reduce capital, or upon liquidation of the company, such tax is payable immediately.

Statement of Income

Stock Dividends. Stock dividends are taxable to corporate recipients as income valued at market. The recipient may record the shares at their nominal value, or preferably the number of shares only without an amount.

The paying company records the stock issued at par.

Directors' Fees and Bonuses. These items are sometimes charged to earned surplus, especially by smaller companies. In the past, they were treated by the paying company for tax purposes as a distribution of profits, the applicable taxes being paid by the company. Beginning in 1962, this practice was abandoned, since distributions to officers and directors became fully taxable to them as individuals.

Tax-effect Accounting. In Mexico, book accounting generally follows tax-basis accounting. However, there is a trend toward obtaining special permission to take depreciation on an accelerated basis for tax purposes, (but not for book purposes), and when this is done, there is a tendency to employ tax-effect accounting if differences are material.

Other. Mexican tax definitions make it difficult for the taxpayer to use his discretion in expensing deferred charges such as organizational and preoperational expenses, as well as tooling purchases in manufacturing. Accordingly, these items are frequently found on balance sheets—even in nominal amounts—as assets subject to a twenty-year amortization or a ten-year depreciation.

Under Mexican tax law, the deduction for bad debt losses is restricted to 1 per cent of sales where the debtors are farmers; 0.1 per cent otherwise, unless the loss has been proved by legal evidence before a court, in which case the total deduction is permitted.

REQUIREMENTS FOR LISTING
ON MEXICAN STOCK EXCHANGE

The first step in registering securities on the Mexican Stock Exchange is the filing of a written application addressed to the Board of Directors of the Exchange, enclosing the following:

1. Financial statements of the company with the opinion of a Mexican contador público

2. Balance sheet and operating statement for the last five years

3. Statement of changes in stockholders' equity from inception, including dividends declared

4. Various documents such as company charter, board minutes, etc.

On approval of this data by the Board of Directors, the company must then submit to the Comisión Nacional de Valores certain other information, including:

1. Balance sheet and profit and loss statement with the opinion of a Mexican contador público relating to the last fiscal year prior to the request for registration (providing this request is filed within the next six months after the date of the financial statements). If the request is filed more than six months after the date of the financial statements, then the financial statements should be those for the six months ending after the date of the last fiscal year.

2. Information comprising the previous five fiscal years (or since the company's incorporation if the company has been in operation for a period of less than five years) showing for each year:
   a. Net profit
   b. Dividends paid
   c. Capital reserves and other reserves
   d. Issues of securities made during the five-year period showing the amount, term, interest rate, guarantees, etc.
   e. Volume and value of the production
   f. Items included under current assets
   g. Details of fixed assets stating the depreciation method followed and the annual depreciation charges

If the request for registration relates to securities issued in a foreign country, in addition to the above requirements, the following conditions should be met among others:

1. The securities must be represented by deposit certificates issued by a Mexican banking institution.

2. The banking institution must agree to furnish to the Mexican Stock Exchange reports in Spanish including all the information relating to the securities.

3. The banking institution must have been appointed by the issuer as its agent in Mexico for the purpose of the payment of dividends relating to the securities issued.

However, Comisión Nacional de Valores has officially stated that not all of the additional conditions required in the case of shares issued in foreign countries will be mandatory providing that (a) the foreign company has installations in Mexico representing a basic industry, (b) the securities are issued to finance such industry, and (c) the foreign company has representatives and offices in the Mexican Republic.

The companies whose securities have been registered with the Mexican Stock Exchange and Comisión Nacional de Valores, must furnish annually, within four months after the close of the fiscal year, the following information:

Balance sheet and statement of profit and loss with the opinion of a Mexican contador público together with the annual report to the stockholders

Statement showing proposed distribution of profits, dividends to be declared and method of payment

Statement of investments in securities, details of issues of debentures, bonds, etc.

Volume and value of production.

There are no regulations covering information to be given prospective purchasers of securities offered privately, or other than through the facilities of the Mexican Stock Exchange.

PERU   8

2

FORMS OF BUSINESS ORGANIZATION

Business organizations in Peru are governed by the Commercial Code of 1902, as subsequently amended, the Civil Code of 1936, and the Banking Law of 1931. Specific legislation has been enacted for the mining and petroleum industries and for electric utilities and insurance companies. The Commercial Code and subsequent legislation regulate the different types of business forms, namely, the sole proprietorship, the partnership, the corporations, and the branch of a foreign corporation. Under the Civil Code of 1936, limited partnerships may be formed.

All types of business organizations other than the individual proprietorship must be officially formed by deed executed and authenticated by a notary public and recorded in the appropriate Public Mercantile Register; subsequent changes must also be notarized and registered. Titles, agreements, etc., may also be registered in the Public Mercantile Register and such documents when registered have preferred acceptance in cases of legal claims.

Foreign enterprises generally adopt the form of a branch of foreign corporation or of a "Sociedad Anónima"; the latter is the legal form which most closely resembles the United States corporation.

Sociedad Anónima (S.A.)

The capital of a Sociedad Anónima consists of shares subscribed by shareholders whose liability is limited to the amount of their subscriptions. The name of the corporation is generally followed by the initials S.A.

Two or more persons may organize a corporation; once a corporation is formed, its shares can be acquired in their entirety by an individual or by another corporation. The law that regulates the Sociedad Anónima does not state minimum capital requirements although some capital must be paid in. Shares may be of any denomination and class but must have a stated nominal value and must be registered until at least 50 per cent of the nominal value has been paid up. Bearer shares cannot be issued in cases where a natural person holds 50 per cent of the capital or where these shares represent more than one-third of the personal wealth of an individual shareholder and his immediate relatives. Shares issued for capital contributed in the form of real estate must remain registered for a period of five years.

Directors do not have to be shareholders, residents or citizens of Perú.

All corporations with a capital of 25,000 Soles (S/25,000) or more must publish an annual financial statement in the *Diario Oficial* (Official Gazette).

Sociedad Civil de Responsabilidad Limitada (S.C.R.L.)

The liability of the members of this type of concern is limited to their capital contributions. The entire capital of the concern must be paid in at inception. It is required to print on all of its forms the amount of its capital and the fact that its members have limited liability.

Branch of Foreign Corporation

A foreign corporation must appoint a representative with appropriate power of attorney who handles the incorporation procedures which require the presentation of various documents including those which prove the legal status of the foreign corporation.

There is no specific capital requirement, and capital assigned to a Peruvian branch does not have to be transferred in cash or other assets, but may be set up by a book entry charging the interoffice account.

There is no legal requirement that directors should be residents of Peru or of Peruvian nationality except for insurance and aviation companies. Branches of foreign corporations do not have to publish their financial statements.

Other Forms of Business Organization

Sociedad Colectiva. This is the equivalent of the unlimited liability partnership, and it may be formed by two or more members. Those who contribute capital are called "socios capitalistas" whereas those who contribute services only are called "socios industriales." Capitalista partners have unlimited liability in regard to third parties in case of liquidation. A partnership must do business under the name of all partners or of one or more of them followed by the words "y Compañía."

Sociedad en Comandita. This is similar to the partnership referred to above, except that it may have one or more partners who contribute capital only and who do not take part in the management of the concern. These silent partners, called "comanditarios," are liable to the extent of their capital contributions. The other partners are called "socios colectivos" and have unlimited liability with respect to third parties in case of liquidation. The name of the partnership is followed by the initials "S. en C."

Business Records

The Commercial Code requires that every business keep the following books: Inventory and balance book, daily journal, general ledger and press-copy of correspondence. In addition, corporations are required to keep minute books and stock registers and anything else required by special laws.

These books must be bound and legalized (rubricated) before use by a judge of a primary court who signs the first page and stamps the court's seal on each folio, which must be prenumbered.

The law which established the Fiscal Registry of Accountants (described later) requires that each daily journal ("Libro Diario") be signed on its front page by the accountant in charge of the accounting records, indicating his category (público, mercantil or práctico), registration number and the date of the commencement of his activities.

The Treasury Department has issued regulations which make the above requirements reasonably flexible in cases where mechanized accounting systems are in operation.

All businesses with a capital exceeding S/100.000 must register their accounting records with the Treasury Department.

THE ACCOUNTING PROFESSION

In the years 1941 and 1943, and after varied legislation on the subject, the government regulated the profession of public accounting and recognized as "contadores públicos" the graduates of accounting courses of Peruvian universities as well as those members of the "Instituto de Contadores del Perú" who, at that time, had been practicing the accounting profession for the past ten years.

In 1959, Law 13253 amended the Commercial Code by establishing that "merchants" (this term comprises all business enterprises) must keep their accounting records with the assistance ("intervención") of either "contadores públicos" or "contadores mercantiles." This law defined the functions of each and authorized those who did not have the qualifications required but who had been signing income tax declarations for the preceding three years to continue performing such functions; these persons are called "contadores prácticos."

There is no law or regulation which, for any purpose, requires the report of an independent public accountant upon financial statements.

Contador Público

This term is the equivalent of the American CPA; the degree is conferred by the universities of Peru and must be registered as such in the "colegio" (institute) where the accountant is domiciled. Practical experience is not required to obtain the degree of contador público.

There are a number of universities in Perú, including the Universidad Nacional Mayor de San Marcos, the Pontífica Universidad Católica del Perú, the Universidad de La Libertad, the Universidad de Arequipa, and the Universidad del Cuzco. To enroll in the accounting courses at these universities, the student must be a high school graduate, and pass a general knowledge and selective examination. Although the curriculum of each of these universities differs, the degree of contador público at the University of San Marcos requires five years of study of subjects generally comparable to those included in similar courses at American universities. Two years of postgraduate study and the submission of a thesis lead to a doctorate degree in public accounting.

Functions. The Supreme Decree 28 of 1960, organized the Colegios de Contadores Públicos and amplified the principal functions of the Contador Público, which were originally outlined in the law of 1959, and indi-

6

cated as the most important areas of his activities. The examination of accounting records and the expression of an opinion on the financial statements prepared therefrom; the certification of transactions, accounts and statements on accounting records; the certification of the authenticity of transactions of an accounting nature and the expression of an opinion thereon; the organization of accounting systems.

Organization of Accounting Firms. This decree also stated the requirements to be observed by public accounting firms, as follows:

(1) The partnership agreement must be granted by public deed which should clearly indicate the joint and several responsibilities of its partners.

(2) The audit reports and professional certificates which the firm issues must be signed by one or more "Contadores Públicos" who represent the firm for that purpose. They must be expressly authorized by the firm by registered public deed. These "Contadores Públicos" must be members of the Colegio and are jointly responsible with the firm they represent for the acts arising from the discharge of their duties and authority vested.

(3) The firm must be registered in the corresponding "Colegio."

Contador Mercantil

Peruvian law provides for the degree of contador mercantil to be conferred by the Department of Education to those who have completed commercial courses at an officially recognized "Instituto Nacional de Comercio" or at a private school duly authorized by that Department. This could be compared to a commercial high school in the United States.

In addition to keeping the accounting records of merchants, as permitted by the law of 1959, a contador mercantil is authorized to sign financial statements for income tax purposes, and he may also perform the functions of a contador público in locations where the number registered is less than three.

Contador Práctico

These are the accountants who do not possess any of the educational qualifications required either for contador público or contador mercantil, but whose function of signing declarations of income for taxation purposes was recognized under the laws of 1943 and 1959.

7

Fiscal Register of Accountants

The "Registro Fiscal de Contadores" was created by the law of 1960, as a newly formed department of the Treasury, to register the names and classifications of all accountants qualified to sign financial statements for tax purposes. There is a central register in Lima and a subsidiary register in each province of the country. The Fiscal Register is composed of three separate sections representing each group of accountants—(públicos, mercantiles and prácticos).

The law which created the Fiscal Register of Accountants states that the tax authorities shall favorable consider any tax returns which may be accompanied by the signature of a contador público, in his capacity as auditor of the taxpayer.

The accountant's registration may be either suspended or canceled if his participation in fraudulent acts in the accounting records of the taxpayer is proven. If the accountant is a contador público, the proceedings will be initiated by the Superintendencia de Contribuciones of the Treasury Department and should be resolved by the colegio to which he belongs. If the accountant is mercantil or práctico disciplinary action is taken by the Treasury Department. Those whose registrations are canceled may not apply for reinstatement until a period of two years has elapsed. The suspensions, cancellations and reinstatements are published in the *Official Gazette*.

Accounting Organizations

Instituto de Contadores del Perú. This, the first Peruvian accountants' association, was organized in 1900. The head office is located in Lima and there are offices in every province.

At present, the membership mainly comprises accountants in private industry and contadores prácticos. They publish a quarterly journal, *El Contador*.

Colegio de Contadores Públicos. A colegio of contadores públicos may be formed in every province where ten or more public accountants are practicing. Their by-laws are subject to the approval of the Treasury Department. Registration of the contador público in the colegio is obligatory for those who practice the profession as independent accountants.

The objectives of the colegio are:

1. To promote professional practice in accordance with their ethics and their socio-economic functions

2. To contribute to the improvement of accounting principles and techniques
3. To cooperate with the public authorities and with other organized professions in matters concerning their specialty
4. To cooperate with foreign entities and corporations and encourage the participation of its members in international professional conferences.

The principal functions assigned by law to the colegio are: to keep a register of its members, to establish and enforce a code of professional ethics, to issue reports on technical matters as requested by public and official institutions, to establish minimum professional fees and to sponsor an academy of professional practice for students and graduates.

At present, there are colegios functioning in Lima, and in the principal provincial capitals. The colegio in Lima was formed as a private organization in 1942, and became the official body under the law of 1960. It now has about 1,500 members. At the Second National Convention of Public Accountants in 1961, a "Federación" was created which combined all the colegios.

The colegio in Lima publishes a newsletter, and a quarterly magazine which contains articles on accounting and auditing subjects.

Asociación de Contadores de Lima. The members of this association are mainly practical accountants (contadores prácticos). They do not engage in what could be understood as professional activities.

Code of Ethics

At the Second National Convention of Public Accountants in 1961, the Code of Professional Ethics submitted by the colegios was approved. The Code includes the following captions:

1. The Public Accountant as a member of a profession
2. Relationship with clients
3. The Public Accountant and the Government
4. The Public Accountant and the Internal Revenue Service
5. Rules of conduct among members
6. Disciplinary measures
7. Code of Ethics' compliance-supervisory bodies.

Although the Code is rather comprehensive and covers the areas of soliciting, contingent fees, fees from the laity, etc., it does not include any rules of conduct comparable to those included under the caption "Technical Standards" of the Code of Professional Ethics of the AICPA.

The disciplinary measures applicable to those who infringe the provisions of the Code, and which are to be enforced by the colegio to which the contador público belongs, range from a simple warning to the exclusion from membership.

To date there have been no cases brought before the colegios.

AUDITING STANDARDS

General and Field Work Standards

Before the Second National Convention of Public Accountants in August of 1961, no minimum auditing standards were prescribed for use by the accounting profession in Perú. At that convention, recommendations were made to the Peruvian practitioners that certain minimum auditing procedures be followed by the contador público in arriving at his opinion on the financial statements of his client. These procedures are:

(1) Comparison of the financial statements to the accounting records. In addition, the auditor should make tests of such records to the extent that he believes necessary, based on his evaluation of the internal control

(2) Observations and physical counts of important assets such as cash, securities, inventories, fixed assets, etc. The auditor should be guided in these cases by the importance of these assets and their control by management. He should take all the necessary measures to determine that all liabilities are reflected in the financial statements

(3) Direct confirmations with third parties through: bank confirmations, circularization tests of accounts receivable and payable, etc., to the extent that he considers necessary and practicable under the circumstances

(4) Examination of important documents and supplementary authorizations, such as: organization deeds, by-laws, minute books, contracts, and the obtaining of certified statements and explanations from management in order to form his opinion.

Extensive promulgation of these minimum auditing procedures was approved, not only for the benefit of the profession but also for those engaged in private and public economic activities.

Prior to the publication of these standards, and perhaps to a considerable extent today, audit procedures emphasized detailed checks of cash and vouchers with a view to disclosing defalcations.

A recent development was the publication, January 1, 1964, of Bulletin No. 1 of the Auditing Committee of the Lima College of Public Accountants. This Committee, under the sponsorship of a new department of the College, was formed to promote and disseminate knowledge of the independent auditor's duties and responsibilities in reporting on his examination of financial statements. The auditing standards proposed in the Bulletin are similar to those stated in the Statements on Auditing Procedure No. 33 of the American Institute of Certified Public Accountants.

Since the period of exposure of these standards has been so brief, there is no information available as to their acceptance by the profession.

Independence. The concept of independence is dealt with in the Code of Ethics, which states that a contador público shall not examine and report upon the financial statements of any company in which he has a financial interest, or of which he is an employee or where there is any type of relationship which could impair his independent judgment. In practice, however, pending more complete dissemination and acceptance of the Code, an understanding of the importance of independence is not widespread. Nevertheless, as a consequence of the work of the Third National Convention of Public Accountants (November 1963), and the resulting publicity, acceptance of the importance of independence is increasing.

Standards of Reporting

There has been no standard form of auditor's report suggested or authorized by government regulation. Bulletin No. 1 of the Lima College (mentioned above), however, suggests that a long-form or a short-form report may be issued, depending upon the purpose for which it is prepared. It states that the auditor's opinion may be unqualified, qualified or he may disclaim an opinion, depending on circumstances.

Consistency and Materiality. Some progress is being made in the recognition of these concepts by the Peruvian practitioner, as a result of the discussions at the Third National Convention and in the quarterly publication of the colegio.

ACCOUNTING PRINCIPLES AND PRACTICES

There has been no official statement of accounting principles either by government agencies or by the Colegio de Contadores Públicos, but there have been discussions on various points in the colegio's quarterly magazine, and a committee of the Lima College of Public Accountants, on Accounting Principles and Practices, has recently been formed and is expected to help in establishing accepted principles.

Form and Content of Financial Statements

Statement Presentation. There is no required or standard form of presentation of financial statements of Peruvian companies. Published statements, required by the regulations affecting corporations, consist of a very condensed balance sheet, with a minimum of disclosure. Various arrangements of the balance sheet items are used; sometimes in order of liquidity, and sometimes in "public utility" form—with the asset side beginning with fixed assets, and the liability side beginning with capital and surplus.

Statements for internal use often give more details of assets than is customary in the United States (petty cash, postage stamps, etc.), and reserves for bad debts, depreciation, and similar reserves are often shown on the liability side of the balance sheet in a special reserve section.

Consolidated Financial Statements

Since consolidated statements are not permitted for income tax purposes, it is unusual that they be prepared for publication or other purposes.

Inventories

Inventories, by law, must be stated at cost. Writedowns to market are not recognized for tax purposes. Cost is generally computed at average or on the first-in-first-out basis. When government controlled prices are

12

involved, cost may include general and administrative expenses, interest, and occasionally selling expenses.

Fixed Assets

The government permitted companies to write up their fixed assets, except land and intangibles, as they appeared on their balance sheets at December 31, 1958, by up to 25 per cent of their net value, and permitted the amount of the restatement to be depreciated over future years.

The Industrial Promotion Law allows restatement of fixed assets if the dollar exchange rate varies by 5 per cent or more in one year. The amount of restatement is debited to the account Restatement-Law 13270, and credits are made to: (a) accrued depreciation, (b) portion applicable to any unpaid amounts, and (c) Restatement Surplus-Law 13270.

Machinery acquired under the above-mentioned Industrial Promotion Law, must be shown under the account Investments-Law 13270, with a corresponding credit, on the liabilities side, to Profits Invested-Law 13270.

Treasury Stock

Purchases of a corporation's own stock must be made out of surplus and treated as a redemption of capital. A corporation may not hold its own stock.

Liability for Severance Pay and Pensions

The liability for severance pay, which is due employees and normally commences ninety days after employment at the rate of one month's pay for each year of service, is usually accrued currently. Severance indemnities of employees hired after July 11, 1962 are limited to S/7000 (Soles) for each year of service. Severance pay for one year of service is accrued after three months of employment; two years after fifteen months, etc.

For employees hired before July 12, 1962, pensions are payable after thirty-five years (in some cases, thirty years) of service, but it is customary to account for these on a cash-payment basis. Presently, all employees and employers pay a percentage of salaries monthly (up to S/7000 per month) to a government entity for future pensions.

Statement of Income

The examination of financial statements in Perú emphasizes the balance sheet, and the statement of profit and loss tends to become a by-product. The latter frequently does not disclose cost of sales, selling and general expenses, etc., but rather classifies such costs under headings such as salaries and wages, materials cost, depreciation and the like.

Interest Income and Expense. As notes receivable are commonly taken as evidence of an account receivable, interest income from this source is likely to be significant. It is taken into income when billed rather than as it accrues.

Interest (other than bank interest) paid on obligations issued to acquire assets is frequently capitalized.

Depreciation. The tax law sets rates for depreciation which are fairly realistic and are generally used. The Industrial Promotion Law now allows accelerated methods of depreciation, in the following circumstances:

1. A greater than usual wearing down, caused by extended operations, of machinery or equipment
2. Machinery or equipment being replaced by others with a larger output or production
3. When dealing with new products in which the government has a special interest in promoting in accordance with the law (special authorization)

Special authorization is required from the Tax Department, which must first consult with the Department of Industries of the Ministry of Promotion and Public Works, so as to issue the corresponding decree.

Authorization for accelerated depreciation applies as from the date it was requested and may not be applied retroactively.

REQUIREMENTS FOR LISTING OF SECURITIES ON THE STOCK EXCHANGE AND PUBLIC SALE OF SECURITIES

It is not usual to attempt to sell securities to the public by means of an offering prospectus, and there are no governmental or other regulations prescribing its contents.

The Lima Stock Exchange (Bolsa de Valores de Lima) is an official exchange with government recognition, but acting on a private basis under the Commercial Code. There are no requirements that financial statements be presented nor that they be reported upon by independent or other accountants.

A bill has been presented (January 1964) to Parliament providing for the establishment of the National Securities Committee which would be charged with ordering, regulating and supervising the Exchange. One of its provisions would require "balance sheets" to be presented, which would be certified by a public accountant or a firm of public accountants acting in the capacity of independent public auditors.

VENEZUELA 9

2

VENEZUELA

FORMS OF BUSINESS ORGANIZATION

The forms of business organization in Venezuela are similar to those of other Spanish-American countries and are provided for in the first ("On Commerce in General") of four sections of the Code of Commerce which was partially reformed in 1955. Other sections of the Code of Commerce deal with maritime commerce, bankruptcies and commercial jurisdiction. Certain professional organizations are regulated under the Civil Code.

The Compañía Anónima and the general partnership have their counterparts in similar forms common in the United States; there are specialized forms of limited partnerships which differ somewhat. The Code of Commerce of Venezuela does not distinguish between foreign and domestic corporations or partnerships; United States companies may engage in business in Venezuela by legal registration of a branch or by organizing a domestic United States corporation registered to do business there. Organizing a subsidiary under Venezuelan law is common, and has certain tax and other advantages.

The government, through various agencies (Banks Superintendency, Treasury, Central Bank, Ministries of Development, Mines and Hydrocarbons, Labor, etc.), supervises the operations of insurance, banking, oil, industrial and other concerns in which it has an interest (see Accounting and Reporting for the Oil Industry, later in this chapter). Industrial enterprises have to be registered in the "Catastro de Industria" (Census of Industry), kept in the Ministry of Development, within a period of ninety days following the start of operation. In order to register in this Catastro, the companies have to submit the constitutive document, list of products to be manufactured, etc. Furthermore, income tax inspectors may inspect the records of any company, and regulations in regard to labor and other matters are provided in social legislation.

3

Compañía Anónima (C.A.)

The most common form of incorporation is the Compañía Anónima which is organized by not less than two incorporators, but has no required minimum number of stockholders. Liability of stockholders is limited to the amount of their subscriptions. All authorized shares must be fully subscribed, a minimum of 20 per cent must be paid for and deposited in a bank, and shares must have a par value. If property other than cash is paid in on subscriptions, its value must be approved by all stockholders, and must be acceptable to the Registrar of Companies.

The constitutive document of a Venezuelan corporation includes matters usually set forth in both the charter and by-laws of a United States corporation. It must be presented to the Court of Commerce in the district of its domicile, published in a local newspaper and inscribed in the Commercial Register. This document must state the compensation and special rights granted to promoters, if any, which may be only in the form of participation in future profits not in excess of 10 per cent and for not more than five years. It must also state the number of comisarios (statutory examiners) who have an unlimited right of inspection of all operations of the corporation.

The legal reserve is provided at 5 per cent of the annual profits until it equals 10 per cent of the capital. This requirement may be higher if so provided in the by-laws, which may also provide other reserves.

Every six months (for banks, every year) the administrators must present financial statements to the comisarios, who must examine them and report upon them to the stockholders at the annual meeting. Ten days after approval by the stockholders, a copy of the financial statements and the report of the comisarios must be filed with the local Court of Commerce.

Compañía de Responsabilidad Limitada (C.R.L.)

This entity resembles a corporation (C.A.) in that the contributors are liable only to the amount of their subscriptions to their participation quotas, divided in units of 1,000 Venezuelan Bolivars or multiples thereof. The capital subscribed must be not less than Bs 20,000 nor more than Bs 2,000,000. Comisarios must be appointed if capital exceeds Bs 500,000.

Unless the instrument of organization provides otherwise, quotaholders wishing to transfer their interest must first offer them to other partners, and in order to transfer to third parties, must have the consent of a majority of partners representing at least three-fourths of the capital. Quotas may not be represented by negotiable shares or securities.

4

Within a maximum of three months after the close of a fiscal period, the managers must prepare a balance sheet and profit and loss statement, and statement of proposed distribution of profits.

Other Forms of Business Organization

Compañia en Nombre Colectivo. This is the usual form of partnership in which all partners are jointly and severally liable for partnership obligations. The partnership agreement must include: the name and domicile of the partnership and of all its partners, the kind of business, and the contributions of partners and methods of sharing profits and losses.

The general partnership is not required to have comisarios.

Compañia en Comandita Simple. In this type there are two classes of partners—general (solidarios) who have joint and several liability for partnership debts, and have exclusive right to management. The liability of silent or limited partners (comanditarios) is limited to a specific amount.

Compañia en Comandita por Acciones. This differs from the above only in that the interests of the limited partners may be represented by shares. The instrument of organization must also specify the amount of capital with limited liability, and the number of comisarios.

Business Records

All businesses (including sole proprietorships) must maintain a journal, general ledger and an "inventory book." Somewhat less elaborate records are required of retail merchants. The journal and the inventory book must be bound and the pages numbered. All other records, including the general ledger, may be maintained in any way which is to the advantage of the company. The Code of Commerce permits the summarization of transactions on a monthly basis. It is therefore the usual practice for the journal to contain only one entry per month summarizing the total debit and credit movements of all major accounts during the month.

At the commencement of operations, the journal and the "inventory book" must be presented to the local Court of Commerce to be signed and dated on the initial page, and all pages must be stamped with the seal of the Court.

5

Corporations and share-issuing limited partnerships must also maintain a stock-transfer book and minute books for directors' and shareholders' meetings, which must be similarly bound and stamped on each page.

COMISARIO (STATUTORY EXAMINER)

The commercial code of Venezuela states in effect that the shareholders of a corporation shall appoint one or more comisarios, who may or may not be shareholders, to prepare a report for presentation at the shareholders' meeting of the following year explaining the results of the examination and the information obtained from management, reporting their observations arising from their examination, and stating their approval (or disapproval) of financial statements and other relevant matters. As mentioned above, the statutory examiners have an unlimited right of inspection of the books and records of the company. They are deemed to be the stockholders' representatives in the financial affairs of the corporation. They are probably subject to civil fraud suits from stockholders or third parties if they make false declarations.

There is no penalty if statutory examiners are not appointed although it is a common practice to appoint the comisarios at the first meeting after the constitution of a company. Any interested party may ask the commercial court to appoint the statutory examiner if one has not been appointed by the shareholders. There are no qualifications for the position of statutory examiner. There is no present requirement that the statutory examiner be a "contador público"; however, more and more domestic as well as foreign corporations are naming practicing public accountants as statutory examiners or at least requesting examinations by practicing public accountants in addition to the work carried on by the statutory examiner.

There is no prescribed form for the statutory examiner's opinion. One form, however, used by public accountants acting as comisarios states that:

The balance sheet and profit and loss statement have been presented to him (comisario) for his opinion

That he has examined such financial statements

That he found the statements in accordance with accounting records and sufficient supporting evidence

That he obtained all necessary information

That he recommends the statements for shareholders' approval.

No mention is made either of accounting principles followed by the company or of auditing procedures used by the comisario.

Since the comisario is not required to have competence in the accounting field or to be independent, any report or opinion issued by him with respect to financial statements does not as a general rule give the same degree of assurance as to the fairness of financial statements as would that of an independent auditor.

THE ACCOUNTING PROFESSION

There are no laws governing the public accounting profession in Venezuela. At present, anyone is permitted to practice as a public accountant. There is no regulatory authority and public accountants are not required to register.

Broadly speaking, it could be said that there are about 300 individuals engaged in public accounting practice in Venezuela, of which approximately 250 work on the auditing staff of international public accounting firms. Of these, about 240 are members of the two leading accounting organizations referred to below. Approximately 160 are members of the Colegio Nacional de Técnicos en Contabilidad and about 80 are members of the Colegio de Contadores Públicos y Administradores Comerciales de Venezuela. In addition there are perhaps 50 practitioners— 25 members of each of the two Colegios—who are engaged in their own private practice either as individuals or as associates in small local firms.

Generally speaking, the services presently performed by the Venezuelan public accountant are the same as those performed by a United States CPA: auditing, income tax assistance, bookkeeping services, etc., and occasionally the handling of detailed administration matters such as employees' social security and income tax retentions. Many of the Venezuelan public accountants perform also the duties of comisario for corporations.

Training of Accountants

Until 1946, the only business training courses available were five-year schools of commerce, which were of high school level and were operated by the government. In 1946, a school of business administration was created at the Central University of Venezuela, but it was not until 1956, that courses in public accounting were introduced.

In 1950, the first group graduated from this school, and until 1959, the graduates were given a degree as Business Administrator-Accountant. In 1956, this school was divided into Business Administration and Accountancy, and in 1960, the university held the first graduation of students following a separate curriculum in accounting. At present, the title granted to graduates of this school is licensee in business administration or business administrator (administrador comercial), and licensee in public accountancy or public accountant (contador público), respectively.

Under the Venezuelan system, admission to a university is subject to a satisfactory completion of the secondary school (five years) with majors in science or humanities. The graduates of this school have the Bachelor's Degree which resembles the European baccalaureate system and can be said to be a combination of American high school and one year of college.

In the case of public accountancy, admission to the school of business administration was originally accorded, in addition to graduates of the secondary school, to graduates from the schools of commerce referred to above and to persons who had ten years' experience in accounting and were able to pass an entrance examination. This third class of admission was rescinded in the Central University in 1958. Since 1963, the Catholic University Andres Bello and the Santa María University permit students to take the first three years of the course in business administration and public accountancy provided they have completed the first three years of secondary school. In order to be candidates for the university degree, however, students will have had to complete the full secondary school (bachillerato).

The university course is a four-year course leading to a degree in business administration or public accountancy. Classes are held in the evening, usually from 6 p.m. to 10 p.m. The curriculum for the first two years is the same; the last two years are devoted to specialization in one of the two fields. The present syllabus for public accountancy includes 2,475 hours of instruction covering general, cost and advanced accounting; auditing and accounting systems; civil, commercial, labor and tax law; economics, finance, mathematics and statistics; business organization and administration, and collateral subjects.

The university, upon the recommendation of public accountants and professors, is considering changes in the curriculum for public accountants which would extend the course to five years. A thorough study of the curriculum in force for public accountants, and a proposed one, were submitted in April of 1960, to the Academic Council of the Faculty of

Economics, upon which the school of business administration and accountancy depends. This study, substantially expanded, was presented to the Seventh National Accounting Convention in 1961.

The proposed curriculum extended the required hours from 2,475 to 3,300; it strengthened such courses as law and economics, and added courses in specialized accounting, theory of internal control and audit reports.

It was also recommended that the degree of "contador público" only be awarded after the candidate has obtained a minimum of two years' experience as a public accountant. Experience could be gained concurrently with the university education or after completion of studies. Although this and other proposed curricula are being considered, no final action has been taken so far.

There are five state and two private universities in Venezuela offering courses leading to a degree in business administration or public accountancy. Up to 1963, there had been approximately 700 graduates.

Professional Accounting Organizations

Colegio Nacional de Técnicos en Contabilidad (National College of Technicians in Accounting). This Colegio, founded in 1942, as the Asociacion de Contadores de Venezuela, is the oldest accounting organization in the country and the majority of practicing accountants are members of it. Current requirements to become a member are the presentation of evidence of recognized accounting studies (university or other institutions—not necessarily official ones) and two years of public or private accounting practice; or several years of public or private practice in responsible accounting positions and, frequently, the presentation of a thesis on accounting, auditing or a related subject. Foreign accountants, holding a CPA or equivalent certificate, may qualify for admission provided they are residents of Venezuela and have a reasonable knowledge of Spanish. The practice of public accountancy is not a prerequisite for membership.

This Colegio, since its foundation, has represented Venezuela in international accounting congresses and is the sponsor and official representative of Venezuela before the Interamerican Accounting Conferences. This organization adopted the Rules of Ethics approved in the Second Interamerican Accounting Conference and made them of compulsory application for its members acting either as independent auditors or as comisarios for corporations. Total membership of this Colegio amounts to approximately 250. Many former members transferred their allegiance to the Colegio de Contadores Públicos y Administradores Comerciales de Venezuela (see below).

Colegio de Contadores Públicos y Administradores Comerciales de Venezuela (*College of Venezuelan Public Accountants and Business Administrators*). This Colegio is made up of graduates in public accountancy or business administration from Venezuelan universities, or those graduates in similar courses in foreign universities who have revalidated their degrees in Venezuela. Graduates of foreign universities are almost always required to take at least two years of the university curriculum. Presently there are about 700 members. As in the previously mentioned Colegio, the practicing of public accountancy is not a prerequisite for membership. As a matter of fact, about 85 per cent of its members work either for private enterprises or government agencies.

Other Accounting Organizations. The Institute of Internal Auditors and the System and Procedures Association have their chapters in Caracas. Their meeting programs are in line with their names, and they have no influence whatsoever either in the practice or the regulation of the accounting profession.

Ethics

Both the Colegio Nacional de Técnicos en Contabilidad and the Colegio de Contadores Públicos y Administradores Comerciales de Venezuela have adopted codes of ethics, which are practically identical. The codes deal with the manner in which members shall practice accountancy and their relations with fellow members and their clients. Specifically, it is prohibited to solicit clients through improper advertising, to base fees on the results of professional service, to accept fees or commissions from or to pay them to the laity, to engage in competitive bidding, to certify *pro forma* projections of earnings, to engage in noncompatible occupations when in the practice of public accounting, and to divulge confidential information obtained in the course of the work.

It is considered injurious to the profession if the accountant, in expressing an opinion upon financial statements which he has examined:

Does not include a material fact not disclosed in the statements, or the statements contain a material fact which is untrue

Becomes liable for professional negligence during the process of his investigations or in the issuance of his report

Failed to obtain sufficient information to allow the issuance of an unqualified opinion, or expresses an opinion when the exceptions are such as to preclude the issuance of an opinion

Fails to disclose the application of accounting principles not generally accepted, or to disclose any material omission of accounting principles applicable in the circumstances.

The provisions of the Code of Ethics relating to the issuance of an opinion based on generally accepted auditing standards and to independence are given under the later heading "Auditing Standards."

Proposed Laws to Regulate the Public Accounting Profession

Various proposals for a law governing public accountancy have been made by several different groups, beginning in 1955, with a regulatory project proposed by the Colegio Nacional de Técnicos en Contabilidad. More recently, both this Colegio and the Colegio de Contadores Públicos y Administradores Comerciales de Venezuela have prepared proposals, of which those of the former were presented to the National Congress at the end of 1961.

Both proposals agree generally that:

1. Comisarios of corporations should be public accountants (with certain limitations).
2. Financial statements of insurance and banking institutions should be certified by public accountants.
3. Financial statements of corporations whose shares are listed on the Stock Exchange should be certified by public accountants.

In the proposal prepared by the Colegio de Contadores Públicos y Administradores Comerciales de Venezuela, the conditions for inscription of foreign professionals are: to be a resident of Venezuela for at least five consecutive years, to revalidate his degree in a Venezuelan university, and to be a citizen of a country in which Venezuelan professionals are allowed to practice the profession.

If this reciprocity condition does not exist the foreign graduate would not be allowed to inscribe his title in the Colegio and, consequently, would be unable to practice even if he had fulfilled the two previous conditions.

In relation to the practice of Venezuelan accountants there are presently unreconciled differences between the two proposals as to whether only one, or more than one, class of persons should be recognized by law as professional public accountants, and also differences in the specified qualifications necessary for recognition as a professional public accountant.

It appears unlikely that the National Congress will take action until the profession as a whole presents a unified proposal.

AUDITING STANDARDS

General and Field Work Standards

The Code of Ethics of both the Colegio Nacional de Técnicos en Contabilidad and the Colegio de Contadores Públicos y Administradores Comerciales de Venezuela states that members of the Colegios will examine the financial statements in accordance with generally accepted auditing standards and that no opinion will be given on such statements if the related examination has not been adequately performed. Although no official pronouncement or codification of such standards has been made, the influence of international auditing firms in Venezuela has had a significant effect on the standards of Venezuelan practitioners. Auditing procedures will normally include confirmation of cash in banks and receivables, and physical observation of inventories.

Independence. The Codes of Ethics of the two professional organizations referred to above state that a public accountant cannot establish a practice unless he assumes a personal and unlimited responsibility; that he has to maintain an independent and impartial judgment in examining and expressing an opinion on financial statements; and that he cannot have any economic or other connection with the corporation to be examined which might in some way affect his independence of judgment.

Standards of Reporting

There are no reporting requirements prescribed either by government agencies or professional organizations and as a consequence there is no standard auditor's report, except that prescribed by the Superintendent of Banks for such financial institutions.

An audit report prepared by Venezuelan auditors usually represents a combination of long-form report, explanations about the work done, and comments on internal control. Reference is very seldom made in the report to "generally accepted auditing standards" or "generally accepted accounting principles" and the consistency in their application. Disclosure of information in footnotes as such is rare, but complementary accounts (cuentas de orden) often disclose contingent liabilities such as guarantees, discounts, collateral held or given, etc.

Consistency. There have been no official pronouncements either by the professional organizations or by government on the consistent application of accounting principles by corporations. As noted before, most of the comisario's reports do not include any reference to the accounting principles used in the preparation of the financial statements subject to examination.

Materiality. There have been no pronouncements on the concept of materiality and its effect on the auditor's work and his opinion on the financial statements.

Disclosure of Subsequent Events. It is not common practice to disclose the existence of events subsequent to the balance-sheet date, which, if disclosed, might have a material effect upon the proper evaluation of financial statements. In general, disclosure of material facts by way of footnote is seldom used.

ACCOUNTING PRINCIPLES AND PRACTICES

In general, accounting practices followed in Venezuela can be described as being in accordance with generally accepted accounting principles as defined in the United States. However, as indicated in the following discussion, commercial, labor and tax legislation and regulations are usually controlling in determining the accounting principles used.

General Form and Content of Financial Statements

Under Venezuelan income tax laws and regulations, financial statements which are a part of tax return forms—which must be signed by the accountant of the corporation in addition to the person who prepares the return and the taxpayer or his representative—are presented in a way similar to American practice: Assets and liabilities are classified as current, fixed, long-term, etc.; "valuation reserves" are shown as deduction from the related asset account, etc. In addition, supplementary schedules showing details of costs and expenses and other financial data are to be presented.

Statement Presentation. As previously mentioned, according to the Code of Commerce the administrators of the corporation should prepare every six months a "summary statement of assets and liabilities condition," which should be put in the hands of the comisarios. Furthermore, the administrators should present to the comisarios the balance sheet of the corporation, together with supporting documents, at least a month in advance of the meeting of shareholders in which such balance sheet will be discussed. The balance sheet "will show with evidence and accuracy the real profits earned and losses incurred." Assets must be stated "at values they really have," but generally this requirement is not followed. Corporate financial statements together with the report of the statutory examiner must be filed with the Court of Commerce within ten days after approval. There is no indication that this filing is anything more than a formality and no prescribed form of presentation exists.

Insurance companies, which are supervised by the Ministry of Development, and banks, supervised by the Superintendant of Banks, are required to publish their financial statements periodically, and the form is rigidly prescribed.

Consolidated Financial Statements. There is no government requirement that consolidated statements be presented. Under the fiscal legislation, companies are treated as separate taxpayers and except for the additional fifty-fifty tax on income from petroleum and mining when consolidation is obligatory, intercompany affiliations are not recognized.

Balance Sheet

Accounts Receivable. Uncollectible accounts written off to expense in the taxable year are deductible for tax purposes. Recoveries of bad debts written off are required to be taken into income of the period in which collected. Allowance for unspecified bad debts cannot be deducted.

Inventories. Inventories must be stated at cost for tax purposes. Cost of materials, merchandise, etc., purchased for resale, processing, or use in Venezuela are deductible for tax purposes as well as related transportation, insurance, normal purchases, commissions calculated as a percentage of cost, taxes and other direct expenses. Pricing should not exceed normal pricing in the supplying market and in any case must be supported by vendors' invoices. "Reserves" or allowances for inventory or other losses are not deductible; however, losses on capital assets destined for the production of income—less insurance recoveries, if any— can be deducted. When an inventory is written down to market, the writedown must be applied to the individual items so that the pricing can be scrutinized, such writedown is not tax-deductable.

Fixed Assets and Depreciation. Depreciation must be taken currently for tax purposes; the taxpayer cannot defer depreciation to be taken up in a year when he has profits. Any method of depreciation which determines the annual charges based on cost and the number of years of useful life is allowed for tax purposes. Straight-line, declining balance and sum-of-the-digits are among the acceptable methods, and the unit of production method is specifically permitted. Once a method has been chosen it may not be changed without the prior authorization of the tax authorities.

In determining the amount to be depreciated, no allowance need be made for salvage value. Maintenance and repairs are deductible expenses provided they do not appreciably prolong the life of the asset or alter its original structure.

Liability for Severance Pay. Under the Venezuela Labor Law there are certain types of payments upon termination of employment not having a fixed duration. Generally, no dismissal indemnities are payable when employment is terminated because of justified cause for dismissal or upon resignation without justified cause. (Justified causes for dismissal and resignation are defined in the Law.) There is no requirement in the law that a provision for these indemnities be created. Nearly all companies accrue for a total or a substantial portion of this contingency, but this provision is not deductible for tax purposes; payments are deductible.

Legal Reserve. Five per cent of net profit for the year must be appropriated for a legal reserve until the reserve reaches ten per cent of subscribed capital stock. There is no precise definition as to the purpose for which the reserve may be used. It is not available for dividends but may be used to absorb losses. It may not be used to acquire treasury bonds or stock.

"Invested Capital" Allowance. The Venezuelan Labor Law provides that, in addition to general expenses, up to 6 per cent of the invested capital can be deducted from the corporation's gross profits in order to compute the base for employees' profit-sharing participation (commonly known as "utilidades"). The term "invested capital" has never been fully clarified, but the consensus appears to be that the following should be included: capital stock paid in, surplus, reserves formed out of unallowable expenses, depreciation reserves (in some cases) and liabilities to parent company or stockholders.

Balances at the beginning of the year or averages for the year may be used for most of the above items. For a branch of a foreign corporation, the head office account is usually taken as "invested capital."

Statement of Income

Cash vs. Accrual Basis. The accrual basis is prescribed for computing taxable income of commercial and industrial activities (including petroleum and mining, agriculture and fishing). Income derived from

15

realty, personal property, professions, remunerations and winnings is taxable when cash is received or available—availability of cash meaning "credits in the account." For credits to constitute income, however, they must represent the ultimate settlement of the debtor's obligations when no subsequent cash payment is contemplated. That means that a credit to the recipient's account on the debtor's books does not necessarily constitute available income.

Profit on Construction Contracts. Profit on construction contracts that take more than a year to complete is determined by estimating the income earned and related costs at the end of the tax year. If the contract takes less than a year, the profit may be taken up in the tax year in which the work is completed.

Profit on Real Estate Development. For real estate development businesses, the cost of sales is determined by adding the cost of urbanizing to the cost of the land and dividing by the number of square meters available for sale to obtain a unit price. This unit price will be applied to the number of square meters sold to obtain the cost of sales.

Profit on Installment Sales. Profit on installment sales is recorded for tax purposes when the sale is made; it is not necessary to await the successive maturities of the installment payments. However, since 1958, the law has specifically permitted recording of real estate credit sales on a cash basis.

Profit or Loss on Disposal of Fixed Assets, etc. The profit and loss from disposal of fixed assets or from incidental activities connected with operations should be accounted for separately, and the records should be so maintained as to show these results.

Treasury Stock. A company's own stock may be purchased out of profits only. Stockholders' approval is necessary to make such a purchase. Such stock may not be held in the treasury indefinitely.

In determining the cost of a company's shares sold, a corporation may add to cost the par value of shares issued by capitalization of earnings.

"Profit for the Year" does not have for many local companies the same meaning as in the United States. These companies frequently prepare a "statement of distribution of profits" in which the following appropriation of "profits" are shown: employees' bonuses, Board of Directors' fees, provision to maintain statutory, valuation and capital "reserves," income tax, etc.

Accounting and Reporting for the Oil Industry

The accounting requirements for the oil industry were prescribed generally under the Law of Hydrocarbons of 1943, and in the Income Tax Law of 1956. Article 68 of the 1943 law states, in effect, that "the Federal Executive has the power to regulate the operations of hydrocarbon concessionaries and to examine the accounts thereof." Oil companies are required to maintain in Venezuela the accounts relative to their industrial operations and those necessary for administrative and fiscal purposes.

Most oil companies maintain separate accounting records for producing and nonproducing concessions.

Sales made at less than posted prices (arbitrarily set by the government) may be required to be increased to posted prices in reporting for tax purposes.

In general, the deduction allowed for depreciation, depletion and amortization is the amount required to amortize the cost of the assets over the period during which it is expected that they will be used to produce income. The group method of calculating depreciation is permitted. No allowance for salvage value is required in determining the amount to be depreciated.

Under the tax law, concession costs, exploration expenses, development costs, indirect costs and any other cost constituting a permanent type of investment may be capitalized for recovery by means of depletion. Depletion allowances are calculated on the unit of production basis which is the ratio of actual production to estimated reserves in a given field. Percentage depletion based on market value of production rather than on cost, such as allowed in the United States, is not permitted in Venezuela. Only the cost of concessions in production may be depleted; however, a producing concession has been defined as any concession wholly or partially located within the proven area of a producing field.

Concession costs consist of payments to third parties for acquisitions, initial exploration and exploitation taxes, annual exploration taxes, legal expenses, registry, maps, surveys, etc., related to acquisition, geological, geophysical and other exploration expenses. All the expenditures of a company prior to obtaining commercial production are usually charged either to an exploration or development account. These are depleted on a company-wide basis.

Nonproducing concessions are usually written off when official renouncement is made to the Venezuelan Government.

Most companies follow the practice of capitalizing intangible drilling costs both in producing and nonproducing areas.

Dry hole costs are either capitalized or considered a loss and charged to expense during the year.

Repairs and maintenance expense, including workovers, which do not increase oil reserves, are expensed.

Purchasing commissions charged by offices outside of Venezuela acting as purchasing agents are generally charged to cost of materials.

Oil inventory costs generally include all costs to place the oil in storage tanks at deep-water terminals. Last-in, first-out is the method of valuation most frequently used.

Oil companies are required to submit the following information to the Ministry of Mines and Hydrocarbons:

1. Monthly	Production report (on which the exploration tax will be computed) and the transportation services rendered to third parties (on which the transportation tax will be computed)
2. Quarterly	Results of operations and estimations, balance sheet, and application of funds
3. Semiannually	Detailed sales report
4. Annually	Financial statements (including consolidated surplus statement and origin and application of funds)
	Statement of production and sales of manufactured products at the year end
	Statement of operations for the year (including statistics, drilling, refining and transportation operations, paid and payable taxes, number of workers, etc.).

In addition, oil companies are required to file, at the request of the Central Bank, the following reports dealing with international transactions:

1. Transactions of the reporting company
2. Computation of net profit payable to foreign investors in respect of their equity in the reporting company
3. Capital transactions of the reporting company
4. Adjusted stockholders' equity movement.

REQUIREMENTS FOR PUBLIC SALE OF SECURITIES

There is no governmental or other supervision of prospectuses used in the sale of securities of corporations to the public. There is little underwriting as such in Venezuela, and the information given to prospective purchasers by brokers handling such sales is based on data supplied by the issuer. There is no requirement for furnishing of financial statements, or that, if any are furnished, they be reported upon by independent public accountants.

REQUIREMENTS FOR LISTING OF SECURITIES ON VENEZUELAN STOCK EXCHANGE

Shares of the compañía anónima and comandita por acciones (limited partnership with shares) can be listed, at their request, on the Caracas Stock Exchange.

The following documents must be submitted:
1. Copy of constitutive document
2. Copy of corporate by-laws
3. Copy of last financial statements and related comisario's report
4. Description of the classes and number of shares issued.

This information must be certified by the company's legal counsel.

To maintain its listing, a company is obliged to submit annual financial statements, showing in particular the amortization and interest payments on long-term indebtedness. Also, the details of any changes in the corporate charter or by-laws must be sent to the Exchange.

BELGIUM | 10

FORMS OF BUSINESS ORGANIZATION

The forms of business organization in Belgium have points of similarity with those in France, since Belgian commercial laws were originally derived from those of France. The principal form of business organization in Belgium is the Société Anonyme (corporation). In addition, business may be carried out as a Société en Commandite par Actions (corporation which has both limited liability stockholders and general partners), Société de Personnes à Responsibilité Limitée (private limited liability company), Société en Commandite Simple (limited partnership), Société en Nom Collectif (general partnership), and Société Cooperative (cooperative). All business enterprises must register with the Register of Commerce.

Business may also be carried out as a branch of a foreign corporation.

Société Anonyme (S.A.)

The Belgian corporation must have not less than seven shareholders; the maximum life of a corporation is thirty years, which is renewable for additional thirty-year periods.

Various types of stock may be issued: for example, "actions ordinaires" (common stock), "actions priviligiées" (preferred stock), and "parts de fondateurs" (founders' shares). There are also "actions de dividende" (dividend stocks), which normally share in earnings but not in capital distributions on liquidation, and "actions de jouissance" (these are shares which, although the original capital investment has been repaid, retain the right to super dividends; they normally do not share in capital distributions on liquidation.) Shares may be in bearer or registered form and need not have a par value. All shares must be subscribed prior to formation; there is no provision for "authorized but unissued stock." Bearer shares must be fully paid before being issued. Registered shares to be paid for in cash may be issued when 20 per cent of the price is

3

paid. If such shares are to be paid for in kind, they must be fully paid before issue. When the number of shareholders falls below seven and such condition persists for more than six months, any interested party may demand dissolution of the company. When the number of shareholders of a corporation is less than two, the corporation is considered to be dissolved by operation of law.

The management of the corporation is in the hands of a Board of Directors, of which there must be at least three members, but who need not be shareholders. They are elected by the shareholders for a term of up to six years and must deposit or have deposited for them a specified number of nominal shares to guarantee performance of their duties.

The Belgian Commercial Code requires that every société anonyme must elect, for a term of up to six years, one or more statutory examiners (commissaires reviseurs), who have an unlimited right of surveillance and control over all operations undertaken by the corporation. The examiners must deposit or have deposited on their behalf guarantees of at least one share each. (Statutory examiners are described more fully under a separate heading.) One of the shareholders, especially in small family companies, is sometimes elected "commissaire."

Corporations must publish their annual financial statements in the Official Gazette *Moniteur Belge*, accompanied by a list of the directors and statutory examiners, the names and addresses of partly paid up shareholders together with the amount remaining unpaid, and a statement showing the distribution of the profits.

Société en Commandite par Actions

This is a combination of the corporation structure with that of a general partnership. This type of company is becoming increasingly rare. The firm's name, preceded or followed by the words société en commandite par actions, may only include the names of the general partners. The liability of the general partners for the corporation debts is joint and several while the liability of the limited stockholders is limited to their share of the capital contribution. The regulations governing a corporation are applicable to this type of organization. Such a société must have at least three commissaires.

Société de Personnes à Responsabilité Limitée (S.P.R.L.)

This form of company is widely used by the small family business

4

attracted by the advantages of limited liability. The liability of the members is limited to the amount of their share subscription.

The company may consist of not less than two nor more than fifty members, and corporate bodies are excluded from membership. The shares are not freely transferable. Belgian company law requires the assent of at least half of the members, holding 75 per cent of the capital, to any share transfer other than to an existing member or close relatives of members. Moreover, the company statutes may impose transfer restrictions more stringent than this. The issued and paid-up capital may not be less than 50,000 Belgian francs. Shares may not have a nominal value of less than 1,000 BF.

The form of an S.P.R.L. cannot be adopted for the business of insurance, savings banks, building societies (mortgage loans), or stock exchange brokers. Bonds and debentures cannot be issued, nor can the shares be quoted on a stock exchange.

An S.P.R.L. can be administered by one or more managers who need not be members. If the number of partners (shareholders) exceeds five, a Commissaire must be elected.

Under the provisions of a Royal Decree of November 4, 1963, an S.P.R.L. having not more than ten members and a capital of not more than three million (B.Frs.) may choose between a tax regime as applicable to a corporation or to individuals. All others are treated in the same way as corporations.

The name of the company must appear in legal and other documents preceded or followed by the words société de personnes a responsibilité limitée, and an indication of the address of the registered office. The financial statements must be deposited with the Commercial Court, but not necessarily published.

The duration of an S.P.R.L. is thirty years, renewable for additional thirty-year periods.

Branch of a Foreign Corporation

Foreign corporations establishing Belgian branches must also apply for a Register of Commerce number authorizing them to trade in the country after producing evidence of publication of the foreign corporation's statutes in the official gazette (*Moniteur Belge*), and the filing of such statutes with the Register of Commerce. The annual financial statements of the foreign corporation (not of the branch) must also be published in the official gazette. A responsible representative domiciled in Belgium, who may be a bank, a Belgian corporation, or a private person must be appointed for the purpose of insuring the payment of taxes.

Other Forms of Business Organization

Société en Commandite Simple. This is a form of partnership with both general and limited partners. The name of the firm consists of the name(s) of the general partners and may not contain the name of a limited partner. Limited partners may take no part in the management; if one of them does so, his liability becomes unlimited with respect to the matters in which he has participated, or if he habitually undertakes managerial duties, he becomes an unlimited partner.

Société en Nom Collectif. All the partners are jointly and severally responsible for the company's liabilities. The partnership name must consist of the names of one or more of the partners.

Business Records

The Commercial Code requires that all enterprises keep an official inventory book, an official journal, and a copy of all correspondence. The official books must be legalized by a judge. This is evidenced by affixing the court's seal to the books in question before any inscriptions are made.

The annual financial statements must be recorded in detail in the inventory book. The journal must contain either in detail or in total the monthly entries posted from the subsidiary account books to the general ledger.

The share register must be kept at the company's registered office.

In addition to the books mentioned above, sales tax and labor legislation require that stamped and approved sales and purchase journals must be kept in accordance with strict regulations, and a personnel register must be kept up to date.

In order to comply with the direct taxation authorities' minimum requirements for information, it is invariably necessary to keep the usual books of account such as the general ledger, cost of sales records, expense analyses, etc.

COMMISSAIRE RÉVISEUR (STATUTORY EXAMINER)

As required in the Commercial Code, shareholders must elect one or more commissaires réviseurs for a period of not more than six years. The commissaires have an unlimited right of surveillance and examination over all the transactions of the company. They need not be of Belgian nationality, reside in Belgium, or have an accounting background. The directors of a corporation must submit to the commissaires réviseurs a statement of assets and liabilities every six months and, in turn, the commissaires réviseurs must present to the annual general meeting a report of this surveillance and any proposals that they consider appropriate. The duties of the statutory examiners are similar to, but in some respects exceed, those of the directors in that the role of the commissaires réviseurs is to observe and, if necessary, to call the attention of the shareholders to the acts of the management, as well as to report on the accounts. Company law (Article 65) states that the report of the commissaire réviseur must include "the propositions they think convenient or necessary to be put to the shareholders' meeting, and they must also record the method by which they controlled the inventories" (inventory of assets and liabilities).

A typical report of a statutory examiner is:

> In accordance with clause .... of the statutes, we have examined the balance sheet at .... as well as the profit and loss account for the year .... and confirm that they are in agreement with the books of account. We have satisfied ourselves as to the existence of cash at banks and investments, and received such information as we required concerning the other items in the accounts.
>
> Our examination having been completed to our satisfaction, we propose that the balance sheet and profit and loss account as submitted by the Board of Directors be adopted by the stockholders.

The report of the usual commissaire réviseur, who is not required to have accounting training, cannot be expected to give the same assurance as to fairness of presentation of financial statements as would that of a professionally trained and independent auditor.

As indicated subsequently, publicly held companies must appoint among its commissaires réviseurs at least one who is a member of the Institut des Réviseurs d'Entreprises.

Provided they are free to carry out the work in accordance with the auditing standards of their respective Institutes, foreign accounting firms practicing in Belgium generally allow their members to be appointed as commissaires réviseurs; the report of the statutory examiner is usually modified to include a reference to the fact that the commissaires réviseurs have been assisted in their audit by the foreign accounting firm to which they belong.

THE ACCOUNTING PROFESSION

There are two recognized groups of independent auditors in Belgium, the Réviseurs de Banque and the Réviseurs d'Entreprises, whose titles are protected by law.

Réviseurs de Banque

The Institut des Réviseurs de Banque was formed in 1935, and its members perform specialized services for banks. Admission to membership is by appointment of the Banking Commission and requires a first-class university standard of education as well as many years' experience in financial enterprises. There are not more than thirty-six members at present, and they are considered the ranking class of independent accountants in Belgium.

While the réviseur de banque is a highly qualified professional in his field, his work is usually of a specialized character relating to banking and finance and does not comprise that which is ordinarily undertaken by an independent public accountant. The members of this Institut may, however, be appointed as a réviseur d'entreprises.

Réviseurs d'Entreprises

Since the law that created the Institut des Réviseurs d'Entreprises required that corporations whose shares are sold publicly must appoint at least one réviseur among its examiners (commissaires), the work of this class of accountants is largely that of the examination of the financial statements of these companies. When a company issues shares for other than cash, the equivalent value given for the shares must be approved by a réviseur d'entreprises.

The réviseur may also perform many of the services undertaken by the Expert Comptable (see following), except that he may not participate in the management of enterprises nor may he be an employee. Any services permitted to him, outside of his legal function as auditor, are done privately and separately from his work as réviseur.

Institut des Réviseurs d'Entreprises. The Institut des Réviseurs d'Entreprises was formed by a government law of 1953, in an attempt to organize the profession, but it has not been very successful since the regulations of the Institut severely restrict the activities of its members. Conditions for admission to the Institut are to some extent similar to those of the Collège National des Experts Comptables (see later discussion), but are much more restrictive. A large number of réviseurs are also members of the Collège.

Ethics. A Royal Decree, dated March 16, 1957, proposed by the Minister of Economic Affairs, established a Code of Ethics for regulating the profession of réviseurs d'entreprises, which, accordingly, has the force of law. Its provisions are summarized as follows:

1. Members must practice under their own names.
2. All publicity is forbidden.
3. They may not participate in the management of any business concerns, even family ones, and may not be involved in any commercial activities.
4. They must respect the rules of professional procedure in relations to their fellow members of the Institute.
5. They must not limit their activities in such a way as to become dependent upon any particular group or authority.
6. They may not accept any missions which are not within the scope of their profession.
7. Members may only be assisted by their partners, their trainees and employees, or by other members of the Institute. In certain cases the Institute can give special authority for departure from this rule.
8. Members may not sign a report upon accounts which have not been verified by them or their partners or staff. In the case of accounts prepared abroad, such accounts may be accepted if they have been examined by someone abroad with an equivalent degree, and reference to this must be made in the member's report.
9. When members give an opinion on accounts they offend the rules of the profession:

9

a. If they omit mentioning an important fact of which they have knowledge and which is not revealed or insufficiently revealed in the accounts, or of which the disclosure is of a nature which could affect the judgment of the reader
b. If they attach to the opinion which they express, qualifications of such a nature that they destroy the value or bearing of the opinion.

Disciplinary procedures are entrusted under the Decree to the Council of the Institute and the procedures and sanctions are detailed in Chapter II of the Decree.

There are other rules which are contained in letters from or statements made by the Institute which are designed to maintain the standing of the profession or to safeguard the members' independence. For example, the réviseur d'entreprises:

1. May not be an employee or sign an employment contract
2. May not be a member of the Board of Directors or be a manager, or proxy holder, or signing clerk in a commercial company
3. Before being able to accept the function of commissaire réviseur in a company, must first obtain permission and authorization from the Institut des Réviseurs d'Entreprises and their agreement to the amount of his remuneration.
4. May not do any form of trading nor accept any duties which belong to other professions, for example, he:
   a. May not hold accounts
   b. May not establish documents relating to the application of Social Laws
   c. May not be an insurance broker
   d. May not give expert opinions or advice on the valuation of real estate, or be an intermediary agent for affairs.

Expert Comptable

The designation expert comptable (accountant) is not protected by law, and anyone may use it. There are a number of expert accountants in Belgium, not members of the Institut des Réviseurs d'Entreprise, who perform professional accounting services and who may or may not be members of the Collège National des Experts Comptables. Recently, government representatives have indicated that legal status will be granted to the expert comptable.

Collège National des Experts Comptables. The Collège was formed in

1950, by grouping some twenty-four representative associations existing in Belgium. Its membership comprises about fifteen hundred accountants of whom about one-third are in public practice (active members); the others are called "agreed members" and are employed in private enterprise or by accounting firms.

Candidates for membership must pass an examination composed of eight parts covering: accounting technique, law, administrative organization, general economics, managerial economics, mathematics and statistics, composition, and ethics. The graduates of any of the courses given by any of the institutions specifically approved by the Collège, or university graduates in economics, financial or actuary courses are exempted from these examinations. These candidates must also pass an examination on practical applications of accounting and must have a five-year training period as an employee of an accountant who is a member of the Collège.

The Collège publishes a monthly journal both in French and Flemish.

The services performed by members of the Collège in Belgium have been outlined by a commission established by the Collège National des Experts Comptables. Some of the areas of interest include:

Advice in the capacity of an expert

Periodic or incidental judgment regarding the state of affairs of companies

Examination of annual accounts

Examination and preparation of cost-price calculations

Advice on the formation, administration, and liquidation of companies

Assistance in the management of enterprises

Advice relative to the transfer and combination of companies.

Ethics. Recently the Collège issued a Code of Ethics which, in ten chapters, discusses such topics as: professional secrets, independence, incompatible occupations, advertising, relations with brother professionals and clients, fees, etc. The position taken is generally similar to that prevailing in other countries; independence is recommended both in letter and spirit, but there is no specific prohibition against having a financial interest in a client.

Since the Code has been in effect a relatively short time, the extent of its acceptance in practice is not known.

Other Organizations of Accountants

Of the remaining organizations of accountants in Belgium, the more important are the Société Royale Chambre Belge des Comptables and the Association Nationale des Comptables de Belgique.

The Société Royale Chambre Belge des Comptables was formed at the turn of the century. Membership is gained by examination extending over a period of approximately seven years, depending upon the ability of the candidate and the time he has available for study, and a diploma is granted on attaining membership. There are no conditions relating to apprenticeship or service with a public accountant, but the vast majority of the candidates do have accounting employment.

The Association Nationale des Comptables de Belgique (A.N.C.B.) was formed in 1958, under the sponsorship of the Collège National, to represent the majority of accountants employed in commerce and in industry who do not qualify for membership in the Collège.

AUDITING STANDARDS

The accounting profession in Belgium has not as yet issued any recommendations on auditing standards and accounting principles similar to those issued by the profession in the United States and United Kingdom. However, the Collège National des Experts Comptables has in preparation a statement (400 pages) setting forth recommended auditing procedures.

General Standards

Adequate public accounting service is not generally available, except possibly from the most progressive experts comptables and the réviseurs d'entreprises. Except in the case of the réviseur, the Belgian auditor is permitted to have financial interests, direct or indirect, in the enterprise which he audits.

Standards of Field Work

1. Field work is frequently limited to verification of the trial balance with the general ledger accounts, examination of the bank statements, and verification of the documents of title to securities.
2. Payment by checks is rare in Belgium, and paid checks are not returned by the banks. Daily statements are mailed to customers, however, and under these arrangements direct confirmations of bank balances are not always considered necessary.
3. It is not usual to request direct confirmation of accounts receivable balances with the debtors, although the practice is spreading.
4. Physical inventories are not always observed.
5. The auditor is not required to review the system of internal control and, hence, his program of audit is not based on the results of such review.

Standards of Reporting

The typical audit report issued by the accounting profession in Belgium, apart from the standard report of the commissaire shown elsewhere in this section, is a discussion in long-form of the composition of the various headings of the balance sheet and earnings statement. It is addressed to the directors of the company and usually does not terminate with a final paragraph stating a formal opinion on the financial statements similar to that of a CPA in the United States.

The reason for this last is that the criterion of the so-called "minimum position" is still generally accepted even by the réviseurs d'entreprise (but not by the réviseur de banque who, however, not being called upon to audit corporations other than banks, does not greatly influence the prevailing standards of practice). Providing that the financial position of a company is at least as good as that shown by the accounts, the accounting profession in Belgium is expected to condone the creation and the withdrawal for use of hidden reserves. As a result, the profession in general is often unable to give a clear-cut opinion as to whether the financial statements fairly present the company's position and results of operations.

Another example of the difficulties facing the profession in Belgium is demonstrated by the treatment of depreciation in published or official accounts. In the absence of adequate profits, depreciation is sometimes not charged because it is considered essentially as an instrument of financial policy. Taxation law is also responsible for this tendency.

The omission of adequate depreciation from the accounts is generally mentioned in a typical commissaire's report but would rarely, if ever, give rise to a qualification of the fair view or correctness of the financial statements.

ACCOUNTING PRINCIPLES AND PRACTICES

Form and Content of Financial Statements

The Commercial Code places the entire responsibility for the valuation of assets and estimate of liabilities on the directors, although it requires that the balance sheet will show fixed assets, current assets, capital, reserves and surplus, debentures, secured liabilities, and unsecured liabilities separately. The Code does not list any further requirements in relation to the form and content of the income statement.

The balance sheet of a company as approved by the shareholders need not and usually does not conform in important particulars with the balance sheet as finally approved by the tax collector.

Consolidated Financial Statements. The practice of preparing consolidated statements is not customarily followed in Belgium.

Pooling of Interests

This method of accounting for business combinations is not followed.

Inventories

Basically, inventories for management purposes are stated at cost, but usually with a generous factor of safety. The Lifo method is not permitted, but tax authorities permit the valuation of raw materials, which are subject to considerable fluctuation in market prices, to be based on such market prices.

Restatement of Fixed Assets

By special legislation passed in 1947, companies were enabled, under certain conditions, to restate their fixed assets and compute depreciation on the increased values. The restatements were credited to a reserve that could be subsequently capitalized.

Statutory Reserve

The law requires corporations to set aside into a legal reserve 5 per cent of their annual profits, until this reserve equals 10 per cent of the corporation's outstanding capital stock. Generally, the statutory reserve may be used only in case of losses or liquidation.

When there are no remaining undistributed profits, the statutory reserve may be used to increase the capital account; if by reason of usage for this or other proper purposes the reserve falls below 10 per cent of the capital, the annual appropriations of 5 per cent of each year's profit must recommence.

Secret Reserves

Directors are not subject to penalties if they allocate profits to an official or hidden reserve, but are liable if they distribute nonexisting profits. The statutory examiner, for example, would report to the shareholders if he believed the inventory valuation was too high, but he would not feel it necessary to report if he believed it to be too low.

Accordingly, many Belgian companies provide reserves which are considered conservative in amount but which would be considered excessive by United States standards.

Liability for Severance Payments

Persons dismissed from service with a company are entitled to varying periods of notice, from three months to more than two years, and in theory serve out the time of notice. In practice, a lump-sum settlement is often made in lieu of notice, but since such liabilities cannot be foreseen, it is customary to account for them on a payment, rather than an accrual basis.

Statement of Income

Tax-effect Accounting. Where there are significant differences between accounting for book and for tax purposes, it is not the general practice to provide for the tax effects of the differences.

Payments to Directors. Payments to directors for fees, services, or commissions are charged to profit and loss. It is quite customary, however, for by-laws to provide that after the statutory reserve and dividends, a percentage of the remaining profits be allocated to the Board of Directors to be distributed among the members as they may agree. These payments are therefore regarded as appropriations of profit, voted by the shareholders similar to dividends, and not as costs to be charged to profit and loss.

REQUIREMENTS FOR PUBLIC SALE OF SECURITIES

The following summarizes the principal requirements to be met by companies wishing to sell securities to the public:

1. Company promoters or management are required to submit to the Banking Commission, at least fifteen days before issue, an information file complying with the latter's requirements.
2. Publication of the intention to make a public issue must be made in the official gazette at least ten days preceding commencement of the offer. The following information is required by the Commercial Code:
   a. Date of act of constitution
   b. Objects clause
   c. Present capital structure
   d. Particulars of unpaid capital
   e. Description and value of assets to be brought in as consideration for issue
   f. Composition of Board of Directors
   g. Most recent balance sheet and profit and loss account.
3. The dossier of information presented to the Bankers Commission usually comprises
   a. Copy of proposed preliminary publication in official gazette referred to above

    b. Schedule of liabilities and contingent liabilities

    c. Purpose of issue

    d. Details of underwriting arrangements

    e. Particulars of shares held by the promoters and underwriters.

4. The Banking Commission may complete its examination of the file by issuing a questionnaire followed by conferences. No inspection of records or audit is requested or undertaken, but penal sanctions are imposed in respect of false information. It is not clear how the latter would normally be established in the absence of reports by independent accountants.

5. Examination of prospectus and other forms of publicity by the Banking Commission with a view to establishing adequacy and accuracy as far as this can be determined without recourse to independent audit reports.

REQUIREMENTS FOR LISTING ON STOCK EXCHANGES

The principal stock exchanges in Belgium are located in Brussels, Antwerp, Liege, and Ghent. The bonds of a company may not be listed unless its shares are also listed.

Domestic companies in Belgium applying for listing on stock exchanges must have a minimum fund of 10 million Belgian francs, capital and reserves, and the balance sheets for the last two years must have been published in the official gazette. Foreign companies, in addition, must obtain a permit from the Ministry of Finance and from the Foreign Exchange Control Authority. The securities must be listed in the country of origin, and the companies must furnish the names of banks responsible for their financial service in Belgium. In regard to both domestic and foreign companies, the Stock Exchange Committee must obtain the formal approval of the listing from the Banking Commission.

DENMARK | 11

I

FORMS OF BUSINESS ORGANIZATION

The forms of business organizations in Denmark are the corporation (joint-stock company), the limited partnership company, the partnership and the sole proprietorship. Also, the operation of a trade or business through a Danish branch of a foreign corporation is a legally recognized form of doing business in Denmark.

Aktieselskab (Joint-stock Company)

Under the Danish Companies Act, No. 123 of April 15, 1930 (as amended), a joint-stock company is defined as any company carrying on a trade or business in which none of the shareholders are personally liable for the obligations of the company over the amount of share capital contributed by them. This is similar to the usual form of corporate entity found in other countries. The name of the company must contain the word "Aktieselskab" (joint-stock company) or an approved abbreviation thereof such as "A/S."

A corporation may be formed by three or more persons. The majority of the founders, but at least three, must be residents of Denmark and Danish citizens or have been residents of Denmark for the preceding five years. All founders must subscribe for at least one share and usually in the amount of at least 500 kroner. Unless specifically authorized otherwise, corporations are required to have a minimum share capital of 10,000 kroner. At least 10 per cent of the share capital (a minimum of 5,000 kroner) must be paid in at the time of registration, the remainder to be paid within one year. Special rules apply to banks and insurance companies.

The Board of Directors must consist of at least three members. If the firm name includes the name of a place in Denmark or national designation, the entire board must be residents of Denmark and Danish citizens or have been residents of Denmark for at least two years. For other companies, only the majority of the board must satisfy the above residency and citizenship requirements. The Companies Act does not specify where the board must hold its meetings. If the share capital exceeds 100,000 kroner, an executive manager or an executive board of managers in charge of administration must be appointed. They are all subject to the same qualifications as to residence and citizenship as the Board of Directors unless they are managing branches abroad, foreign managers of subsidiaries of foreign corporations may obtain exemption from these requirements.

Corporations must be audited annually by independent auditors chosen at a general stockholders meeting. If the company's shares are quoted on an exchange, there must be more than one auditor and at least one must be a state-authorized public accountant. If a company's shares are not listed, owners of one-third of the share capital may require auditing by a state-authorized public accountant. One annual meeting of the stockholders will be held in Denmark at which the annual accounts are to be presented.

Frequently, the by-laws of pension funds under the supervision of the State Insurance Board provide that the auditors of such funds shall be state-authorized, although Danish law merely requires that the auditor of a pension fund be a "competent auditor."

Kommandit Aktieselskab (Limited Partnership Company)

This is an arrangement between one or more individuals in partnership with a joint-stock company. The individual partners cannot be shareholders in the corporate partner. The liability of the corporate partner is restricted to the amount of its share capital whereas the individual partners are fully responsible. At least three other promoters besides the fully responsible partners will take part in the formation of a limited partnership company. It is, in general, subject to the same regulations which are applicable to corporations. The constitution or by-laws and the application for registration must specify the names of the fully responsible partners, the amount of capital subscribed by them and their shares of gains and losses. The limited partnership company must be identified as such in its name by the words "Kommandit Aktieselskab." There are very few limited partnership companies in existence because of an unfavorable tax status.

4

Branch of a Foreign Corporation

A foreign corporation may do business in Denmark through a branch located in Denmark provided this same right is accorded Danish corporations by the country of domicile of the foreign corporation. In registering a Danish branch of a foreign corporation, the name of the branch must indicate its nationality and that it is a foreign joint-stock company. The manager of the Danish branch must be given power of attorney and must be responsible for compliance with Danish law. He must satisfy the same qualifications as to residence and citizenship as the Board of Directors of Danish corporations, but an exemption may readily be obtained.

Other Forms of Business Organization

Partnership and Sole Proprietorship. These forms of business enterprises are generally similar to those commonly found in other countries. Partnerships as such are not subject to taxation. The partners are taxed individually on their proportionate share of the partnership revenue and capital.

Cooperative Societies and Foundations. Cooperative societies are particularly important in agriculture. Foundations are also important.

Business Records

The Bookkeeping Act of June 5, 1959, permits the use of a loose-leaf bookkeeping system, provided adequate controls are introduced to prevent its misuse.

Limited companies are required by law to keep:

1. Status book—contains the annual balance sheet and income statement signed by management not later than six months after the end of the financial year
2. Minute book—contains proceedings of stockholders' and directors' meetings
3. Audit note book—contains a report by the auditors after each examination
4. Share register—must be authorized by the registrar of companies
5. Register of share transactions by directors and executive managers

The official accounts of the company must be filed with the registrar of companies and the tax authorities.

QUALIFIED AUDITOR

The Companies Act sets out certain regulations concerning the audit of a joint-stock company. Generally, any joint-stock company shall be audited by one or more qualified auditors. A qualified auditor, according to Section 52 of the Companies Act of April 15, 1930 (as amended), is anyone who is of age, of good repute, and not divested of the management of his estate. Qualified auditors must not be in the service of the company, nor be members of the Board of Directors or managing directors, nor be in the employ (under any form) of any member of the Board of Directors, managing directors, bookkeeper or cashier, or be related by blood or marriage to any of the above parties.

Furthermore, the regulations specifically state that appointed auditors must have access to all the books and accounts of the company and be entitled to examine the cash in hand and holdings of securities and inventories. The Board of Directors and managing directors are bound to give the auditors any information they might demand for the verification of the correctness of the accounts.

As previously mentioned, the Companies Act provides that certain designated companies must be audited by one or more qualified auditors and, in specified cases, one must be a state-authorized public accountant. In practice, qualified auditors are almost invariably state-authorized public accountants.

THE ACCOUNTING PROFESSION

General

Professional auditors, as such, were unknown in Denmark until the close of the nineteenth century when a few accounting and auditing firms were organized. Early in the 1900's, the larger business enterprises began to utilize the corporate form of doing business, which, in turn, led to a demand for professional accounting services. On May 14, 1909, the King signed Denmark's first law concerning authorized auditors. Also, the transition of the larger enterprises into joint-stock companies necessitated the enactment of regulations which were embodied in several Companies Acts. The one currently in effect is the Companies Act of April 15, 1930 (as amended), which requires certain designated companies to have their financial statements examined by one or more qualified auditors, one of whom must be state-authorized if the companies' shares are included in the official stock exchange list. State-authorized public accountants are also required in the case of banks, insurance companies and credit societies lending on mortgages.

Statsautoriseret Revisor

The Business Act of April 28, 1931, and the Ministry of Trade Proclamation No. 273 of July 25, 1962, and Proclamation No. 116 of April 6, 1933, provide certain regulations concerning state-authorized public accountants. Proclamation No. 273 deals with examinations of state-authorized public accountants and Proclamation No. 116 deals with the professional activities, duties and liabilities of state-authorized public accountants.

The license to practice as a state-authorized public accountant is granted by the Ministry of Trade, Industry and Shipping upon fulfilling specific requirements and passing certain examinations as described below.

Examination for State-authorized Public Accountant. The state-authorized public accountant examination is given by a board consisting of seven members. The members are appointed by the Minister of Commerce to serve for three years. One member represents the Ministry of Commerce, one represents the universities, one represents the Tax Department, two represent industry and, finally, two members are state-authorized public accountants. A candidate for the examination must satisfy the following requirements:

1. Be a Danish subject
2. Be a resident of Denmark
3. Be over 25 years of age
4. Not have been declared incapable of managing his own affairs and must be in full control of his estate
5. Have had at least three-years' experience in the performance of ordinary accounting work in the office of a state-authorized public accountant.

The examination is given in two sections. The first section consists of two theoretical parts—Part A in economics and trade law and Part B in accounting theory, auditing and taxation. The second section consists of accounting practice. The candidate must have three years experience before taking Theory Part A of the examination and one year must elapse after passing Part A before he may take Part B. Both theoretical parts must be passed before taking the examination in practice.

With respect to the first section, two written tests and one oral test must be passed in the subject of auditing, whereas one written test and one oral test must be passed in the other subjects. However, in the case of candidates who have been granted a diploma in accounting by a school of economics and business administration, the first section consists of the tests in auditing only if not more than six years have expired since the diploma was awarded. At the present time, more than 90 per cent of the candidates have been granted the academic diploma, and this percentage continues to rise.

The examination in practice comprises four written and one oral test made up of problems in areas in which the state-authorized public accountant is expected to be skilled. The average age of these candidates is between thirty and thirty-two, and they generally remain with an auditing firm about two or three years before being admitted to partnership or starting their own practice.

The examination is held once a year. Candidates must sit for Theory Part B within four years after they have passed Theory Part A and must sit for Practice within six years after they have passed Theory Part B. A candidate may not take any part of the examination more than three times. Candidates who have passed the examination receive a certificate issued by the board.

Requirements for Practice as a State-authorized Public Accountant. The Business Act of April 28, 1931 (as amended), specifies certain requirements that must be met before an individual will be granted a license to practice as a state-authorized public accountant. After passing the required examination, the candidate must sign a solemn declaration that he will diligently and faithfully perform the work entrusted to him and that he will conscientiously fulfill all the duties of a state-authorized public accountant.

Professional Activities, Duties and Liabilities of a State-authorized Public Accountant. Proclamation No. 116 of April 6, 1933, sets out certain regulations concerning professional activities, duties and liabilities of state-authorized public accountants. Some of the more important provisions are:

A state-authorized public accountant:

Must not be employed in or associated with any business other than accounting and auditing

Must not be a member of management or on the Board of Directors of a trade or industrial enterprise

8

Must not participate in a trade or industrial company

Must not be related to the client either directly or through employees in a position of trust with the client

Must not reveal anything with which he has become acquainted in the course of his business

Must not enter into partnership with or be employed by auditors who are not state-authorized

Must not carry on a joint business venture with attorneys-at-law

May form a joint-stock company of accountants provided that the majority of the Board of Directors and all members of management are state-authorized public accountants.

In addition to the foregoing provisions, the proclamation provides that a state-authorized public accountant may employ any number of state-authorized accountants or assistants who have had three years experience with a state-authorized accountant. In addition, he is permitted to hire up to three inexperienced assistants for each state-authorized accountant in his employ. He must file a return each year with the Ministry of Commerce, Industry and Shipping, reporting the number of state-authorized accountants engaged in his practice and the number of registered accounting assistants. A registered assistant (including both the experienced and inexperienced assistants mentioned above) must be at least eighteen years of age and employed in the profession of accounting. In January 1964, about 2,000 assistants were employed by 630 practicing accountants. There were an additional sixty state-authorized accountants not in public practice.

When there is more than one auditor required to audit a particular company and one is required to be state-authorized, then the other elected auditor cannot be on the staff of the elected state-authorized auditor, be in the same auditing company or be in the same partnership of auditors.

Foreningen af Statsautoriserede Revisorer

The Institute was founded on January 12, 1912, and is subject to the by-laws of the organization which were adopted at the first general meeting on the founding date and thereafter amended periodically through 1961. The objects of the Institute are:

To bring together state-authorized public accountants in all matters affecting their common professional interest

To protect the professional and general interest of accountants in external as well as internal affairs

To supervise and contribute to the fulfilling of the general and special duties of accountants and to enhance the reputation and ability of the profession.

The advisory committee of the Institute is frequently employed by the courts and authorities to give expert opinions on accountancy matters and these opinions, together with the work of the research committee, are analagous to the American Institute's statements on auditing standards and accounting principles, although few have been issued to date.

Membership in the Institute is limited to state-authorized public accountants (with certain exceptions for honorary members). Members are entitled to use the initials "F.S.R." and the stamp of the Institute. A state-authorized accountant who ceases to practice will be entitled to retain his membership unless his business or position is in conflict with the status of membership.

Generally, the advisory committee on behalf of the Institute will deliver opinions on matters concerning accountancy and auditing submitted to the Institute by one or more of its members, by the legislature, the executive authorities or the courts. Decisive opinions on these matters require the agreement of a majority of the members of the committee. A report on each matter is to be entered in a minute book, recording the opinions given by the committee, disclosing dissenting votes and any other relevant information. Generally, this report together with the opinions are published in the official publication of the Institute— *Revision og Regnskabsvaesen* (Auditing and Accountancy).

Ethics. At an extraordinary general meeting on June 14, 1954, the Institute adopted a Code of Professional Ethics which are deemed to form part of the by-laws of the Institute.

Members of the Institute are bound to observe the following rules as set out by the Code of Professional Ethics:

Members will act in accordance with the best professional standards and comply with the rules and regulations of the Institute.

Advertising will be permitted in connection with the commencement of a practice, a change in address, taking over a practice, partners joining or retiring, but must be restricted to necessary information.

Individual press advertising is regarded as undesirable.

If members wish to advertise, they must be restricted to name, occupation, address, telephone numbers and office hours.

There are various other restrictions on advertising.

An audit must not be performed gratuitously or for an unreasonably low fee except where warranted.

Agreements must not be made where the amount of the fee is related to the results obtained.

Members must neither receive nor pay commissions on client transactions.

Any member succeeding a state-authorized accountant on an engagement must ascertain why his predecessor discontinued the engagement.

A member must not offer employment to an employee of a colleague. This does not apply to advertisements or unsolicited applications.

Members must not criticize the work of a colleague unless the colleague has first been advised of the criticism.

Complaints of infringement of these rules are to be submitted to an arbitration committee of the Institute, consisting of five members, which will hear the complaints and attempt to settle the dispute.

Functions of the State-authorized Public Accountant. Under Danish law, state-authorized accountants are required to be employed as auditors of corporations listed on the stock exchange as well as banks, certain insurance societies and other institutions governed by statute. The assistance of a state-authorized accountant is usually required for purposes of preparing declarations on applications for loans, for financing programs and on work for public institutions.

In addition the examination of financial statements for the purpose of reporting thereon the state-authorized public accountant may:

1. Act as an intermediary between directors and stockholders, between creditors and the public, and between the audited company and the public
2. Act as an expert consultant in modernizing bookkeeping systems, preparing budgets and budgetary controls

3. Make certain company analyses, render certain reports to management or give a critique on company administration
4. Assist in a price settlement dispute or make declarations to price controlling authorities (monopoly control) and to certain government agencies
5. Prepare tax returns for clients, although he is not required to do so by the law
6. Act as independent adviser in economic and commercial relations since obtaining many public loans and subsidies depends on the cooperation of state-authorized public accountants.

AUDITING STANDARDS

The practice of public accounting in Denmark is, in general, limited to qualified auditors previously described. The qualified auditor is usually but not necessarily a state-authorized public accountant. However, he must meet certain previously specified qualifications. The profession of public accounting, as practiced by state-authorized public accountants, is specifically regulated as to qualifications, duties, and responsibilities by the Acts and Proclamations as set out under "The Accounting Profession" part of this chapter.

General Standards

As mentioned previously under the "Requirements for Practice as a State-authorized Public Accountant," the requirements for license as a state-authorized public accountant assure adequate education, training and proficiency through the provisions of the Business Act and Proclamations as mentioned above. The state-authorized public accountant must not give any declaration or certificate on matters of accounts without having investigated the case sufficiently so that an opinion can be formed as to the accuracy of the declaration or certificate.

Standards of Field Work

Generally, an auditing register (described below) is kept by the state-authorized public accountant. The auditing register can either be required by law or provided by the company's by-laws (for companies) or requested by the client (for other businesses). The auditing register will contain the following information:

1. What audit work has been executed
2. What period is covered by the audit
3. Whether the auditor has been able to fulfill his obligations to the company
4. Whether he has received all information requested toward establishing the validity of the accounts
5. Whether he considers the accounts to have been drawn up in accordance with the law and the company's by-laws.
6. If the accounts are prepared for use as a basis for tax assessment this should be so stated, and if the accountant's approval is requested, he will include a special declaration that the accounts are in conformity with tax provisions.

Generally, a field audit by a Danish state-authorized public accountant is divided between interim and year-end work. There has been a departure from the detailed checking of accounts and underlying records toward the examination of internal control. The primary responsibility for proper controls and procedures lies with management, but the auditors review them to determine that they are functioning properly.

As mentioned previously, the advisory committee of the Institute issues opinions on auditing standards and accounting principles which are used as a guide by the members.

The following audit procedures are generally applied by the state-authorized public accountant in obtaining sufficient evidential matter as a basis for forming an opinion regarding the financial statements:

1. A count of cash on hand
2. Confirmation of bank accounts
3. A count of securities
4. Accounts receivable are not usually confirmed, but other tests are performed to substantiate their accuracy.
5. Observation of physical inventory is not usually done, but test counts of the year-end book inventory are generally made
6. Provisions for uncollectible accounts are evaluated as to adequacy
7. A physical examination of buildings and machinery is rarely made
8. A determination that all known and estimated liabilities are provided for in the accounts.

Standards of Reporting

The endorsement made by Danish state-authorized public accountants on the company's annual accounts is usually very brief and can vary considerably. A sample endorsement follows:

> The above Profit and Loss account and Balance Sheet are in accordance with the books of the company which have been examined by the undersigned auditors.

Audit Records

As mentioned under field standards, an auditing register is generally required to be kept either by the Companies Act, by the company's by-laws or by request of the client. In joint-stock companies, this register must be submitted to the Board of Directors whereas the stockholders do not have access to the register. Therefore, if the auditor feels that his critical comments are important enough to be brought to the attention of stockholders and creditors, he must make his comments in his endorsement of the annual accounts. In addition, the auditing register often contains comprehensive comments on the progress of the business as well as an analysis of the audit itself. These comments are designed to inform management and the Board of Directors of the auditor's view concerning the earnings of the company, whether operational analyses are kept up to date, whether budgets are prepared to guide the business during the year, and whether periodic reviews are made of these analyses and budgets for purposes of evaluating variances. Many Danish companies regard this register as a valuable support of management and the Board of Directors.

ACCOUNTING PRINCIPLES AND PRACTICES

The advisory committee of the Institute of State-authorized Public Accountants is the unofficial authority for pronouncements of generally accepted accounting principles and practices in Denmark. Officially, the Companies Act of April 15, 1930 (as amended), sets out certain provisions for reflecting accounts in the balance sheet and profit and loss statement. In addition, the Bookkeeping Act of June 5, 1959, has had some minor influence on accounting matters.

Form and Content of Financial Statements

The presentation of the balance sheet varies considerably among companies, and there is no generally recognized form. In some cases, the order of presentation is similar to that of public utility companies in the United States, such as in the following order:

Assets	*Equity and Liabilities*
Fixed assets	Equity section
Long-term investment	Long-term debt
Accounts receivable	Accruals
Securities	Accounts payable
Cash	

Current assets and current liabilities are not generally set out as separate subtotals. Mortgages and pledges created by the company and any surety or guarantee entered into and not expressly covered must be stated separately.

Consolidated Statements. Consolidated financial statements are not ordinarily prepared in Denmark for submission in reports to shareholders, but are very often prepared for Boards of Directors. Investments in subsidiaries are usually recorded at cost.

Pooling of Interests

The accounting concept "pooling of interests" as applied to mergers and consolidations of corporations is not recognized in Denmark.

Marketable Securities

Securities which are included in the official stock exchange list must not be stated at an amount exceeding the buying rate quoted at the end of the financial year.

Inventories

It is an accepted practice to state the inventory at an amount which is as much as 35 per cent below the lower of cost or market, which is also allowed for tax purposes. The extent of such secret reserve, which may vary from year to year, is rarely disclosed. Inventory costs of manufacturing concerns ordinarily do not include overhead costs. The Lifo method of valuing inventory is not permitted in Denmark.

Fixed Assets

The Companies Act provides that a write-up of fixed assets will be permitted if the amount is used for writing down other fixed assets, for covering operating deficits or for allocation to a special reserve which must only be used for such purposes. If the amounts written up are used to cover a deficit, this must be expressly stated in the accounts. It is an accepted practice to use excessive rates of depreciation in financial statements prepared for submission to shareholders. It is also an accepted practice to compute depreciation of assets before they are placed in service. There is no general practice with respect to capitalizing indirect costs on fixed assets constructed by a company for its own use.

Organization Expenses and Goodwill

Organization expenses to the extent not written off immediately will be written off to profit and loss for income tax purposes at not less than 15 per cent per annum. Purchased goodwill is required to be amortized at the rate of 15 per cent per annum.

Bond Discount and Premiums

Bond discount and premiums are not ordinarily deferred on the balance sheet except when arising from mortgages. They are customarily written off directly to profit and loss.

Reserves

Depreciation Reserves. Depreciation reserves are not customarily shown separately on the balance sheet, but are usually netted against the related assets. Hidden or secret reserves are generally not permitted except with respect to undervaluation of inventories and fixed assets (specifically buildings, machinery and ships). As a rule, it is not permissable to charge income with provisions for reserves which are not actually required for a specific purpose, and yet provision is sometimes made for depreciation on future purchases of fixed assets.

Statutory Reserves. Statutory reserves are required by the Companies Act which provides that 10 per cent of the annual profits remaining after provision for depreciation or for covering deficits from previous years will be set aside in a "statutory reserve" until this reserve equals one-tenth of share capital. Thereafter, the annual provision will be 5 per cent of the annual profits. To the extent that the reserve has not reached one-fourth of the share capital, any premium received from the issuance of stock in excess of amounts used to cover expenses incurred in the formation of the company or an increase in share capital, will be added to this reserve. The statutory reserve must only be used to cover a deficit, insofar as the deficit cannot be covered out of the surplus of the year or out of the company's reserves other than the statutory reserve. If the statutory reserve does not amount to one-tenth of the share capital, the dividend to the shareholders must not exceed 6 per cent annually.

Treasury Stock

A joint-stock company must not acquire or receive as security its own shares in an amount exceeding 10 per cent of share capital. This limitation shall not apply if the shares are acquired for the purpose of reducing share capital. The acquired shares must be accounted for as a special item with a statement of their par (or nominal) value. If the company has received its own shares in security of any claim, the nominal value of such shares must be stated in the accounts.

Statement of Income

Presentation of the income statement varies considerably in Denmark. As a general rule, only gross profit from business operations is shown. Other income is shown separately by type. General and administrative expenses, depreciation, income taxes and other special items are generally shown as separate items.

Also a combined statement of income and earned surplus is usually included with a detailed explanation as to the disposition of the opening balance of earned surplus and net income for the year.

Tax-effect Accounting. The concept of tax-effect accounting is not generally applied in Denmark.

Income Tax Expense. It is not customary to provide for income tax on current income, but rather to charge income taxes to expense as paid.

Stock Dividends. Stock dividends are accounted for by the issuing company on the basis of par (or nominal) value of the shares issued.

REQUIREMENTS FOR PUBLIC SALE OF SECURITIES

A Danish company offering securities for sale to the public will usually have a prospectus, excluding financial statements, published in a financial newspaper. If the issuing company is listed on a stock exchange, the prospectus and the financial statements (audited by two auditors, one of whom must be a state-authorized public accountant) will be reviewed by the stock exchange board. These financial statements are available to prospective buyers for a small fee. If the issuing company is not listed, the financial statements may be signed by any "qualified auditor."

A prospectus must include, in addition to general information about the company, the following facts:

1. The purpose for which the capital is being raised
2. Face value of new shares and the amount at which they are being offered for sale to the public
3. Method of payment for new shares by subscribers
4. Rules for over-subscription of the new issue.

REQUIREMENTS FOR LISTING OF SECURITIES ON THE STOCK EXCHANGE

A stock exchange board reviews all applications for listing securities on the stock exchange. Financial statements for at least one year must be filed with the listing application. Such statements must be audited by two auditors, one of whom must be a state-authorized public accountant. A company filing a listing application must have capital stock of at least kroner 2,000,000.

The financial statements of registered joint-stock companies are filed annually with the registrar of such companies where they are accessible to the public. Many companies publish their annual financial statements in financial newspapers.

FRANCE 12

I

FORMS OF BUSINESS ORGANIZATION

Business in France is conducted by individual proprietorships, various forms of partnerships, and certain types of corporations. Foreigners wishing to do business in France may do so by establishing a branch in France, or by forming a French subsidiary company, such as a Société Anonyme or a Société à Responsabilité Limitée. A branch of a foreign corporation may be established in France by complying with certain legal formalities, which include filing of the company charter and by-laws with a French commercial court, inscription in the Register of Commerce and filing annual accounts with tax authorities. A subsidiary may be organized as a French corporation, having a separate legal identity and being subject to the same legal and tax treatment as a domestic French company.

The Société Anonyme (S. A.)

The usual French corporation, which is very similar to a United States corporation, is the société anonyme. It is a corporate entity, and must be created for a definite period of time, usually not beyond ninety-nine years. First, the articles of incorporation (statuts) must be prepared, which include provisions similar to those of both the charter and the by-laws of a United States corporation; then, capital stock is issued and the first stockholders' meeting is held. From the accounting standpoint, the important action of this first meeting is the appointment (for one year) of the commissaire(s) aux comptes; subsequently, he is appointed for a three-year term. The duties of the commissaire aux comptes are discussed later.

The Société à Responsabilite Limitee (S. à R. L.)

A limited liability company (société à responsabilité limitée), which has the features of both a partnership and a corporation, is suited to the requirements of a small or medium-sized business, has relatively few shareholders, and is not permitted to obtain capital from the public. It constitutes a legal entity, and the liability of shareholders is limited to the amount of capital which they have paid in. The life of the company is stated in the articles of incorporation (statuts); if it is unlimited, any shareholder may dissolve the company at will. There must be a minimum of two partners and a minimum capital of Frs. 10,000. The shareholders appoint a manager (gérant), who may be one of them, and who has a separate contract which places him in a strong position.

Other Forms of Business Organization

The sole proprietorship and the general partnership (Société en Nom Collectif) are very similar in law and custom to comparable organizations in the United States. The general partnership, under French law, constitutes a separate legal entity; even so, the partners are taxed individually, not as a partnership entity. Its name must include the name of at least one of its partners, and, if only one name is used, it must be followed by "et compagnie." It is a French enterprise even if all of the partners are aliens.

A partnership may include limited partners, in which case it is termed "Société en Commandite Simple." Its general partners (commandités) with unlimited liability are similar to those of the société en nom collectif; the limited partners' (commanditaires) liability is limited to the amounts contributed to the firm, and they cannot participate in the management. The general and the limited partners may only transfer their interests with the unanimous approval of all partners. This form of organization is not in general use. Another form of partnership with limited partners is the "Société en Commandite par Actions." Here the interests of the limited partners (commanditaires) are represented by transferable shares of stock.

There are also joint ventures (associations en participation), of which the financial syndicate (syndicat financier) and the underwriters' syndicate (syndicat d'émission) are examples. A somewhat specialized entity is the Société à Capital Variable, which is used principally by co-operatives, whose purpose is similar to farm and other types of co-operatives in the United States. It may increase capital by contributions from existing or new participants, and the participants may withdraw their capital at any time.

Business Records

The basic records required by the Code of Commerce are the general journal and a book of balances (livre d'inventaire). The latter is comparable to a trial balance book, in which are also recorded the annual balance sheet and profit and loss account. In addition, the Code of Labor requires a payroll journal (livre de paye). These three records must be prenumbered and stamped by a judge or mayor. There are other records which have to be maintained to conform with tax, social, commercial, customs and other regulations. The nominative share transfer ledger is commonly used, but many other records are of limited use.

Le Plan Général, a standard accounting system (described later), approved by the French government, requires the maintenance of a general ledger, and recommends the use of such subsidiary journals, ledgers, etc., as may be necessary for a particular firm.

COMMISSAIRE AUX COMPTES (STATUTORY EXAMINER)

The basic law of 1867, as amended, provides that all companies (sociétés anonyme) must have their accounts examined by one or more commissaires aux comptes, who are appointed by the stockholders for one year at the first meeting, and thereafter for three years. A private (closely held) company may appoint any person not specifically disqualified (see below), but a publicly held company must appoint at least one commissaire from a list drawn up by a special committee under the jurisdiction of the local court of appeal. The expert comptable (see later discussion) is eligible for inclusion on this list but there are many appointed who have no advanced knowledge of accounting.

The diploma of commissaire aux comptes has been given, since 1936, to persons who pass a qualifying examination in bookkeeping, accounting, mercantile and company law and taxation, which is less stringent than that required of the expert comptable.

Possession of this diploma is not, however, a prerequisite for inclusion on the list of commissaires aux comptes.

Persons Disqualified

Since a principal qualification of the commissaire aux comptes is stated to be that of independence, relatives of directors or of persons contributing assets other than cash for capital stock, persons receiving salary or remuneration in any form from the company, spouses of these persons, and persons in certain other categories are disqualified from holding that office.

Company law forbids a director of a company to hold the function of commissaire in that same company, and during five years after the end of his term of office a commissaire is prohibited from being a director of a company in which he was the commissaire, or of any associated company.

Functions

Under French law, the commissaire aux comptes is officially responsible for the independent audit function. He may not allow another person to substitute for him, but he may act jointly with another commissaire (adjoint), or he may have an assistant (suppléant). His duties and responsibilities are stated in the law in some detail, but not the manner in which they are to be carried out.

The commissaire aux comptes is required to report to the stockholders upon the financial statements presented to them by the Board of Directors at the annual meeting. He is not expected to prepare them. Such financial statements must be submitted to the commissaire at least forty days before the annual meeting.

The commissaire has other duties prescribed by law which differ from those assigned to the United States or United Kingdom auditor. For example, he may call a general meeting of shareholders in case of emergency; he is required to report on contracts and agreements of the company, known to him, in which directors are directly or indirectly involved; he must reveal to the public prosecutor any criminal acts of the company or its officers of which he has knowledge.

Examining Procedures

The duties and powers of the commissaire aux comptes as provided by law are such that it would appear that he is permitted, if not expected, to perform an examination of financial statements in a manner not too different from that customary in the United States, except that he does not observe the taking of physical inventories nor does he confirm accounts receivable by correspondence with the debtors.

However, the fees suggested by the Federation des Associations de Commissaires de Sociétés Inscrits par les Cours d'Appel are low. The suggested fee for one commissaire, for a company with capital, reserves and loans of $20,000,000 is $2,200 with increases up to 50 per cent if three commissaires are appointed. It seems apparent that an examination of financial statements in the sense understood in the United States cannot be made with such fee limitations.

Reports of the Commissaire aux Comptes (Statutory Examiner)

There is no standard form of report prescribed for the statutory examiner in France, comparable to that of the AICPA in the United States or that required by the Companies Act in the United Kingdom.

Under the provisions of the law of 1867, as amended March 4, 1943, the statutory examiner submits two reports to the annual meeting of stockholders, a general report and a special report.

The general report deals with whether the accounting information contained in the board's report to the shareholders is correct, and whether it has been consistently presented in comparison with the preceding year; it also comments on the board's proposals for disposition of profits. The general report is often in "long form."

The special report deals exclusively with contracts or agreements between the company and any of its directors (either directly or indirectly); the report must state whether these contracts or agreements were initially approved by the board and how they affect the company.

It is apparent that the commissaire aux comptes, as such, is not required to have the training or experience in accounting and auditing which is expected of the independent auditor in the United States or the United Kingdom (although if he is an expert comptable he may have had such training or experience). Any report issued by the commissaire need not, and usually does not, give the same assurance as to the fairness of presentation of financial statements as would that of the independent certified or chartered accountant.

Organizations of the Commissaires aux Comptes

It has been stated that companies having public shareholdings must select their commissaires from a list established by each local court of appeal. To appear on this list, the person must be an accepted member of the Compagnie des Commissaires des Sociétés. Any one of the following may be a member: A holder of the state diploma of expert comptable; a government employee having a knowledge of accounting; a financial expert attached to the Court of Appeal for more than five years; one who has acted as an accountant in a business for at least ten years; a licensed member of a government technical school; an auditor of companies for more than ten years; or one who has passed the examination for the diploma of Commissaire aux Comptes.

There has also been organized the Fédération des Associations de Commissaires de Sociétés Inscrits par les Cours d'Appel (Federation of Associations of Commissaires of Companies Registered by the Courts of Appeal).

THE ACCOUNTING PROFESSION IN FRANCE

There are two main classes of professional accountants in France, the expert comptable and the comptable àgréé, each of which has differing educational and training qualifications and differing fields of practice. These classes were created under the Decree of September 19, 1945, as L'Ordre des Experts Comptables et des Comptable Agréés, with the object of "assuring the defense of the honor and the independence of the professions which it represents."

As most of these two classes of professional accountants in practice at the present time obtained their titles under the above Decree, the following discussion of educational and experience requirements are those prescribed under its provisions. Certain modifications of this Decree were issued in 1963, effective January 1, 1964, and are summarized in later paragraphs.

The Expert Comptable

The Decree defines the expert comptable as one who is considered: "the technician who, in his own name and under his responsibility, engages in the usual profession of organizing, verifying, appraising and correcting accounts and accounting of every nature." It also states that: "The expert comptable may also analyze, by means of accounting technique, the position and functioning of enterprises under their different economic, legal and financial aspects. He reports on his verifications, conclusions and suggestions."

An expert comptable must be registered as a member of the Order, he must be a French citizen, of good character, twenty-five years of age, and have obtained the diploma of expert comptable issued by the National Minister of Education. Even though he has obtained this diploma, he cannot be inscribed on the roll of the Order unless he is engaged in the practice of public accounting as a principal. He may not take a salaried position, even in the office of another expert comptable, except with specific permission of the Order.

Foreigners with accepted qualifications may practice in France as experts comptables provided a convention or agreement has been concluded between France and the country concerned.

Education and Training. The first step toward obtaining the diploma of expert comptable is a preliminary examination (first part) which may not be taken before the year in which the candidate reaches nineteen years of age, and which must be passed before the candidate may become "articled." The first preliminary examination consists of a written and an oral examination. The written portion includes two compositions, one on law and one on economics, and an examination in accounting. There follows an oral examination given by members of L'Ordre des Experts Comptables et des Comptables Agréés and other qualified persons designated by the Minister of National Education. Such an examination devotes fifteen minutes to each of seven subjects— civil law, commercial law, constitutional law and finance, civil procedure, economics, mathematics and accounting techniques.

Having passed the first preliminary examination, the candidate may become articled, and during this period is under the supervision of a monitor (controleur de stage). With the latter's approval, the term of articleship may be served in the office of an expert comptable, or in the Ministry of Economic and Financial Affairs, or with a professional accounting organization; there are provisions for serving a portion of the time otherwise. The year of service following the second part of the preliminary examination must be with a French qualified accountant in France or its Community.

After two years' studentship (articled service), the applicant may take the second part of the preliminary examination. The written portion of this examination is similar to that of the first part, but is more advanced. The subjects covered in the oral portion are commercial law, penal law in general and penal legislation as applied to commerce, economics, statistics, French taxation, and accounting techniques.

The period of articled service is ordinarily three years, but may be extended, at the request of the candidate, for a period of up to three additional years. In certain instances the period may be reduced by one year for persons with long practical experience or for one holding certain high degree diplomas, with the approval of the Superior Council of the Order. At least one year of training must elapse between passing the second part of the preliminary examination and the final examination, and of course the period of the articles must be completed before the final examination is taken.

After having passed the preliminary examination, the candidate for the degree may be recognized by the Council of the Order as an "expert comptable stagiaire"; he is not a member of the Order but is subject to its supervision and discipline.

In preparation for the final examination, the candidate takes courses during his articled period. These may be correspondence courses, or courses provided by attending classes at the two principal institutions for this purpose, which are located in Paris—L'Ecole Nationale d'Organization Economique et Sociale (a private institution), and L'Institut de Technique Comptable—Le Conservatoire des Arts et Métiers (sponsored by the governmental body).

Further, during the articled period, his progress is supervised by his monitor, to whom he makes quarterly reports of progress based on a diary of the candidate's professional activities. At the end of the articled period, the monitor decides whether the candidate is ready for the final examination.

The final examination, which is given in Paris and other principal cities once each year, is in two parts; in addition, as a last requirement, a thesis must be presented to the examining board.

The first part of the final examination is written, and eight hours is allotted for its completion. It consists of a composition dealing with a public accountant's service to a business enterprise and, in effect, is a case study involving numerous accounting problems. The second part is oral and consists of twenty-minute periods of questioning on business management, auditing, statistics, regulation of the profession and professional obligations, and special aspects of accounting investigations carried out upon the orders of the courts.

The subject of the thesis, which is the last obligation of the candidate, must be submitted to the examining board for approval six months before the thesis is presented. The completed thesis may be presented at the time of the final examination, but usually this is done at a subsequent session of the board, at which time the candidate is required to defend his thesis. When the thesis is accepted, all other requirements having been met, the diploma is issued to the candidate. He is then accepted into membership of L'Ordre des Experts Comptables et des Comptables Agréés provided he practices as a public accountant.

Although the program for obtaining the diploma of expert comptable appears comprehensive, there is some indication of dissatisfaction with its results by the profession in France. It appears that the percentage of candidates, for the first preliminary examination, who finally obtain the diploma, is small, and the number of new candidates presenting themselves is declining. As previously stated, changes in the above requirements designed to correct some of these conditions have recently been promulgated.

Functions. The expert comptable, as such, is not primarily concerned with auditing. Since France is essentially a country of small-sized companies, closely or family held, the practice of the expert comptable deals very largely with the problems of small and medium business firms. He functions mainly as a business advisor from a management and controllership standpoint, rather than as an independent auditor giving an opinion upon the fairness of financial statements. A principal function is to advise his clients with respect to accounting and reporting methods which result in minimizing tax liabilities.

The tradition of French business, as in most of Europe, is that of secrecy in business matters. While this viewpoint is being eroded, it undoubtedly has affected the practice of the expert comptable in France in that he has been limited in his work to those areas specifically authorized by management except when he functions as a commissaire aux comptes.

A barrier to the development of French accounting and auditing practice is the rule of the Order that each member may not utilize the services of more than five salaried accountants, exclusive of experts comptables stagiaires (Rules, Title One, Section III, Art. 19). This requirement effectively impedes if not prevents the development of firms of experts comptables on a scale necessary to conduct examinations of financial statements of large companies in accordance with the standards and procedures common in the United States and the United Kingdom.

Training of auditors in such methods is impeded because the stagiaires may spend only one year of their required experience with United States or United Kingdom—oriented firms of accountants, and, as noted above, if an expert comptable accepts a salaried position with such a firm he may no longer be inscribed on the rolls of the Order.

Independence. The Decree of 1945, establishing L'Ordre des Experts Comptables et de Comptables Agréés, provides in Article 22 that: The functions of members of the Order are incompatible with any occupation or any act, the nature of which would affect their independence, and in particular:

> He may not accept any salaried employment, even with another expert comptable.

He may not enter into any business transaction or act as a business intermediary.

He may not perform any function in any commercial enterprise.

He is forbidden to act as a commercial intermediary, to draw up contracts, to represent persons in courts, or his clients before public administrations, or do any accounting work in enterprises in which he possesses, either directly or indirectly, a participation estimated as being substantial.

He is forbidden to work for a company if he and/or persons employed by him are retained as commissaire aux comptes of that company.

Finally, members of the Institute are not allowed to spend the major part of their activity for the benefit of only one enterprise or one financial group of companies.

The foregoing interdictions or restrictions also apply to the member's spouse, his salaried employees and any person acting on his behalf.

When an expert comptable accepts appointment as commissaire aux comptes of a company, it is understood that he will, in the course of his duties, give advice on tax matters, management, law, etc. He may not, however, as an expert comptable functioning as commissaire aux comptes, accept a definite and independent assignment to do such work. For this reason, partners and staff of French offices of United Kingdom and United States firms usually prefer not to accept such an appointment, except in the case of companies very closely held.

The Comptable Agréé

As defined in the Decree of September 19, 1945, the Comptable Agréé is one who: "is considered as the technician who, in his own name and under his responsibility, engages in the usual profession of keeping, centralizing, opening, closing, and supervising accounting and accounts of every nature."

He must be a French citizen, of good character, and twenty-two years of age. He must have successfully passed the preliminary examination (Parts one and two) for the degree of expert comptable, and have had three years of professional practice, approved as sufficient by the Council of the Order. He must also become a member of L'Ordre des Experts Comptables et des Comptables Agréés, thus becoming subject to its rules and disciplinary authority.

The work of the comptable àgréé is somewhat comparable to that of bookkeepers or accountants in commerce and industry; they do not perform independent auditing functions in the sense understood in the United States or United Kingdom.

Recent Revisions of Education and Experience Requirements

Under decrees issued in August and October 1963, the educational and experience requirements for the titles of expert comptable and comptable agréé were revised and became effective January 1, 1964. There were a number of "escape clauses" included, applicable to persons having qualifications under previous decrees and to persons in process of obtaining titles under the 1945 decree; these are omitted from the following summarization of the principal provisions of the new decrees.

A. *The Expert Comptable.* To be inscribed as an expert comptable in the list of members of L'Ordre des Experts Comptables et des Comptables Agréés, the candidate must obtain the newly authorized "Diplôme d'Expertise Comptable" (diploma of Expertise in Accounting), which is presented to persons who successively:

1. Have completed three years of apprenticeship as a stagiaire or articled clerk.

> To be admitted as a stagiaire, the candidate must be nineteen years of age and have obtained the diploma of "Etudes Comptables Supérieures" (Higher Accounting Studies—see below under "Comptable Agréé).

2. Have obtained the following certificates:

> Le Certificat Supérieur de Révision Comptable (higher auditing certificate)

and one of the following:

> Le certificat supérieur juridique et fiscal (certificate of advanced law and tax law)

> Le certificat supérieur d'organisation et de gestion des entreprises (higher certificate of business organization and management)

> Le certificat supérieur de relations économiques Européennes et Internationales (certificate in advanced study of European and International economic relations).

3. Have passed an oral examination upon a thesis submitted within a period of five years beginning January 1 of the year following receipt of the second certificate.

It will be noted that the diploma of Expertise Comptable is now substituted for the former diploma of Expert Comptable.

The examination syllabus for the new diplôme d'Études Comptables Supérieurs and that for the higher diplôme d'Expertise Comptable were published in January and March 1964, respectively. They include both written and oral sections.

With the agreement of the Council of the Order, the three-year term of articleship may be served as follows:

1. One year, at least, in the office of an expert comptable
2. With an official of the Ministry of Economic and Financial affairs designated to control the economic and financial interests belonging to the State
3. Up to one year with a comptable àgréé, or with a foreign practitioner authorized to practice as an expert comptable or comptable àgréé
4. With a commercial enterprise in which the accounting is controlled by a member of the Order
5. With the Conseil Nationale de la Comptabilité
6. Abroad, with the agreement of the Superior Council of the Order, either with a foreign practitioner of a standing comparable to that of an expert comptable or of a French firm of accountants or with one or several private enterprises whose accounting is controlled by the said practitioners.

B. The Comptable Agréé. To be inscribed as a comptable agréé in the list of members of L'Ordre des Experts Comptables et des Comptables Agréé, the candidate must:

1. Be twenty-five years of age
2. Have the diploma of Études Comptables Supérieures (advanced accounting studies) issued by the National Minister of Education
3. Have two years' practical professional accounting experience judged sufficient by the Council of the Order, acquired with an expert comptable or a comptable agréé or in a public or private enterprise.

The diploma of Études Comptables Supérieures requires the possession of certificates indicating passing of examinations in études comptables (accounting studies), études économiques (economic studies) and études juridiques (legal studies).

During a temporary period, persons who hold the diploma of "Technicien Supérieur de la Comptabilité" (superior technician in accounting)—decree of February 26, 1962—or the diploma of Technicien de la Comptabilité (technician in accounting)—decree of February 19, 1952— and who have had two years' approved experience, may also be inscribed as comptables agréés on the list of members of the Order. Also persons who hold the former Brevet professionnel de Comptable or who have passed the former Examen préliminaire au Diplôme d'Expert Comptable (Preliminary examination for the diploma of expert comptable) and who have had two years' approved experience, may be inscribed as comptable agréés on the list of members of the Order.

C. *Summary of Changes.* The principal changes introduced by the new decrees are:

1. For the diploma of expertise comptable:
   a. The increase in required age of candidate, for obtaining the diploma, from twenty-two to twenty-five years, notwithstanding the age of nineteen required for being articled.
   b. The introduction of an obligatory certificate of higher auditing.
   c. The substitution of the diploma of études comptables supérieures for the passing of the (former) preliminary examination (Parts one and two).
   d. The introduction of higher certificates (optional) for law and tax legislation, for business organization and management, and for European and international economic relations.

2. For the inscription as a comptable agréé:
   a. The substitution of the diploma of Études Comptables Supérieures for those of Technicien Supérieur de la Comptabilité and Technicien de la Comptabilité.
   b. The increase in required age of candidates from twenty-two to twenty-five years.
   c. The decrease in required years of experience from three to two. However, persons who hold the former brevet professionnel de comptable must now have two years' experience whereas formerly no experience was required.

Organization of Accounting Firms in France

For the most part, public accounting in France is carried on by one expert comptable with one or more assistants. The practice of the profession in the form of a partnership, limited liability companies, or a sociéte à responsabilité limitée is also permitted, provided certain conditions are fulfilled.

Organizations of Accountants

The organization of accountants in France corresponding more nearly to the American Institute of CPAs is L'Ordre des Experts Comptables et des Comptables Agréés, instituted in 1942, and formalized by decree in September, 1945, which law also governs its administration and discipline. Its members are those who have received the diploma of expert comptable or have fulfilled the requirements to become a comptable àgréé. Initially, many practicing accountants were given their diplomas or admitted to the Order without passing an examination. Its approximately twenty branches are each administered by a local council and, in turn, are under the control of a national council.

An important feature relating to L'Ordre des Experts Comptables et Comptables Agréés is that government officials (Commissaires du Gouvernement) are present at sessions of the Order and they have the power to bring decisions of the Order before the court.

In addition to the foregoing, there are various organizations of accountants in France whose membership or purposes are more specialized. Recently, the Institut Français des Experts Comptables Diplomés par l'État was formed by the merger of the following three organizations: Chambre Nationale des Experts Comptables Diplomés par L'État; Compagnie Nationale des Experts Comptables; and the Union Professionelle des Sociétés Fiduciaires d'Expertise Comptable.

The first aim of the Institute is to tighten relations between its members and to safeguard their monetary and moral interests together with the diplomas and title of expert comptable.

There is also the Société des Experts Comptables Français. Essentially of a cultural nature, it arranges the French participation in the various European conferences of public accountants held under the sponsorship of the Union Européenne des Experts Comptables Economiques et Financiers (U.E.C.). A main purpose of the Société is the formation of a European association of accountants. A phased plan has been adopted to achieve this aim by 1965.

In addition, the Société de Comptabilité de France is an association which is concerned with the training of professionals practicing as assistant accountants, accountants, chief accountants and public accountants. There is also the Compagnie des Chefs de Comptabilité (Chief Accountants).

Ethics

The Council of the Order has adopted a "Code des Devoirs Professionnels" (Ethics) which, in thirty-five articles, discusses the duties of the members as individuals in the exercise of their profession. It also discusses members' relations with other members, with their clients, with the Order itself, with government representatives, and with their articled clerks. The provisions of some of these articles, such as those dealing with employment of assistants and those dealing with independence, have been mentioned under previous headings of this section. Other provisions of general interest are paraphrased as follows:

Personal advertising is forbidden.

Use of titles, decorations and diplomas is regulated.

Members may not speak ill of another member; they may not accept an engagement previously held by another member without first conferring with such member.

The members must fulfill conscientiously and devotedly the duties entrusted to them by clients.

Members have the right to minimize by proper means taxes payable by clients, but they must not participate in any deceit of the fiscal authorities.

The fact that one member recommends another does not authorize division of the fee.

Fees may not be based on the financial results (gross sales, etc.) of the client.

Members of the Order take the following oath:
I swear to exercise my profession with conscience and honesty, to respect and make others respect the laws in connection with my work.

There are provisions for various penalties to be imposed, after due process, upon members who act in contradiction of the Code, which acts are interpreted to be a violation of the above oath.

AUDITING STANDARDS

The accounting profession in France does not have as a guide for its work a statement of auditing standards in a form such as that published by the AICPA as Statements on Auditing Procedure No. 33—Auditing Standards and Procedures. As previously stated, both the commissaire aux comptes and the expert comptable are expected to maintain an independent mental attitude towards their work.

The Order has recently issued two publications: (1) *Le Commissaire aux Comptes dans les Sociétés Françaises* (The Commissaire and French business companies). This is a work of 457 pages and deals at some length with the laws governing the appointment of the commissaire, his independence and the technical aspects of his duties. A description of various auditing procedures is given, and there are frequent references to United States and United Kingdom practices. It is stated that the Commissaire is permitted to choose the methods and means to assure himself of the regularity and correctness of the accounts. (2) *Les Diligence Normale en Matière de Travail Comptable* (Normal Procedures in the Accountant's Work). This substantial work covers the legal basis of the expert comptable's work with commentary on the legislative text and rules of the Order and suggestions as to methods of procedure. It includes a sample questionnaire on Internal Control.

It should be stated, however, that this publication in no way represents an official guide to the French practitioner on how to do his work. It has been produced merely with the intention of provoking discussion with a view to subsequent publication of definite recommendations by the order in a manner similar to those issued by the professional organizations in the United Kingdom and the United States.

General Standards

Training and Proficiency. The expert comptable, as previously described, undergoes scholastic and apprenticeship training which purports to adequately prepare him for his work.

The Commissaire aux Comptes need not have any special training in accounting and auditing.

Due Care in Performance of Work. The Code of Devoirs of the Expert Comptable refers to the necessity for conscientious and devoted attention to client's affairs, and French law holds a Commissaire aux Comptes responsible when he does not carry out his duties with due care.

Standards of Field Work

There is no statement of the French accounting profession comparable to that of the AICPA which defines standards of field work in terms of adequacy of planning, impact of materiality and relative risk, and competence of evidential matter.

It is not customary to confirm accounts receivable balances by correspondence nor to observe the taking of physical inventories.

There are references in the publication *Le Commissaire aux Comptes dans les Sociétés Françaises* to the need for an auditor (commissaire) to have knowledge of the quality and weakness of the system of internal control of the enterprise being audited.

Standards of Reporting

The reports required of the commissaire aux comptes have been described in a previous section. There are no specific requirements as to the form and content of the report of the expert comptable.

ACCOUNTING PRINCIPLES AND PRACTICES

The Plan Général (discussed hereafter) and the French tax law are the most influential factors in shaping the accounting principles applied in the preparation and presentation of financial statements in France.

The influence of the accounting profession, to date, apparently has not been as great as that of the profession in the United States and the United Kingdom. The basic framework of French accounting is similar to that in other areas, but there are certain dissimilarities of which the reader of French financial statements should be aware. The principal differences are discussed herein.

Form and Content of Financial Statements

Statement Presentation. In general, the French balance sheet as prescribed by the Plan Général follows those of United States public utility companies: the assets on the left, beginning with fixed assets and ending with current assets; the liabilities and capital on the right, beginning with capital and surplus, then long-term debt, and ending with current liabilities.

There is no combined statement of income and earned surplus, as known in the United States. Instead, the statement of operating profit and loss (similar to the nineteenth-century "trading account") includes sales, purchases, inventories, costs, other income, etc. The balance of "operating profit" is carried to a "statement of income and profit and loss" which includes income taxes, prior years' adjustments, nonrecurring items, etc.

Another variation from United States practice is that the financial statements presented by the directors to the annual meeting of shareholders, and which are reported upon by the Commissaire aux Comptes, are not what would be considered in the United States as the "final" figures. The purpose is to present to the stockholders a statement showing the amount of income for the year available for distribution as dividends to stockholders, as tantième (bonus) to directors, and for appropriation for various reserves. The shareholders then approve the various distributions and appropriations. The financial statements customarily printed and distributed are those as presented to shareholders; sometimes an additional balance sheet is circulated showing the disposition of net income as approved by the shareholders.

The "Plan Comptable Général." The desirability of reasonable comparability of financial data by company and industry has long been recognized by the government as well as by accountants in France, and French accounting thought has favored the establishment of a uniform chart of accounts adaptable to all industry.

To this end, in April 1946, the government established a Commission for Accounting Standardization (Commission de Normalisation des Comptabilités), which developed a standard accounting system under the name "Plan Comptable Général." The Plan was approved by order of the Minister of National Economic Affairs in 1947. At the same time there was created the Conseil National de la Comptabilité, a consultative body under the Minister of Economic Affairs, composed of representatives from different ministries, L'Ordre National des Experts Comptables, the Société de Comptabilité de France, different professional groups, and certain staff members from the profession. The duties of this commission are to provide a continuing review of the Plan and to suggest revisions when deemed necessary. Such revisions were made in 1950 and 1957. The latter revision is now in current use.

The decree of 1947, obligated certain government or quasi-government corporations and others to institute the Plan (appropriately modified as a "Plan Particulier"), for example: Certain government departments (e.g., National Health Service); public corporations (French Railways, Electricité de France); enterprises in which the state or a public agency owns at least 20 per cent of the capital stock; firms which have received ten million dollars or more in aid from the state; and firms operating under a measure of government control (such as certain cooperatives).

A decree of August 1958, obliges firms which have taken advantage of the tax law permitting certain revaluations of assets to conform to certain accounting rules (specified in the Plan) relating to nomenclature and to the classification of certain items.

Concerns which have had to comply with this latter requirement usually also prepare their balance sheets which are presented to stockholders in the same form; however, whether or not this is in fact a statutory requirement for the presentation of accounts to stockholders has not yet been made clear.

The Plan may be imposed on a particular industry when it has presented and obtained approval of a Plan Particulier, which has been prepared within the over-all framework of the Plan Général.

The stated objectives of the Plan are to provide more precise accounting data which will:

Promote more reliable national economic and fiscal policies

Assist in eliminating fiscal inequalities

Minimize social misunderstandings by informing the public of the true distribution of natonal wealth

Provide data for the study of market trends

Improve healthy competition

Aid in the development of fairer taxation

Provide shareholders, suppliers and bankers with an opportunity to exercise their judgment more satisfactorily

Aid governmental authorities in exercising controls

Provide a clear and prompt view of financial results

Permit analysis and comparison of manufacturing costs.

21

The statement has been made (F. M. Richard, 7th International Congress of Accountants) that 90 per cent of big concerns, 60 per cent of middle-sized firms and 40 per cent of small businesses have adopted the Plan as a basis for their accounting. Moreover, it appears that their number will be increased during the next few years. Under a law of December 28, 1959, it is provided that the Plan Comptable Général will be obligatory for all firms meeting certain conditions. It is provided that committees of management and technicians of various industries be formed under the supervision of the Conseil Superieur de la Comptabilité, to draft Plans Particular suitable to their business. The Conseil will report to the Ministre des Finances et des Affaires Economiques distinguishing between those parts of the proposed Plan which should be made obligatory and those which are merely recommended.

The Plan Comptable Général includes:

A detailed chart of accounts, numbered on a decimal system, from which the periodical financial statements may readily be prepared. (Title I, chapters 1 and 2.)

The general rules, definitions and functions of the accounts included in Classes 1 through 8. (Title II, chapters 1-4.) This portion is analogous to the text material in the United States' Utility, Railroad, etc., classifications.

A discussion of the cost accounting procedures provided in Class 9 of the Plan. (Title III, chapters 1-7.)

Throughout these sections of the Plan (Titles I, II and III) are placed a number of model financial statements and statistical reports. The last section of the Plan includes the texts of various pronouncements and decrees relating to the preparation and implementation of the Plan, the latest bearing the date of December 28, 1959. While a detailed discussion of the Plan is not contemplated here, the following summary of the main groups of accounts will indicate the general scheme of the Plan:

Group I   Capital stock, surplus, surplus reserves, donated surplus, reserves for liabilities, long-term liabilities, intercompany and branch accounts

Group II   Fixed assets: organization expenses, property, plant and equipment, construction work in progress, property subject to war damage claims, long-term loans receivable, investments and related reserves for loss in value, and guarantee deposits

Group III   Inventories: goods for resale, raw materials, materials and supplies, salvage stock, semifinished product, finished goods, work in process, packing materials, and related reserves for loss in value

Group IV   Accounts receivable and payable: accounts payable, suppliers; accounts receivable, customers; employee accounts, accounts with the state, accounts with shareholders and partners, subsidiaries or parent company, miscellaneous receivables and payables, accrued liabilities, prepaid expenses and deferred credits, suspense accounts

Group V   Financial accounts: short-term borrowings, short-term loans to others, bills and notes payable, bills and notes receivable, checks and coupons receivable, miscellaneous investments and government securities, cash on deposit, cash on hand, internal cash transfers

Group VI   Operating expenses: purchases, payroll, taxes, subcontractors' costs, transportation and traveling, administrative and selling expenses, interest, depreciation

Group VII   Operating income: sales, sales of scrap and returnable containers, allowances on sales, allowances and rebates received, miscellaneous income, financial income

Group VIII   Profit and loss: results of operations, prior years' adjustments, extraordinary gains or losses, appropriations to reserves (nontrading or exceptional), income taxes, results of period awaiting appropriation, opening and closing balance sheet accounts

Group IX   Cost accounts

Group X   Special accounts: contingent assets and contingent liabilities.

Offsetting of Accounts. The Plan Général provides that Group IV includes both accounts receivable and payable; in Group V are included both short-term borrowings and lendings, as well as notes payable and receivable. While these groups are usually properly classified as assets or liabilities on published balance sheets, it is not always certain that complete segregation has been made. Reserves (see below) provided by approval of shareholders at the annual meeting are sometimes deducted from a related asset rather than classified according to the provisions of the Plan Général.

Consolidated Financial Statements. There is no requirement in France that consolidated or group accounts be prepared or published, although they are sometimes prepared for internal purposes. It is also not required nor is it customary that parent company statements be accompanied by the financial statements of unconsolidated subsidiaries, nor with information comparing parent company investment with underlying net assets of such companies, nor dividends received by the parent compared with profits or losses of unconsolidated subsidiaries for the period.

Pooling of Interests

The "pooling of interests" concept is not known in France. The French law concerning mergers of corporations is complicated and not within the scope of this discussion.

Investments

Investments in stocks of other companies were permitted under various decrees in the past to be revalued free of tax; current balance sheet amounts were revised to equal the lower of (1) quoted market or net assets per share and (2) acquisition cost multiplied by the applicable index coefficient of the year of acquisition. The increase is included in the revaluation reserve.

Inventories

The general basis for stating inventories under French law is cost. (There is no provision for the use of Lifo.) Cost may be reduced to market should this be lower than cost for raw materials having known quotations. Cost or market may also be reduced when the items concerned are known to have deteriorated, to have changed in style, or to be slow moving, in which cases they are valued at estimated realizable prices.

The reductions from the cost or market basis are set up in appropriate reserve accounts as suggested in the Plan Général, and such reserves are shown as a reduction from the asset on French balance sheets, on which the basis of valuation is not stated since it is generally understood that cost or market is used.

Various methods have been permitted for revaluation of inventories in order to eliminate the effects of inflation on taxable income. The tax reform law of December 28, 1959, provided for the discontinuance of all previous legislation in this respect with the exception of the "Provision pour fluctuations des Cours" (Provision for price variations) which is only utilized by enterprises having inventories of raw materials the prices of which are influenced by international markets and the franc value of foreign currency.

The afore-mentioned law of 1959, further permitted the setting up of a reserve for increase in prices of over 10 per cent on products other than those included in the price variation reserve referred to above. The tax exemption in this case, however, is merely postponed for a period of six years.

The reserves provided for (a) price variations and (b) replacement are shown on the liability side of the balance sheet.

Fixed Assets

It is not customary to state the basis of stating fixed assets even though the basis is frequently not historical cost.

Inflation of currency in France since 1920, and especially since 1945, has forced various government-sponsored methods designed to cushion its effect upon business. Various decrees, the last in 1959, permitted companies to revalue their fixed assets based on a price-index principle, the resulting writeup being credited to a revaluation reserve. All companies whose average sales for the three accounting periods ending before December 29, 1959, that exceeded five million francs were obliged to revalue their fixed assets to the maximum extent. Companies with lesser average sales had the option to revalue all or part of their fixed assets, but most companies took full advantage of the permission to revalue to the maximum permitted.

Earlier decrees dealing with revaluation of fixed assets exempted revaluation reserves from tax; a tax law of December 1959, did impose a special tax of 3 per cent on revaluation reserves, but freed them from any future liability to income tax and, as before, left them distributable as (1) stock dividends (subject to the registration tax in the circumstances described below) and (2) as cash dividends (subject to withholding tax) to the extent that such reserves may be considered realized. The meaning of the word "realized" is not, however, defined in French law. The reserves may be capitalized without payment of the 7.20 per cent registration tax if effected before January 1, 1966.

The depreciation reserve is revalued by formula at the same time and by application of the same indices as the plant, and the resulting increase is charged to the revaluation reserve. Thereafter, annual depreciation provisions are calculated on the net increased plant values.

25

Surplus Reserves

Included under this general heading are items such as: Premium on capital stock, legal reserve, optional reserves, reserve for replacement of inventories, special revaluation reserve and grants from state or public institutions.

Each year, all companies (S.A. or S.à R.L.) are required to set aside as a legal reserve 5 per cent of net profits, less tax, until the total reaches 10 per cent of the nominal capital. The legal reserve may be used to compensate an accumulated loss, in which case the company must rebuild the reserve by making appropriations in the prescribed manner out of future profits.

During the period from the Second World War through 1959, various methods were permitted for periodic revaluation of inventories, with the objective of eliminating the effects of inflation on taxable income. The resulting increases were credited to reserve accounts entitled "Réserve de renouvellement des stocks," "Réserve pour stock indispensable," or "Réserve de dotation sur stocks" until the law of December 28, 1959, taxed these reserves at a reduced rate. Thereafter they became free reserves and to a large extent have disappeared from French company balance sheets.

The "Optional reserves" are those which the shareholders at the annual meeting decide should be appropriated out of that year's profits. The reserve resulting from revaluations of fixed assets was discussed above.

In general, the reserves included in this section are (1) equivalent to paid-in or donated surplus, or are (2) those which are optional with the company and when the offsetting charge is treated as an appropriation of profit.

Included in this section is the "Balance of Profit and Loss Account Brought Forward"; in public companies, most of the year's profit is customarily distributed as dividends to stockholders, bonus to directors (tantième), or appropriated to some reserve. Consequently, the balance carried forward is usually a minor amount. The term "earned surplus" has no equivalent in French accounting; indeed, there is no comparable concept. In the French view, all earnings should be distributed as dividends to shareholders, as bonuses to directors (tantième), or appropriated as reserves indicating the purposes for which the earnings are retained.

Liability Reserves

Although included in the "Capital" section of the Plan Général, these reserves are provided by charges to tax-deductible expense, and they represent legal liabilities. Among them are: Provisions for risks, such as litigation, guarantees of product, self-insurance, losses on purchases for future delivery, fines and penalties, exchange losses; provision for restoration or reconditioning of rented premises at expiration of lease; provision for expenses to be spread over several periods; and provision for pensions to employees.

Contingent Liabilities

While it is a general custom in France to discount notes receivable before the due date, it is not usual to mention the resulting contingent liability. Neither is it customary to disclose guarantees nor liens on assets.

Capital Stock and Stock Dividends

All capital shares of French companies (with an unimportant exception) have a nominal or par value. No-par stock is unknown in France.

Capital may be increased by a vote of the shareholders at extraordinary general meetings by issuing additional shares or by increasing the par value of existing shares, in which case and at such time an amount equal to the par value of the additional shares, or the increase in par value, is transferred from reserves (unappropriated surplus) to capital. Since in all such cases the par value is the measure of the amount transferred, and not the market value as is the case in the United States with respect to stock dividends, it is not necessary in France to attempt to distinguish between a "stock split" and a "stock dividend."

The Statement of Income

Sales and Cost of Sales. Sales and cost of sales are not required to be reported in the financial statements, but "turnover" figures are usually given in the directors' report.

Depreciation. Prior to 1960, the straight-line method of depreciation was the method used for both book and tax purposes. It was then supplemented with a variety of special depreciation allowances, generally as a modification of the straight-line method.

Under a law of December 28, 1959 (amended), the declining-balance method of computing depreciation is permitted, applicable to machinery and equipment purchased or produced after December 31, 1959, such as: Equipment and tooling used in industrial, manufacturing, transforming or transport operations; handling equipment; water or air cleaning installations; steam, heat or energy-producing installations; safety installations or installations of a medico-social nature; office machines, except typewriters; equipment and tooling used in scientific or technical research; warehousing and storing installations, with the exception of related premises; and buildings and equipment of hotel enterprises.

Note that hotel buildings are the exception to the exclusion of structures from the permitted categories.

Specifically excluded from the application of the declining-balance method are: Items which were acquired or produced prior to January 1, 1960; items acquired secondhand or whose normal service life is less than three years; and private lodgings, industrial sites, professional premises, buildings (other than hotels), and generally any item which does not specifically fall into one of the above-listed categories.

Assets acquired or constructed prior to 1960, and those listed above as not being eligible for the declining-balance method, are to continue to be depreciated by the straight-line method.

Depreciation rates normally accepted for tax purposes are:

Industrial buildings, such as factories, warehouses, etc.	5%
Commercial buildings, such as offices	2%-5%
Dwellings	2%-4%
Plant equipment (machines) and tools	10%-15%
Office furniture	10%
Autos and trucks	20%-25%

When demonstrated to the satisfaction of the tax authorities, higher rates may be allowed when necessary to reflect abnormal wear and tear or obsolescence. Upon abandonment of an asset, the undepreciated balance may be charged off.

The declining-balance rates prescribed vary from 1.5 to 2.5 times the straight-line rates, depending on the estimated length of the service life, as follows:

Estimated useful life	Multiple applied to straight-line rate
Three or four years	1.5
Five or six years	2
Over six years	2.5

For example, an item purchased in 1960, with a ten-year life (straight-line rate 10 per cent) would carry a declining-balance rate of 25 per cent. In the year of acquisition, an entire year's depreciation may be taken, regardless of the month in which acquired.

When the declining-balance method produces an amount for a year less than the amount obtained by dividing the residual balance by the remaining years of life (a straight-line method), the latter method may be used.

A further provision permits a company to elect to continue depreciating under the former provisions of the law during the period 1960-1964, but it must be applied to all acquisitions during that period. This is presumably to provide a transitional period for companies which would otherwise lose beneficial tax deductions.

To qualify as a tax deduction, depreciation must be recorded on the books. If, however, a loss for the year is shown before deducting depreciation, such depreciation need not be deducted but may be carried forward to the first subsequent profitable year. Current depreciation is deducted before applying any of the deferred depreciation. When there is a profit for the year before depreciation, but not sufficient to cover the entire provision for depreciation, the company need not deduct the excess of depreciation over profit before depreciation. Such excess may likewise be deferred and deducted in subsequent years under special rules.

A company, which has not revalued its fixed assets under prior legislation that no longer exists, may defer depreciation and carry it forward without time limitation against future taxable profits *only* if it is *not* recorded on the books in the year to which it relates. A company, which has revalued its assets, is not bound by this restriction; it may charge depreciation as part of a loss and preserve the right to deduct that depreciation in spite of a usual five-year limitation for carry-forward of losses.

Gain on Sale of Depreciable Assets. Gain on sale of depreciable assets is computed in the usual manner by comparing net book amount (either original cost less depreciation or revalued depreciated cost) with selling price. If the proceeds (computed as selling price plus depreciation previously deducted) are invested within three years in other fixed assets, or in at last 20 per cent of the outstanding shares of another company, no tax is then paid on the gain. However, the gain is applied to reduce the cost of the new asset, resulting in smaller depreciation deductions on any depreciable property so acquired in subsequent years. During the "holding period," the gain is credited to a special reserve account.

If reinvestment is made in such assets as land, shares in other companies, intangibles, etc., on which amortization or depreciation is not normally computed or allowable, or in long-term assets for which depreciation is deductible over an extended period, or if reinvestment is again made when these assets are sold, the result, in effect, is that payment of tax is deferred indefinitely or spread over a long period.

Certain investments in other companies are treated as "fixed assets" for the purpose of computing gains on their sale. The rules are similar to those above for depreciable assets.

Tantième (Bonus) Paid to Directors. Tantième (bonus) paid to unsalaried directors is considered as a distribution of profits, and is not a tax deduction to the paying company. No director other than the Président Directeur Général and the Directeur Général Adjoint may be a salaried employee.

Tax-effect Accounting. In France, there are no significant differences between book deductions from income and tax deductions. As indicated previously, depreciation deducted for tax purposes must be similarly recorded on the books. Accordingly, the problem does not normally arise of giving tax effect in the books to tax-return deductions which are charged to income on the books in another period. Exceptions may arise when (a) excessive depreciation has been provided in prior year(s) and (b) provision has been made for vacation pay costs currently, but, which may be deducted for tax purposes only when paid.

REQUIREMENTS FOR PUBLIC SALE OF SECURITIES

Underwritings of public issues are handled in France through banks. There are no official specifications as to form and content of financial statements to be furnished the prospective investor, nor for any report upon them by an independent auditor.

REQUIREMENTS FOR LISTING OF SECURITIES ON THE STOCK EXCHANGE (BOURSE)

The Paris Stock Exchange (Bourse) admits securities to trading through action by its Comité des Bourses de Valeurs (Committee on Stock List) upon filing of a document or series of documents corresponding to the "Listing Application" of the New York Stock Exchange, which contains much the same basic data and technical information about the securities to be listed. The points of interest from an accounting standpoint are:

An undertaking to publish quarterly, essential information concerning the activities of the enterprise, *particularly the sales figures*

A detailed memorandum on the industrial or commercial activities of the firm, accompanied by a comparative balance sheet based on the last three balance sheets, together with an explanation of the variation of the principal items from one fiscal period to another

A memorandum stating plans for investment and calls on surplus capital

A list of subsidiaries and their holdings, with reference to their activity, showing their capital and percentages of stock held

A statement of dividends distributed

A balance sheet, a profit and loss statement, directors' report, minutes of meetings of the shareholders for the last ten fiscal periods with supporting documents for the last five fiscal periods.

It does not appear that any of the financial data—balance sheets or profit and loss statements—are required to be reported upon by an independent accountant.

GERMANY 13

1

FORMS OF BUSINESS ORGANIZATION

Business in Germany is conducted under the usual forms of organization: single proprietorship, partnership, and several forms of corporate organization. Foreigners may freely organize new corporations or acquire control of existing corporations. A foreign corporation may also conduct its business through branch offices. This also requires a government permit and registration in the Commercial Register. In practice, tax and other considerations have for the most part led foreign corporations to operate through a subsidiary rather than a branch.

Aktiengesellschaft (AG)

The German AG most closely resembles the usual United States corporation. There must be five incorporators, whose minimum capital is Deutsch marks 100,000. The capital is divided into shares which can be freely transferred; the par value must be DM 100 or a multiple thereof. No-par value shares are not permitted under German law. Shares or bearer shares may be registered.

The law (Companies Act) regulates in considerable detail the conduct of corporate affairs, including accounting. The AG has two independent governing bodies—the "Vorstand" (board of directors or management) and the "Aufsichsrat" (supervisory board exercising control and giving instructions to the management). These bodies act with independent personal responsibility. The financial statements of the AG must be examined by independent qualified accountants (Wirtschaftprüfer), filed with the local trade registry, and published in the *Federal Gazette*.

Gesellschaft mit beschränkter Haftung (GmbH)

There is no exact legal counterpart to the German GmbH in the United States. In actuality, a small corporation in the United States is run much the same way as a German GmbH.

The capital of a GmbH must be at least DM 20,000. There must be at least two incorporators. Each member must subscribe at least DM 500 and additional subscriptions must be in multiples of DM 100. The liability of the members of the GmbH is limited to the amount of their subscription.

Share certificates are rarely issued. Transfer of interests may be restricted by contract so that the personal relationship between the members may be maintained. One person may acquire all the interests of the other members; in other words, a one-man GmbH is possible.

Rules and regulations for the conduct of corporate affairs are less strict than for the AG, allowing much latitude and informality. Except for banks, there is no requirement for examination by independent accountants and for the publication of financial statements.

Therefore, unless there is expectation that recourse to public financing through stock or debt issues may be had in the future, the GmbH is the legal form most advantageous for United States firms operating in Germany.

Business Records

The Commercial Code requires that each business keep suitable records in a living language (not necessarily German) in bound form; erasures and alterations which would make the original entry illegible are forbidden.

Despite the legal requirement of bound books, loose leaf accounting and ledgerless accounting have been sanctioned through practice and have lately been accepted by the taxing authorities subject to certain conditions.

THE ACCOUNTING PROFESSION

In Germany there are two classes of accountants serving the public, Wirtschaftsprüfer (WP) and Vereidigte Buchprüfer (VBP). Then there are accountants whose work is exclusively directed toward taxes: Steuerberater (StB) and Steurerbevollmächtiger (StBev). There are many WPs and VBPs who are also StBs.

In general, professional standards of the WP and the VBP are similar, but the educational and minimum age requirements differ. Generally, legally required audits may only be performed by WPs.

The new federal Accountancy Law passed in 1961 has the effect of ultimately extinguishing the VBP class: No more VBPs will be licensed; persons now licensed may become WPs by taking an oral examination.

Wirtschaftsprüfer

The Wirtschaftsprüfer most closely resembles a certified public accountant in scope of services, professional standards and ethics, and educational and other entrance requirements.

To become a WP, a candidate must have the necessary personal and professional qualifications and must pass an examination. He must normally be of German nationality or from a foreign country which grants reciprocity to Germans, and have the necessary educational and experience requirements.

Graduation from a university with a major in law, economics, business, or engineering is required. Before entering the university, the students spend four years in an elementary school and nine years in a secondary school, the curriculum of which is college preparatory. Following the period of formal study, a candidate for WP needs six years of practical experience, of which at least four years must be with a WP. Candidates who have not graduated from a university are acceptable if they have had at least ten years' practical experience in the profession. As a practical matter, it is almost impossible to fulfill all requirements before the age of 30; most persons are first admitted at age 35.

The examination covers the following areas:

1. Theory and practice of accounts and business administration
2. Business law (more detailed knowledge is required than just such fundamentals as are necessary in the United States)
3. Tax law
4. Law and ethics of the profession
5. Legal requirements and auditing practice.

The candidate must prepare a thesis and submit to a written and an oral examination. A candidate who fails must generally wait at least one year before applying again. Usually a candidate may not reapply after three failures. After passing the examination, the candidate is licensed by the government.

The profession may be practiced in the form of a partnership or in corporate form, AG or GmbH.

Ethics.

The Wirtschaftprüferkammer (Chamber of Accountants, see page 9) is authorized to issue rules for the exercise of the profession, and holds disciplinary hearings on complaint of violation of the following rules:

1. Compatible occupations: The WP must practice his profession as his main occupation. Certain occupations are not compatible with the profession, such as participation in commercial or other business enterprises or in finance companies; employment by corporations, including being a member of the management of corporations other than Wirtschaftprüfensgesellschaften; and being a government employee, except as a teacher. Specifically mentioned as being compatible with the profession are consultation services, teaching assignments, and free-lance writing.

2. Independence: The profession in Germany recognizes independence both in the subjective and the objective sense. A WP may not accept an engagement when he is doubtful about his impartiality. But a WP also must refuse an engagement when there are reasonable grounds for an outsider to doubt his independence. As illustrations of this latter situation, it is stated that a WP is not considered independent if he or his wife or their brothers or sisters have a material investment in or are indebted in a material amount to the company to be audited (or its parents or any subsidiary) or when he or his wife is closely related to the owner, a member of the board of directors, or the managers of the enterprise audited.

The Institut der Wirtschaftsprüfer issued a pronouncement that there is normally no reason to infer lack of independence from the fact that the WP: (a) assisted in the preparation of the financial statements (the key word is "assisted"—a WP may not examine financial statements prepared solely by him); (b) examined financial statements of prior years; (c) acted as consultant for the client in accounting, tax, or management services; (4) represented the client in accounting or tax matters with government agencies or third parties; (e) has issued for the client advisory opinions in accounting or tax matters; (f) was a witness or expert witness in a law suit to which the client is a party; (g) examined the parent company of the client.

On the other hand, a WP would not be considered independent if he exercised a management function for his client or if his activities were such that they made him the equivalent of an employee.

3. Confidential relationship with client: The prohibition against disclosure of secrets of clients is not only a professional duty, but a breach is a criminal offense subject to fine and/or imprisonment. The criminal sanction also applies to the professional staff of the WP. Matters revealed to a WP in his professional capacity are generally privileged communications in civil as well as in criminal proceedings.

4. Advertising and solicitation: There are the usual rules against advertising, e.g., announcements may be inserted only in a newspaper covering the region in which the WP is active, the size must not be larger than 2 x 3.5 inches, it must be dignified and must be restricted to establishment of practice, change of address, admission of a partner, and similar matters; circulars may be sent only to existing clients. A WP may not solicit clients; of course, he may answer requests.

5. Personal responsibility: According to the principle of personal responsibility, a WP is required to reach his own conclusions and express his own opinions. He must therefore use care in selection of assistants, assign to them only tasks which they are qualified to perform, and supervise them to the extent that he can form his own opinion. An accounting firm may not require a WP to sign an opinion if he has personal reservations.

    Under German law, a WP has unlimited liability to third parties only for knowingly signing false statements and has liability for negligence only to his client, limited to DM 100,000 (to be increased to DM 250,000).

6. Conscientiousness: The WP must conduct himself so as to justify the confidence which the public has in him because of his official status, and at all times maintain loyalty toward his clients. In the performance of his work, he must act as his conscience dictates; he must conform not only to legal requirements but also to professional ethics. He must exercise due care and scrupulous attention to the affairs of his client. Examination procedures and extent of examination are governed by legal and professional requirements and are not subject to instructions of the client.

Functions. The legally required, annual audits of an Aktiengesellschaft (corporation) must be performed by a WP, as must those of banks, insurance companies, home building and loan associations, and public utilities, regardless of the legal form in which they are conducted. The WP gives advice in tax matters and represents his clients before the tax authorities. A difference from practice in most other countries is that the WP is permitted to render legal advice to his clients, provided such advice is related to business law in connection with his professional mission. As a result, many German WPs have fully qualified lawyers as members of their staff.

Vereidigte Buchprüfer (VBP)

VBPs are also in public practice and licensed by the government. The extent of the examination comprises the same areas as that for the Wirtschaftsprüfer but is less penetrating. The minimum age is twenty-eight years. There is no requirement for academic study. Prerequisite for taking the examination is generally five years of practical experience, including three years of experience in the employ of a VBP. Academic studies may be substituted for part of the practical experience requirements. The examination is similar to the one for WP: a thesis, a written examination and an oral examination. Subjects covered are accounting, commercial law and tax law. A candidate is expected to be fully familiar with accounting and tax law and the fundamentals of commercial law.

The VBP is generally subject to the same rules of ethics as the WP. He also may practice in the corporate form subject to the same restrictions. He may render the same kind of professional services as the WP except that annual audits (of an AG) required by law may only be performed by WPs. As previously indicated, under the federal Accountancy Law (1961), the classification of VPB will eventually be extinguished.

Steuerberater (StB)

The StB is an expert in tax law and practice. The requirements are similar to those for a WP, including academic study, practice requirements and an examination of the same general character held by the tax authorities with special emphasis on tax law. For that reason many WPs are also StBs and vice versa.

8

Steuerbevollmächtiger (StBev)

The StBev is enrolled to assist clients in tax matters, generally limited to practice before local tax offices. Requirements to become a StBev are comparatively few.

Organizations of Accountants

Wirtschaftsprüferkammer (Chamber of Accountants). As required by the law dated July 24, 1961, concerning the professional organization of accountants (Wirtschaftsprüferodnung) all Wirtschaftsprüfer and certain other practicing accountants must be members of the Wirtschaftsprüferkammer, a public corporation. The main task of this corporation is to protect and promote the professional interest of its members and to supervise their professional activity.

Institut der Wirtschaftsprüfer. Prior to the establishment of the Wirtschaftsprüferkammer, the Wirtschaftsprüfer were already professionally organized in the Institut der Wirtschaftsprüfer. While the Wirtschaftsprüferkammer is concerned with all professional matters, the Institut der Wirtschaftsprüfer is confined to technical questions, especially to the interpretation and application of legal provisions and of accounting principles.

The German Institute traces its history back to 1930. Its voluntary membership included almost all WPs in Germany.

The Vereidigte Buchprüfer are now also incorporated in the Institut der Wirtschaftsprüfer. The Institute publishes a journal twice a month and bulletins and opinions on technical matters. Although such technical opinions are not legally binding, they do exert some influence because they could have some weight in a court of law. The Institute also owns a publishing company.

The principal committee of the Institute, dealing with professional matters is the "Accounting and Auditing Committee," which has the following subcommittees for:

Banks

Insurance companies

Governmental units

Bankruptcy

Legal and trusteeship matters

Tax matters

Business economics

A collection of bulletins and opinions was published by the Institute in 1956. Subsequent bulletins are published in the journal. The following few titles of bulletins and opinions give an indication of some of the subject matters covered:

"Utilization of Internal Auditing by the Auditor"

"Accountants' Report in Case of Legally Required Audits"

"Accountants' Report in Cases of Other than Legally Required Audits"

"Qualifications and Exceptions"

"Regular Audits and Examinations in Connection with Defalcations"

"Valuation of Fixed Assets No Longer Used in Production"

"Reserves with Regard to Current Assets"

"Report on Special Examinations"

"Post-balance Sheet Events"

The Institute issued a recommended contract between the client and auditor which is generally made part of the written contract for audits. If negligence is claimed by the client in connection with the audit of an AG (corporation), the WP's liability is limited by law to DM 100,000. Consequently, the recommended contract between a WP and his client contains a similar provision.

Other Organizations. The organization of the VBP is the Bundesverband der vereidigten Buchprüfer. There is no federal organization of StBs but there are several regional ones.

AUDITING STANDARDS

In Germany, there is no codification of generally accepted auditing standards and necessary audit procedures. However, there are in existence certain norms, partially based on provisions incorporated in the law, partially based on pronouncements of the German Institute, and partially based on literature and usage. The Wirtschaftsprüferkammer (Chamber of Accountants), under the new (1961) law, has the duty to issue professional directives, which are being compiled and are expected to be published in 1964.

General Standards. The equivalent of American general standards is contained in a pronouncement of the German Institute approved by the membership in 1958 and partially incorporated in the Wirtschaftsprüferordung (Accountancy Law) passed in 1961. The first of the general standards is met by the principle of personal responsibility discussed *supra* under professional "Ethics," item (5). The second general standard is met by the principle of independence discussed there under item (2). The third general standard is discussed under item (6).

Standards of Field Work. There is no codification of standards of field work although there are several specific areas commented on in the literature and in pronouncements of the German Institute. These are discussed below in relation to their counterpart in the pronouncements of the American Institute.

1. *First standard (AICPA)*

   The second part of the first standard of field work (proper supervision of assistants) is explicitly stated above under professional ethics item (5). The first part of this standard (adequate planning of work) has no exact counterpart in German law or official pronouncements. It is obvious that for internal reasons WP firms of all but the smallest size must of necessity do a certain amount of planning, if only for the sake of proper utilization of the staff. Proper planning and the use of an audit program have lately been discussed more extensively in the literature.

   The idea of interim examinations is specifically allowed by a provision of the law. The extent of audit work which may be performed before the fiscal year's end is apparently not settled. Some items are the checking of additions to and deductions from fixed assets and other balance sheet items to the interim point so that the year-end work can be confined to transactions for the remainder of the year. Depending on his individual judgment, the auditor may confine himself to a general review of the accounts from the time of the interim examination (followed by a more detailed examination of this period at the next interim examination) or perform the detailed examination of the period at the year's end.

The interim examination will sometimes contain tests of the accounting process by testing systematically and in detail a block of transactions in each of the major areas, e.g., cash receipts and disbursements, sales and accounts receivable, purchases and inventories.

2. *Second standard (AICPA)*

The review of the system of internal control is not required as such under German law. However, literature and practice have put increased emphasis on internal control as a basis for conducting an examination. For example, in the 1963 edition of the *WP Handbook,* there is one section devoted to a systematic explanation of the principles of internal control and how to examine the existing system. It closely follows American literature on the subject.

At present, the examination of the system of internal control is not the basic cornerstone of an audit and no systematic review is required or made. Of course, review and consideration of internal control is a part of the examination of the various accounts. It is generally recognized that the extent of examination procedures depends on existing internal control. The German Institute issued a bulletin dealing with this aspect as long ago as 1934. But in the absence of a formal requirement for a systematic review, the attention paid to internal control is limited as compared with American practice.

In one of its bulletins, the German Institute states that an ordinary audit is not designed to discover defalcations. If, however, the auditor becomes suspicious, he must notify his client of the suspicious circumstances, otherwise he may become liable to his client. Liability may also arise if the auditor does not use due care in his examination and as a result does not discover or recognize circumstances which might have aroused his suspicion.

3. *Third standard (AICPA)*

The standard of competence of evidential matter is different in Germany, mainly with respect to audit procedures regarding confirmation of receivables and bank balances and observation of physical inventories.

Observation of physical inventories is not a required procedure and not usually practiced. The German auditor will inquire into the instructions given for the taking of inventories, he will inspect original inventory sheets and trace them into the inventory compilation, and obtain an inventory certificate from the management.

Confirmation of receivables is generally not practiced in Germany. Evidence is obtained by examination of company documents. Equally, independent confirmation of bank accounts or accounts payable is unusual. Possibly bank confirmation loses some of its importance, inasmuch as banks send statements, but not cancelled checks, daily.

It is standard practice to request a letter of representation from the management, usually in the form suggested by the Institute. The letter contains representations that all the records submitted for examination were complete, that all assets and liabilities were set forth in the balance sheet at their proper valuation, that all contracts, law suits and disputes which might affect the financial statements were disclosed, etc.

There is no legal requirement for the management to sign the letter. There is, however, a legal requirement that the management give all information necessary for the conduct of the examination so that the auditor may elicit through specific inquiry all the information contained usually in the letter of representation. The letter is considered an expediency rather than a necessity.

In general, the auditor may rely on the representations of management, except when circumstances arouse his suspicions. In such case, it is his responsibility to satisfy himself by additional procedures to the extent possible. On the other hand, a representation by management can never take the place of necessary audit procedures. Representations are important in those situations where the information is not subject to audit substantiation.

Standards of Reporting. Standards of reporting, as well as the accounting principles discussed in the following section, evolved in response to the requirements of the Companies Act. They are prescribed by law for corporations (AG). However, they have been extended in practice generally to financial statements of other companies, although they are probably less binding and more flexible in those cases.

The accountants' report recommended by the German Institute is universally used. It states that "on the basis of the examination of the books and records of the client and explanations received from the management, the accounting and the financial statements are in accordance with legal requirements." Legal requirements deal generally with valuation and proper classification and will be discussed later.

The accountants' report follows the legal language contained in the

Companies Act. It differs from American practice, in that it is ostensibly a statement of fact rather than of the auditor's opinion. However, the literature emphasizes that the report is based on an examination which is necessarily limited so that it is self-evident that it is not absolute truth, but only a subjective evaluation of the evidence. The addition of the phrase "in our opinion" would not limit the responsibility of the auditor; it is implicit under the circumstances.

The law specifically mentions qualified opinions and the denial of an opinion. A qualification must be clearly stated; if possible, an indication of the magnitude of the affected area should be given. Not every disagreement between the auditor and the management requires a qualification. The decision whether disclosure is sufficient, or whether a qualification or, possibly, a disclaimer is necessary depends on the magnitude and importance of the items. It is a matter of professional judgment of the auditor. Some situations mentioned in the literature as requiring qualifications are:

Incorrect classifications of major items

Overvaluation of assets

Nondisclosure or understatement of liabilities and risks

Failure to disclose material post-balance sheet events in the narrative section of the financial report

Omission of, or incorrectly stated comments prescribed by law.

The German audit report contains no reference to consistency. It is recognized, of course, that management has wide discretion in valuing assets and so to establish "hidden reserves." In general, there is no requirement to disclose the establishment of such reserves, but disclosure is suggested when the reserves are taken back into income.

Long-form Report. The short-form report fulfills the attest function of the auditor. In addition, the auditor is required, in the case of AGs, to issue a long-form report which is generally detailed and contains not only statements of fact, but also judgments on the various items included in the balance sheet and earnings statement. The report is intended for the supervisory board (Aufsichtrat) and is used by them as an aid in reaching their own conclusions on problems of management.

This report must state whether the accounting process and accounting principles during the year as well as the financial statements are in accordance with legal requirements. It must also state whether the management answered all requests for information and supplied all necessary documents and other items of substantiation.

Practice has established the general outline and contents of this report.

It contains many details that in American practice would be contained in the audit working papers.

The report usually comprises two parts. The first contains general remarks dealing comprehensively with sales and production volume, capacity and utilization of facilities, work force, etc., mainly in comparison with the preceding year. Expansion plans and other financial plans are also discussed. The second gives details of the composition and, in some cases, the movement of the items of the balance sheet and statement of profit and loss.

This report will normally also comment on major violations of principles of good internal control, but will not contain more routine suggestions for minor changes in accounting and internal control procedures.

ACCOUNTING PRINCIPLES AND PRACTICES

Form and Content of Financial Statements

The form of financial statements is set forth in considerable detail in the Companies Act. There is frequent discussion in the literature as to how specific items are to be classified. The Act specifies that the prescribed classifications must be followed unless the business requires a different classification which must be equally informative. The legal classifications are considered minimum requirements; a more detailed presentation is permissible; it may indeed be necessary for clarity of presentation. Specifically prohibited is the offsetting of liabilities and assets.

The balance sheet is presented in the form which in the United States is used for utilities:

Assets	*Liabilities*
Fixed assets	Capital stock
Current assets:	Reserves
Inventories	Liabilities
Securities	
Receivables	
Cash	

An analysis of fixed assets transactions is presented on the face of the balance sheet. Different from American practice, depreciation is usually deducted from the assets and not accumulated in a separate account.

The earnings statement has been historically presented in account form as follows:

Costs and expenses	Income
Salaries and wages	Sales, less material cost of
Pensions and other em-	goods sold
ployment benefits	Interest income, less inter-
Depreciation	est expense
Interest	Other income, net
Taxes	
Other expenses	
Net earnings	
TOTAL	

This form is similar to the single step earnings statement with expenses classified in functional classification and a considerable netting of cost and expense items against revenues.

However, in 1959, the Companies Act was changed with a view toward making the earnings statement more revealing. In general, offsets of costs and expenses against revenue items are prohibited. One effect of this prohibition is that now total sales must be disclosed. The new law also authorized instead of the account form an earnings statement more similar to the one used in the United States, which deducts from net sales cost of goods sold to arrive at a gross profit and then follows with other expenses, miscellaneous income, and expenses.

Under the Companies Act, an integral part of the annual report by management in addition to the financial statement is a narrative section. This text material contains: (1) a business portion; i.e., comments on the general state of the enterprise, its competitive position and prospects for the future, and important post-balance sheet events, and (2) a financial portion; i.e., explanations and comments on the financial statements.

The distinction between the business portion of the text material and the financial portion is important for the auditor. The financial part is subject to his examination and his opinion extends to it; the business part is not covered by his opinion. However, the management is required to submit this portion to the auditor for his review, and he is responsible for determining that none of the information is misleading. The accountants' report would be qualified if misleading information were not corrected.

The business portion deals with results of the past year and prospects for the coming year, with competitive position, with orders on hand, and such items; it would discuss, for example, the opening of new branches during the past year and plans for additional branches in the future.

The law requires specifically that it reveal post-balance sheet events of major importance. This requirement is especially significant because the annual report is normally issued three to five months after the end of the fiscal year. Types of major events to be reported would be: significant price changes, important new contracts, acquisition of real estate, acquisition of a new business, and major losses.

The financial section is designed to supplement and explain the financial statements, specifically "changes since the last report," e.g., a substantial change in the level of inventories or a change in classification within the financial statements. Also to be disclosed under this provision are changes in consistency in the application of accounting principles if material; e.g., a change in depreciation method.

In addition to these general provisions, the law contains a list of specific items which must be disclosed, among them the acquisition of treasury stock, assets pledged, contingent liabilities, guarantees, and relationship with affiliates.

Financial statements together with the narrative section and the audit report must be submitted to the stockholders' meeting, filed with the local trade registry, and published in the *Federal Gazette*. They may be submitted voluntarily to banks or other interested parties. The financial statements together with the audit report, but not the narrative section, are also published in the commercial press.

It may be seen that the financial part of the narrative section fulfills to some degree the function of footnotes in American practice. However, disclosure requirements are not as firmly established and clearly developed. In some respects the requirements go beyond those established in the United States.

Consolidated Financial Statements. The Companies Act authorizes consolidated statements, but rules and regulations under the Act have not been issued. The bigger firms prepare consolidated statements for internal use. A few also publish consolidated statements. Accordingly, practice has established few generally accepted rules.

There is some controversy about the principles of inclusion and exclusion. Ownership of a majority of the outstanding stock is generally considered a necessary condition. Ownership of 50 per cent of the stock is sometimes considered sufficient, if the remainder of the stock is widely dispersed. Banks, insurance companies, and finance companies should not be consolidated, according to some authorities.

There is also controversy over the elimination of intercompany profits remaining in the accounts of the constituent companies, especially when there are minority interests present. A few authorities maintain that such elimination is unnecessary.

While affiliated companies generally issue separate statements, certain disclosures must be made with respect to affiliations. The narrative part of the financial statements must disclose the relationship to parents and other affiliates and the basis for the relationship, such as stock ownership, common ownership, or contractual relationship. The balance sheet must disclose investments in affiliates together with other long-term investments, as well as receivables from and payables to them. For both receivables and payables, no distinction is made as to balances arising from normal business transactions or from other sources, such as intercompany dividends, interest, rent, etc; the balances from all intercompany transactions are reflected in one account for receivables and one for payables, each of them summarizing the net receivables or the net payables of each affiliate. The earnings statements must disclose dividends and interest (in one figure) from affiliates and other long-term investments. The narrative should comment on these items and make a general statement as to relationships with affiliated companies. Frequently, the disclosure requirements are satisfied by a simple statement that no changes have occurred since the previous year.

Accounting Practices

German theory and practice recognizes that the balance sheet contains mostly items that are deferred for later transfer into the earnings statement. From this follows the principle of balance sheet continuity, i.e., the closing balance sheet of one period is the opening balance sheet of the next. This principle is, however, accepted strictly as a formal principle. For example, an item written down at the end of the year is carried forward at that valuation into the next year, but if the item is still on hand at the end of the next year, it does not necessarily remain at the written down valuation, and may be revalued within the limits of the acquisition cost or manufacturing cost, respectively. If a material revaluation is made, the amount of write-up must be disclosed. This is different from American practice where a write-down to market of an inventory item will establish the carrying value of the item for the next inventory.

The law also established the principle of completeness, i.e., the balance sheet must contain all assets and liabilities. For example, intangibles purchased must be shown; a liability for which the statute of limitation has tolled must be shown, if the corporation does not intend to avail itself of its right to refuse payment; assets acquired under conditional sales contracts are to be set up, conversely the seller must record the receivable and eliminate the cost of the asset sold.

General Principles of Valuation

Acquisition cost or production cost is the highest allowable value for assets; unrealized gains may not be recorded. The German law also recognizes the principle of conservatism and requires that current assets be written down to a lower replacement or reproduction cost or net realizable value. These principles seem very close to American practice, but there is much greater leeway in Germany as to the extent to which assets may lawfully be written down. In general, it is permissible to understate assets (although not to overstate liabilities) if the company's management considers that there are valid business reasons for doing so.

The application of German tax law also often leads to an understatement of assets in financial statements prepared for commercial purposes. The chief examples are accelerated depreciation for various types of fixed assets and inventory reserves of up to 20 per cent on certain imported products. Normally, advantage can only be taken of these tax reliefs if the amounts concerned are provided for in the financial statements.

In making the cost-market comparison, it is generally necessary to deal with individual items. For example, if two different securities are owned, it is not permissible to compare the total cost with the total market value and therefore offset a loss in value of one security against an increase in value of the other. Some groupings are acceptable in the case of fungible goods or goods of a similar nature.

Basically, market value is determined as of the balance-sheet date. However, losses and drop in prices between the balance-sheet date and the date of valuation should be recognized to the extent that they affect goods on hand or liabilities on the balance-sheet date. For example, if a debtor goes into bankruptcy after the balance-sheet date, the receivable should be reduced in value if it is considered that the debtor was already in difficulty at the balance-sheet date.

Inventories

Raw material cost includes freight-in, duty, and other expenditures to bring the material into place and is to be reduced by trade discounts and, according to some authorities, cash discounts.

Cost of work in process and finished goods includes material, labor and overhead. Material cost is usually determined by the average method, but Fifo, Lifo, and base stock methods are not acceptable for tax purposes. Changes in the method of valuation are allowed; if the amounts are material, the change should be disclosed in the narrative section of the annual report, although opinions vary as to the extent to which disclosure is necessary in practice.

German tax law requires that physical inventories be taken at the close of each taxable year. Inventories may be counted at an earlier date and brought forward to the year end only if controlled as to interim activity on perpetual inventory quantity records. Inventories of work-in-process may be unacceptable if counted at other than year-end dates, unless perpetual records are maintained as to quantities of specific items throughout the manufacturing process.

Accounts Receivable

Uncollectible accounts should be written off. For doubtful accounts it is necessary to provide a reserve. In general, a specific reserve is provided for individual accounts and a general reserve for the remainder of the accounts.

Long-term accounts carrying no or a low rate of interest are preferably set up at the discounted amount. Foreign receivables should be set up based on the rate of exchange at the balance-sheet date or at the date of acquisition, whichever is lower. Consideration must be given to exchange restrictions.

Long-term Debt

Such debt must be shown at the amount to be paid. Debt discount and expenses are to be shown on the asset side to be amortized over the life of the debt. If a part of the debt is retired at an early date, a proportionate amount of debt discount and expense must be written off. The amount should be written off to maturity. Assets pledged as security should be disclosed in the narrative section of the annual report. Bonds repurchased which may be reissued are to be shown on the asset side among securities. Long-term liabilities which carry a low rate of interest or no interest may be carried at their face value or at their discounted value; the discount may be carried on the asset side.

Legal Reserve

The law makes provision for the establishment of a legal reserve for the safety of creditors. In general, 5 per cent of net earnings must be set aside until the reserve reaches 10 per cent (or a higher amount provided in the by-laws) of the capital stock account. The reserve may be utilized only to cover operating losses or a write-down of assets.

Capital Stock

Capital stock is to be shown at par value. Each issue of stock with different rights is to be set forth separately. Disclosure of the number of authorized shares appears not on the face of the balance sheet but in the narrative. Treasury shares are shown on the asset side. Subscriptions receivable for capital stock are also shown on the asset side.

REQUIREMENTS FOR LISTING OF SECURITIES ON THE STOCK EXCHANGES AND PUBLIC SALE OF SECURITIES

At present there are eight stock exchanges in Germany. These are supervised through authority of the State in which the exchange is located (Börsenaufsicht). The listing of securities on an exchange is governed by the Stock Exchange Law as amended and supplemented. Application for listing of securities is made to an admissions committee of the stock exchange by a member bank which also acts as a broker. The committee passes on the adequacy and completeness of the information submitted, but does not investigate and does not take responsibility for the correctness of the information. The responsibility for the correctness of the information rests with the bank and the issuer.

The issue of bonds and debentures requires approval of the Federal Ministry of Economics in consultation with the competent supreme authorities of the state in which the issuer resides. The issue of shares no longer requires approval.

An application for listing on an exchange must be accompanied by certain documents among which are:

A prospectus signed by the applicant and the participating bank

Annual reports of the company for the last three fiscal years

A copy of the last previous prospectus, if any, and

Under certain circumstances, a copy of the latest quarterly financial statements following the annual report.

The prospectus includes items such as:

Excerpts from the Articles of Incorporation

A copy of the financial statements for the latest year

Information as to the activities of the company

Comments of the management on the financial statements presented and on the present and future prospects of the company

Information on investments in other companies

In the case of debentures details must also be set forth as to the conditions under which the debentures are issued.

In practice, the details of disclosure are agreed upon in consultation between the issuer, the bank, and the stock exchange. The prospectus must be published. After publication has been made, the bank then applies for the official listing of the securities. The application must also be published.

Requirements for listing on an exchange are not too well defined by regulations or general practice. Disclosures, while more extensive than those supplied in the annual report, are somewhat less than those normally found in American listing applications and prospectuses.

GREECE   **14**

I

FORMS OF BUSINESS ORGANIZATION

The same types of business organizations are found in Greece as are found in other European countries and the United Kingdom—the single proprietorship, the partnership and the corporation.

A foreign corporation wishing to establish a branch in Greece may do so after complying with certain formalities, or it may form a subsidiary under Greek law, which will then be subject to the prevailing regulations governing similar Greek enterprises. There are no special corporation laws relating to foreign owned Greek corporations; there are a number of provisions in Greek law intended to encourage foreign investment in companies designed to promote national production and to contribute to national progress.

The Corporation

This is the usual form which, upon incorporation, becomes a legal entity, and the liability of its shareholders is limited to the amount of capital contributed by each.

The corporation may be formed by two or more persons under a notarial document (Memorandum of Association), which includes the articles of incorporation. This memorandum is signed by each subscriber, and sets forth the number of shares subscribed by each, the name of the company (last word must be "Limited"), the registered office, and the purposes of the company. The minimum capital requirement is 5,000,000 drachmas, and in any case at least that amount must be paid in. Subject to this minimum, when higher amounts of capital are subscribed, 25 per cent of the subscriptions must be paid within two months of incorporation and the balance within ten years, as provided in the Articles. If any part of the capital is to be obtained by public subscription, the minimum

3

capital requirement is 10,000,000 drachmas, all of which must be paid up in full. Public subscription may be effected only through a bank. The Memorandum of Association is filed with the Ministry of Commerce, and is published together with the Ministry's approval in the *Official Gazette*.

A copy of the balance sheet, the directors report and the auditors' report (the latter being that of a certified public accountant of Greece when required) are to be submitted to the Ministry of Commerce at least twenty days before the date of the general meeting. They are also published in the *Bulletin of Public Companies* and in certain specified newspapers. Within twenty days after adoption by the general meeting, a copy of the adopted balance sheet is submitted to the Ministry of Commerce.

The Limited Liability Company

This form corresponds to the British "private company" or to the French "Société à Responsibilité Limitée," and is intended for smaller organizations with limited capital and few participants. It may be formed by two or more persons using the same initial documents as required for the joint-stock company. The attested copy, however, is filed with the Secretariat of the Court of First Instance, and a summary is published in the *Official Gazette*.

The minimum capital is 200,000 drachmas, to be fully paid. The member's liability cannot exceed the amount of his share contribution.

The Board of Directors of a company of limited liability is obligated to publish a balance sheet in the *Official Gazette* and in certain specified newspapers at least twenty days before the general meeting.

The Partnership

The general partnership (Société en Nom Collectif) is formed by two or more (usually a maximum of twenty) persons by a written agreement filed with the Secretariat of the Court of First Instance. The partners are jointly and severally liable for the debts of the partnership.

The limited partnership (Société en Commandite) is governed by a Memorandum of Association and is composed of general partners, who are jointly and severally liable for partnership debts, and limited partners, (whose names may not appear in the firm name), whose liability is limited to the amount of their contributions.

4

Business Records

For tax purposes, companies are categorized according to size. For instance, "Category D" companies are those which meet the following requirements:

Have annual sales of foodstuffs exceeding 5,000,000 drachmas or

Have annual sales of goods exceeding 4,200,000 drachmas or

Have annual income from services exceeding 500,000 drachmas and

Are limited liability companies.

The records listed below are required to be maintained by "Category D" companies. Except for items 5 and 6, the records must be "visaed" by the fiscal authorities before any entries are made therein. The laws also prescribe time schedules within which transactions must be recorded:

1. Cash book
2. General journal(s) (for transactions other than cash)
3. Summary journal (total or control accounts for entries in 1 and 2 above)
4. General ledger
5. Analytical ledgers of general ledger accounts
6. Cost (inventory) book
7. Year-end general inventory and balance sheet book
8. Memorandum books for checks, bills payable and receivable (Columnar form prescribed by law—but the information may be incorporated in books 1 and 2 above)
9. Production book and cost analysis (unless cost records are integrated with general accounting system).

Limited companies must also keep minute books of the general assembly and directors' meetings.

There are certain records prescribed for smaller organizations in Categories A, B, and C.

THE ACCOUNTING PROFESSION

In ancient Greece, accountants who examined and approved accounts of government officials were themselves highly placed officials. It was not until quite recently, however, that an accounting profession composed of specially trained and educated persons, equipped to examine and report upon commercial and industrial enterprises as well as upon government activities, was organized.

Although the Greek Companies' Act (1920) provided that limited liability companies were obliged to have their annual statement of accounts audited by two "auditors" appointed by the General Meeting of Shareholders, there was no specification of the required qualifications for such appointment, nor of the kind of examination to be made. As a result, auditors were usually not equipped to make an audit in the present-day accepted sense, and, in most cases, the financial statements were signed after comparison with the books of account.

After World War II both the British and later the American Economic Missions required reliable information about the financial and economic situation in Greece. Out of the British experience there was established in 1949, the "British Accounting Advisors to Greece," one of whose tasks was: "to assist in the establishment of a Greek Institute and profession of audit accounting." After many discussions, a law was passed in 1955, establishing an accounting profession in Greece; this was the same year in which the contract with the British Accounting Advisors expired. Two of these advisers remained to advise the government during the formative stages of the project.

Soma Horokoton Logiston (Institute of Certified Public Accountants of Greece)

Literally, the name of the Institute is that of "Sworn-in Accountants," as each member, assistant and articled clerk, after admission, must take the following oath:

> I solemnly swear that I shall be faithful to my country, to the King of Greece, to the Constitution and to all the laws of the country and shall honestly and conscientiously fulfill my duty.

The member is known as an "Orokotos Logistic" (Sworn-in Accountant), but the usual English translation is "Certified Public Accountant of Greece" (C.P.A.G.).

The Institute was established as an autonomous body to foster the development of the accounting profession in Greece. It is governed by a Supervisory Board consisting of the chairman and eight members who will be:

A professor of the Graduate School of Commercial and Economic Studies.

A member of the Supreme Fiscal and Audit Court of Greece.

Five prominent officials.

A Certified Public Accountant of Greece who has been elected by his colleagues as their President.

A qualified accountant (a British Chartered Accountant who has the position of Technical Adviser to the Institute may be appointed).

The main functions of the Supervisory Board comprise the following:

Appoint members, assistants and articled clerks

Regulate the examinations

Compile operating procedures (with advice from the Technical Adviser)

Fix fees

Maintain disciplinary provisions

Fix rates of emolument for professional and administrative personnel.

Initial Organization. Initially the Supervisory Board selected ten individuals from numerous applicants for the post of certified public (sworn-in) accountant. These applicants had certain academic qualifications and experience. Subsequently there have been two additional appointments from candidates outside of the Institute.

The first appointments to the posts of assistant CPA and articled clerks were made from applicants holding the equivalent of a Bachelor of Science Degree in Economics, and who passed certain written and oral examinations.

The law provided that in the first year the number of members should be ten; it might be increased to twenty-five after two years, and thereafter the number would be determined by Royal Decree. At present, there are 111 members, consisting of fifteen CPAs of Greece, eighteen assistant CPAs, and seventy-eight articled clerks.

Each member may employ no more than three assistants and ten articled clerks.

7

Advancement to Certified Public Accountant of Greece. The original appointment to the posts of assistant CPA and articled clerks were made after written examinations given by the professors of the Graduate School of Commercial and Economic Studies. The oral examinations were held by a panel consisting of accounting and law professors and members of the Supervisory Council of the Institute.

Promotion from one grade to the next higher is made when the work-load of the Institute requires it. The persons considered for promotion to the next rank must have completed the following periods of service for each grade: articled clerk (B) three years, articled clerk (A) five years, and assistant CPA three years. So far no written examinations have been required for promotion; such promotions are based on a report of a subcommittee to the Supervisory Council.

Recruitments of Articled Clerks. Candidates for entry into the profession must possess the degree equivalent to Bachelor of Science in Economics, and must pass a written examination covering accounting, commercial law and taxation, and an oral examination on accounting and foreign languages. Four such examinations have been held in the last two years.

Functions of the Certified Public Accountants of Greece

The law establishing the Institute also lists the functions, both obligatory and "facultative," which the members of the Institute must or may perform (condensed):

Obligatory:

To report upon subjects of a financial and administrative nature which require knowledge of accountancy

To conduct audits of public institutions other than municipalities

To make examinations required by law courts

To conduct audits of limited companies, listed on the Exchange or in which the government has an interest, when authorized by the Minister of Commerce

To audit insurance companies' accounts when required by the Minister of Trade.

Facultative:

To act as "auditor" of a limited liability company (not listed on the Stock Exchange) as prescribed by the Companies' Act of 1920. If a company makes such appointment, there need be but one auditor instead of two.

To make special examinations by appointment by the Currency Committee of the Bank of Greece.

To make examinations of limited liability companies on request of banks or other lending institutions when a loan of over 200,000 drachmas is involved.

In 1959, a ministerial decision required all limited liability companies whose shares were officially listed on the Stock Exchange to have an audit by members of the Institute.

In addition, the members may engage in furnishing tax and finance advisory services, conducting investigations of proposed acquisitions of businesses, and similar activities.

Functions of the Institute of Certified Public Accountants of Greece

The operations of the Institute are unique as compared with corresponding institutes and associations of accountants in other countries. At the time of its inception, there were few Greeks with a high standard of experience in auditing, and the organization and training of a body of professional accountants was considered an important task of the Institute. It was therefore established by law as a quasi-governmental institution and was granted certain subsidies by the government for its initial development.

There are one or two foreign firms of practicing accountants in Greece offering services to foreign clients, and a number of small practitioners offering monthly bookkeeping and tax services. There are no firms of independent certified public accountants of Greece, as the accounting and auditing work described under "Functions" above is performed by members of the Institute under its direction, much as though the Institute itself constituted a firm of public accountants as is understood in other countries. The Technical Adviser to the Supervisory Council might be analogous to the senior partner of a conventional accounting firm; the members (CPAs of Greece) have offices and staff assigned to them within the premises of the Institute according to the resolutions of the Supervisory Council. Once assigned, the staff usually remains with the designated CPA. The Institute has a central administration and common facilities for typing, communications, etc.

Under the law, all requests for audits or other professional work are submitted to the Supervisory Council, which in turn appoints a CPAG to carry out the required work. This central control is to ensure an even flow and spread of work throughout the various offices of the CPAGs. Except when fees are fixed by government agencies, or by the courts authorizing the work, fees for work done are assessed by the Supervisory Council on recommendation of the Technical Adviser. The CPAGs, the Assistant CPAGs and articled clerks receive monthly salaries based on rank, period of service, merit and similar considerations.

All reports and statements of opinion for regular audit and accounting work are signed by the certified public accountant of Greece responsible for the work, and are submitted to the client through the Supervisory Council. The covering letters are passed to the Technical Adviser who endorses the copy with any appropriate notes arising from his review of the assignment. The covering letters are then signed by the Chairman of the Supervisory Council.

It is expected that, with a steady increase in the demand for the services of independent public accountants, and the increased supply of trained accountants through the educational and training programs of the Institute, the profession might establish itself independently of the Institute as in other countries, so that the Institute may confine its efforts to the educational, training and technical aspects of its work.

Ethics

The Institute adopted a Code (Standards) of Ethics in 1961, which compares favorably with similar codes of other countries. Among the more important provisions regarding the certified public accountant of Greece are the following (condensed):

> He will not engage in any business or activity incompatible or inconsistent with his professional work. (The Act itself lists the following as incompatible professions: Merchant; civil servant, judge or notary; employment by a private or public enterprise; administrative managing director or an accountant of a limited liability company; the pursuit of any other profession.)

> He will not be a partner of or engage the services of a person not approved by the Institute.

> He will not advertise his services or attainments.

> He will not enter into competitive bidding for professional work, nor solicit clients in a manner not warranted by personal relations with such clients.

If approached by a prospective client to supplant a previous auditor, he will communicate with the latter before accepting the engagement.

He may be held guilty of an act discreditable to the profession for the following reasons:

Is materially negligent in performing his work

Fails to disclose a material fact known to him which would make misleading the financial statements on which he is stating an opinion

Fails to obtain the information and explanations necessary to express an unqualified opinion, but nevertheless does so

Fails to disclose in his opinion any deviation from prescribed auditing standards

Violates the confidential relationship between himself and his client.

Independence. The Code of Ethics also provides that the certified public accountant of Greece will not audit the accounts of a concern under the following circumstances:

If he is an official or employee of the concern

Has a financial interest in the concern which is material in relation to either the capital of the concern or his family wealth

Purchases shares or other securities of the concern while he is acting as its auditor

Has any financial relationship with officers or employees of his client such as lending or borrowing.

In addition, the Standards of Auditing (discussed later) state that the auditor should conduct his work with impartiality, that he should not accept gifts or favors directly or indirectly from his client, that he should not have any financial relationship with his client, and that in maintaining an attitude of independence, he will be guided by the Standards of Ethics adopted by the Institute.

The statement of "Standards" also indicates that the impartiality of the auditor would not necessarily be impaired by the fact that he had designed or participated in the design of the accounting system of the organization which he is auditing.

AUDITING STANDARDS

Under the direction of the Technical Adviser to the Supervisory Board of the Institute, a Statement of Auditing Standards, which was adopted by the Institute on January 30, 1961, was prepared. In addition to the Standards of Ethics and reference to impartiality, previously discussed, the standards are described under three headings—Basic Standards, Standards of Performance, and Standards of Reporting. A textbook, *Auditing*, written by Mr. L. A. Mattingly, Technical Adviser, has been published. This book describes recommended audit procedures in some detail.

Basic Standards

These standards comprise the requirements that are imposed by the Institute of Certified Public Accountants of Greece, composed of persons who have qualified by education and experience to be so appointed by the Supervisory Board. In conducting his work, the certified public accountant of Greece is responsible for selection, instruction and supervision of his assistants, and must bring reasonable skill and diligence to bear on his work. The matter of impartiality is covered under this heading.

Standards of Performance

The importance of the CPAG basing his work on a thorough evaluation of internal control procedures, and consideration of the factor of materiality in planning an audit program is stressed. The audit procedures should be selected so as to form a logical basis for his opinion on the financial statements, and his working papers should provide evidence that his work has been performed in accordance with the prescribed standards. Confirmation of assets by correspondence with responsible third parties is recommended. Although confirmation of accounts receivable by this method is not specifically mentioned, it is generally considered to be mandatory. Provided adequate tests have been made of the accuracy of the stated amounts of physical assets, statements of responsible officials may be accepted, but physical inspection of some of the assets is required.

12

The importance of inquiries as to events which have occurred subsequent to the balance-sheet date, and which might reflect a material change in the fairness of presentation, is especially referred to. Specifically, the possible effects of post balance-sheet events on the valuation of inventories and receivables are given as examples.

Standards of Reporting

This standard states that the ultimate objective of an auditor's examination of financial statements is to express an opinion as to the fairness thereof, except in cases where, due to absence of material evidence, the auditor is unable to express an opinion on the financial statements. In such cases, he should state in his report:

1. Whether or not, in his opinion, the statements and any notes forming an integral part thereof, fairly present the financial position and the results of the period covered, in conformity with accepted accounting principles
2. Whether or not the principles of accounting used by the concern under audit were consistent with those of the previous period
3. Whether or not his examination was made in accordance with the standards of auditing accepted by the Institute of Certified Public Accountants of Greece
4. Whether or not the concern under audit had kept the books of account prescribed by law
5. Whether or not the financial statements were in agreement with those books of account
6. Any material disclosures which are not shown on the financial statements.

In further explanation of the application of these reporting requirements, it is stated that the auditor must express his opinion in clear and generally understood terms, and must furnish the reader with information complete in all material respects. If, because of the absence of material evidence, he is unable to satisfy himself as to the fairness of the financial statements, he must state such inability and his reasons therefor. If absence of evidence or inability to carry out certain audit procedures are not so material as to require denial of opinion, the auditor may qualify his opinion, stating clearly the extent of his exception.

If financial data is to be prepared without audit by the Certified Public Accountant of Greece, and if his name is to be associated with such data, he must state clearly on the statements that they have been prepared from data without audit. The Certified Public Accountant of Greece must not associate his name with forecasts of profits or financial position in such a manner that may lead the reader to believe that he vouches for their accuracy.

The following is the English version of the unqualified form of audit opinion used by the Certified Public Accountant of Greece:

To the Shareholders of XYZ Company, S.A.:

In my opinion, based upon my examination, the accompanying financial statements (with their notes), fairly present the financial position of XYZ Company, S.A., at 31st December, 196.., and the results of its operations for the year then ended in conformity with legal requirements and accepted accounting principles applied on a basis consistent with that of the previous year.

My examination was made in accordance with the requirements of Article 37 of the Companies' Act of Greece (No. 2190) and also in conformity with the Standards of Auditing accepted by the Institute of Certified Public Accountants of Greece and accordingly included such tests of accounting records and other auditing procedures as I considered to be necessary in the circumstances. I obtained all the information and explanations (including statements of all branch operations) which I needed for the purpose of my audit.

I have found that the books of account (and production cost books) as required by existing laws have been kept by your Company, and that the accompanying financial statements are in agreement therewith.

(Signed)

Other Pronouncements of the Institute

In addition to the "Standards" discussed above, the Institute has published a series of "Technical Notes" for the guidance of its members. These include questionnaires on internal control for various types of business, audit program guides, standardized working papers, guides to reporting, and statement presentation, etc.

ACCOUNTING PRINCIPLES AND PRACTICES

The Institute has not yet published pronouncements specifically relating to accounting principles or rules. Such published rules as are available are contained in the Greek Companies' Act (as amended), of which the more significant are described below.

Accounting Principles

The Greek Companies' Act states certain "Principles of Valuation" which must be followed. For example:

1. Inventories are to be stated at the lower of cost or market.
2. Investments in the following shall be shown at cost:
   Greek Government bonds

   Debentures issued by Greek corporations

   National Bank of Greece

   Greek Limited Companies secured "in rem."
3. Fixed assets will be shown at cost, including cost of improvements, less accumulated depreciation, which is to be provided in proportion to the wear and tear of the company's assets and the probable duration of their use.
4. Uncollectible claims (accounts receivable) are to be written off, and doubtful claims shown at their estimated realizable value.
5. Debentures issued by the company are to be shown as liabilities at their redemption price; the difference between this price and the issue price may be deferred and written off over the life of the debentures.

Form and Content of Financial Statements

The Act prescribes the form of financial statements in some detail. A summary of these requirements is as follows:

Balance Sheet:

Assets side:

Fixed assets:

Stated by main captions, including intangibles, investments and long-term receivables

Current assets:

Inventories (by main classifications)

Circulating assets—current receivables, securities, prepaid expenses

Available assets:

Cash in banks and on hand

Accumulated deficit from operations

Liabilities side:

Capital and reserves:

Stated by main captions, including surplus from revaluation

Provisions for possible decline in value of assets not shown as deductions from the appropriate items, and provisions for contingent liabilities

Obligations:

Stated by main captions, e.g., long-term debt (maturing after one year), short-term debt, dividends payable, and income of the following year

Retained earnings

Contingent assets and liabilities.

Profit and Loss (*Results of the Year*). This statement must follow the balance sheet, must be complete and clear, and must show the actual profits and losses sustained. The items to be shown separately are stated hereunder:

Gross profit after deducting cost of goods sold:

Less:

Administrative expenses

Finance charges

Selling expenses of goods and services

Profit from normal operations of the company:

Add or deduct:

Income from other businesses

Interest payable

Abnormal benefits or profits

Balance

Less:

Abnormal charges

Losses or provisions not includible in cost of sales

Balance

Less income tax

Profit and loss for the year ("Results of the Year").

Losses accruing during the year must be charged to profit and loss of that year, and must be estimated if not exactly known. Special losses, by permission of the Ministry of Commerce, may be deferred and written off in amounts equivalent to one-third of the succeeding annual profits. During the period of write-off, dividends may not exceed 5 per cent on the paid-up share capital, and such payments will not exceed five years.

The Act then states that the account "Results of the Year" (Profit and Loss Account) will be followed by a schedule showing the way net profits were appropriated. There should appear therein the balance of undistributed profits or loss of preceding years as an addition to or deduction from the aggregate of the net profits for the closing year.

The above requirements as to statement presentation are effective beginning with the year 1963.

Other Provisions Affecting Statement Presentation:

1. The balance sheet and results of the year are to be prepared in comparative form.
2. Liens on fixed assets are to be described as to nature and extent.
3. Amounts due from shareholders on account of subscriptions to capital stock, and amounts due from directors, are to be shown separately.
4. Account titles in financial statements must clearly indicate their contents; the accounts must contain only like items, and asset and liability items, whether alike or not, may not be offset one against the other.
5. The accounts representing accumulated depreciation of fixed assets or long-term obligations, will be deducted from the related items.
6. Administration expenses will not be shown as assets on the balance sheet, except that research expenses and organization expenses may be so treated if, by company statute or resolution of the general meeting, they are to be amortized over a period not exceeding ten years.
7. If a company has issued no par value or founders' shares, this fact must be stated on the balance sheet.
8. There are special requirements as to items to be shown in the financial statements of insurance companies.
9. Banks, commercial and similar enterprises may arrange their assets on the balance sheet in order of liquidity.
10. A public company with branches must prepare combined financial statements after adjustment for intracompany balances.

Consolidated Financial Statements. There is no requirement of Greek company law to prepare consolidated financial statements of a parent company and its subsidiary companies.

Statutory Reserve

Article 44 of the Greek Limited Companies' Act provides that at least one-twentieth of the net profits should be deducted annually for the formation of a Statutory Reserve, until such reserve equals at least one-third of the share capital. This reserve may only be used to absorb a deficit in the profit and loss account prior to the payment of any dividends.

REQUIREMENTS FOR LISTING ON THE STOCK EXCHANGE AND PUBLIC SALE OF SECURITIES

While there are requirements for financial statements to be furnished in connection with Stock Exchange listing and prospectuses, the provisions of the law are general in scope. For the convenience of its members, the Institute has issued "Technical Notes" on this subject, which list items that it believes should be dealt with in reports for this purpose.

ITALY | 15

FORMS OF BUSINESS ORGANIZATION

The various forms of business organization are regulated by the provisions of the Civil Code and are classified into Imprese Individuali (sole proprietorships) and Società (partnerships and companies).

Foreign investors usually adopt the form of an Italian corporation (Società per Azioni) and less frequently operate as a branch of a foreign corporation.

The Italian Government has established certain fields of activity in which foreign investment is restricted, *viz*: shipyards, aircraft manufacture, airline operations, banks, and insurance companies.

Società per Azioni (S.p.A.)

This is the form of business organization that most closely resembles the American corporation. It must have a minimum capital of one million lire, which must be fully subscribed, and at least three-tenths of the cash proceeds from the subscriptions must be deposited in the Banca d'Italia before registration. Once the registration has been completed the deposit is returned to the corporation. Capital and bond issues over five hundred million lire are also subject to the approval of the Treasury Department.

The Civil Code authorizes four different classes of shares: common (ordinarie), preferred (privilegiate), benefit (di godimento), and employees' shares (azioni a favore dei prestatori di lavoro). Preferred shares may not exceed 50 per cent of the total capital stock. When employees' shares are issued, the capital stock must be increased by the stated value of such shares. Shares may not be issued for less than par value and must be registered. "Bearer" shares are not permitted except in Sicily, Sardinia, and in certain other cases. Upon formation, an Italian corporation must have at least two stockholders. Subsequently, the corporation may have only one stockholder, but in such a case the sole stockholder assumes unlimited liability for debts or the corporation from the date upon which he became the sole shareholder.

With certain exceptions, debentures outstanding may not exceed the par value of paid-up capital stock.

Neither shareholders nor directors need be Italian nationals or residents. There is no provision in the law regarding the number of directors. Every corporation must have a statutory board of auditors, whose functions are described later.

The directors are required to submit annual financial statements, together with their report, to the board of auditors at least thirty days before the date set for the shareholders' meeting, which assembly should not take place later than four months, and in particular cases six months, after the close of the annual operations. Such documents and the transcript of the shareholders' approval thereof must be filed with the Registrar of Enterprises within thirty days.

The Civil Code provides that if a corporation sustains losses which are in excess of one-third of its capital, and if the losses in excess of one-third of the capital are not recovered in the succeeding year, the company must reduce its capital proportionately. If by reason of such losses, the capital is reduced below the statutory minimum (presently one million lire), it must be brought back to that minimum or the legal form of organization must be changed.

Branch of a Foreign Corporation

As in the case of other forms of business organization, duly legalized copies of the articles of incorporation and the by-laws as well as the Board of Directors' resolution authorizing the branch must be filed with the Registrar of Enterprises of the corresponding district, together with the names of the persons who will represent the foreign corporation in Italy. Pending the establishment of the Registry of Enterprises the above documents must be filed with the court having jurisdiction over the foreign corporation's principal office in Italy. Thereafter, the branch must register with the Chamber of Commerce, which will assign a registration number, generally appearing on the business stationery of the company. A copy of its annual financial statements must be filed with the Registrar, subject to the same rules that apply to Italian corporations. The branch form is not usually adopted by foreign investors mainly because there are no substantial advantages as compared to the organization of an Italian corporation and also because of the problem in allocating costs to the branch for tax purposes.

Other Forms of Business Organization

Società in Nome Collettivo. This is the equivalent of the unlimited partnership, in which all partners are jointly and severally liable. The association is not dissolved upon the death of a partner unless the articles of partnership so provide.

Società in Accomandita Semplice. This is a limited partnership in which the general partners are jointly and severally liable, while the limited or silent partners are liable up to the amounts of their contributions, which cannot be in the form of shares. A partner's equity may be fully transferred if partners representing a majority of the capital so agree. When the partnership's equity is represented by shares, it is called Società in Accomandita per Azioni, which is a legal entity.

Società a Responsabilità Limitata. This is a legal entity similar to a limited liability partnership in which the firm is liable only to the extent of its own assets, and each member is liable up to the limit of his capital contribution, which cannot be represented by shares, although the partners' interests may be easily transferred. The required minimum capital is fifty thousand lire, and this type of partnership may not issue bonds.

Business Records

The Civil Code prescribes that all commercial enterprises must keep a journal (in which all transactions are recorded in chronological order), and an inventory book (in which the annual financial statements must be transcribed). These are considered official records, and before they are put into use they must be numbered and authenticated by a public notary or by the court. Corporations must also keep certain other books such as minutes of directors' and shareholders' meetings, a stock register, minutes of the board of auditors' meetings, etc. There are other books which are required by tax and labor laws. Among these are the following:

1. Record of fixed asset additions, retirements, and depreciation
2. Chronological record of certain payments to third parties (individuals) for commissions, fees, interest, etc.
3. Raw materials, goods in process, etc., used in the production process (yearly summary of inventory movement)
4. Payrolls and personnel records
5. Chart of accounts with notes of basis adopted for valuing assets.

5

All the books and documents must be kept for a period of at least ten years.

COLLEGIO SINDACALE (THE BOARD OF AUDITORS)

The Civil Code provides that corporations must have a board of auditors to control the management, audit the accounts, check compliance with the provisions of the Code and, in general, safeguard the interests of the stockholders. The board is composed of three or five auditors and two alternates (called sindaci), who need not be shareholders, are elected for a period of three years, and may be re-elected. Corporations with a capital stock of fifty million lire or more must select at least one of the auditors from the official list of auditors (ruolo dei revisori ufficiali dei conti—see discussion later in this section); if the board is composed of five auditors, not less than two of them must be selected from the official list and, in either case, one of the alternates must be so selected. The chairman of the board of auditors must be chosen from those selected from the official list. Relatives of the directors by blood or marriage within the fourth degree, and persons connected with the corporation or its subsidiaries by a continuous relationship involving remunerated work (employee status), may not be appointed auditors.

The board of auditors must meet at least once every quarter and make obligatory examinations of cash and securities. The examinations performed by the auditors must be recorded in the minute book of the meetings and resolutions of the board of auditors.

Auditors must attend meetings of the board of directors and shareholders and are jointly liable with the directors for the latters' acts and omissions whenever injury would not have occurred if the auditors had exercised due vigilance.

A typical report of the board of auditors may read as follows:

> The balance sheet and income statement at . . . . which the Board of Directors presents to you, closes with a profit of Lire. . . . . . and appears to us, following a close examination, prepared on the basis of the accounting results and in accordance with legal provisions, by which the criteria for the valuation of the assets have been observed.

6

In view of the fact that the accounting, the records, the cash and the securities, on the basis of our periodic examination, have been found to be kept correctly, we conclude, recommending for your approval, the balance sheet, the income statement and the proposal of the Board of Directors to distribute the profit.

We thank you for the faith with which you have honored us.

The duties of the statutory auditor are prescribed by the Civil Code, but no auditing methods are suggested or recommended. In addition, the chairman of the board of auditors must sign the income tax returns filed by the company (which includes the official financial statements).

As indicated above, one (or in some cases, two) member of the board of auditors must be a person whose name appears on the Official List of Auditors, and all of them may be capable of giving good commercial, legal, or tax advice to management. Nevertheless, they do not claim to, nor are they expected to make an examination of the financial statements such as would be required of an independent chartered or certified public accountant in order to give an expert and informed opinion upon the fairness of presentation of such financial statements.

Foreign accounting firms sometimes allow their members to accept appointments as sindaci, where the concerned corporations are audited by such accounting firms in accordance with generally accepted standards in the United States or Great Britain.

THE ACCOUNTING PROFESSION

The accounting profession in Italy is not organized in a form similar to the profession in the United States or the United Kingdom; its development has been mainly governed by the regulations of the Ministry of Justice, which has established the purposes, duties, and fees to be charged, and the rules pertaining to the conduct of the profession. The provisions of the Civil Code concerning the functions and composition of the board of auditors of corporations have also contributed to the development of the accounting profession.

There are two categories of professional accountants in Italy: the Dottore Commercialista (Doctor of Commerce) and the Ragionieri e Perito Commerciale (Accountant and Commercial Expert). The activities of each body are governed by two separate laws both passed by the Italian Parliament on October 27, 1953. There are differences in the educational and professional backgrounds of each, and the law specifies the activities each may undertake, but, in practice, little distinction is made.

Upon fulfilling the prescribed conditions, both categories of accountants may be registered in the respective official lists (albi professionali), described later.

There are very few large local accounting firms in Italy; most of the work is done by individual practitioners, who, for the most part, do bookkeeping work, act as tax advisors, prepare official financial statements of companies, and do detailed auditing work limited to certain accounts. They are sometimes organized in corporate form.

Dottore Commercialista (Doctor of Commerce)

This is a designation which may be obtained by admission to membership in the Ordine dei Dottori Commercialisti (Order of Doctors of Commerce). Membership in the Order is available to graduates of a four-year university course leading to the degree of Dottore in Scienze Economiche e Commerciale (Doctor of Economic and Commercial Science). In general, the course covers economics, accounting, banking, and public, civic, and commercial law. The university graduate must present a doctoral thesis on a subject which must be accepted by the Ministry of Education, and he must pass an oral examination by a Board of Professors appointed by the state. To become a member of the Order, he must also pass a special state examination, which may be taken immediately after completing his university studies. There is no requirement for practical experience.

Most persons studying for the Dottore degree are graduates of the Ragioniere (accountant) schools and thus also possess the ragioniere's diploma (see below).

Ordine dei Dottori Commercialisti. The Order has a national society which is divided into local societies to which qualified university graduates may be admitted upon passing the necessary state examinations. A member must be an Italian citizen or a citizen of a foreign country granting reciprocal arrangements. Foreign degrees or diplomas may be recognized as the equivalent of Italian diplomas.

The Order comprises two categories: (1) those in public practice, who may also register in the "official list," and (2) those who are not in public practice. It is organized in every district with at least fifteen dottori commercialisti and is governed by a local and national council.

A member of the Ordine dei Dottore Commercialisti is empowered to deal with:

1. Administration and liquidation of business concerns, of personal estates, and of specific assets
2. Appraisals and surveys and technical advice
3. Administrative inspections and audits
4. Verification of and all other enquiries concerning the reliability of financial statements, of accounting entries, and of all accounting documents of business concerns
5. Settlement and liquidation of damages
6. Statutory audits of trading companies
7. Tax advice and representing clients before tax authorities.

Ragioniere e Perito Commerciale (Accountant and Commercial Expert)

To obtain the above diploma, the student must have completed five years of elementary school and three years of junior high school, and have graduated from a five-year business high school (which includes courses in accounting, mathematics, business law, etc., but not auditing), and have passed a government controlled examination. This diploma in itself does not entitle the holder to membership in the Collegio dei Ragionieri nor to be inscribed on the "official list" of auditors. (See following.)

Collegio dei Ragionieri e Periti Commerciali (College of Accountants and Commercial Appraisers). The Collegio is organized in a manner similar to that of the Ordine dei Dottori Commercialisti, with local collegi having their local councils which elect the National Council (Consiglio Nazionale).

The qualifications for membership in the Collegio dei Ragionieri are:

1. Italian citizenship
2. Diploma as a ragioniere
3. Two years practical experience in the office of a member of the Collegio dei Ragionieri, or of a member of the Ordine dei Dottore Commercialisti in public practice
4. Successful completion of a state controlled written and oral examination concerning the provisions and procedures contained in the Civil Code, and on tax and accounting problems.

The principal activities of the Collegio dei Ragionieri are:

9

1. The administration of the admission of new members including the verification of prerequisites and conducting the examinations
2. The enforcement of laws limiting the professional activities of members and reporting infringements by nonmembers of activities reserved only for members
3. Acting as lobbyists for the profession
4. Ruling on members' fees disputed by clients; if approval of the Collegio is granted, it is possible to obtain rapid collection by special legal process. Most of the fees are set by law which either provides fixed rates or gives minimums and maximums.

It is the responsibility of the Collegio dei Ragionieri to see that new members meet the requirements prescribed by law.

A member of the Ragionieri e Periti Commerciali body is empowered to undertake:

1. Administration and liquidation of business concerns, of personal estates, and of specific assets
2. Appraisals, surveys and technical advice
3. Auditing of books of account of business concerns and all enquiries concerning financial statements, accounts, accounting entries, and accounting documents of business concerns
4. Settlement and liquidation of marine losses
5. Statutory audits of trading companies and other bodies
6. Distribution of personal estates, preparation of the relative projects and plans of liquidation in judicial cases
7. Preparation of systems of account for private and public concerns, reorganization of accounting systems
8. Calculation of production costs for industrial enterprises and preparation of data on accounting and administrative matters
9. Tax advice and representing clients before tax authorities.

It is evident that there is little distinction between the defined activities of the dottore and the ragioniere. In practice, so far as is known, no distinction is made.

Ethics

While no official code of ethics has been issued, it is generally held that neither the dottore nor the ragioniere may carry on an industrial or commercial business, nor serve as directors of a company where they also act as auditors, or divulge the affairs of the client.

Ruolo dei Revisori Ufficiali dei Conti (Official Register of Auditors)

Membership in either the Ordine dei Dottori Commercialisti or the Ordine dei Ragionieri e Periti Commerciali does not automatically provide registration in the appropriate professional official lists (albi professionali), but such registration can be obtained by any person who is of Italian nationality and has been admitted to a local organization (collegio) of the Ragioniere e Periti Commerciali body or a local organization (ordine) of the Dottori Commercialisti body.

As previously stated, at least one active member of the board of auditors of a company whose capital is less than Lire 50,000,000 must be a person so registered. In the case of companies with a capital of Lire 50,000,000 or more, at least one of the active members (two, if there are five active members) must be selected from the official list of auditors (ruolo dei revisori ufficiali dei conti).

Persons seeking registration on this list are required:

1. To be of Italian nationality
2. To have served for at least five years as an active statutory auditor or as a director, administrative or accounting officer (dirigente) of a limited company having a capital stock of not less than Lire 50,000,000, or to have satisfactorily performed other similar duties.

The above term of five years is reduced either to three years in the case of persons previously included for at least five years in the roll of the Dottori Commercialisti or to four years in the case of persons previously included for at least six years in the roll of Ragionieri e Periti Commerciali. In case the persons are not members of the roll of dottori or of ragionieri, the above period of five years is increased to ten years.

It will be noted that the official list contains persons who are not required to have professional experience in the examination of and reporting upon financial statements in the sense understood in the United States and the United Kingdom.

Società Fiduciarie e di Revisione (Fiduciary and Auditing Companies)

This type of organization is common in Switzerland, and there are several subsidiaries of Swiss companies in Italy. It is defined by law as being any enterprise which (1) administers property of third parties, (2) performs audits of businesses or management services, and (3) represents shareholders and bondholders. The enterprise cannot serve as a member of the board of auditors of a corporation, act as a trustee in bankruptcy, or serve in any capacity which is created as the result of a personal appointment with personal responsibility. The società fiduciarie e di revisione may take the form of a corporation or a partnership. They are under the surveillance of the Ministry of Industry and Commerce with whom they must file annual financial statements. One-half of the capital must be invested in government securities, or securities guaranteed by the state, up to a maximum amount of Lire 500,000.

The international auditing firms with offices in Italy are regulated by the laws pertaining to società fiduciarie e di revisione.

AUDITING STANDARDS

Since audits by independent public accountants are not customary with Italian business firms, and the accounting profession has not been organized as an institute or other self-regulating body usually present in most countries, there is very little that may be said with reference to standards of auditing. International accounting firms practicing in Italy use, in general, the standards of their countries of origin.

Independence

The only reference to the independence concept is found in the Civil Code which mentions the circumstances precluding the appointment of persons to the board of auditors. There is no prohibition against holding a financial interest in the enterprise subject to the auditor's examination.

Standards of Field Work

The Italian practitioner does not generally perform any of the following auditing procedures:

1. Review of internal control

2. Obtain direct confirmation from banks. (It is not a common practice of banks to return paid checks.)
3. Confirm receivables and payables
4. Observe physical inventories
5. Make detailed test of transactions
6. Review subsequent events.

Standards of Reporting

Since most of the audit services performed by the Italian practitioner are in connection with his appointment as a member of the board of auditors, the accounting profession has not developed a typical form of audit report other than the report of the statutory auditors previously referred to.

As has been explained before, the prescribed content and accounting basis of financial statements in Italy are those listed in the Civil Code and those enforced in tax regulations, and there is no significance attached to their consistent application. The standards of disclosure are limited to those applicable under the same circumstances.

ACCOUNTING PRINCIPLES AND PRACTICES

The accounting profession in Italy has not issued any recommendations regarding accounting principles. The Civil Code, however, prescribes the contents of the balance sheet and the principles of valuation of assets and liabilities. In addition, rules of valuation and disclosure are frequently enforced through tax regulations.

Form and Content of Financial Statements

Statement Presentation

Balance Sheet. The balance sheet follows the traditional form of assets on the left side and liabilities on the right side. The Civil Code prescribes that items shall be classified under the following heads:

Assets:

Stock subscriptions owing by shareholders

Land and buildings

Machinery and equipment

Furniture and fixtures

Patents and copyrights

Trademarks and goodwill

Inventories of raw materials and merchandise

Cash on hand

Cash at banks

Fixed revenue securities

Investments

Treasury stock

Accounts receivable—customers

Accounts receivable from affiliated companies

Other receivables

Memorandum accounts (per contra)

Note—Although not mentioned in the above classification, prepaid and deferred expenses are usually shown separately, with an apappropriate description. The Civil Code recognizes the principle of apportioning certain charges over more than one year.

Liabilities:

Capital stock

Statutory (legal) reserve

Other reserves

Reserve for amortization and depreciation of fixed assets

Reserve for severance indemnities

Liabilities for which collateral security given

Trade accounts payable

Amounts owing to bankers and other lenders

Amounts owing to affiliated companies

Bonds issued

Other liabilities

Memorandum accounts (per contra)

The offsetting of accounts in the balance sheet is not permitted. Notes to financial statements, such as those disclosing contingent liabilities, material lease commitments, and material subsequent events are rarely, if ever, appended.

In the subsequent paragraphs, the bases of valuation prescribed in the Civil Code for certain assets is given. If special reasons make it necessary to depart from such prescribed bases, the directors and the board of auditors are required to state them, justifying each individual case when reporting to shareholders on the accounts.

Consolidated Financial Statements. Consolidated financial statements are not generally prepared. Investments in affiliates are shown at or below cost, and it is not customary to indicate a comparison of underlying net assets nor to compare parent company income from dividends of affiliates with related net income of such affiliates.

Pooling of Interests

The method of accounting for certain types of mergers or consolidations of companies on the basis of pooling of interests is not often followed in Italy.

Accounts Receivable

Although the Civil Code calls for stating accounts receivable at net realizable values, tax legislation does not allow provisions for bad debts. Specific accounts must be proved to be uncollectible.

Inventories

Inventories must be valued at cost or market, whichever is lower (however, the basis of valuation is not generally disclosed in the balance sheet.) An ultra-conservative view of market value is not uncommon.

Securities

Securities must be appraised, taking into account their current market values; investments in affiliates must not be valued in excess of their underlying book values.

Fixed Assets

Basis of Valuation. Fixed assets must not be stated at more than cost. Reserves must be shown on the liabilities side.

Financing Costs. Financing costs during initial construction of a plant are generally capitalized; after commencement of operations, further costs of such nature are generally charged to expense but are frequently disallowed for income tax purposes.

Capitalization of Certain Expenditures. Extraordinary repairs and maintenance are capitalized and amortized over a period of years, the annual amortizations being tax deductible.

Restatement of Fixed Assets and Related Reserves. In past years, up to 1953, several laws were enacted permitting the restatement of fixed assets to partially compensate for the decline in purchasing power of the lira.

In 1952, a restatement in terms of post-World War II monetary values was authorized for plant, equipment, related reserves, investments, etc., and, in certain circumstances, inventories.

At the same time, stockholders' equity accounts were required to be revalued, but not restated on the books, by applying coefficients to each year's increase. Any excess of asset revaluations over the increase in stockholder's equity revaluation was taxable under certain circumstances. As a result, most companies limited the amount of asset revaluations to the amount which was nontaxable.

The restatement law called for a segregation of the restatement reserves as to: (1) an amount equal to the restatement of capital stock and the statutory reserve, and (2) the difference, if any.

Goodwill and Other Intangibles

Goodwill may be recorded only when purchased and must be written off within a reasonable number of years, based on the prudent judgment of the directors and with the approval of the board of auditors.

Intangibles must be stated at cost as reduced by appropriate amounts of annual amortization.

Bond Discount and Other Deferred Charges

Bond discount must be written off in accordance with the corresponding amortization schedules.

Preliminary expenses deferred must be written off in a period not exceeding five years.

Treasury Stock

Treasury stock must be shown separately.

Statutory Reserve

Corporations are required to segregate into a special reserve at least 5 per cent of their annual net profits until the reserve has reached 20 per cent of the capital issued. This reserve may be used to absorb losses, but must thereafter be restored to the minimum required.

Secret Reserves

Both Italian jurisprudence and tax laws make frequent reference to secret reserves, which historically have been more or less condoned. However, in 1954, special authority was given to disclose these reserves on the books without incurring tax liability, unless the reserves were utilized by transfer to capital or distributed. Many companies have taken advantage of this.

Taxed Reserves

Sometimes this caption is used to reflect the counterpart of items disallowed by tax authorities and then capitalized in the books.

Surplus

Financial statements consist of a balance sheet and a profit-and-loss statement; the surplus statement is practically never presented.

The Statement of Income

The Civil Code does not prescribe any specific form or content for the income statement, which is usually presented in account form; that is, income on the credit side and expenses on the debit side. A typical income statement is generally quite condensed and usually starts with the gross profit, although there is a trend among larger companies toward furnishing more information.

Cost and Inventory Accounting. Many corporations accumulate costs and expenses in production accounts, and only at the end of the year is the closing inventory recorded. Practice varies considerably regarding overhead allocation to the ending inventories. Standard cost techniques are gaining wider acceptance.

Costing of Raw Material Issues. Italian fiscal law requires that issues of raw materials and supplies be charged to production on a last-in, first-out basis.

Depreciation. The provision for depreciation in any year is generally based on the normal maximum rates allowed by the tax authorities. It is usually provided at the maximum rates, however, only in years when a profit is shown. Losses on disposition of fixed assets are deductible for income tax purposes.

In addition to normal depreciation, Italian tax law recognizes provisions for accelerated depreciation up to 15 per cent per annum, but not aggregating more than 40 per cent of cost in the first four years from the date of acquisition of depreciable plant and equipment.

Income Tax Expense. The larger companies provide for income tax liability on the accrual basis. In some cases, such provision represents a general appropriation unrelated to the taxable income of the current year; or it may represent a charge to income for taxes paid on a cash basis, to which may be added a provision for final or estimated official assessments received during the year for current or prior years' income taxes.

Bonuses to Directors. When the by-laws of a corporation stipulate that a percentage of profits is distributable to directors, the amount so distributed is generally charged to earned surplus.

REQUIREMENTS FOR PUBLIC SALE
OF SECURITIES—PROSPECTUS

The Civil Code prescribes that a corporation may be financed through public subscription on the basis of a prospectus describing its purposes, capital, status of subscribed shares, principal provisions of the certificate of incorporation, and promoters' share in profits, etc. The prospectus carrying the signatures of the promoters must be deposited with a public notary prior to its release and distribution, after the requirements of the Civil Code have been complied with.

The promoters are entitled to reserve 10 per cent of the annual net profits of the corporation on their own behalf for a period not exceeding five years.

There are no specific regulations concerning data which must be furnished for a prospective investor.

REQUIREMENTS FOR LISTING
ON THE STOCK EXCHANGES

Stock exchanges in Italy are managed by the local Chamber of Commerce and are subject to the supervision of the Treasury Department.

The requirements for the first registration are mainly that the provisions of the Civil Code have been fulfilled, that operations for the two preceding years have been profitable, and that evidence be presented that the shareholders have approved the financial statements of those two years; there should be no dividend or interest payments in arrears. A company must have a minimum capital of Lire 1,000,000,000 in order to have its securities listed on the Milan exchange. Foreign companies must publish their balance sheets for the two preceding years in the *Official Gazette*.

When an additional issue is being listed, the only requirement is that the Treasury Department authorize the issue when the capital is in excess of Lire 500,000,000.

SWEDEN 16

FORMS OF BUSINESS ORGANIZATION

The forms of business organization in Sweden are the limited liability company, the partnership, the sole proprietorship, and the cooperative. The latter is of special importance in Sweden, although similar organizations are, of course, not uncommon in other countries.

Aktiebolag (The Limited Liability Corporation)

This is a corporate entity corresponding to the usual form in other countries. The legislation applicable to the Aktiebolag is contained in the Stock Companies Act of 1944, which was effective January 1, 1948.

A minimum of three legally competent Swedish citizens, or entities resident in Sweden, may form a corporation. After incorporation, the number of shareholders may be reduced to one.

The name of the company as specified in the by-laws must contain the word "Aktiebolag" and is commonly abbreviated "AB."

The minimum capital is SK 5000, represented by shares of (usually) not less than SK 50, and, except in special instances, the shares must be registered. The liability of the shareholder is limited to the par value of shares subscribed. All shares must be paid up within two years of incorporation.

At the constituent meeting called by the incorporators, a Board of Directors is elected consisting of one or more members. If the maximum authorized capital exceeds SK 500,000, at least three directors must be elected and a managing director, who need not be a member of the board, appointed. The corporation is considered formed when the meeting has adopted the by-laws and voted its formation.

The shareholders must appoint one or more auditors to examine and report upon the balance sheet and profit and loss statement. The auditors are also required to report upon the administration of the company. If the maximum authorized capital exceeds SK 500,000, at least two auditors must be appointed, and if such capital is SK 2 million or more at least one of the statutory auditors must be Swedish Authorized Public Accountant (A.P.A.). With the permission of the Royal Board of Trade (Kammerskollegium), a foreign citizen may act as the second auditor. The qualifications and duties of the A.P.A. are discussed in a later section.

Even in respect of minor corporations, an A.P.A. or an approved examiner of accounts (see later discussion), must be appointed at the request of shareholders holding at least one-tenth of the share capital.

The Stock Corporation Act requires that the Board of Directors and the managing director submit a report which includes financial statements (balance sheet at year end and profit and loss for that year) and the management's report on administration to the annual meeting of shareholders. The auditors must report upon these documents, which, after approval by the shareholders, are filed with the Royal Swedish Patent and Registration Office in Stockholm where they may be inspected by anyone. The managing director of a parent corporation must also present to the board and to the auditors (but not to the shareholders) a consolidated balance sheet and/or a statement on group affairs.

Subsidiary or Branch of a Foreign Corporation

Prior to 1956, a foreign enterprise wishing to carry on business in Sweden was generally limited to doing so only through a Swedish subsidiary. Under the Law of 1955, effective January 1, 1956, a foreign corporation may establish a branch in Sweden by obtaining permission from the Swedish government, which is granted provided the applicant company is operating in the country of its origin. There are certain activities which are not permitted, such as the manufacture of war materials, domestic air transportation, or shipping in Swedish vessels. In general, the laws applicable to Swedish companies are equally applicable to branches of foreign corporations doing business in Sweden. The branch must appoint a Swedish authorized public accountant as auditor.

Other Forms of Business Organization

Ekonomisk Förening (Cooperatives). This legal form of organization is reserved for cooperative enterprises—both agricultural and consumer cooperatives are important in the Swedish economy and have between two and three million members. They are required to furnish their members with annual financial statments and usually furnish them to the public on request.

4

The Cooperative Societies Act of 1951, states that auditors must be appointed to examine and report upon the annual financial statements. The auditor must have such experience of bookkeeping and knowledge of economic conditions as his appointment requires, but he need not be an authorized public accountant or an approved examiner of accounts. It is customary for the larger cooperative societies to appoint an authorized public accountant.

Partnerships. The partnership form is not as common in Sweden as in other countries because the capital requirements for the corporate form are minimal and corporations are easily and inexpensively organized.

There are three forms of partnership—the simple partnership (Enkeltbolag), the regular partnership (Handelsbolag) and the joint-stock partnership (Kommanditbolag). The simple partnership need not be registered in the commercial register, but the name under which the Handelsbolag carries on business must be registered. All partners have unlimited liability toward third persons.

The joint-stock partnership has both active and silent partners. Active partners are jointly and severally liable for partnership debts but silent partners are liable only to the extent of their capital.

Business Records

The Bookkeeping Act (1929) prescribes that certain bound books be kept—specifically, the journal in which day-to-day transactions, or to a certain extent summaries of such transactions, are recorded and the inventory book in which the assets and liabilities are recorded at the end of the year. Limited liability companies are required to maintain a share register. Generally, there must be kept such additional records as are necessary, depending on the size and nature of the operations.

THE ACCOUNTING PROFESSION

For many years, articles of association of limited companies in Sweden have made provision for audits of the accounts. The Companies Act of 1895, prescribed that the board's administration and the company's accounts be examined by one or more auditors. These auditors were often persons with business experience, but seldom were skilled in accounting matters. During the early twentieth century, however, the beginnings of an accounting profession occurred. In 1909, the Stockholm School of Economics offered a university education which comprised business administration (accounting and finance), economics and business law. The profession was established by action of the Stockholm Chamber of Commerce in 1912, when it adopted its first statutes for authorization of public accountants. In Sweden, the chambers of commerce (of which there are twelve—one in each of the Swedish districts) are private organizations, authorized by the Crown. Their duty is to look after the interests of economic life, and, among other things, they report on draft bills after their consideration by the appropriate legislative committee of the Riksdag.

Auktoriserad Revisor (Authorized Public Accountant)

Each of the twelve chambers of commerce is empowered to issue the authorization to practice the profession of public accounting. The Authorized Public Accountant will possess such knowledge and experience as will enable him to undertake audits and examine accounts and economic administration, even when the questions connected therewith are of a complicated, unusual or far-reaching nature.

The chamber of commerce may admit as an A.P.A. any Swedish man or woman who:

1. Is age twenty-five, and preferably not over fifty-five.
2. Is not under any restriction as to his or her person or property.
3. Has received an economics degree (Bachelor of Commerce Degree) at a Swedish school of economics with the special provision that the examination for that degree included economics, business administration and law (with special emphasis on accounting, auditing and business law), and that certain qualified grades had been obtained in business administration and law.
4. Has proved his or her aptitude for the profession by work in practice, i.e., duly certified service with an authorized public accountant for not less than five years.

It is possible to obtain authorization without the degree mentioned in 3 above, by passing a special examination in the same subjects given by professors of a Swedish school of economics; in practice, this route is seldom used.

Having complied with the above requirements and having been authorized as a public accountant, the applicant makes the following declaration to the chamber:

6

I, ..., hereby promise on my faith and honor, as a public accountant authorized by the .... Chamber of Commerce, to carry out audits entrusted to me with honesty and zeal, carefully and to the best of my ability, implicity to observe the secrecy incumbent upon an accountant, and otherwise in every particular to comply with the regulations laid down in respect of my office.

After this declaration has been filed, the chamber issues the accountant's certificate.

In Sweden, while there are no special professional examinations required, all authorized accountants have passed rigorous university examinations. There was no "grandfather clause" admitting practicing accountants without the qualifications specified at the time the chambers established the procedures.

To coordinate the processing of applications received by the twelve chambers of commerce, there has been established the Central Accountants' Board of the Chambers of Commerce, which passes on all applications for authorized public accountant and recommends to the chambers whether the application should be approved.

It is stipulated that the authorized public accountant may not carry on any business as a merchant or agent, nor may he be an active partner in a business enterprise of any kind. He may not hold a salaried public or private office. He may, of course, be a partner or employee of another A.P.A. The chamber of commerce may grant exceptions from this rule, but permission is usually granted only for teaching activities. If an A.P.A. should accept a salaried position in industry, his authorization would be revoked. In Sweden, therefore, a person entitled to use the designation, authorized public accountant, is always an independent professional accountant.

The statutes of the chambers of commerce provide that an A.P.A. may not undertake the audit of a business enterprise of which he is an officer, or is in a subordinate, or dependent position in relation to persons in the administration, or control of the enterprise, or if he has more than a negligible financial interest in the enterprise, or if there are any other special circumstances likely to shake confidence in his impartiality in the performance of his duties.

As in other countries, A.P.A.s may practice as individuals, with one or more assistants (who may be A.P.A.s or approved examiners), or in partnership with several other A.P.A.s. Also, a number of Swedish auditing firms are organized as limited companies, of which the shareholders and board members must all be A.P.A.s. Regardless of the form chosen, a partnership or corporation may not be appointed as auditor of a limited liability company—the appointment is always of an individual A.P.A.

Foreningen Auktoriserade Revisorer
(The Authorized Public Accountants Association)

This Association was founded in 1923, and the present "Statutes" were adopted in 1945. Membership is composed of those who:

Possess a Swedish chamber of commerce authorization as a public accountant

Have practiced as such satisfactorily for at least one year immediately prior to application for membership and continue to practice thereafter

Have a reputation for integrity and are considered suitable for membership.

Of the total (363) authorized public accountants, 274 are members of the Association (January 1964).

The objectives of the Association are to maintain a high-principled and professionally skilled corps of A.P.A.s, to promote sound principles and rational methods of auditing, accounting and business administration, to safeguard the professional interests of its members, and to foster a spirit of solidarity and mutual understanding among its members.

Ethics

The Association has included in its statutes a number of statements bearing on the ethical conduct of its members, which essentially cover the matters spelled out in the Code of Ethics of the American Institute of Certified Public Accountants. They are (condensed):

A member shall carry out conscientiously and to the best of his ability the tasks entrusted to him with honesty, diligence and care.

A member may not reveal information obtained in the course of his professional work, or make use of it to his own or another's advantage.

A member may not, in addition to his accountancy work, carry on any other business that may adversely affect his independence, or is otherwise incompatible with his position as an A.P.A.

A member must not undertake to report upon a business firm in which he has direct or indirect interest—such interest includes holding one or more shares or participating rights in the firm; he must not place himself in circumstances that may disqualify him by law to act as a judge.

8

Advertising is limited to brief announcements in newspapers or periodicals not exceeding twelve in any one year.

There are other unwritten but generally observed rules of conduct. An A.P.A. who is asked to replace another person as auditor of a company should confer with his predecessor prior to accepting the engagement as to whether there may be any reason why he should decline the appointment. It is considered a breach of professional etiquette to approach a prospective client with offers of unreasonably low fees or promises of better service than is offered by other colleagues. A member of the Association may not offer employment to an employee of a colleague without first having conferred with the latter. He may not undertake an audit of a business enterprise where he or his firm has performed bookkeeping work.

Disciplinary Procedure

The statutes state that a member who in the course of his work deliberately commits a wrong or who otherwise acts dishonestly, or who in some other way disregards the duties incumbent upon him as a member, may be given a warning, a caution or may be expelled from membership in the Association, depending on the seriousness of the offense and whether there are mitigating circumstances. The resolution of the Council may be appealed to the Board of the Association.

Penalties Imposed Under the Companies Act

The Companies Act provides penalties (in the form of fines or imprisonment) upon the authorized public accountant if, in an audit report or in the financial statements, he intentionally or through gross negligence gives incorrect, incomplete or misleading information, or fails to criticize management although there is reason, therefor. He may be fined if he disregards the regulations concerning the contents of the audit report or the certificate on the financial statements.

Functions of the Authorized Public Accountant

The A.P.A., when appointed as one of the official auditors of a limited liability company, examines its annual financial statements as submitted by the management to the annual meeting of shareholders, and reports upon his examination of such financial statements. The Companies Act specifies certain duties of the independent auditor: To examine the books and all other accountings, to read minutes of board and stockholder meetings, to conduct or inspect inventories of cash and other assets, to examine the company's system of internal control, to examine the annual financial statements and the annual business report.

Although not legally compelled to do so, many smaller Swedish companies appoint an A.P.A. as one of their auditors.

One of the duties of the auditor in Sweden (whether or not he is an A.P.A.) is to examine and report upon the administration of the company's affairs. This is, of course, an unusual function of the independent auditor from the point of view of most other countries. The purpose presumably is to bring to the notice of stockholders any administrative measures that might affect the shareholders' decision whether or not to grant to the board its annual discharge from responsibility.

The authorized public accountant in Sweden also carries out valuations, investigations, organizational commissions, and assignments as arbitrators; occasionally he may act as administrator of property, administrator of estates and trustee in bankruptcy.

The Swedish auditor incurs heavy responsibility for preparation of income tax returns if taxable income has been understated. Therefore, accountants usually prepare income tax returns only when they have a very detailed knowledge of the data on which the return is based, which they may have when they are also auditors for the concern. They do, however, consult with their clients on tax matters and assist in investigation of tax cases.

Godkanda Granskningsman (Approved Examiner of Accounts)

This classification of accountants is also recognized by the chambers of commerce. The approved examiner of accounts is expected to possess "such knowledge and experience as will enable him to examine accounts and consider simple administrative questions connected with such examination."

In addition to the qualifications as to age and good character required of the A.P.A., the approved examiner must possess good knowledge of bookkeeping, and the laws governing annual reports and taxation, and have displayed an aptitude for accountancy work. The necessary knowledge may be evidenced by an examination certificate issued by a school of commerce or a junior college of commerce, or by the nature of the practical work in which he or she has been engaged. Such practical work will comprise at least five years in a responsible position with a large business enterprise, or as a clerk to an authorized public accountant. He is required to file a declaration with the chamber of commerce identical to that filed by the authorized public accountant. There are now about 650 approved examiners in Sweden.

The approved examiner may be appointed auditor of a limited company, except where the Companies Act requires the appointment of an A.P.A., or he may act as an assistant to an A.P.A. He is permitted to carry on auditing work in addition to other employment, and usually does so.

Svenska Revisorsamfundet (The Swedish Accountants Association)

This Association includes the approved examiners as well as other accountants in Sweden, including a few A.P.A.s.

The qualifications for membership in this Association are the same as those given above for the approved examiner of accounts. The applicant is required to make the following declaration to the Association:

> I, ..., hereby promise on my faith and honor, as a member of the Swedish Accountants Association, to carry out audits entrusted to me with honesty and zeal, carefully and to the best of my ability, implicitly to observe the secrecy encumbered upon an accountant, and otherwise in any particular to comply with the regulations laid down in respect of my office.

AUDITING STANDARDS

Any Swedish citizen may practice accounting in Sweden, and with the exception of larger companies, as previously described, the auditors of limited companies need not be qualified accountants. The profession of independent public accounting as practiced by the authorized public accountants does have standards enunciated both in the statutes of the chambers of commerce and of the A.P.A. Association, although these are not "codified" in any one statement.

General Standards

The requirements for admission as an A.P.A. assure adequate training and proficiency of the auditor, and the necessity for an independent attitude is stressed in the aforementioned statutes. The Association has stated that honesty, diligence, and due care are requisite in the performance of the auditor's work.

Standards of Field Work

Emphasis is laid on the review of internal control. The Board of Directors has primary responsibility for the existence of a satisfactory system, but the auditors must review it to determine whether it is functioning properly and, if not, to so report to the management.

In larger companies, a detailed audit of all transactions is done by internal auditors, but in smaller ones the elected auditor may perform it. Many A.P.A.s now consider that, based upon a comprehensive review of internal control and upon a review of the work of the internal auditors, the work of the A.P.A. may consist of tests of the transactions during the year combined with examination of year-end balances. In smaller companies where internal control is weak and there are no internal auditors, some auditors consider it necessary to make a detailed audit of transactions for the year.

There is no specific provision for confirming accounts receivable with the debtors, though it is common practice to do so. As previously noted, the Companies Act specifies that the auditor should "conduct or inspect inventories of cash and other assets." Observation of physical inventory-taking is not obligatory, but it is often carried out.

Standards of Reporting

There are two aspects of the auditors' report in Sweden: first, the auditor must sign the balance sheet and profit and loss statement for identification; and, second, he must present a separate audit report. The signature on the financial statements may be accompanied by a simple statement, saying, "Reference being hereby made to the audit report, it is certified that this balance sheet is in accordance with the books."

As to the separate audit report, there is no established or fixed form of wording. The Companies Act, however, does specify the matters to be covered by such report. The more important of these are (condensed):

> The results of the auditor's examination, specifically whether the auditor has any reservations regarding the company's financial statements, its bookkeeping, the safeguarding of its assets, or the administration of the company's affairs, and if there are such reservations, the reasons for them

> Whether the auditor recommends approval of the balance sheet; whether he recommends that the managing director and the board be discharged from responsibility for the administration for the cur-

rent year, and whether he concurs in the management's proposals for the distribution of profit and loss for the year, including the due appropriations to legal reserves

Whether there has been a writeup of fixed assets (as permitted under certain provisions of the Companies Act), or whether current assets are recorded above cost

Whether there has also been an examination of certain legally defined pension funds.

If the company reported upon is a parent company, certain other statements must be made in the auditor's report: (1) whether the legal rules concerning consolidated statements and preparation of a special statement on ownership of subsidiary company shares, intercompany accounts, property pledged by a subsidiary, etc., have been observed, and (2) If a dividend is proposed, whether it is considered to be in conflict with sound business practice considering the financial position of the group and the results of its activities as a whole.

An example of the auditor's report upon a large Swedish Company follows:

Statutory Audit Report upon the accounts of ABC Company at December 31, 19___.

In our capacity as auditors to the ABC Company we hereby submit the following report for the year 19. . .

We have examined the Annual Report, studied the accounts, the minutes and other documents containing information as to the financial position and the management of the corporation, and made such other inquiries as we considered necessary.

The detailed checking of the records has been carried out by the Corporation's internal audit department who have reported to us on their examination.

The provisions of the Companies Act concerning shareholdings and group reporting have been complied with.

In the course of the audit there appeared no reason for remarks to be made upon the Annual Report, the bookkeeping or the verification of assets, or upon the management.

The Board of Directors and the Managing Director propose that the profits according to the balance sheet be appropriated as follows:

Transfer to General Reserve . . . . .Kr.
Dividend to Shareholders of Kr. per Share . . . . ”
Carried Forward . . . . ”

Kronor _____

This proposal does not conflict with the provisions of the Corpora-ration Act concerning appropriations to legal reserves or with sound business practice.

We recommend:
that the balance sheet as at 31st December 19.., included in the Annual Report and signed by us, be adopted, that the profits be ap-propriated as proposed above, and that the Board of Directors and the Managing Director be granted discharge from liability for their management for the period covered by the annual report.

Stockholm,

_____   _____
Authorized Public Accountant   Authorized Public Accountant

Since there has been no authoritative statement in Sweden of codified auditing standards or of accounting principles, no specific reference to these concepts appears in the reports of Swedish auditors. The matter of consistency is referred to in the section following.

REPORT OF THE BOARD OF DIRECTORS AND MANAGING DIRECTOR

This report on administration, in Swedish practice, is required for all limited companies, regardless of size and number of stockholders; it is submitted to the auditors for review and report; it is presented at the annual meeting and filed with the registration authority, where it is open to public inspection. It is considered a part of the financial state-ments and is the vehicle for much of the disclosure of the company's affairs. Some of the matters which are required by the Companies Act to be disclosed in this report are:

The assessed values of real estate for tax purposes, and the fire in-surance coverage of real estate, machinery and plant.

The average number of workers and the average number of other employees.

The total amount of salaries and wages for the period covered by the financial statements, showing separately (1) manual workers, (2) board and management personnel, and (3) all other.

Reasons for, and amount of any writeup of fixed assets, and utilization of resulting reserve.

A proposal by management for the distribution of profit to the legal reserves.

When the reporting is that of a parent company, the group's total distributable profits must be included.

If any current asset is carried at an amount higher than cost, but which can be justified as in accordance with generally accepted accounting principles and sound business practice, the fact must be stated and reasons therefor given.

Certain changes in accounting practices as compared with the previous year must be disclosed:

Any change in classification of assets as to current or fixed

Any change of major importance in principles of computing depreciation

Undervaluation of inventories is considered in conformity with sound business practice, but if changes in the amount of such reserves has a material effect on net income, the direction and magnitude must be disclosed. (In recent years there has been a tendency among leading corporations to give full information about secret reserves in inventories.)

There are certain other items which may be included in the report of the management, if it can be done "without detriment to the corporation." They are:

Net sales

Other matters of importance such as changes in the activities of the corporation by opening new branches or new sales markets, and substantial property or subsidiary acquisitions.

Post-balance sheet events of importance.

ACCOUNTING PRINCIPLES AND PRACTICES

The Swedish Authorized Public Accountants Association has issued various recommendations relating to accounting principles and practices, but as they do not have legislative or other backing, they have not had the influence or general acceptance that are found in like pronouncements of similar organizations in some other countries. The general principle guiding accounting practices, which is mentioned both in the National Bookkeeping Law and the Companies Act, is that they must be exercised "in accordance with generally accepted accounting principles and sound business practice." As to valuation of assets this is often applied in practice as the "principle of lowest value."

The Swedish tax law has significant influence on accounting practices because taxable income is determined from the actual book entries of the taxpayer with certain exceptions where special rules on depreciation are followed.

The two laws in Sweden which have the greatest influence on accounting matters are the Bookkeeping Law (Bokforingslagen, 1929) and the Companies Act (effective January 1, 1948). The former applies generally to the keeping of business records, bookkeeping procedures, and kind of information to be shown in such records. The latter deals with valuations, certain accounting practices, and prescribes standard statement classifications.

The Swedish Association of Metalworking Industries has issued a Standard Chart of Accounts, which, while directed to this industry, has had wide influence on accounting in general, with special reference to cost accounting.

Finally, it is considered "sound business practice" in Sweden to level out income from year to year, and this practice is recognized as proper by the income tax law by allowing the taxpayer (1) to undervalue inventories, (2) to over or underprovide for depreciation, within certain limits, at company discretion, and (3) to make discretionary allocations to investment fund reserves up to 40 per cent of net profit before taxes.

Form and Content of Financial Statements

The Companies Act prescribes in some detail the items to be shown on the financial statements. In general, the order is similar to that of public utility companies in the United States—on the assets side of the balance sheet, fixed assets first (plant and equipment, patents, goodwill, long-term investments), followed by current assets. On the liability side, capital first, followed by legal and general reserves, special reserves, depreciation reserves, long-term debt, current liabilities, and, finally, unappropriated profits. The Association of A.P.A.s has recommended the order more commonly used in the U.S.A., that is: current items first, descending to fixed assets and capital on the respective sides. A number of published balance sheets of the larger companies in Sweden follow the latter form.

Consolidated Financial Statements. The managing director presents to the board and to the auditors a consolidated balance sheet or a "group" statement. There is no legal requirement for these statements to be presented at the annual meeting of the parent company, but the management's report must state the result of the group's operations in order that such meeting may take this factor into consideration.

The rules of consolidation stated in the Companies Act are similar to those customary in the U.S.A.—intercompany accounts and intercompany profits in inventories are eliminated and the investments in and dividends received from unconsolidated subsidiaries are disclosed in comparison to the underlying net assets and earnings for the year. Goodwill arising in consolidation is usually deducted from surplus at acquisition or from free reserves; negative goodwill is treated as an undistributable reserve.

When the statements presented are those of a parent company, and unless the information is given in the balance sheet, the managing director must also present to the shareholders a special statement of group affairs, which contains:

Each subsidiary's holdings of shares in other affiliates

Total amount of parent company's payables to and receivables from each of its subsidiaries

Each subsidiary's payables to and receivables from other subsidiaries

Contingent liabilities assumed by a subsidiary on behalf of the parent or another subsidiary

The book amount of property pledged by a subsidiary as security for indebtedness of the parent or another subsidiary

If a detailed statement of the parent company's investment in shares of subsidiaries is not shown on the balance sheet, it must be given here by indicating the name of the subsidiaries, the number of shares held, and the book value of the shares.

Unless special permission is granted, the latest balance sheet of each subsidiary must be appended to the balance sheet of the parent company.

Notes to Financial Statements. The use of "Notes to Financial Statements" is not highly developed. This is due to the fact that information required to be given (see below), as well as other types of disclosure, is more often included in the report of the management. The following is required to be disclosed and sometimes is shown on or in a note to the balance sheet:

The balance-sheet value of pledged assets with separate amounts for:

Mortgages on real estate

Chattel mortgages

Mortgages on ships, and

Mortgages on other movable property

The total amount of contingent liabilities resulting from accommodation endorsements, guarantees, etc., and (separately) the amount of discounted notes

Pension obligations (see under "Pension Costs").

Pooling of Interests

The accounting concept of "pooling of interests" as applied to mergers and consolidations of corporations is not recognized in Sweden.

Current Assets

General. The general rule for valuation of current assets (including marketable securities and inventories) is that they be stated at no more than the lower of cost or market, but "good business practice" may permit a lower valuation.

Accounts Receivable. Accounts receivable are required to be stated at the amount deemed collectible and worthless accounts must be written off.

Portions of accounts deemed uncollectible may be written off, either by reducing the recorded amount of the receivable or by establishing a reserve, which may be deducted from the asset or included on the liability side. An estimated provision such as a percentage of sales or recorded amount of receivables is not permitted by tax law, except in the case of installment sale receivables. It is not common practice to show separately either the amount by which receivables have been reduced, or the "value correction" reserve.

Claims against members of the board, the managing director, or the auditors, must be shown separately if they exceed either SK 10,000 or 2 per cent of the corporation's net worth as shown by its balance sheet. Receivables from and liabilities to subsidiaries must be shown separately.

Inventories. The Companies Act prescribes the lower of first-in-first-out cost or market basis for valuation of inventories.

The income tax law, which requires that the tax-computed inventory be recorded on the books, provides for three methods of inventory valuation:

1. The initial inventory computation, after deducting obsolete or unsalable items, may be reduced by as much as 60 per cent.
2. The 60 per cent rule may be applied to the average inventory of the two preceding years. If the inventories have declined markedly in the recent years, it is possible that the inventory reduction applied to the closing inventory could produce a negative closing inventory. If so, it would be shown on the credit side of the balance sheet.
3. The third method deals solely with inventories of raw materials or staple commodities. The management has the option of the lowest market price of the current period or the lowest price of any of the nine preceding periods. This latter lowest price can then be further reduced by 30 per cent. If this method is selected, it precludes the use of Method 2. But Method 1, however, can still be used for the other part of the inventory.

It should be stated that not all companies use any of these methods, and even those that do, do not always write the inventory down to the lowest amount allowed. It will be seen that there is a wide range of choice for inventory valuations for a Swedish company. There is also no uniformity in the balance-sheet classification of the resulting inventory reductions. In some cases, they are deducted from the inventory and, in a few others, are shown on the liability side among the reserves. If such reserve is restored in a subsequent year, the amount so restored is subject to income tax.

Fixed Assets

Fixed assets may not be shown at more than cost (but see below as to "enduring value"). If "true value" is found to be materially lower than cost less accumulated depreciation, a special depreciation allowance must be provided unless an increase in the depreciation rate can be considered sufficient, according to generally accepted accounting principles and sound business practice.

Fixed assets considered to have an *enduring value* substantially in excess of the amount at which they were shown in the last preceding balance sheet may be written up to not more than such *enduring value* if the amount by which they are increased is used for (1) necessary writing down of other fixed assets or (2) an increase of capital by the issue of bonus shares. Real estate may not be written up to an amount exceeding the latest assessed value for tax purposes.

Unless fixed assets are stated at cost, the report of the management (which is considered a part of the financial statements) must disclose whether there has been a writeup of fixed assets, the amount thereof, and the disposition, if any, of the resulting increase.

Goodwill, Patents, Trademarks, etc.

The purchase cost of acquiring from a third party such intangibles as trademarks, trade names or similar items must be written off for both book and tax purposes generally over a ten-year period. Patents are amortizable over their remaining life.

Prepaid and Deferred Charges

It is not required that these items be shown separately on the balance sheet; they may be grouped with "other current claims."

Corporate organization expenses are not tax deductible and may not be capitalized. Research expenses and expenses of advertising and selling in connection with introducing a new product may be capitalized and written off over five years or longer "if justified by generally accepted bookkeeping practices and sound business practice."

Bond Discount and Premiums

Discounts on outstanding debt may be amortized over the life of the related issue or they may be charged off directly to expense. Premiums are usually shown as a liability and amortized over the life of the related issue.

Reserves

Depreciation Reserve. The Companies Act classification shows the accumulated depreciation on the liability side of the balance sheet. On the other hand, the Association recommends that depreciation be shown separately as a deduction from the related assets. However, many companies show the net book amount on the asset side.

Investment Fund Reserve. Business corporations are permitted by the government to set aside, at their own discretion, up to 40 per cent of their pretax net business income as an investment reserve for economic stabilization. The amount so set aside is deductible for both national and local taxes and up to 46 per cent of the total reserve must be deposited in the Swedish National Bank, without interest. In general, it may be used, when so authorized by the Labor Market Board, for construction of buildings, acquisition of new machinery and equipment, the purchase of inventory and development of mineral deposits. The total cost of the asset so acquired is then reduced by the amount of the investment fund set aside for the purpose; only the net balance of the asset is subject to depreciation.

There is no ceiling on the total amount or in the number of years during which the investment reserve may be set aside. There are a number of special provisions in the tax law relating to the usage of the reserve in certain circumstances.

Statutory Reserve. The Swedish Companies Act requires that companies set aside annually 10 per cent of net income to provide a legal reserve until such reserve equals 20 per cent of the outstanding capital at par. This can be used only to cover losses which cannot be met in any other way.

If total liabilities (as defined in the Act) exceed the sum of legal reserve and the capital stock, the company must provide a "supplementary legal reserve," the computation of which is specified in the Act. There is also a restriction on the payment of dividends from current earnings when circumstances require provision of a supplementary reserve. The Act provides for dissolution of the supplementary reserve when the net worth exceeds legal liabilities, and specifies to what extent and the manner in which the reduction in such reserve may be treated.

Premium on Capital Stock

If capital stock is sold at a premium, such premium must be added to the legal reserve.

Treasury Stock. The Companies Act prohibits the purchase of a corporation's own shares either by itself or by a subsidiary, unless the stockholders authorize and approve a reduction of outstanding capital stock.

Statement of Earned Surplus

The Swedish financial statements do not include a statement of surplus due to the fact that they are prepared before the annual meeting has approved the dividend and distributions to reserves. The balance sheet shows the surplus at the beginning of the year, the dividends and distributions approved during the current year from that balance, and the amount available for the current year distributions as follows:

Profit on balance sheet December 31, 1961		SK 500,000
Deduct, approved at 1962 annual meeting:		
Appropriated to legal reserve	SK 50,000	
Dividend to shareholders	150,000	200,000
Unappropriated earnings from previous year		300,000
Profit for the year 1962		600,000
	Total	SK 900,000

A further statement may be added to indicate the proposed distributions for the current year:

At the disposal of the 1963 annual meeting		SK 900,000
Disposal proposed by the board:		
Appropriated to legal reserve	SK 60,000	
Dividend to shareholders	200,000	
To be carried forward	640,000	SK 900,000

Statement of Income

The Companies Act states the items to be included in the profit and loss account, with the proviso that whenever it may be considered necessary according to generally accepted accounting principles and sound business practice a further breakdown will be given. The specific items listed are:

Income:

Income from the company's business operations, segregated between any independent operations which may be carried on, unless such segregation is found to be detrimental to the corporation

Dividends received, showing separately dividends received from subsidiaries

Interest income, showing separately interest received from subsidiaries

Profits on sales of fixed assets, unless under the circumstances a different accounting is permitted by generally accepted accounting principles and sound business practice

Other income, not resulting from business operations.

Gratuitous or other extraordinary receipts.

Expenses:

Loss from business operations, or from operations which must be reported separately (see income, above)

Interest expense, showing separately interest paid to subsidiaries.

Income taxes

Depreciation of fixed assets, or appropriations to a value correction account for fixed assets, classified in accordance with the fixed asset accounts on the balance sheet

Losses on sales of fixed assets, unless under the circumstances a different accounting is permitted by generally accepted accounting principles and sound business practice

General administrative expenses

Extraordinary expenses and losses

Net profit (loss) for the year.

Sales and Cost of Sales. It will be noted that the amount of sales is not required to be reported in the profit and loss statement; however, if not considered detrimental to the corporation, the sales figure must be included in the report of the management. Similarly, cost of sales is not required, although management must include in its report the total amount of wages and other remuneration, apportioned as to workers, the board, the managing director, and others in managerial positions, as well as other employees of the company. The profit and loss statement, therefore usually begins with the "gross profit" figure, which is often arrived at after deducting selling expenses.

Pension Costs. All persons gainfully employed receive pensions, the cost of which is borne by the employers. Up to a certain level the pensions are handled by the state, but in the case of white-collar employees, amounts above this level are usually insured or covered by a pension fund arrangement entered into by a very large number of companies in industry and commerce. Actuarial computations for uninsured pensions, have to be made each year. The annual cost of pensions for which no provision has been made must be shown.

Tax-effect Accounting. Since book accounting is usually nearly identical with tax accounting in Sweden, the question of allocation of income taxes (deferred or "latent" taxes) seldom arises.

Depreciation. As a general rule, depreciation must be computed on cost, not on replacement or appraised value, and "book depreciation" of machinery and equipment must be recorded on the books if claimed for income tax purpose.

Depreciation on buildings is limited to an amount based on the estimated useful life and, for tax purposes, normally ranges from 2 per cent to 4 per cent per annum.

Depreciation on machinery and equipment, however, is guided by quite liberal rules. There are two permissible methods: "book depreciation" and "planned depreciation." The rules permit changing from one method to the other in certain circumstances.

The book depreciation method provides only ceilings or maximums. The taxpayer may take less than the maximum allowable in any year, and thus postpone deductions to a later year. Most large companies use the book depreciation method. The maximum deduction in any one year is established by either of two alternatives, which may be elected by management. These are (1) the 30 per cent declining-balance rule and (2) the 20 per cent straight-line rule. It is not required to follow the same alternative in each successive year. Under the declining-balance method, over half (51 per cent) of the cost of machinery can be written off in two years; under the straight-line method the entire cost is written off over five years.

Under the planned-depreciation method, the depreciation deducted on the tax return need not coincide with that charged on the books. Essentially, it represents a straight-line method based on estimated useful lives of the various classes of assets. It is useful when a company is reporting losses or small profits, because any planned depreciation in any year which is in excess of that amount required to reduce the taxable profit to zero can be carried forward indefinitely, until a net taxable profit is shown.

Depreciation on buildings may be computed either on cost or on "assessment value." The assessment value is used when cost is unknown, or, as in the case of old buildings, when cost is considerably lower than "assessment value."

There is no requirement for disclosure of the method of computing depreciation, but if a change in the method is of major importance, it must be commented upon in the management's report.

General and Administrative Expense. There has been no authoritative statement of expenses to be included in this classification, and there is quite a wide variety of practice in this area. However, a corporation is expected to be consistent in its treatment of this expense from year to year.

Stock Dividends. Stock dividends are usually issued in large amounts and accounted for at their par value by the issuer. The recipient as a rule would not adjust the cost of his investment.

REQUIREMENTS FOR SALE OF SECURITIES TO PUBLIC AND FOR LISTING OF SECURITIES ON THE STOCK EXCHANGE

Sale of a limited liability company's securities to the public is ordinarily handled through a commercial bank, which determines information to be furnished to a prospective purchaser. There are no governmental regulations which prescribe requirements for the data to be furnished. Any financial data included in the data furnished prospective purchasers is submitted by the Board of Directors.

Applications for the listing of shares on the Stock Exchange are made in writing to the Council of the Stock Exchange by a member of the Stock Exchange or by the management of the company whose shares are to be listed, and the details are usually handled by a Swedish bank. Shares of companies whose share capital is less than SK 5,000,000 kronor may not be registered; neither may bonds or debentures if the nominal amount of the loan to be listed is less than SK 5,000,000.

In addition to the usual data as to the shares to be listed, it is required that the company's annual report and the auditor's report be submitted for the last five accounting years, although in special cases the Council may permit listing when the annual report and the auditor's report cover only one year. It is not required that applications for listing of bonds and deferred or other debentures be accompanied by such reports, unless the company does not have its shares listed; in the latter case, the company's annual reports and auditors' reports for the last two accounting years must be submitted.

The general provisions regarding the auditors and their reports, previously discussed, are applicable; since the capital of a company wishing to list its shares must be at least SK 5,000,000, one of the statutory auditors must be an authorized public accountant.

As previously stated, all annual reports of Swedish companies are available for inspection by the public in the Royal Swedish Patent and Registration Office.

SWITZERLAND | **17**

FORMS OF BUSINESS ORGANIZATION

The principal forms of business organization in Switzerland are the stock corporation "Aktiengesellschaft" and the limited liability company "Gesellschaft mit beschränkter Haftung." Business may also be carried out as a registered branch of a foreign corporation. In addition, a company may operate as a partnership limited by shares "Kommanditaktiengesellschaft," cooperative society "Genossenschaft," limited partnership "Kommanditgesellschaft," general partnership "Kollektivgesellschaft," and as a single proprietorship "Einzelfirma."

Aktiengesellschaft (A.G.)

The most popular form of business organization is the stock corporation which most closely resembles a United States corporation. The Swiss stock corporation must be formed by at least three incorporators, who may be corporate bodies. The articles of incorporation are drawn up according to the Federal requirements and in the language of the canton (state) in which the corporation is domiciled. (There are twenty-five cantons and each one has a "Register of Commerce" which is open for inspection by the public. Some cantons maintain more than one register, separately for each district. The important entries in the "Register of Commerce" are published in the official *Swiss Commercial Gazette*.) The contents of the articles are in general terms similar to those of other countries. A resolution of the incorporation meeting which would contain the articles of incorporation must be authenticated by a notary and recorded in the Register of Commerce. Resolutions to change or amend the articles of incorporation must be approved by the shareholders in a general meeting, and also be authenticated by a notary and recorded in the Register of Commerce. Upon registration the corporation is free to commence operations officially. With the exception

3

of banks, finance and insurance companies, annual financial statements of corporations need not be published or recorded in the Register of Commerce.

Swiss law does not provide for "authorized and unissued" stock. All of the stock of a Swiss corporation must be fully subscribed at the time of formation. One-fifth of the par value or at least 20,000 Swiss Francs of the capital must be paid in prior to the incorporation meeting and the balance is payable on call. A stock corporation must have a minimum capital of S.Fr. 50,000 divided into shares with a par value of at least S.Fr. 100. No-par shares are prohibited, shares may not be issued at a discount and no class of stock may be denied voting rights. Each share is entitled to one vote. However, since shares of differing value may be issued, each vote may not represent the same amount of capital contribution. Stock may be registered or issued to bearer. If the latter, shares must be fully paid before they may be issued. Preferred shares may also be issued giving preference in profit distributions, pre-emptive rights and special rights in the event of liquidation. Swiss corporations may restrict ownership of their shares, e.g., to Swiss residents or entities.

The stock corporation is managed by its Board of Directors (Verwaltungsrat) or by a single director. Directors must hold qualifying shares and are elected by the shareholders. The first members of the board are named at the incorporation meeting and serve for up to three years. Thereafter directors are elected for periods up to six years. A majority of the directors must be citizens and residents of Switzerland. If there is a single director, he must be a citizen and resident of Switzerland. If this requirement is not met the corporation may be required to cease operations. The board may delegate to board members (Delegierte) or nonboard members (Direktoren) the power to act in the name of the company.

The shareholders finally approve the amount recommended by the directors to be distributed as a dividend as well as the directors' profit participation.

Gesellschaft mit beschränkter Haftung (G.m.b.H.)

The Swiss limited liability company constitutes a legal entity and the liability of its members is limited to their subscribed capital. In the event of bankruptcy the members become liable directly to the creditors for any unpaid share subscriptions. Management of this type of company follows the rules of partnership. The name of a limited liability company must contain the abbreviation (G.m.b.H. or in French—S.à.r.l.). The capital must be at least S.Fr. 20,000, but not more than S.Fr. 2 million

4

and is divided into fixed shares of S.Fr. 1,000 each. As in the case of the stock corporation, all of the shares must be subscribed.

The names of members and the shares in Swiss Francs held by each must be entered in a special company register and reported to the Cantonal Register of Companies each year. Depending on the articles of formation, the limited liability company may or may not appoint an auditor. The annual financial statements need not be published, except when the company engages in banking, financial or insurance activities. Unless otherwise provided for in the articles of incorporation, profits and losses are distributed on the basis of the amounts paid in on subscriptions for capital shares.

Branch of a Foreign Corporation

In order to operate as a branch of a foreign corporation in Switzerland, it is usually necessary to register with the Registry of Commerce in the canton in which the branch will be domiciled. Registration consists of furnishing information regarding the foreign corporation, such as the names of members of the Board of Directors, state of incorporation, copy of its articles of incorporation, trade name, and name, place of birth and address of Swiss branch manager. This person must live in Switzerland but need not be a Swiss national. The branch must maintain its own accounting records.

Other Forms of Business Organization

Kommanditaktiengesellschaft. In the partnership limited by shares, one or more of the members are jointly and severally liable to the creditors for an unlimited amount while the liability of the limited partners is limited to the amount of their capital contribution. Those members with unlimited liability form the Board of Directors of the company.

Genossenschaft. The Swiss cooperative corresponds to cooperatives in the United States, except that it cannot have a fixed capital. Its liability is generally limited to its changing capital.

Kommanditgesellschaft. This corresponds to the United States limited partnership. It has both general partners who have unlimited liability and limited partners whose liability is limited to the amount of capital

5

which they have agreed to contribute. Only individuals may be general partners, while corporations or other partnerships may be limited partners. Registration is required for this type of partnership. Limited partners have nothing to do with the management of the partnership but do have a right to obtain the annual accounts and to examine, or have examined, its books and records.

Kollektivgesellschaft. This corresponds to the United States general partnership in which all partners are jointly and severally liable for partnership debts. Only individuals may be members of this type of partnership which must be registered with the Registry of Commerce.

Einzelfirma. A single proprietorship must be registered with the Register of Commerce unless its annual gross turnover is less than S.Fr. 50,000. A trade name must be used if the proprietorship is registered and also books and records must be kept.

Business Records

Those business organizations which are subject to registration must keep proper books. The books required vary according to the character and extent of the business but must reveal the financial position of the firm through inclusion of all debits and credits connected with the business, and must show the results of operations on an annual basis.

These books as well as all related documents and correspondence must be made available as legal evidence if necessary.

It is not required that firm's books be officially stamped. Books may be kept in any currency but the annual financial statements must be expressed in Swiss currency.

STATUTORY AUDITOR

The Swiss Code of Obligations (referred to hereafter as the Code or OR) requires that one or more statutory auditors (Kontrollstelle) be elected by the shareholders. The power and duties of the statutory auditor are discussed in more detail later.

THE ACCOUNTING PROFESSION

There are two official organizations of accountants in Switzerland. These are the "Vereinigung Eidgenössischer Diplomierter Buchhalter" (Union of Federally Certified Bookkeepers) and the "Schweizerische Kammer für Revisionswesen" (Swiss Chamber of Auditing).

The certified bookkeepers are normally employed by private companies as chief bookkeepers or company accountants. Normally they are not concerned with auditing and have had no specific audit training. Accordingly, the following discussion is limited to a description of the "Schweizerische Kammer für Revisionswesen," the organization of professional accountants.

The accounting profession (with reference in particular to auditing) is not as formally controlled in Switzerland as in the United States. Anyone can act as an auditor, whether or not he has any professional qualifications, except in the relatively few instances, discussed later, when the law requires an independent accountant (unabhängiger büchersachverständiger) be appointed as auditor. However, the practice of appointing qualified members of the accountants' professional organization to perform audits is increasing.

Schweizerische Kammer für Revisionswesen

The Schweizerische Kammer für Revisionswesen (Swiss Chamber of Auditing) is the principal body of control of the accounting profession in Switzerland. The Chamber was formed in 1925, and is composed of three basic groups:

1. Verband Schweizerischer Bücherexperten (VSB)
   (The Society of Swiss Certified Accountants)
2. The Union of Accounting and Auditing Firms
3. The group of Audit Associations for Banks and Savings Banks.

The purpose of the Chamber is, on the one hand, to examine candidates for the title of certified accountant (see below) and, on the other hand, to further the interests of the profession, and to protect its reputation, honor, and independence.

Ethics. The Chamber has issued rules of professional conduct, which include the following to which the members agree:

7

1. To practice their profession independently and in accordance with the law and in particular to engage in no activity which could influence their impartiality toward their client
2. To accept no assignments which are in conflict with the responsibilities of the profession
3. To accept no gifts or other benefits which could affect an objective judgment
4. Not to disclose professional secrets
5. To advertise only in a discreet and professional manner
6. Not to compete for clients in an unethical manner.

A violator of these rules is brought before a professional court of honor which may issue reprimands, impose fines and possibly order expulsion from membership in the Chamber.

Eidgenössische Diplomierte Bücherexperten

The title of "Diplomierter Bücherexperte" is gained by passing a professional examination which is prepared and given every two years by the Schweizerische Kammer für Revisionswesen under the control of the Ministry of Economics. The candidate must have three years experience in accounting with two of these in auditing before taking the preliminary examination. Then after successfully completing the preliminary examination and obtaining three additional years of experience the candidate is eligible to take the final examination. Prior to taking this examination he must solve a practice-set type problem at home. This problem consists of the preparation of a long-form report which requires a knowledge of statistics, mathematics and business organization as well as auditing. A judgment as to the economic position of the firm must also be written. The examination itself covers in part these same problem areas and in addition economics, law and taxation.

The names of candidates who successfully complete the final examination are entered in the official register. They may join the "Verband Schweizerischer Bücherexperten" (Society of Swiss Certified Accountants) and are entitled to use the initials V.S.B. after their names. The Society was established in 1913, and has about 550 members. It has also issued rules of professional conduct which are similar to those of the Kammer, given above.

In Switzerland only the title "Diplomierter Bücherexperte" is protected and not the practice of the profession.

Sociétés Fiduciaries (Accounting and Auditing Firms)

The Swiss national firms of accountants are almost all organized as corporations and, in addition, offer services of a fiduciary as well as a professional accounting nature. A firm of accountants may be organized in any form recognized by law. To become a member of the Union of Accounting and Auditing Firms a firm must be organized as a legal entity with a capital of at least S.Fr. 100,000. The services which members of these fiduciary societies, as well as members of the V.S.B. may offer, include the following:

Statutory auditors

Auditing the accounts of banks if a member of the panel authorized to perform bank audits

Preparing and filing tax returns

Tax consultants

Executors and trustees

Management consultants

Business organization analysts—drawing up articles of incorporation

Fiscal experts

Legal advisers to business

Court-appointed bankruptcy or fraud experts

Industrial analysts

Directors (where an individual is not actually the statutory auditor)

Formal management of companies and foundations

Bookkeeping and accounting.

LEGAL REQUIREMENTS FOR EXAMINATION OF FINANCIAL STATEMENTS

Stock corporations and cooperative societies must by law have their financial statements examined as described below. Other types of business organizations may appoint statutory auditors if this requirement is set forth in the articles of organization.

The following details relate to the stock corporation since it is the most important form of business organization. There are three basic types of examination: (a) The examination by the statutory auditor (Swiss Code of Obligations "OR" 728 et seq.), (b) the examination by independent professional auditors (OR 723), and (c) the examination in the event of a reduction in capital (OR 732).

The Examination by the Statutory Auditor (OR 728 et seq.)

The statutory auditor may not be a member of the Board of Directors or an employee of the company being audited. Accounting or fiduciary firms may act as statutory auditors. They are initially elected for one year and subsequently may be elected for terms of not more than three years. In voting for the statutory auditor, multiple voting rights may not be used.

The statutory auditor named in the articles of formation must file a written consent at the Registry of Commerce. The statutory auditor does not need to have any professional qualifications or meet any legal requirements; he is not considered an independent contractor as might be the case in the United States under similar circumstances, but he does have an essential role in the corporation as the control authority. The power and duties of the statutory auditor are discussed below.

Financial statements must be examined by the statutory auditor before they are submitted to the annual general meeting of the shareholders. The requirement of examination given by law to the statutory auditor is described (OR 728) in the following words (as translated):

> The auditors determine whether the balance sheet and profit and loss statement agree with the books, whether the books are properly kept and whether the information as to the operating results and the financial position of the company complies with the requirements of the law as to valuation and with any special provisions of the articles of the corporation.

The Board of Directors must make the books and supporting documents available to the auditors and, if requested, furnish explanations about the inventory and its valuation principles or any other matters pertinent to the examination.

The statutory auditor has the right to attend the general meeting, and he must submit a short-form report to the general meeting of stockholders wherein the results of the audit examination must be stated. OR 729 requires that this report recommend either the acceptance of the balance sheet, with or without qualifications, or the rejection of the balance sheet by having it referred back to the directors. The auditors also advise on the directors' proposal regarding the distribution of the profits. The report of the statutory auditor is important because the general meeting cannot pass any resolution concerning the balance sheet unless this report has been submitted to it.

The auditor's report need not be accompanied by the financial statements but it is common practice that this be done.

Any irregularity of management or violation of provisions laid down by the law or by the articles discovered by the auditor in the course of his examination is to be brought to the attention of the officer superior to the person responsible for the delinquency and to the chairman of the board, and in serious cases even to the general meeting. The auditor may be held responsible for any loss or damage resulting from an improper discharge of his duties.

Despite the responsibility given to the auditor and the heavy demands placed upon him by law, anyone can be appointed as statutory auditor because the law, as already mentioned, has not laid down any rules concerning the qualification of the person so appointed. Very often professional accountants with or without certificates, or fiduciary societies, are appointed as statutory auditors.

The Examination by Independent Professional Auditors (OR 723)

The lawmakers were aware of the insufficient qualifications of many persons permitted to be selected as statutory auditors and, therefore, in the public interest and in the interest of creditors wrote into law stricter audit requirements for stock companies over a certain size. In accordance with OR 723, the directors of a corporation are required to have their company's balance sheet examined by independent professional accountants if their company has a share capital of five million francs or more; or has unredeemed bonds payable; or invites the public to entrust money to them.

The law does not make clear what type of examination is required of such independent professional accountants, but one may assume that the principles of examination mentioned in OR 728 are also applicable in this case and that this examination will be expected to be carried out in a professional manner, as would be expected from qualified professional persons.

The report of these experts is to be submitted to the Board of Directors and the company's statutory auditors (OR 723). This report will usually be given in a long-form presentation and will include detailed information on each major account and usually also an outline of the audit procedures followed.

The law speaks of independent professional accountants. In contrast to the statutory auditor, specialized knowledge and professional experience is required; however, this accountant does not have to be certified. Of course certified accountants, fiduciary societies, or other organizations which meet the professional and independency requirements can be named.

The Examination in the Event of a Reduction in Capital (OR 732)

When stock capital is reduced without being concurrently offset by new fully paid-in capital, the interests of the firm's creditors may be endangered. The law therefore requires that the general meeting of stockholders may not decide upon a reduction in the firm's capital unless an audit report is presented which states that the demands of the creditors will be fully covered by the assets even after the capital is reduced.

This audit report must be prepared by a fiduciary society or an auditors' association accredited by the Swiss Federal Council for this purpose.

Bank Audits

The federal law on commercial and savings banks of November 8, 1934, requires a careful examination of banks consistent with their special position in the economy. The examination must be made each year and include a report. Only the audit associations and thirteen fiduciary societies have been given the right to perform these examinations. It is considered preferable that the auditors in charge of these examinations, who are appointed by the associations or societies, be certified.

AUDITING STANDARDS

General Standards

The Schweizerische Kammer für Revisionswesen has not yet promulgated any compilation of generally accepted auditing standards. Recently, however, the Kammer named a committee to prepare a compilation of auditing standards applicable to Swiss conditions.

Although the statutory auditor may not be a director or an employee of the company being audited, he may be a shareholder or have some other financial interest in such company. Only in the case of banks is the statutory auditor required to maintain independence.

Article 730 of the Code (OR 730) states that auditors and bookkeeping experts are prohibited from communicating to individual shareholders or to third parties any information obtained in carrying out their duties.

Standards of Field Work

There is no statute which defines auditing procedures in Switzerland, nor are there any other standards promulgated similar to those of the American Institute of C.P.A.'s, Bulletin No. 33. The following differences in auditing procedures exist in Switzerland:

1. The auditor will not request direct confirmation of bank balances, accounts receivable and accounts payable and will not observe the taking of physical inventories unless specifically asked to do these audit steps. The Swiss auditor satisfies himself as to the correctness of the bank balances, the validity of accounts receivable balances, and the completeness and correct evaluation of the inventory by tests of available company records.

2. The accounting system and the system of internal control are only studied to the extent necessary to write the audit program and to determine the amount of testing required.

3. The auditor will rely on verbal confirmations of management that the financial statements include all those assets and liabilities which are known and ascertainable.

Standards of Reporting

The standards of reporting of the statutory auditor of Switzerland have been established by the Code (OR 729) which requires that the auditor certify that the financial statements truly reflect the company's financial condition as stated in the books, that the books have been properly kept and that the results of operations and the financial position of the company are shown in conformity with legal and statutory valuation principles.

The statutory auditor must recommend, further, either acceptance of the financial statements with or without reservations, or their rejection by having them returned to the Board of Directors.

He must also state whether or not the recommendations made by the Board of Directors as to the distribution of profits are in accordance with the requirements of law.

There is no standard form of audit report. An example of an unqualified auditor's report complying with OR 728/29 follows:

To the General Meeting of the shareholders of Company X:

As duly appointed statutory auditors of your company we have examined the Balance Sheet at December 31, 196.. and Profit and Loss account for the business year 196.. submitted to us and have found them to be in agreement with the company's books. As a result of our audit we confirm that the books have been properly kept and that the financial statements fairly present the company's financial position at December 31, 196.. and the results of its operation in conformity with the principles of evaluation prescribed by the law and the company's articles of association.

Based on our findings, we recommend that the financial statements be adopted without reservation and that the directors' proposal set out below for dealing with the available retained earnings be accepted:

Appropriation to legal reserve	0.000
Distribution of a dividend of 10 per cent	0.000
To be carried forward	0.000
	0.000

Zurich, (date)   Yours very truly,
                                                      ABC A.G.

The statutory auditor who is not a professional accountant will usually submit only this report, whereas a certified accountant acting as a statutory auditor will often supplement this short report with a long-form report. This will include a discussion of his audit findings and an analysis of the various important balance sheet and profit and loss accounts. This long-form report is given, however, only to the Board of Directors and not to the stockholders. Occasionally the long-form report will include a description of the audit procedures followed. No rule requires this. However, in the case of the report of the independent certified accountant acting under the provisions of OR 723, the audit procedures followed would ordinarily be described, since there are no generally accepted auditing standards to which reference can be made. Further, the report prepared under terms of OR 723 must not only be presented to the Board of Directors but also to the statutory auditor, when the latter is not also the certified public accountant.

Consistency. In the application of accounting principles, consistency is not expressly required by the Code or any other regulation. Nonetheless, the balance sheet is to be prepared in a complete, plain, and neatly arranged manner so that the principle of consistency is in this way partly followed. Consistency as a principle is in conflict with the accepted accounting practice in Switzerland relating to the right to increase or reduce secret reserves which gives a great flexibility in the valuation of some assets.

Materiality. Although the principle of materiality is never expressly stated, the auditor, whether a statutory auditor or an independent professional accountant (or acting in both capacities), must judge in the case of each discrepancy whether it is to be mentioned orally, written into long-form report, or even in important cases written into the statutory report.

DIRECTORS' REPORT (BUSINESS REPORT)

The directors must submit to the general meeting a written business report on the financial position of the firm, the operations of the company and the results of the year. This report should also include a proposal concerning the payment of dividends and the disposition made of the remaining profits.

The business report is not subject to examination by the statutory auditors.

ACCOUNTING PRINCIPLES AND PRACTICES

Form and Content of Financial Statements

The accounting rules and practices in Switzerland are based on the applicable articles of the Swiss Federal Code of Obligations. In addition, the Schweizerische Kammer für Revisionswesen and the professional accounting organizations actively promote the application of generally accepted accounting principles.

Statement Presentation

In Switzerland, the usual arrangement of the financial statements is for assets to be shown on the left side and liabilities and capital on the right side. There are no rules concerning in what order the various accounts are to be shown on the balance sheet. The only rule in the law says that "the statement of profit and loss and the balance sheet are to be complete, clear, neatly arranged and in accordance with recognized commercial principles." The order of the items on financial statements is usually in accordance with their liquidity. This would result in a balance sheet similar to the following:

Assets:

    Cash on hand and in banks
    Accounts receivable
    Raw materials
    Finished goods and work in process
    Furniture and fixtures
    Machinery and equipment
    Buildings
    Investments
    Prepaid expenses, etc.
    Patents

Liabilities:

    Accounts payable
    Accrued liabilities
    Medium and long-term liabilities
    Retained earnings
    Legal reserve
    Special reserves
    Share capital

However, the order of listing in which the assets side begins with fixed assets, and the liability side with share capital, is also seen frequently. It should also be noted that valuation allowances, such as for bad debts, depreciation, and the like, are often included under liabilities rather than deducted from the related asset.

Legal Rules of Valuation. The law prescribes principles of valuation in order to prevent an overvaluation of the assets. The highest permissible valuation of assets is given as follows:

Inventories:　　　　　　　　　　At unit cost or market value, whichever is lower

Fixed assets:
Furniture and fixtures
Machinery and equipment　　　　At cost less appropriate depreciation
Buildings
(the amount of insurance coverage for fixed assets must be set forth on the balance sheet)

Investments:
In quoted marketable securities　　At their average quoted value during the month preceding the date of the balance sheet

In nonquoted securities　　　　At cost plus accrued interest or dividends and less any reserve for decline in value

Consolidated Financial Statements. Consolidated financial statements are not required to be prepared in Switzerland.

Pooling of Interests

The "pooling of interests" concept has no accounting significance in Switzerland. Regardless of the type of merger, the assets of the merged company are recorded in the books of the merging company in accordance with tax regulations.

Inventories

Companies which maintain complete inventory records with sufficient details of quantities and prices and bases for such prices, may value inventories for tax purposes at a minimum value of up to one-third below cost or market, whichever is lower. For corporate purposes, there is no minimum.

Fixed Assets

When money is borrowed to finance the construction of new facilities, it is not customary to capitalize interest charges or loan discounts, although hydro-electric and some other companies do so.

Organization Expenses

Organization expenses are usually charged directly to profit and loss. However, certain organization costs as provided for in the company's by-laws or as authorized by the shareholders, and the stamp tax on shares issued, may be deferred and amortized over five years.

Liability for Income Tax

The income tax system in most of the Swiss cantons is one in which the taxes due and levied in a year are determined on the basis of the prior year's income. Therefore, the amount accrued for income taxes at the end of a fiscal year in Switzerland is that based on the income of the prior year. No accrual is made for taxes based on the income of the current year, since there is no legal liability for tax on that year's income at the current balance sheet date, although there is a liability in the economic sense.

A determination of this economic tax liability is complicated in Switzerland since the Confederation and many cantons compute taxes on the average income of a two-year period preceding a two-year assessment period, and also because tax payments are deductible for purposes of federal and certain cantonal income taxes.

Funded Debt

Bonds are shown at principal amount and must be set out separately. Bond discounts must be amortized to the due date.

Contingent Liabilities

Contingent liabilities arising from guaranteeing loans to third parties, purchase or sales commitments and other types of contingent liabilities should be set forth on the balance sheet or in a schedule attached thereto. Important subsequent events should also be disclosed in the body of the report rather than in footnotes, which are not used in Swiss reports. Disclosure of commitments under leases is not required.

Legal Reserve

Under Swiss law a company must create a legal reserve of 5 per cent of annual net profits to accumulate 20 per cent of paid-in capital. In addition to this, an amount equivalent to 10 per cent of those dividends exceeding 5 per cent of capital must also be credited to the reserve. Such reserve is also credited with net gain on reissue of defaulted share subscriptions, and with the difference between the selling price and nominal value of new shares issued. To the extent of 50 per cent of the capital, the legal reserve can only be used to cover losses or to maintain the company in times of deficit, to avoid unemployment or to mitigate its consequences.

Secret Reserves

The Code fixes an upper but not a lower limit for valuation of assets, and the basis for valuation is not shown on the balance sheet. Further, it is permitted that silent or secret reserves may be created "if this seems desirable for assuring the continued prosperity of the company." However, such reserves must be brought to the attention of the statutory auditor, but he is not allowed to disclose them in his report without the board's consent. The tax authorities accept for the most part provisions for and utilizations of secret reserves.

Statement of Profit and Loss

There is no uniform practice as to form of presentation of the profit and loss statement in Switzerland. Often sales and cost of sales are shown separately but sometimes only the gross profit on sales is shown.

Depreciation. Depreciation may be applied on cost less accumulated depreciation (declining-balance method). On this basis, normal depreciation rates would be:

office furniture and fixtures	20 per cent
industrial machinery	25 per cent
motor vehicles	30 per cent

Frequently, too, depreciation is based on cost, in which case the rates used would be half of the above rates. The tax authorities may permit considerably higher rates of depreciation.

Because of inflationary trends in the Swiss construction industry, the tax authorities may, in special cases, allow the depreciation of real property before it is placed in service. Otherwise depreciation commences when such property is placed in service.

Tax-effect Accounting. As indicated previously, there may be differences between amounts charged to income on the books and that permitted for income tax purposes, although tax depreciation may not exceed book depreciation. It is not usual to make corresponding allocation of income taxes to future periods.

Payments to Directors. The customary profit participations of the members of the Board of Directors are considered as appropriations of the annual net profits and are not deductible for tax purposes.

REQUIREMENTS FOR PUBLIC SALE OF SECURITIES

The company must issue a statement and publish a printed report on the financial position and operations. This report is placed at the disposal of shareholders at the bank which submits the application for listing.

The company must furnish the Exchange with twelve copies of its prospectus which must be published once in a daily paper and show:

1. Name, domicile and purpose of the company and the date of its inception

2. Total amount of capital, surplus and reserves; classes of stock outstanding and voting rights
3. List of directors and names of statutory auditors
4. Details of dividends paid during preceding five years
5. Details of bonded debt outstanding
6. Last balance sheet and profit and loss account
7. Details of the company's most important subsidiaries with a statement of their capital and bonded debt
8. Summary of company's operations in case more than six months have passed since the last general meeting of shareholders
9. Terms of issue
10. Purpose of issue.

The company must also submit twelve copies of its last published annual report, its articles of association, as well as a facsimile of the stock certificates in use.

Thereafter, the company has an obligation to submit annual reports to the Stock Exchange Association Committee and to notify the Committee of any changes in the articles of association.

REQUIREMENTS FOR LISTING OF SECURITIES ON STOCK EXCHANGES

The principal international stock exchanges are in Zurich, Basle, and Geneva, and there are exchanges of domestic importance in other cities of Switzerland. These exchanges are governed by the Local Association of Stock Exchange Members and supervised by the Federal Association of Stock Exchanges. In Switzerland there is a regulation concerning the listing of securities, which is administered by the "Association of Stock Exchanges." These regulations give all the requirements which must be met in order for a security to be admitted to the exchange. The most important of these requirements are:

1. The company must issue a statement and publish a printed report on its operations to be placed at the disposal of shareholders and bondholders at the bank which submitted the application for listing.

2. The company must furnish the Exchange with twelve copies of its prospectus, which must be published, and show:

    a. Details of dividends paid during the preceding five years.
    b. Details of the company's most important subsidiaries with a statement of their capital and bonded debt.
    c. Details of securities being listed.

3. The company must also submit twelve copies of its last published annual report, its articles of association, as well as a facsimile of the stock certificates in use.

4. Thereafter, the company has an obligation to submit annual reports to the Stock Exchange Association Committee and to notify the Committee of any changes in the articles of association.

5. In order for a company's securities to be admitted for trading, the total par value of the security must be at least S.Fr. 500,000 for a domestic issue and twice that much for a foreign issue. Where bonds are to be issued, the capital must be equal to the value of bonds to be issued if under S.Fr. 1 million—and if over that amount the capital must be at least S.Fr. 1 million. The company must have completed one year of operations, and the financial report for that year should be available. All interest and dividends are payable free of bank charges at the places where the securities are listed.

THE NETHERLANDS | 18

1

FORMS OF BUSINESS ORGANIZATION

As in the United States, there are three main forms of business organization in The Netherlands—the corporation, the partnership, and the sole proprietorship. The Commercial Code also provides a legal entity for "cooperatives," which function largely in agriculture, both as consumer and production organizations.

Foreign corporations wishing to establish a business in The Netherlands usually do so by organizing a Netherlands subsidiary. Application is made to the Nederlandsche Bank by a lawyer, auditor, or other interested party for a license to establish the business. If the purpose is to manufacture in The Netherlands, approval of the Ministry of Economic Affairs is also necessary. There is no legal difference between such a subsidiary and a Dutch company owned by citizens of The Netherlands.

Naamloze Vennootschap

The Limited Liability Company is established by notarial deed containing the articles of incorporation, which must be received by the Minister of Justice with no objections, recorded with The Chamber of Commerce in the district of domicile, and published in the *Official Gazette*.

The capital is furnished by at least two persons, and is represented by shares of par value (no-par shares are not recognized.) At least 20 per cent of the capital must be subscribed by the founders, of which at least 10 per cent is paid in. The corporation is a legal entity, and the liability of its shareholders is limited to the amounts subscribed to its capital. The name of the company shall begin or end with the words Naamloze Vennootschap or the letters "N.V."

The Netherlands Commercial Code provides that the shareholders of a corporation or the Board of Directors may appoint an expert to audit

3

the books and report to the stockholders on the company's balance sheet and the profit and loss statement with the explanatory comments that are submitted by the management. The Code states that the shareholders will not be bound by any list of candidates. There are no specific qualifications required of the "expert," unless provided for in the Articles of Incorporation. Usually appointment is made by the directors or by management.

There is no requirement for publication of financial statements except that the following must file their financial statements with the office of the Chamber of Commerce:

Companies whose shares or debentures are listed on certain stock exchanges

Companies authorized by their articles of incorporation to issue bearer shares to an aggregate amount exceeding 50,000 guilders

Companies having bearer bonds outstanding

Banking and insurance companies (life insurance companies are subject to special rules and have prescribed forms of financial statements.)

Partnerships

In addition to the usual form of general partnership (Venootschap onder Firma), there is a form of partnership (Commanditaire Vennootschap) in which the managing partners carry unlimited liability, and the limited (silent) partners, who may not take active part in the management of the partnership, have their liability limited to the amount of their participation. The capital contributed by the limited partners may be represented by shares, in which case the form is called "Commanditaire Vennootschap op Aandelen." Professional men such as auditors and lawyers practice in partnerships called "Maatschap."

Business Records

The Netherlands Commercial Code (Art. 6) merely provides that everyone carrying on a business must keep proper records so that his assets and liabilities may be ascertained at any time.

THE ACCOUNTING PROFESSION

In The Netherlands there was no legal regulation of the accounting profession as to title or as to practice of the profession until mid 1963. In that year, the Registered Accountants Act was enacted, of which, however, only the transitory provisions have been put into force. (See discussion following.)

There is no legal or other requirement for the professional examination of financial statements of limited liability companies by qualified auditors and their reporting thereon (except for pension funds, savings funds and life insurance companies); anyone can call himself an accountant and carry on any kind of accounting or tax work for which he can find clients. This will be true also after the new law has been put into full operation. The new law only protects the title and the profession of the "registeraccountant."

A State Committee is at present considering proposals for a revision of the Commercial Code. One may expect that the question of whether or not audits will be made obligatory for all or some classes (e.g., those listed on the stock exchange) of companies will be considered. Because of international relationships (e.g., the Rome Treaty), it appears unlikely that such compulsory audits, if adopted by legislation, will be performed by "registeraccountants."

The New Law

The law is meant to unite all accountants who fulfill the requirements laid down by the act for registration in the Netherlands Institute of Registeraccountants. These requirements are the possession of an accountant's diploma obtained at one of the Dutch universities or of the accountant's diploma granted by the Netherlands Institute of Registeraccountants, or, during a transition period, proof of at least ten years' practice of the accounting profession. Members of the Netherlands Institute of Accountants (N.I.v.A.) and of the Association of University Trained Accountants will, in general, qualify for registration.

A transition period is provided, during which time certain provisions of the act become effective; these mainly concern the setting up of a committee in charge of approving applications for registration. The Register will not be opened until three years after this committee has commenced its work, and thereafter those registered may use the title "Registeraccountant."

The title "Registeraccountant" will be protected, but anyone may still call himself an accountant. Another committee will also consider regulations for those who use the title "Accountant" but who do not qualify for Registration, and whose practice is mainly concerned with small business.

The Minister of Economic Affairs has promulgated the Rules for the professional conduct of the members of the Netherlands Institute of Registeraccountants as an aid to the committee, which will have to consider applications for the Register, and as a guide for professional conduct at the time the new law is put into operation.

There is no essential difference between the rules of the present N.I.v.A. and those of the future N.I.v.R.A. in respect to partnerships. The Council of the future N.I.v.R.A., however, has the authority to grant a dispensation permitting a Netherlands registeraccountant to form a partnership with a foreign nonregisteraccountant. Such dispensation, however, can only be granted if the professional organization, of which the nonregisteraccountant is a member, has been approved by the general meeting of members of the N.I.v.R.A.

Present Standing of the Profession

The practice of professional public accounting is highly developed in The Netherlands, comparable to the profession in other highly industrialized countries. This progress is due very largely to the efforts of The Netherlands Institute of Accountants, whose members may sign themselves "Members of N.I.v.A." This designation is equivalent to the United States' "C.P.A." or the United Kingdom's "C.A.," and the Institute members are recognized in The Netherlands as belonging to a respected profession.

The Netherlands Institute of Accountants

General. The Institute, dating from 1895, undertakes the training of prospective members, regulates the profession, and disciplines its membership. Its members, composed of those holding its accountancy diploma or a similar diploma awarded by a Netherlands university, constitute a very important part of the accountancy profession in The Netherlands.

6

There are approximately 1,950 members of the Institute, of whom about half are engaged in public practice.

Requirements for the Accountancy Diploma. Persons of good repute who have graduated from a secondary or grammar school (Hogere Burgerschool or Gymnasium) may be enrolled by the Institute as "student-members" (assistenten). These student-members, usually while employed on the staff of a Dutch firm of accountants who are members of the Institute, pursue a course of evening study. The curriculum of the Institute is in two phases, which usually covers a minimum of eight years, as follows:

> Courses of study of three and one-half years duration, leading to the intermediate examinations in civil law, mathematics, social economics and Part I of theory and practice of business economics

> Courses of study of four years duration, leading to the intermediate examinations in tax law, Part II of theory and practice of business economics, theory and practice of methods and systems of accounting and the theory and practice of auditing

> Finally, the candidate must present a subject approved by the President of the Board of Examiners, upon which he will be thoroughly examined. Study time is estimated to be half a year.

The Institute organizes courses designed to prepare applicants for the required examinations. As a rule the student-members follow these particular courses, although they may prepare for the required examinations otherwise, as by a private tutor.

There are five universities in The Netherlands which grant the Accountancy Diploma to those graduates of economics who also have completed post-graduate study in accountancy. The Institute recognizes this diploma as meeting its requirements for membership.

Disciplinary Functions. A Discipline Committee of the Institute, upon complaint or upon request of the Council, examines whether a member has been guilty of actions which impair the reputation of auditors, such as serious negligence in the execution of his profession, acts incompatible with good faith, or offenses against the rules and regulations of the Institute. This Committee may, upon a judgement of guilt, impose various penalties ranging from a reprimand to expulsion from the Institute. An Appeals Committee may revise the adjudications of the Discipline Committee. The judgments of these committees are published, and may in certain circumstances constitute an important directive to members of the Institute.

The Association of University-trained Accountants

This Association (Vereniging van Academisch Gevormde Accountants) is composed of persons holding the Accountants Diploma from a university or college. Such persons, on becoming members of the Institute or of the Association, have not had the practical experience which the student-members of the Institute normally obtain; they do have greater background in academic subjects and in economics. Of the total having this degree, about two hundred and fifty are members of the Association, and about one hundred and seventy are members of the Institute.

Other Organizations of Accountants in The Netherlands

There are about ten other organizations of persons doing some kind of accounting work in The Netherlands, such as those engaged in book-keeping work and tax work. As indicated previously, at the present time there is no statutory regulation as regards the use of the title of "Accountant" or of the exercise of that profession. However, the authorities and the business community have learned over the years to recognize the importance of membership in the Institute (N.I.v.A.) and the Association (V.A.G.A.)

Ethics

The Institute and the Association have adopted identical Rules of Conduct and Codes of Ethics. In addition to the requirements as to independence, discussed later, the Code of Ethics includes the following (condensed):

Members will not:

Engage in any activity detrimental to the status of the profession

Report upon an account wholly or in part prepared by themselves, relatives, partners, or employees

Act as promoters

Advertise or permit advertising on their behalf

Pay commissions for procurement of business

Accept commissions

Accept remuneration depending on the results of their work

Offer their services except in response to personal invitation to do so. If they are succeeding a previously engaged auditor, the latter must be consulted.

Functions of the Members of the Institute and the Association

The members conduct examinations of all types of business organizations and issue opinions upon their financial statements. Even though there is no legal requirement that such examinations be made and published, most Dutch concerns engage independent accountants to do so; the majority of companies listed on the stock exchange are examined, nearly all of them by members of the Institute or Association. The Netherlands auditor is expected to advise his clients on business as well as on accounting matters; for this reason the curriculum of the Institute emphasizes studies in economics. In addition, the auditor is expected to give his clients much the same type of management services and tax advice as are customary in the United States. The larger accounting firms are affiliated with tax counsel firms which act as tax counsel directly with the accounting firm's clients.

AUDITING STANDARDS

The auditing standards observed by the outside auditor in The Netherlands (members of the Institute or the Association) are not enunciated in the same way as those of the American Institute's Statement on Auditing Standards and Procedures. However, the Netherlands Institute has published Rules on Professional Activities, which cover essentially the General Standards and Standards of Field Work of the American Institute of C.P.A.s.

Although the outside auditor in The Netherlands recognizes that a proper study and evaluation of internal control is an important part of the audit procedure, he does not rely to the same extent on internal control as do many of his foreign colleagues. Particular stress is placed on the independent verification of various organic relations between the flows of monies and of goods. This usually involves a greater volume of detailed checking of transactions, particularly expenditures, than is customary in the United States or in the United Kingdom. Attendance at physical stocktaking is an essential requirement, but not the circularization of accounts receivable because of the way the Dutch banking system operates. There is now a trend towards greater reliance on internal control because of improvements in internal control procedures.

9

General Standards

The Rules on Professional Activities state (Art. 2, Part I) that members are required to perform their work honestly, accurately, and impartially. The technical training of the members and student-members has been described above; the reputation of members of both professional accounting bodies is high as to proficiency in auditing.

The requirement of the Rules as to impartiality is also referred to in the Code of Ethics, which states that members may not act on behalf of any person, corporate body or institution if they have any interest therein which would affect their impartiality. They would be deemed to have such interest if they have a substantial financial interest in, or fulfill any employment with (other than as outside auditor), or are directors of the enterprise under examination. The obligation of the members of the Institute and the Association to preserve an independent attitude towards their work is taken very seriously. Members may only practice on their own account, in partnership with, or as an employee of another member; they may not practice under a corporate form.

Standards of Field Work

The standards enunciated by the American Institute's Statement on Auditing Standards and Procedures under this heading—i.e., planning and supervision of work, study of internal control, and competence of evidential matter, are also recognized by the profession in The Netherlands. The Rules state that (condensed): Members are required to assure themselves that their partners and other members associated in their work comply with the Rules for Professional Activities and the Code of Ethics and those underlying the working programs of the partnership. The review and evaluation of internal control is not specifically mentioned in the Rules; the attitude of The Netherlands' auditor is referred to under the heading "General" above. The Rules state (as to comptence of evidential matter) "that members will perform their professional activities in such a way that their execution provides a reliable basis for their statements on the results of such activities."

Standards of Reporting

The members' responsibilities as to their reports are stated in the Rules for Professional Activities, and may be summarized as follows:

As to reports in general, members shall state the results of their activities so that a true and fair view of such results is obtained; a report, even if it is a mere signature, implies unqualified concurrence with the document covered, unless the contrary is specifically stated in a proviso starting with the words "subject to." The proviso must state the matters to which exception is taken so that the import is clear. If the proviso is such as to negative the purport of the report or to detract materially from the report, the member will not give a corroborative report.

If a member's report relates to a document forming a part of a set of documents published together, his report will be deemed to cover statements, information and explanations made in other documents in the set which relate to the document to which his report relates.

As to reports relating to annual accounts, they will cover the balance sheet, profit and loss account and explanatory notes. Such reports corroborate that the annual accounts have been drawn up in accordance with good commercial practice and affirm the existence and valuation of assets and liabilities and the description of the individual items.

The auditor may approve the financial statements, approve with a clearly defined exception, state disapproval with clearly defined reasons for such disapproval, or disclaim an opinion when he has been unable to obtain sufficient competent evidential matter.

Form of Report. The Netherlands Institute has not recommended a specific form of auditor's report. The Rules state that a "report" means any statement, either written or oral, which expresses an opinion or from which an opinion may be inferred. Often, if not usually, the report consists merely of the auditor's written signature on the financial statements; it may be accompanied by the words "audited and approved," or merely "approved." A view widely held in The Netherlands is that approval of the statements is signified by the auditor's signature. There is general agreement that the short form report should not state any audit procedures which were applied or not applied because this would mean nothing to the "interested layman." A more elaborate report is sometimes given; it usually is submitted to the directors or to the management.

The meaning of the phrase "good commercial practice" as used in the Rules (see above) is discussed later under "Accounting Principles." As to consistency in their application, this concept is not specifically referred to in the Rules, although there is a general requirement that the financial statements and the related notes give an "accurate picture" (fair view) of the financial position and the results of operations.

ACCOUNTING PRINCIPLES AND PRACTICES

There has been no statement of "generally accepted accounting principles" issued in The Netherlands comparable to those issued by the American Institute of C.P.A.s or to the publications of the Institute of Chartered Accountants in England and Wales. Although the Rules for Professional Activities refer to the auditor's corroboration that the accounts have been drawn up "in accordance with good commercial practice," the Netherlands accountant feels that this duty is fulfilled if he finds that the adopted principles in a given case are acceptable and are, in his opinion, in accordance with what is customarily done in the branch of trade concerned.

The Committee of Advice on Professional Matters of the Institute gives advice in individual cases and issues reports upon problems of a general nature, which are advisory only. In 1955, certain Recommendations were published by a study committee sponsored by the Dutch Employers Organizations, which publication was followed by a revised edition issued in 1962. These covered such matters as revaluation of assets, pension liabilities, comparative figures, consolidated accounts, and a number of other matters. It is stated that these recommendations have been adopted in many cases.

It is common practice to prepare separate financial statements for "fiscal" (tax) purposes in accordance with the requirements of the tax laws; these may show substantial deviations from financial statements prepared for publication or general shareholders' meeting purposes. It is perhaps for this reason that tax rules have had less influence on "generally accepted accounting principles" in The Netherlands than in some other countries.

Form and Content of Financial Statements

Statement Presentation

The form of balance sheet is that usually found in the United States for public utility companies—assets on the left, capital and liabilities on the right. In the case of industrial enterprises, assets are generally arranged with fixed assets as the first item, and descending in order of liquidity with cash as the last item. The right-hand side begins with capital and capital reserves, followed by liabilities and provisions, and closes with profit available for disposition by the stockholders.

The legal requirements of statement presentation for limited liability companies are minimal and are stated in Article 42 of the Commercial Code. These requirements are: a balance sheet and profit and loss statement, together with explanatory notes stating the standard adopted for valuing the movable and immovable assets of the company. The statements must be signed by the managing officers and directors and presented to the general meeting of shareholders for their approval. There are no requirements as to the content of the profit and loss account, but the balance sheet must separately show the following:

1. Cash on hand, in banks, and postal clearing balances
2. Investments in other enterprises and amounts receivable from them
3. Securities listed on the Stock Exchange (except those under b)
4. Securities not so listed (except those under b)
5. Accounts receivable (not includable under a and b)
6. Inventories of raw material, work in process and finished goods
7. Land and buildings, machinery and plant
8. Intangible assets
9. Deferred income
10. Prepaid and deferred items
11. Due on subscriptions to capital stock

Special acts prescribe in great detail the form and content of annual accounts of life insurance companies, pension funds, and savings funds.

Comparative Financial Statements. It is considered good practice in The Netherlands to prepare comparative financial statements.

Consolidated Financial Statements. Competent authority suggests that consolidated financial statements are frequently essential to an understanding of unconsolidated statements, and that both consolidated and unconsolidated statements should be published. Many of the larger Dutch companies which have subsidiaries do so.

Inventories

While in general the "lower of cost or market" basis for stating inventories is considered the more acceptable procedure, the practice of stating inventories at less than this amount is not uncommon. Inventory cost usually includes overheads, but they may be omitted. "Lifo" and "base stock" methods are permitted for tax purposes and are also used for book purposes.

Fixed Assets

There is no prohibition against revaluing fixed assets on the basis of current cost, and this is sometimes done. Such revaluation would be disclosed in the annual report. The increased value is credited to a revaluation reserve, which is not taxable, nor is depreciation allowed for tax purposes on the written up fixed asset base.

Debt Discount and Expense

Although such items are normally deferred over the life of the respective issues, it is also considered good practice to charge them to income in the year incurred.

Liability Under Long-term Leases

Material commitments under long-term leases are not required to be disclosed, although such disclosure has been recommended by the Institute's Committee of Advice on Professional Matters.

Reserves

It is customary for many Dutch companies, when authorized by their Articles of Association, to charge to income provisions for reserves having no specific purpose. Such reserves are not deductible for tax purposes, nor taxable if restored to income.

Statement of Profit and Loss

The profit and loss statement, which may be either in account form or statement form, is usually quite condensed, and sometimes includes items which in the United States would be shown in the surplus summary. The 1962 Report of the Dutch Employers Organizations recommended, however, that a clear-cut distinction be made between the computation of profit and the appropriation of profit. Sales and cost of sales are seldom stated in published financial statements. There is no legal requirement for a statutory reserve, but it is customary to allocate most of the year's income, after dividends, to various reserves or to a general reserve. The figure of undistributed earnings on Dutch balance sheets is often a minimal amount.

"Current-value" Accounting. Probably because of the influence of economic thought on the development of accounting principles in The Netherlands, it is considered proper if indeed not preferable to charge income with the current (or replacement) cost of goods and services utilized to produce such income. This involves computing depreciation on the basis of current value of fixed assets and the costing of inventory used at its current value (approximately Lifo method). Many Dutch accountants feel that only by matching cost, measured by current value against the net proceeds of goods sold or services rendered, can the true net income of the period be computed.

Investment Allowance. The Netherlands tax law provides for "Investment Allowances" of 5 per cent for the first two years on specified plant additions. For tax purposes these investment allowances are treated as operating expenses, but do not reduce allowable depreciation. There is a disinvestment addition of 5 per cent per year for the first ten years on the proceeds of sales of fixed assets for which, in prior years, an investment allowance has been granted.

Depreciation. The straight-line and declining-balance depreciation methods are commonly used for book purposes. Depreciation may commence when the purchase contract is concluded. When "current value" accounting is adopted, depreciation recorded on the higher replacement valuations of fixed assets will exceed that permitted for tax purposes, which is restricted to the cost basis.

Directors' and Management's Bonuses. Bonuses to directors and management are sometimes regarded as distributions of profit, especially when so provided in the company's articles of incorporation. They are, therefore, sometimes shown as an appropriation of net income for the year in the statement of profit and loss. Generally, they are deductible for tax purposes.

Stock Dividends. Stock dividends are accounted for by the issuing company on the basis of par value. The recipient is taxed on income based on par value, unless the distribution was from paid-in surplus, in which case it is tax free.

15

REQUIREMENTS FOR LISTING OF SECURITIES ON THE STOCK EXCHANGE AND PUBLIC SALE OF SECURITIES

The requirements for a prospectus offering shares or debentures to the public are contained in paragraph fourteen of the regulations issued by the "Vereeniging voor den Effectenhandel" (Stock Exchange Association), a semi-official body which manages the Stock Exchange under the supervision of the Ministry of Finance. The provisions relating to accounting matters include:

> For issues not previously listed on the Stock Exchange, an analysis of capital stock and surplus accounts from the inception of the company
>
> Balance sheets and income statements for the last two years and financial information for the current year to date. If the issuer is a foreign corporation, the financial statements must cover the last five years.

The balance sheets and income statements of a Dutch company must be accompanied by an auditor's certificate, except when the management of the Stock Exchange waives this requirement. This is sometimes done when the company does not have an auditor, since there is no legal or other requirement that a Dutch company have one. When an auditor's certificate is included, the accountant must give his written consent to its inclusion in the prospectus.

An application for listing securities must follow directly after issuing a prospectus, and is made through a bank which is a member of the Stock Exchange Association. It must be accompanied by the prospectus, but there are no other accounting and reporting requirements. Once its securities are listed on the Stock Exchange, the company has an obligation to publish annual accounts.

Report of the Board of Directors 15

FORMS OF BUSINESS ORGANIZATION

The forms of business familiar to United States readers are also found in the United Kingdom, as United States laws are generally derived from the British. There are, of course, significant differences, but the sole proprietorship, the partnership and the limited liability company are generally similar.

Companies in the United Kingdom are governed by a "Companies Act." The "Jenkins Committee" has recently concluded investigations into the workings of this Act, and has made numerous recommendations which may be incorporated into a new Companies Act in the foreseeable future.

Companies

With the exception of certain special types of companies, the formation and dissolution of all incorporated companies in the United Kingdom are controlled by the provisions of the Companies Act (1948), the latest in a series of Acts regulating companies. The Act distinguishes between "public" and "private" companies, and there is a subdivision of the latter designated as an "exempt private company."

The Public Company. This corporate body corresponds closely to the publicly held United States corporation. It may be formed by seven or more persons, and may have an unlimited number of shareholders. The liability of its members is limited to the amount, if any, unpaid on shares held by them (company limited by shares), or to such amount as the members undertake to contribute to the assets in the event of its being wound up (company limited by guarantee). In either case, the name of the company must end with the word "Limited" or the abbreviation "Ltd." At present, shares with no-par-value may not be issued.

Every company must appoint an auditor or auditors eligible for appointment as having qualifications (discussed later) or authorized individually by the Board of Trade (a government department headed by a cabinet minister), who reports to the members upon the annual accounts submitted to the annual general meeting. An annual return must be made to the Registrar of Companies which includes the annual accounts laid before the general meeting of shareholders, certified as a true copy by a director and the secretary, and a certified copy of the report of auditors thereon and the report of the directors.

A company must have at least two directors who are appointed by the shareholders, and in whom is vested the management of the company.

With certain exceptions, any company offering shares or debentures for sale to the public must issue a prospectus containing the information specified in the Fourth Schedule of the Companies Act, which is comparable in many respects to that required under the United States Securities Act of 1933.

The Private Company. The private company is comparable with the closely held United States company. Its members are limited to fifty (exclusive of employees and past employees who have continued to be members). The articles of incorporation must limit the right of members to transfer their shares, which is usually done by requiring the consent of the directors. The private company may not offer its shares or debentures to the public; they must be placed privately, often with members of a family, friends or business acquaintances. An auditor or auditors must be appointed under the same conditions as for a public company.

The private company has certain privileges, among which are: It need have no more than two shareholders, nor more than one director; it need not hold a "statutory meeting" or file a statutory report; it need not publish annual accounts, but they must be furnished to shareholders and debentureholders, and filed with the Registrar of Companies.

The Exempt Private Company. Many private companies (largely family owned) are of this type. To obtain this status, the company must certify annually that: No body corporate is the holder of any shares or debentures (with certain exceptions); no person other than the holders have any interest in any of the shares or debentures; the number of debentureholders does not exceed fifty; no body corporate is a director; no arrangement exists whereby the company's policy can be determined by persons other than directors, members or debentureholders or trustees for debentureholders; and that the company has complied with the regulations governing its "private" status.

In addition to the privileges granted to all private companies, exempt private companies need not file with the annual return a balance sheet

4

and profit and loss statement, nor a directors' report nor an auditor's report. While an auditor must be appointed, he need not be a person qualified for appointment under the Companies Act. The provision of the Companies Act that he may not be an officer or servant of the company, or of a body corporate, applies, though the auditor of an exempt private company may be a partner or employee of an officer or servant of the company. Instead of printed copies of certain resolutions and agreements required to be filed with the Registrar, copies in some other approved form will be accepted.

Branch of a Foreign Corporation

A foreign company, wishing to establish a branch in the United Kingdom, must first obtain formal Treasury Department approval through the latter's agent, the Bank of England. There must then be filed with the Registrar of Companies: (a) the name and address of the person(s) resident in the United Kingdom upon whom legal process against the company may be served, (b) particulars of the directors of the company, (c) a certified copy of the company's charter and by-laws, and (d) a copy of subsequent annual accounts of the foreign company complying with the provisions of the Companies Act.

In practice, accounts drawn up in accordance with the laws and procedures of a country where the accounting standards do not differ materially from those prevailing in the United Kingdom (as for example, those of the United States), are accepted by the Registrar.

Partnerships

The Companies Act provides that a partnership which is organized for the purposes of profit and has more than twenty partners must register as a company under the Act. If the partnership is in the banking business, it must register if the number of partners exceeds ten. Partnerships in general are governed by the Partnership Act of 1890.

Business Records

Section 147 of the Companies Act (1948) requires that every company will keep proper books of account to show all amounts received and expended and the matters in respect of which the receipt and expenditure take place, all sales and purchases of goods and the assets and liabilities of the company. It states further that proper books of

5

account will not be deemed to be kept "if there are not kept such books of account as are necessary to give a true and fair view of the state of the company's affairs and to explain its transactions." It is provided that records may be kept in looseleaf or other form provided adequate precautions are taken for guarding against falsification and for facilitating its discovery.

THE ACCOUNTING PROFESSION

The practice of accounting as a profession, as we know it today, was born in the United Kingdom beginning in the early or middle nineteenth century, although recognition of the "professional accountant" is implied by his employ on insolvency cases arising under the Scottish Bankruptcy Act of 1696. A directory of accountants was available in Edinburgh in 1773.

As a result of many business failures in earlier years, various methods of dealing with liquidation of bankrupt estates were enacted, culminating in the Bankruptcy Act of 1869, which in effect transferred the administration of insolvent estates to professional accountants. At first, therefore, accountancy practice was largely concerned with bankruptcy, liquidations and receiverships. However, in 1883, a new Bankruptcy Act established the office of "Official Receiver," which led to some reduction in the insolvency business of the professional accountant.

The decline in this type of work, however, was soon offset by increased demands for accounting and auditing work. The introduction of the "limited liability" company by the Companies Act of 1855, and the consolidation of various Acts affecting companies in the Companies Act of 1862 (which for the first time required registration for most companies), led to the formation of a great many companies operating on a much greater scale than formerly. Such companies needed improved accounting methods and procedures to control their operations, which service the professional accountants were able to supply. In addition, their field of examination and reporting upon financial statements was extended by an increasing recognition that companies which raised capital from the public must provide their shareholders with reports by auditors on their accounts so that shareholders might have reasonable assurance that the accounts presented by the directors were fair and the profits shown by them were truly available for distribution.

This trend was accentuated in 1879, by the Company Act requirement that banks, and in 1900, that all companies, must appoint auditors.

The first Royal Charter was granted in 1854, to the Society of Accountants of Edinburgh (since merged in 1951 with other Scottish bodies to form the Institute of Chartered Accountants of Scotland). The Institute of Chartered Accountants in England and Wales was incorporated by Royal Charter in 1880. These Institutes have been the model for the accountancy profession in the countries comprising the Commonwealth, and have greatly influenced the development of the profession in many other countries. Some other accounting bodies have since been organized in the United Kingdom.

In the United Kingdom admission to and control over the activities of the members of these societies (comprising the accounting profession in that country) are in the hands of the societies themselves, rather than in governmental or educational institutions. The four main accounting societies in the United Kingdom which are presently recognized under the Companies Act (1948) are:

The Institute of Chartered Accountants in England and Wales

The Institute of Chartered Accountants of Scotland

The Institute of Chartered Accountants in Ireland

The Association of Certified and Corporate Accountants.

The Chartered Accountant

The title of "chartered accountant" (Fellow, F.C.A., or Associate, A.C.A.) may be used by persons obtaining membership in the Institutes of England and Wales, and of Ireland. The Institute of Scotland does not distinguish between "Fellow" and "Associate," and its members are designated C.A. The discussion which follows indicates the requirements for membership in the Institute of England and Wales; those of Scotland and Ireland differ in minor details.

The preparation for membership in the Institute is basically a five-year apprenticeship system reduced to three years for graduates of United Kingdom universities and to four years for those who have achieved a specified educational standard intermediate between the three-year and five-year candidates. The candidate serves in the office of a chartered accountant under "articles," the terms of which are subject to the rules of and the supervision of the Institute.

To be eligible for admission to articles, the candidate must have reached the age of sixteen, and have met certain general educational requirements. It is not required that he be a citizen of the United Kingdom. The selection of persons to be articled (generally, a maximum of four in service at any one time per member), is made by the member who must be in public practice.

The Examinations. In addition to practical training, which is the responsibility of the principal, the articled clerk must pass certain examinations. After two years' articled service (one year when the service period has been reduced from five to three years because of possession of a university degree), the candidate may sit for the intermediate examination covring accounting, auditing, taxation, elementary cost accounting, law and general commercial knowledge. Before the end of his articled service he must pass the final examination (Parts I and II), which includes advanced accounting, auditing, taxation, general financial knowledge, cost accounting, and English law relating to companies, liquidations, receiverships, contracts, sales, bankruptcy, trusts and similar matters.

Preparation for the examinations is the responsibility of the candidate, who is required to become a member of one of the chartered accountant student societies. These societies arrange lectures on accounting subjects, and in some cases classes for instruction. Most articled clerks take a correspondence course, which may be supplemented by attendance at evening and daytime classes offered by technical and commercial colleges, and by private tuition. The candidate is entitled to leave of absence of at least one month before each of the examinations and the Council of the Institute recommends an additional two months for each examination.

Articled Service. As indicated above, the period of articled service varies from three to five years. The principal to whom an articled clerk is apprenticed is expected to arrange work assignments so as to provide the maximum possible experience for the clerk. While service cannot commence other than in the United Kingdom, it may be served in other locations for not more than six months, and the clerk may spend periods of not more than six months in all in an industrial, commercial or other suitable organization. The total period allowed for study, service outside the country and in other than public accounting may not exceed one-third of the term of service.

The term of articled service may be reduced to three years if the candidate is a graduate of a university of the United Kingdom. Non-university students, aged eighteen, with certain superior academic attainments may be articled for four years. There is also in effect the so-called "University Scheme," under which certain universities of England and Wales provide courses over a period of two-and three-quarter years, which with three years' service as an articled clerk, completes the time requirements for both the university degree and membership in the Institute. Participants in the University Scheme are exempted from the intermediate examination, but are required to take and pass the final examination.

In November 1963, some relatively minor revisions were instituted in the above requirements.

Organizations of Accountants

The Institute of Chartered Accountants in England and Wales. The Institute is composed of members who, after serving as articled clerks and after having passed certain examinations as outlined above, have been admitted as Associates (A.C.A.); and of those Associates who have been admitted as Fellows (F.C.A.) after having either: (a) been in public practice for at least five years or (b) completed ten years of membership in the Institute. A membership may be suspended or revoked by the Disciplinary Committee of the Institute if the member is found to have violated any related provisions of the Royal Charters. There is also a special class of membership (F.S.A.A. and A.S.A.A.) for members who hold or obtain the qualification formerly granted by the Society of Incorporated Accountants (see below).

The Institute has issued a number of "Recommendations on Accounting Principles" as well as a series of directives on "Professional Conduct." It publishes a monthly magazine (*Accountancy*). In 1961 a further series of recommendations on "Auditing" were instituted.

In 1957, the Society of Incorporated Accountants (incorporated under the Companies Act in 1885), was integrated with the Chartered Institutes. It had branches in Scotland, Ireland, Wales, Australia, South Africa and India, and issued the designation Fellow (Associate) of the Society of Accountants and Auditors (F.S.A.A. and A.S.A.A.). Its members were either those who: (a) had served under articles or (b) had served as accountancy clerks to a member of any approved body who was in public practice, or was chief financial officer to a municipality or county. Its members had also passed examinations which did not differ greatly from those of the Chartered Institutes.

The Institutes of Scotland and Ireland. These Institutes are similar to the Institute of Chartered Accountants in England and Wales in structure and services to their members. The Scottish Institute recognizes services under articles with a member practicing as a public accountant in any part of the United Kingdom.

9

The Association of Certified and Corporate Accountants. Admission to this organization is by examination after service under articles, normally for five years, either with a practicing accountant or in the finance and accounting department of a commercial or industrial company, in one of the nationalized industries or in local government, if that employment has been approved by the Council of the Association as providing accounting experience of adequate scope and character.

Other Organizations of Accountants. There are certain other organizations of accountants in the United Kingdom which serve specialized fields of accountancy. Examples are The Institute of Municipal Treasurers and Accountants and The Institute of Cost and Works Accountants.

Functions of the Chartered Accountant

The United Kingdom chartered accountant examines and reports upon financial statements of business enterprises. Under the Companies Act of 1948, every company except exempt private companies formed under its provisions must appoint an auditor who is a member of an accountancy body recognized by the Board of Trade or who is individually authorized by the Board as having similar qualifications obtained abroad or having experience specified in the Act. The accountancy bodies so recognized are the three Chartered Institutes (England and Wales, Scotland, and Ireland) and the Association of Certified and Corporate Accountants. Several hundred overseas accountants have also been individually authorized by the Board of Trade as having the requisite qualifications obtained abroad.

The United Kingdom chartered accountant advises clients on tax matters, prepares returns, and discusses proposed changes in returns with the Inspector of Taxes. He provides management services of various kinds for his clients, and undertakes special investigations for specific purposes on behalf of managements or for government departments.

There are some activities in which the United Kingdom chartered accountant often engages but which would not be customary for a CPA in the United States. He may act as liquidator or receiver of a company or as a trustee in bankruptcy. He may do the work of the secretary of a company, act as a registrar and transfer agent of its shares and debentures, or as appraiser of shares (especially of private companies) for estate tax, for sale, and other purposes.

Ethics

One of the fundamental objects of the Institute, as expressed in the Royal Charter of 1880, is to compel the observance of strict rules of conduct as a condition of membership. The Institute has not, however, promulgated any official Code of Ethics similar to that of the American Institute of CPAs (but see page 13 as to independence). Nevertheless, very similar rules are embodied in the five fundamental rules included as Clause 20 of the Supplemental Royal Charter of 1948, certain of the provisions of Clause 21, and in various statements of the Council of the Institute. The five rules of the Charter may be briefly summarized as:

1. A member will not allow a nonmember to practice in his name unless he is in partnership with that nonmember.
2. A member in practice will not share a fee with a nonmember who is not his partner or employee.
3. A member in practice will not accept fees or profits of a nonmember who is not his partner or employee.
4. A member in employment may not carry on public accountancy work in his own name on behalf of an employer who is not a chartered accountant in practice but whose business is such as would ordinarily be performed by a member of the Institute in practice.
5. A member in practice may not carry on any business incompatible with the practice of accountancy.

Clause 21 of the Charter provides disciplinary action against a member who (condensed):

1. Violates any fundamental rule of the Institute applicable to him
2. Has been guilty of any act or default discreditable to a public accountant or a member of the Institute
3. Has committed felony, misdemeanor or fraud
4. Is adjudged a bankrupt, fails to satisfy a judgment or makes an assignment for the benefit of creditors
5. Willfully commits any breach of the by-laws of the Institute.

The Council from time to time has issued statements bearing on matters of professional ethics affecting its members. Some of the more important of these cover the following subjects: changes in appointment of auditors, contingent fees, professional designations, publicity, practice as an incorporated company, special reports, relations with other professions, professional confidence, and independence.

Appointment of Auditors

The directors of a company may appoint the auditors at any time before the first annual general meeting of the shareholders, but if this is not done, the shareholders will appoint the auditors on that occasion.

If the shareholders have not appointed auditors, the Board of Trade must be notified, and that Board will fill the vacancy.

The shareholders of every company have the duty, at each annual general meeting, to appoint an auditor or auditors, who will hold office from that meeting until the conclusion of the next annual general meeting. Although the auditor is technically reappointed annually, it is not necessary that a resolution to that effect be passed at each annual general meeting, provided that there have been no positive steps to the contrary, that he is duly qualified, and that he has not given notice of his unwillingness to be reappointed. Directors may fill a casual vacancy in the office of auditor, such as may occur by reason of the death or incapacity of the auditor.

A change in auditors may be suggested by any shareholder, provided notice of the intention to propose a resolution to that effect is given not less than twenty-eight days before the annual general meeting. The company must, at least twenty-one days before the meeting, notify the shareholders and the retiring auditor of this intention. The retiring auditor has the right to make representations in writing to the company, to have them sent to the shareholders, and to be present and to be heard at the general meeting on the resolution and on any other matters which concern him as an auditor.

While not covered in the Companies Act, the rules of the Institute require that the proposed auditor communicate with the retiring auditor, primarily to determine whether there is any professional reason why the proposed engagement should not be accepted.

It is considered that when a firm of auditors is appointed, the appointment is of all the constituent partners, and that each must satisfy the requirements of the Act as to eligibility.

Remuneration of Auditors

The remuneration of the auditor is fixed by the company "or in such a manner as the company in general meeting determines." In practice, the company often delegates to the directors the duty of arranging the auditor's remuneration in consultation with the company's duly appointed auditors. The Act specifies that any expenses reimbursed to the auditor are to be treated as remuneration. If the remuneration is not expressly fixed by resolution of the company in general meeting, it must be disclosed under separate heading in the accounts.

The remuneration here referred to is that for his work in his capacity as auditor; it does not refer to other types of accounting or tax work for which arrangements are made with the directors or other company officials.

AUDITING STANDARDS

General Standards and Standards of Field Work

The Institute of Chartered Accountants in England and Wales has published a statement (1961) entitled *General Principles of Auditing,* which covers in essence the matters dealt with under the headings "General" and "Standards of Field Work" in the American Institute's publication "Auditing Standards and Procedures." The Institute of Chartered Accountants has always emphasized the need for training of personnel, due care in the performance of work, proper planning and supervision, the importance of internal control, and the obtaining of competent evidential matter. These matters are discussed in the statement referred to and in many articles and discussions by members.

Inventories and Receivables. There is no official pronouncement of the Institute requiring the presence of the auditor at inventory-taking, nor for the direct confirmation of accounts receivable with the debtor. However, many chartered accountants do feel that occasional or periodical observations of inventory-taking are desirable, especially in connection with an initial examination, and do make such observations. It is not usual to correspond with debtors, but other auditing procedures are utilized. Both these activities would usually also be done in the case of a United Kingdom subsidiary of a United States company.

Liability Certificates and Other Representations of Management. Two directors are required to sign, on behalf of the Board of Directors, the financial statements presented to the annual meeting of stockholders; most chartered accountants do not consider it necessary to obtain separate representations from officers of the company.

Independence. Paragraph 6 of the Institute's statement states that (the auditors) "must approach their work as auditors with an independent outlook and must do nothing which would impair that independence."

The fact that under the Companies Act auditors are appointed by the shareholders, and not by directors or management, contributes to the independent status of the company's auditor. The Companies Act also provides that none of the following will be qualified for appointment as auditor of a company:

(a) An officer or servant of the company
(b) A person who is a partner of or in the employment of an officer or servant of the company (except in the case of an "exempt private company")

(c) A body corporate

(d) Any person disqualified under (a), (b) or (c) for appointment as auditor of that company's subsidiary or parent company, or who would be so disqualified if the body corporate was a company.

It is not lawful for one of the partners to be a director of a client public company in which the firm serves as auditor; an exempt private company, however, may appoint as auditor one of the partners who is not a director. Many United Kingdom accounting firms believe that the latter, though permissible, is not desirable.

There is no prohibition against the appointment as auditor of a person who is a blood relative of an officer of the company, nor against the auditor having a financial interest in the company. Many firms, while not objecting to partners or staff holding an investment in client companies, prohibit short-term trading in their securities. Purchases or sales based on confidential information obtained in the course of an audit of the company would be considered misconduct.

It is not usually considered that the independence of a firm is impaired if staff members other than those engaged on an audit of a client write up its books.

Standards of Reporting

The content of the auditors' report upon the accounts, i.e., the balance sheet and profit and loss statements submitted to the annual general meeting of shareholders of a public company is specified in the Ninth Schedule of the Companies Act of 1948. They must state (condensed): Whether they have received all the information and explanations which they required; whether proper books of account have been kept by the company; whether the financial statements are in agreement with the books of account; whether, in their opinion, the financial statements give a true and fair view of the state of affairs and the profit (loss) of the company; and whether, in their opinion, the accounts comply with the Companies Act, 1948.

The Institute of Chartered Accountants has suggested in the *Members' Handbook* a form of auditors' report which, in the opinion of counsel, satisfies the provisions of the Act. There are a number of variations of the form in use, and it requires modification when there are branches or subsidiaries, some of which may have been audited by others, or when consolidated statements are presented.

There is no requirement that reference be made to adherence to generally accepted auditing standards or to conformity with and consistency of application of generally accepted accounting principles. When

14

preparing a report upon a United Kingdom subsidiary of a United State's parent company, however, the accountant usually is expected to include statements with respect to such matters in his report.

Consistency. As to consistency, the Companies Act provides that the profit and loss account will show when any item therein is affected by any change in the basis of accounting. If there has been such change, the auditor must cover it in his report unless it were shown on the face of the statements or in a footnote.

Disclosure of Subsequent Events. The British view is that the financial statements are issued as at a given date, and that, in general, subsequent events should not be reflected in the accounts. Later information regarding such items as the valuation of receivables or inventories may be useful in determining their proper amounts at the balance-sheet date. Disclosure of subsequent events would usually be considered necessary if such events are so material that informed decisions on financial matters cannot be made by shareholders without considering the accounts in light of these events. Subsequent events such as disposal of a substantial part of the business, would normally be disclosed in the directors' report or in the chairman's statement accompanying the accounts.

Reporting on Dividend Proposals, etc. Often the accounts of a United Kingdom subsidiary of a United States parent company are required for parent company purposes prior to the holding of the annual general meeting of the subsidiary, and therefore prior to the approval of the accounts by the board and prior to the approval by the annual general meeting of the dividends to be paid and appropriations of profit and loss proposed by the directors. In this case, the auditors' report may contain the qualification, "With the exception that they do not give effect to transfers to and from reserves and dividends which may later be proposed by the directors, it is our opinion that. . . ."

Report of the Board of Directors

It is compulsory under the Act to attach to every balance sheet laid before the company in general meeting, a report by the directors with respect to the company's affairs, and stating the amount, if any, which

15

the directors recommend to be paid as a dividend, and the amount, if any, which they propose to allocate to or from reserves. The directors are also required to report any change in the nature of the company's business or in the classes of business in which the company has an interest, provided such information "will not in the directors' opinion be harmful to the business of the company."

The directors are empowered to pay interim dividends without reference to or approval of the shareholders; as to the year-end or final dividends, the shareholders may approve or reduce the amount recommended by the directors, but they may not increase it.

ACCOUNTING PRINCIPLES AND PRACTICES

The establishment of "generally accepted accounting principles" in the United Kingdom is left largely to the accounting profession, except as provided for in the Companies Act. They are contained in the "Recommendations on Accounting Principles" and in other pronouncements included in the *Members' Handbook*, published by the Institute of Chartered Accountants in England and Wales, as well as publications of other professional accountants' societies. The Institute's recommendations are not binding on its members and depend for recognition on their being generally accepted by the business community.

Form and Content of Financial Statements

In the United Kingdom, balance sheets are frequently issued in account form, with liabilities and capital on the left and assets on the right; however, the statement form is not uncommon. The order of the items is usually similar to that of a United States utility company, i.e., on the liability side capital and surplus first, followed by long-term debt and current liabilities; on the asset side, fixed assets first, followed by investments and current assets. The profit and loss statement is sometimes in account form, although the statement form is now being used more frequently.

The content of financial statements is prescribed in various sections of the Companies Act, and in the Eighth Schedule to that Act. As indicated previously, the auditor must state in his report whether the financial statements give the information required by the Act in the manner prescribed. The basic requirement as stated in Section 149 of the Act is that the balance sheet give a true and fair view of the state of affairs of the company at the close of its financial year, and that the profit and loss account give a true and fair view of its profit or loss for the financial year. There are various clauses in the Act which permit flexibility in the application of the Act's provisions, under proper circumstances and after complying with certain requirements. It is not intended that the presentation of financial statements be reduced to the mere filling out of forms.

Comparative Statements. The Act requires that prior year figures be given for both balance sheet and profit and loss items. The Institute recommends that where an item appears in a note to the statements the corresponding amount for the previous year also be shown.

Consolidated Statements. The presentation of the financial statements of a company which has subsidiaries is dealt with in the Companies Act by requiring the preparation of "group" accounts. In general this means "consolidated" financial statements, but Section 151 of the Act permits the directors to authorize variations if the same or equivalent information can be made available to the shareholders in another form. These might take the form of partial consolidation, separate statements of certain subsidiaries, supplemental information given in notes, etc.

It is required that the parent company balance sheet be given in addition to the "group" accounts. While a separate profit and loss account of the parent company is not required, it is necessary to indicate how much of the consolidated profit was directly attributable to the operations of the parent company.

Where there are unconsolidated subsidiaries, the consolidated accounts must show the investment in and indebtedness of or to those subsidiaries as separate items. When consolidated accounts are not submitted there must also be shown: (a) the reasons why subsidiaries are not dealt with in group accounts; (b) the net aggregate amount of the unconsolidated subsidiaries' profits or losses attributable to the holding company and its consolidated subsidiaries, but not dealt with in the consolidated accounts, distinguishing between the profits or losses of the current year and those of earlier years since acquisition; (c) information corresponding to that shown in (b) above, in respect of the profits and losses dealt with in the consolidated accounts; and (d) any material qualifications in the audit reports on the accounts of the unconsolidated subsidiaries. The above information is required whether or not some form of group accounts other than consolidated accounts is prepared in respect of the companies concerned. Only in very restricted circumstances laid down by the Act is a company exempted from preparing group accounts in respect of all its subsidiaries.

Excess (or Deficiency) of Cost of Investment Over Net Assets of Subsidiary at Date of Acquisition. When the cost of an acquired subsidiary's stock exceeds its net assets at date of acquisition, United Kingdom practice is to classify such excess in the consolidated balance sheet as "goodwill," "net premium on acquisition of shares in subsidiaries," "cost of control," etc. When it has been determined by independent appraisal that the fixed assets of the acquired subsidiary are understated on its books, it is considered acceptable to adjust the fixed assets' valuation on the books of the subsidiary at the time of acquisition, thus reducing or eliminating the goodwill arising in consolidation. (The same result would be attained in United States practice in a consolidation entry.)

When there are several subsidiaries, some of which in consolidation produce positive and some negative goodwill, it is customary in the United Kingdom to offset one against the other, producing either net "goodwill" or, if negative, shown separately or, if not material, included with "capital reserves."

Pooling of Interests

The accounting technique referred to in the United States as a "pooling of interests," applicable in certain circumstances when one company is acquired by or merged into another company, is not recognized as such in the United Kingdom.

However, the United Kingdom does recognize that a different accounting treatment may be accorded an "acquisition" than is accorded a "merger." A merger is described as the acquisition by one company of the shares of another, wholly or mainly for shares in the acquiring company, when the activities of the two companies are allied or complementary, and when there is an intention to retain the basic management of the acquired company. These conditions are similar to those required for a "pooling of interests" in the United States. In general, the accounting treatment is similar to that of the pooling concept, except that such treatment relating to the values assigned to shares acquired and those issued and the treatment of the resulting difference may not agree with the treatment accorded in the United States. Details of the possible alternate treatment acceptable in the United Kingdom are outside the scope of this study.

Current Assets

Loans to Directors, Officers, and Employees. Except under certain conditions, and except in the case of an exempt private company, loans to a director may not be made, other than advances for expenditures incurred or to be incurred by him in connection with his duties as director.

The amount of loans made to a director or officer during the year must be disclosed in the financial statements, unless it is a loan made in the ordinary course of business by a company whose business includes the lending of money. A loan to an employee need not be disclosed.

Inventories. There is no statutory requirement that the basis of stating inventory be given, but the Institute suggests that an appropriate description of the basis of stating inventory on the balance sheet is desirable. The Institute recommendation is that stock-in-trade be carried at cost (with or without overhead addition), but not in excess of realizable or replacement value, except that in the case of tea, rubber-producing companies and some mining companies, stock-in-trade may be carried at selling prices less selling costs. The comparison of cost and net realizable or replacement value may be made on the basis of (a) item-by-item, (b) group-by-group, or (c) in the aggregate.

The base stock and Lifo method are permissible, but since they are not recognized for income tax purposes, they are seldom used.

Directors' Statement Regarding Current Assets. If, in the directors' opinion, any of the current assets do not have a value, or realization in the ordinary course of business, at least equal to the amount at which they are stated, this fact must be disclosed in a note to the financial statements or in a report or statement annexed thereto.

Fixed Assets

While the Institute's "Recommendation on Accounting Principles" (N.15) continues to favor historical cost as the basis for reporting fixed assets, there is no prohibition against substituting values based on independent appraisals. Subsequent depreciation should be computed and charged to income on the higher appraised values of the fixed assets; for income tax purposes depreciation is permitted only on cost and at rates prescribed by the revenue authorities.

The Companies Act requires that the method or methods used to arrive at the amount of fixed assets under each heading will be stated. It appears that the description "at valuation or cost" applied to the gross amount of fixed assets complies with this section, although the best practice requires disclosure of more than the minimum information.

The increment resulting from an upward appraisal of fixed assets is usually credited to the capital reserve account. There are differing legal decisions on the question whether or not a company is permitted to distribute a surplus of this kind, but the Jenkins Committee on company law, having considered evidence from the Institutes of England and Wales and of Scotland, were of the opinion that such surplus should not be directly or indirectly available for distribution. Surplus may be utilized for distribution of bonus shares.

Interest and Overhead During Construction. Except in the case of businesses engaged in property development, "Interest during Construction" is rarely charged to the cost for fixed assets in the United Kingdom, and if charged, the amount is based on interest actually paid. The cost of fixed assets constructed by the company's employees may or may not include overhead applicable to the work; there has been no generally accepted rule issued on this point.

Goodwill and Other Intagibles

Unless circumstances indicate that these items should be written down in order to present a true and fair view of the accounts, they may either be retained in the accounts at cost, or written down or off by charge usually to undistributed profits or to capital reserves. However, whatever treatment is followed is disclosed as a matter of good practice. It is not required by Companies Act that the method used to arrive at the balance of goodwill as shown on the balance sheet be stated.

Deferred Charges

Debt Discount and Expense. These items are usually written off to revenue reserves when they are incurred, although the method of amortization over the life of the related issue is permissable. The Act permits a charge to share premium account.

Organization (Preliminary) Expenses. Preliminary expenses are required by the Act to be separately stated in the balance sheet "so far as they are not written off." There is no requirement for amortization of this type of deferred item, but it is usually written off over a short period.

Liabilities

Unearned Revenues. In the United States, amounts received in advance for subscriptions, etc., are classified as deferred income, after deducting the estimated cost of earning such revenues in the ensuing period or periods. In the United Kingdom, the entire amount is either separately disclosed and classified or grouped with current liabilities.

Liability Under Long-term Leases. It is not usual to disclose liabilities on long-term leases in United Kingdom financial statements.

Pension Liability. The Institute of Chartered Accountants in England and Wales recommends that, where there is an obligation to provide pensions or other retirement benefits which are not covered by contributions to a retirement benefits plan, provision should be made for the related liability if the amount is material; if no such provision has been made, disclosure of the facts should be made in a footnote to the financial statements. If, at the time a pension plan is established, the cost of past service has not been provided and paid in full, the amount of such unpaid cost should be disclosed in the financial statements of each succeeding year until the total of such cost is paid or provided for.

Provisions and Reserves

The Companies Act distinguishes between balance-sheet items entitled, respectively, "provisions" and "reserves." The source of a "provision" is a charge against current income in arriving at profits; the source of a "reserve" is an appropriation of profits. A provision may represent a valuation allowance (for bad debts, depreciation, etc.) or an amount to provide for a known liability of which the amount "cannot be determined with substantial accuracy." If the amount could be reasonably determined, it would be classified as an accrued liability.

Reserves, in turn, are divided into "revenue" reserves and "capital" reserves.

Revenue Reserves. Revenue reserves are appropriations from profits or surplus, and represent revenue earned in the past which is available for disposal in the future.

Some of the purposes for revenue reserves are to put aside earnings to provide for possible future loss years, to equalize dividends (reserve to be drawn upon in loss years), and to put aside funds for redemption of debt (until date of redemption).

Capital Reserves. The term "capital reserves" is defined in the Act as being one which "does not include any amount regarded as free for distribution through the profit and loss account." There would be included in capital reserves items such as:

Premium on capital stock paid in

Amounts reserved for replacement of plant at higher prices

Profit accumulated for redemption of debentures, when redemption has been effected

Surplus arising from revaluation of fixed assets

Surplus of subsidiaries at dates of acquisition.

The Act provides that the share premium account (premium on capital stock paid in) which is a capital reserve, may only be applied in the following ways: (a) paying up an issue of bonus shares (stock dividend); (b) writing off preliminary expenses or the expenses of an issue of shares or debentures; and (c) providing the premium payable on the redemption of any redeemable preference shares or debentures of the company. The share premium account is otherwise treated as part of the share capital of the company which cannot be reduced or repaid without consent of the court.

Redemption of Preference Shares. The Act also provides that when preference shares are redeemed out of profits, an amount equivalent to their par value must be transferred from profit and loss to "Capital Redemption Reserve Fund." This reserve may be utilized only for the issue of "bonus shares" (stock dividend).

Preference shares may also be redeemed out of the proceeds of a new issue.

If such shares are redeemed at a premium, the premium must be charged to profit and loss, or against the existing balance of a prior share premium account.

Secret Reserves. The Act prohibits the creation of "secret reserves" by requiring disclosure of the additions to and reductions of both revenue and capital reserves under each of their individual headings. Further, the provision for depreciation, renewals or dimnution in value of assets, or provisions for any known liability which is in excess of that which, in the opinion of the directors, is reasonably necessary for the purpose, must be shown as a reserve and not as a provision.

The Act excepts from the above restrictions banking, discount, assurance and, through powers granted to the Board of Trade, also grants certain exemptions to special types of shipping companies. The Board of Trade may permit companies not to disclose certain reserves if satisfied that such disclosure would be prejudicial to the company's interests.

22

Stock Options

Stock options are sometimes granted in the United Kingdom. The Companies Act requires that, in such cases, there be disclosed in the annual accounts by a note or in a statement or report annexed thereto, the number, description and amount of shares under option, the period during which the option is exercisable, and the price to be paid for shares under such option.

Stock Dividends

In the United Kingdom, bonus shares (stock dividends) are accounted for at par by the issuer, and the amount thereof may be charged to either revenue or capital reserves as authorized by the Board of Directors. They are usually substantial in amount and are not issued in lieu of cash dividends.

Normally, no adjustment is made in the book amount of investment when stock dividends are received by a corporation. If an adjustment is made, an amount equivalent to par value may be credited to a capital reserve. They may also be credited to income, although some professional accountants within the United Kingdom would take exception to this treatment.

Profit and Loss Statement

Sales and Cost of Sales. The Companies Act (1948) does not require disclosure of sales or cost of sales. Most companies' published reports begin with a figure representing profit before taxation, or with the trading profit followed by other items of which the Companies Act requires disclosure. In many cases, sales or "turnover" are reported in the directors' reports or chairman's speech, but cost of sales is rarely disclosed.

Items to Be Disclosed Under Companies Act (1948). Certain items are required to be shown separately in the profit and loss account or in notes thereto. The items required to be shown include:

Charges
> The amount charged to revenue for depreciation, renewals or diminution in value of fixed assets. If such charge is provided by some method other than depreciation or provision for renewals, or is not provided for, the method used or the fact that it is not

provided must be disclosed.

The amount of interest on the company's debentures and other fixed loans.

Taxation

The amounts of charges for taxation on profits, and the basis on which the charge for United Kingdom income tax is computed.

Appropriations

The amounts provided for redemption of redeemable preference shares and for redemption of loans

The amount, if material, set aside or proposed to be set aside to, or withdrawn from, reserves

The amount, if material, set aside for provisions other than depreciation, etc., and the amount withdrawn from such provisions and not applied for the purposes thereof.

Other

The aggregate amount of dividends paid or proposed, stating whether the amount shown is before or after deduction of income tax

Any material respects in which any items shown in the profit and loss account are affected by transactions of a sort not usually undertaken by the company or otherwise by circumstances of an exceptional or nonrecurrent nature, or by a change in the basis of accounting.

Directors' Emoluments. The aggregate amount of directors' emoluments must be disclosed in the accounts or a statement annexed thereto. There must be included in this figure amounts received from the company and its subsidiaries by directors of the holding company for services, and for such of their expenses as are charged and treated as emoluments for income tax purposes and contributions under any pension plan scheme.

This amount must distinguish between sums received as director and other emoluments, such as that received as a salaried officer.

Remuneration of Auditors. If the remuneration of auditors for their examination is not fixed by the company in general meeting, the amount thereof, including reimbursed expenses, must be shown under separate heading in the profit and loss account.

Depreciation and Depletion. The straight-line and the reducing-balance methods of computing depreciation are the most common. The latter is the method generally used for income tax purposes.

The Institute recommends that if additional provisions are made for obsolescence that cannot be foreseen, or for a possible increase in cost of replacement, they should be treated as appropriations of profits to a capital reserve not available for distribution.

Provision for depletion of wasting assets (mines, wells, quarries, etc.), is recommended by the Institute, but if the practice of a particular company is not to make such provision, it should be made clear to the shareholders that dividends distributed to them are, in part, a return of capital.

Provision for Income Tax. The fiscal year for United Kingdom income tax begins on April 6, an income tax for that year is generally based on the accounting year of the taxpayer ended within the preceding "tax year." For a calendar year company, therefore, its tax based upon the income of the year 1962, is assessed for the "tax year" ended April 5, 1964 (1963/4), and is payable on January 1, 1964.

The Institute recommends that profit and loss be charged in each year with a provision for income tax based on the profits for that year, and should be so described. It further recommends that the balance sheet should include under appropriate captions as a current liability for future income tax, amounts representing the full amount of unpaid taxes on profits to date.

The portion of such unpaid taxes representing the liability for tax on the profits of calendar year 1961, payable January 1, 1963, is a "provision" includible in the liability section; the portion representing "future liability" for taxes based on profits for calendar year 1962, but applicable to the "tax year" 63/64, and payable January 1, 1964, has been the subject of discussion as to whether it is a "provision" (liability) or revenue reserve. Against its classification as a liability is the fact that considerable time elapses between its creation and its settlement, so that future losses or changes in tax laws may substantially change its amount. The Institute's recommendation, however, is that it should be shown as a separate item, captioned "Future Income Tax," on the balance sheet, and not aggregated with other reserves.

In any case, the Act requires that there should be shown by footnote or otherwise the basis on which the amounts included for income tax have been computed. Accounting practice recognizes that if the full amount computed on profits to date is not set aside that fact should be made clear.

Allocation of Income Tax. In addition to annual depreciation allowed for tax purposes, which is not usually the amount recorded on the books, the tax laws permit the deduction of an additional "initial allowance" (accelerated depreciation) applicable to the acquisition of certain new assets, which is usually not recorded on the books. The total annual depreciation and initial allowance (known as "capital allowances") taken over the life of the asset may not exceed its cost less salvage. The initial allowance is granted irrespective of the amount provided for depreciation for accounting purposes.

In the early years of the asset's life and especially when intial allowances are received, the tax deduction may exceed the book depreciation, and the Institute recommends that the income tax deferred by such procedure be set aside and shown as a separate item in the balance sheet, described as "Tax Equalization Reserve" and grouped with "Future Income Tax."

Investment Allowances. The United Kingdom laws also provide for "investment allowances" in varying percentages applicable to certain classifications of assets, which reduce the amount of income tax and profits tax due.

The Institute considers that such tax savings should reduce the current charge to taxes in the profit and loss account, and, if the savings are material, the extent to which the tax charge is relieved by them should be shown in the profit and loss account or in a note thereto. As a matter of financial policy, the company may make a corresponding transfer from profits to a capital revenue reserve. The Institute considers that allocation of the tax saving over the life of the assets is not appropriate.

Extraordinary Charges and Credits. The Institute's "Recommendations" (No. N.18 par. 43) deals with the treatment in the profit and loss or surplus account of "items of an exceptional or non-recurrent nature." They should be dealt with:

> In such a way as to show in the particular circumstances a true and fair view of the result of the year and, apart from tax adjustments relative to earlier years, which, if material, should be separately disclosed, may be dealt with as follows:
>
> (a) Where the items arise from the trading operations of the company, they may be dealt with in arriving at the trading surplus or deficit and disclosed separately by way of note or separate inset on the face of the account
>
> (b) They may be shown separately in the section of the account which includes other income and nontrading expenditure of the year
>
> (c) They may be shown separately after the "profit after taxation"
>
> (d) They may, in appropriate circumstances, be omitted from the profit and loss account and taken directly to a reserve.

The recommendation of the Institute does not mention the criteria for distinguishing between a charge to income for the year and a charge to surplus as does the American Institute's Bulletin No. 43, (p. 63), which states that items of this character chargeable to surplus are those which are material in relation to the company's net income and are not clearly identifiable with or do not result from the usual or typical business operations of the period. This, however, is covered in part by the requirements already mentioned under the profit and loss statement.

REQUIREMENTS FOR LISTING ON THE STOCK EXCHANGE, LONDON, AND FOR PROSPECTUSES UNDER THE COMPANIES ACT

Since in almost all cases the issuance of a prospectus in connection with an offer to sell new securities is accompanied with an application for listing such securities for trading on the Stock Exchange, the requirements for both are considered jointly. The prospectus must conform to the requirements of the Fourth Schedule of the Companies Act, and the listing application with the requirements of the Stock Exchange.

The accountant's report covers:

Profits and losses for ten years

Assets and liabilities

Rate of dividends for the past five years

Aggregate emoluments of directors for the last accounting period

If the accounts have not been made up and audited to a date within three months of the date of issue, the report must state this fact

Other relevant matters.

The statement of profits and losses is presented on a group basis. The statement of assets and liabilities must be presented for both the parent company alone and the consolidated group.

Further, the statement of profit and loss, while based on those shown in the annual accounts, may reflect adjustments as between years of the ten-year period resulting from changes in the basis of accounting during such period, allocation to the proper period of subsequently arising items of income and expenditure, and other matters requiring adjustment. There must be filed with the Stock Exchange a statement setting forth the adjustments made and the reasons therefor in order that the statement may fairly serve the purpose for which it is prepared.

If the proceeds of sale are to be applied to the purchase of a business or a company which will become a subsidiary, a report by accountants (not necessarily the company's auditors) upon such business or company covering profits and losses for the past five years and the assets and liabilities at the end of the latest year must be furnished.

The reporting accountants are required to file the following assurances or data: (a) letter of consent to the appearance of their report in the context of the prospectus; (b) that they are satisfied with the evidence of stocktaking throughout the period under review; (c) that proper provision for depreciation of fixed assets has been made; (d) information concerning the equalization of taxation; and (e) in the case of a company with material overseas interests, separate information on income derived therefrom and assets employed. Information must also be furnished regarding any restrictions on remittance of profits or repatriation of capital.

The prospectus in the United Kingdom contains a statement which will not be found in one issued in the United States. This is the statement of future prospects which is the responsibility of the directors of the company offering securities for sale.

Since the prospectus must contain a statement that the independent accountants have consented to the publication of their report in the context in which it appears, it is generally considered that the accountants, before giving this consent, need to examine the grounds on which the statement is based.

If the company desiring to issue new securities is one with present securities listed on the Stock Exchange, London, there is issued an "advertised statement," which informs the public about the securities for which a quotation is being sought on the Exchange and which will then be available to the public for purchase. The statement is governed by the rules of the Exchange and not by the Companies Act.

FORMS OF BUSINESS ORGANIZATION

The forms of business organization in the Republic of South Africa are similar to those found in the United Kingdom, the principal ones being private and public companies with limited liability. Regulations governing their formation and operation are prescribed in the South African Companies Act, 1926, as amended through 1963. This act is similar to the British Companies Act of 1948, with special modifications for South Africa.

In addition to the two types of companies stated above, business may be carried out as a partnership or as a sole proprietorship.

Every company, public or private, foreign or domestic, and any association, syndicate or partnership, consisting of over twenty persons, operating in South Africa must be registered with the Registrar of Companies in Pretoria, except foreign banks and insurance companies which must be registered with the Registrars of Banks and Insurance, respectively.

The Public Company

This form of organization most closely resembles the usual United States publicly held corporation. It must be formed by a minimum of seven shareholders, but there is no limit to the total number of shareholders. There is a requirement that a public company have at least two directors who must deliver to the Registrar of Companies written consent to act as directors. A company registered with limited liability must have "Limited" in its name.

To form a public or private company an original and two notarized copies of the memorandum and articles of association, a statement of the registered address of the company and evidence of payment of a tax on nominal capital must be presented to the Registrar of Companies. South African law does not provide for shares of no-par value. Directors of public companies must show evidence that they have subscribed to or contracted in writing to take up qualification shares, if required by the articles of association.

Before a public company may issue shares, it must file with the Registrar of Companies a prospectus (described later) or a statement in lieu of a prospectus where shares are not going to be issued publicly. It must obtain a certificate from the Registrar of Companies in order to commence business. A statutory report giving certain details of subscription to shares, cash received, names and addresses of directors and officers and estimated preliminary and flotation expenses of the company must be prepared and presented to the registrar and to the shareholders of the company at the statutory meeting.

The public company is subject to compulsory annual audit and its annual balance sheet and profit and loss account, auditor's and directors' report, as well as its annual summary pertaining to share capital are required to be filed with the registrar's office.

The Private Company

This type of company is formed to obtain the advantage of limited liability for family businesses, small closely held businesses and for subsidiaries of other companies. It may be formed by two or more persons. The number of members is limited to fifty, excluding employees and former employees. Transfer of shares of a private company is restricted and such a company in South Africa may not issue shares or debentures publicly. A private company must add to its name the words "Proprietary" and "Limited" or the Afrikaans equivalents.

Although a private company is subject to compulsory annual audit, it is neither required to file its annual balance sheet and profit and loss account publicly nor to file a statutory report nor to hold a statutory meeting. It is, however, required to file an annual summary (described later), and to have at least one director. It may commence business immediately after registration without specific authorization.

Branch of a Foreign Company

All banks and insurance companies are governed by special laws, whether they are incorporated in South Africa or are branches of foreign companies. Any other foreign company may establish a place of business and carry on its activities without forming a local subsidiary. It must publicly file its annual balance sheet and profit and loss account.

4

However, most foreign companies operate through local subsidiaries in the Republic of South Africa, rather than through branches.

Other Forms of Business Organization

In addition to the two types of limited liability corporations, a partnership or an individual proprietorship may be used to carry on business. Except in Natal and the Transvaal, a partnership is not required to register. Two to twenty persons may form a partnership by agreement, either oral or written. Each partner is jointly and severally liable for all debts contracted by the partnership.

Two of the provinces have a special type of partnership where the liability of certain special partners is limited. The general partners are jointly and severally liable for partnership debts up to and beyond that which pertains to the special partners.

Business Records

The Companies Act states that every company shall keep in one of the two official languages (English or Afrikaans) such books of account as are necessary to exhibit a "true and fair view" of the company's affairs. The books and accounts may be kept at the registered office of the company or elsewhere at the discretion of the directors. If accounting records are maintained outside of South Africa, which is unusual, returns must be sent to South Africa and retained there to show with reasonable accuracy the financial position of the company at least every twelve months. These returns must permit the preparation of the company's financial statements in accordance with the Act.

PUBLIC OFFICER

Every company must appoint a public officer who must be approved by the Commissioner of Inland Revenue. The public officer is usually the secretary of the company but may be another employee or a person from outside of the company. The duty of the public officer is to take responsibility for the preparation of the tax return, to sign it on behalf of the company and to act as a liaison with the tax office in all matters pertaining to the taxes of the company. The auditor may not be the public officer of the company he audits and therefore may not sign the tax return, but he may assist in its preparation.

Since a balance sheet issued by a company must always have the auditor's report attached to it, it follows that such report is included in the balance sheet accompanying a tax return. There is no legal requirement that such report be attached to other than corporate tax returns. Financial statements, however, must be satisfactory to the tax authorities and they may request audited accounts from companies.

THE ACCOUNTING PROFESSION

General

The accounting profession in South Africa dates from the early part of this century when societies of accountants were formed in the republic of the Transvaal and the Orange Free State and the Cape and Natal colonies (all four became provinces upon formation of the Union of South Africa in 1910). The founders of these organizations were in most cases members of the Institute of Chartered Accountants in England and Wales, or the Institute of Chartered Accountants of Scotland or the Society of Incorporated Accountants and Auditors, and the local societies were modeled along lines that adhered closely to these institutes.

In Transvaal and Natal, ordinances were passed which required practicing accountants to be registered members of the societies, and prohibiting anyone from practicing as an accountant or auditor or signing a balance sheet and profit and loss account unless he was so registered. It was not until 1951, however, that such registration was mandatory throughout the Republic.

Chartered Accountant (S.A.)

In 1927, parliament passed "The Chartered Accountants Designation (Private) Act No. 13" which permitted the members of the four societies (discussed later) the sole right to the use of the designation "Chartered Accountant (S.A.)." The members of these societies are not all in public practice; perhaps half of them are in full-time employment in industry or otherwise. There is no distinction as to title or classification of membership whether the member is in public practice or engaged in some other capacity.

Public Accountants' and Auditors' Act, 1951, as Amended. This Act was designed to govern those members of the accountancy profession (largely chartered accountants) who are engaged in the practice of public accounting. It specified certain qualifications for those entitled to register under the Act, and restricted the practice of public accounting to persons who did, in fact, register.

The administration of the Act is under a "Public Accountants' and Auditors' Board," composed of representatives of the chartered societies, educators, and four members nominated by the central government. The Board's powers include that of regulating required service under articles of clerkship, conducting the final qualifying examination, regulating initial and annual fees for registration, the prescription of degrees, diplomas and other qualifications which will entitle any person to exemption from compliance with any of the requirements. The Board also prescribes what will constitute improper conduct, imposes sanctions for such actions, and publishes a journal relating to accounting and auditing matters.

Requirements for registration as an accountant and auditor for a person resident in the Republic are that he:

1. Must submit application and pay the required fee
2. Must be not less than twenty-one years old
3. Must have served under articles of clerkship for the prescribed period and have passed the prescribed examinations. (Length of time of clerkship and number of examinations may be reduced by obtaining a university degree).

The law provides for certain substitutions for item 3 above for persons who were members of the societies or equivalent societies on or before January 1, 1950, or who were eligible for membership therein at the time the law was passed.

The Board may register as nonresident accountants and auditors members of certain other professional bodies, including members of the American Institute of Certified Public Accountants.

Service Under Articles. In order to enter into "Articles of Clerkship," the applicant must satisfy the Board that he has passed the matriculation examination of the Joint Matriculation Board or an equivalent examination. The period of articled clerkship which must be served is five years, unless the applicant holds a university degree, in which case the period is usually reduced to three years. During this five year period the applicant is expected to obtain a Certificate on the Theory of Ac-

7

countancy by preparing for, taking and passing four intermediate examinations given by recognized South African universities. He is also expected to take and pass a final qualifying examination conducted by the "Public Accountants' and Auditors' Board." These examinations may be taken in either English or Afrikaans.

The applicant can prepare for the intermediate examinations by attending approximately ten hours of classes weekly at local universities or he may take a correspondence course from the University of South Africa in Pretoria.

The applicant and the public accountant with whom he is articled must sign an agreement called "Articles of Clerkship" on a form prescribed by the Board. The form is then filed with the Board and upon completion of clerkship the public accountant must endorse the articles to the effect that the period of service has been completed to his entire satisfaction.

Functions of Chartered Accountants in Public Practice. In addition to accepting appointments as auditors, chartered accountants also perform secretarial work, act as tax consultants, accept appointments as trustees, act in liquidations, act as consultants on systems work, and also offer assistance in the field of financial management. They may also act as directors in those companies for which they are not the auditor, or they may be cost consultants or financial experts.

Disciplinary Rules. The Board is empowered to inquire into and deal with any complaint laid before it with respect to any registered accountant and auditor who:

> ... commits any offense involving dishonesty, is dishonest in the performance of any duties in connection with his professional work, assists in evading any taxes payable, signs any false statement knowing it to be false, knowingly or recklessly prepares or maintains any false books of account, divulges any confidential information, accepts fees contingent upon the result of his work, accepts commissions or brokerage on work referred to others, permits his name to be used in connection with estimates of future earnings, or solicits professional work by solicitation or advertising.

The Companies Act also created penalties for infractions of the Board's disciplinary rules summarized above. The Board may remove or suspend any registrant who is found guilty of contraventions of the Act or of unprofessional conduct.

Ethics. The Code of Professional Etiquette promulgated by the Board requires that before accepting an engagement previously undertaken by another registered accountant and auditor, the latter shall be consulted by the auditor who has been approached to succeed to the engagement.

The Code also covers the basis for quoting fees, publishing of articles on professional subjects, criticisms of other registered accountants and auditors, and recruitment of staff employed by fellow accountants.

Appointment of Auditors

The Companies Act provides that every company at each annual general meeting of shareholders will appoint one or more auditors (who must be "registered") to act from the end of that meeting until the end of the following annual meeting. The auditors are considered to be representatives of the shareholders and as such are looked upon by the shareholders for an opinion as to whether or not the final accounts and balance sheet as presented by the directors truly and fairly reflect the affairs of the company.

The Act states that the auditor will have access to the books, accounts and vouchers at all times and will have the right to obtain whatever information or explanations from the officers of the company which, in the auditor's opinion, are necessary for the performance of his duties. He is entitled to attend any general meeting of the company and may speak on matters pertaining to him as auditor.

It is obligatory that the auditor's report to be read at the annual general meeting of shareholders, unless all the members present agree to the contrary. No company balance sheet may be issued or published without the auditor's report being attached thereto.

Professional Accounting Organizations

As stated previously, each of the four provinces of the Republic of South Africa have a legally constituted accountants' society whose members have the right to be designated "chartered accountants." These societies, which have approximately 4,000 members, are the following:

The Transvaal Society of Accountants

The Cape Society of Accountants and Auditors

The Natal Society of Accountants

The Society of Accountants and Auditors in the Orange Free State.

After passage of the Public Accountants' and Auditors' Act (1951),

9

these chartered societies continued as voluntary provincial societies to deal with professional research and matters within the provinces.

The Act provides that in addition to any other requirements prescribed by any society for admission, any person who has been registered as an accountant and auditor under the Act is entitled to membership in such society provided his registration was acquired by serving under articles of clerkship and passing the prescribed examinations, or alternatively, passing the final qualifying examination and having not less than six years' experience in the office of a practicing public accountant.

These societies have occasionally published pamphlets and technical papers. The Transvaal Society of Accountants in 1959, published an address by two members entitled "Some Thoughts Toward the Formulation of a Code of Auditing Procedure." Each chartered society has its own code of etiquette which is generally based on those of the English societies. There are no classes of members of the societies such as fellows or associates. Each member is a chartered accountant (S.A. or C.A. only).

In 1945, the above societies and the Rhodesian society formed the Joint Council of the Societies of Chartered Accountants whose main functions are as follows:

1. To act as an advisory council to the societies and to coordinate their activities more closely and effectively.
2. To promote the prestige of the profession by encouraging a high standard of professional and general education and knowledge
3. To deal at the request of the societies with matters affecting the profession which require consideration on a national rather than on a provincial level
4. To provide for research in South Africa in accounting, auditing and kindred matters
5. To develop on behalf of the societies a public relations organization.

This joint council was responsible for sponsoring the first congress of South African accountants in 1955, the second in 1960, and is preparing for the third in 1965.

The members of the branches of the "Society of Incorporated Accountants and Auditors" in Capetown, Johannesburg and Durban have been assimilated into the chartered societies.

AUDITING STANDARDS

General Standards

The Joint Council of the Societies of Chartered Accountants of South Africa has recently issued (1964) Statement A 1 "Auditing Principles and Standards" which essentially covers the general and field work standards of the American Institute of CPAs, including references to independence, internal control, materialty, and the auditor's responsibility for discovery of fraud. The auditor must, of course, conduct his examination so as to enable him to report upon the accounts in accordance with the provision of the Companies Act and the provisions of Section 26 of the Public Accountants' and Auditors' Act.

Independence. The Companies Act provides that the following will be disqualified from appointment as auditor of a company:

1. An officer or servant of the company or of any other company performing secretarial work for the company
2. A person who is a partner of, or employs, or is in the employment of, an officer or servant of the company
3. A person who, by himself, or with his partner or employee, habitually or regularly, performs the duties of secretary or bookkeeper to the company
4. A body corporate.

There is no specific provision against the auditor's having a financial interest in the company he is auditing, but this practice is discouraged by several of the larger firms of accountants. Rule 3 above is interpreted to mean that while the auditor may not keep the books of a public company, he may prepare the closing entries and the financial statements. Under certain circumstances an auditor of a private company could also superintend or keep its books.

Standards of Field Work

There is no statute which defines auditing procedures in the Republic of South Africa, but as indicated above, a statement concerning such procedures has recently been issued by the Joint Council. The auditor has attained and follows a high standard of professional competence in South Africa.

The auditor is not required to confirm receivables, although more and more practitioners are doing so. There is no requirement that the auditor witness the taking of physical inventories, although this practice also is usually followed. A separate review of internal accounting control is not usually performed in connection with the preparation of the audit program, except in the case of larger firms or at the special request of the client.

Standards of Reporting

The standards of reporting of the auditor in the Republic of South Africa are governed mainly by the Companies Act, as amended, the Insurance, Banking, Building Societies Act and other legislation. There is no standard form of audit report. Most practitioners choose to use the actual wording of the section of the Act in making the statements that are required to be made, followed by their opinion.

The usual form of auditor's unqualified report, which complies with the requirements of the Companies Act is as follows:

> We have examined, to the extent to which we have considered necessary, the books and accounts and vouchers of the company and have satisfied ourselves of the existence of the securities. We have obtained all the information and explanations which to the best of our knowledge and belief, were necessary for the purpose of our audit. In our opinion, proper books of account have been kept by the company, so far as appears from our examination of those books.

> The foregoing balance sheet and profit and loss account are in agreement with the books of account and in our opinion and to the best of our information and according to the explanations given to us, the said accounts give the information required by the Companies Act, 1926, as amended, in the manner so required and the balance sheet gives a true and fair view of the state of the company's affairs as at December 31, 19. . and the profit and loss account gives a true and fair view of the profit for the year ended on that date.

An auditor of a holding company must report on consolidated statements and certify that they reflect a "true and fair view" of the affairs of the group from the point of view of the members of the holding company.

Consistency. The Companies Act requires disclosure by footnote or in the body of the accounts of any inconsistent application in the basis of accounting.

12

Materiality. The South African chartered accountant has the same concept of materiality and its effect on his work and on his opinion on the financial statements as does a CPA in the United States. The Companies Act, while not actually defining the word, makes several references to materiality as does the Public Accountants' and Auditors' Act in the form, "Material Irregularity."

DIRECTORS' REPORT

The Companies Act requires that the directors prepare and present a report on the state of affairs of the company at each annual general meeting of shareholders. This report, which must be either in English or Afrikaans, is to be presented in addition to the profit and loss account and balance sheet as at the end of the financial year. This report should include a statement as to dividends paid, declared or proposed, the amount to be transferred to "reserves" and the amount of directors' remuneration recommended. It must state any change during the course of the year in the nature of the company's business or in the composition of the Board of Directors of the company or any of its subsidiaries. It must also disclose the particulars of material changes in the assets and liabilities of the company which may have taken place between the date of the balance sheet and the date of the report and which would materially affect the financial statements. The report must also state the details of any subscriptions of shares or debentures during the year, the number of shares or debentures subscribed for, the consideration received by the company, and the date of the subscription.

ACCOUNTING PRINCIPLES AND PRACTICES

Form and Content of Financial Statements

The accounting rules and practices in South Africa are based upon the Companies Act. The eighth schedule of this Act lists the requirements which must be followed in the preparation of financial statements. In addition, the Public Accountants' and Auditors' Board, the Joint Council and the councils of each society actively promote the application of generally accepted accounting principles.

Statement Presentation. The general arrangement of financial statements in South Africa is similar to that in the United Kingdom—capital and liabilities on the left side and assets on the right side.

Balance Sheet. The following information must be specified in the balance sheet account or in notes thereto:

1. Classes and amount of each class of share capital authorized and issued
2. Amount and earliest date of redemption of any redeemable preference shares, and the redemption price
3. Any share capital on which interest has been paid out of capital and the rate of interest
4. Particulars of options on unissued shares, showing number of shares, description, option price, and the period during which the option is exercisable
5. Details of any shares which may be issued by the directors
6. Period and amount in arrears on cumulative preferred stock
7. Particulars of any redeemed debentures which the company has the power to reissue
8. Basis on which foreign currencies have been translated into South African currency, where the amount of assets and liabilities affected is material
9. If the directors believe that current assets have a net realizable value less than that stated in the accounts, a statement to this effect
10. The market value of nontrade investments if it differs from the amount shown in the balance sheet
11. Details of any assets pledged to guarantee debts of third parties
12. The aggregate amount of estimated liability for contingencies
13. The aggregate amount of unrecorded commitments for capital expenditures
14. Fixed assets must be distinguished from current assets. Where an asset is not distinguished as fixed or current, the asset must be specifically described. The aggregate amount provided or written off since the date of acquisition of the fixed assets for depreciation or diminution must be stated.

The following expenditures, which may be carried forward, must be disclosed insofar as they are not written off:

1. Preliminary expenses
2. Expenses incurred on any issue of shares or debentures
3. Commission for procuring subscriptions for shares or debentures
4. Discount on debentures.

14

With the exception of the provision for depreciation, reasonable provisions for bad debt, discount, etc., may be deducted from assets without disclosure. Provision for estimated liabilities must be separately disclosed.

Profit and Loss Statement. The statement of profit and loss of commercial companies does not usually show sales and cost of sales. It must show separately exceptional or nonrecurring transactions, compensation paid to present and past directors, auditor's remuneration (unless approved at the annual general meeting), profits or losses on share transactions, income from investments, aggregate amount of dividends paid or proposed, profits or losses on selling nontrade or fixed assets, and, separately, interest on debentures, fixed loans, other borrowed monies, and particulars of taxation charges.

The Companies Act, 1926, also requires that disclosure be made if depreciation is not provided for or if it is provided by a method other than a charge to profit and loss. If there is no provision for taxes, there must be a statement to this effect giving the reason therefor and the period for which no provision has been made.

Comparative Financial Statements. The Act requires that comparative figures be presented for the immediately preceding period.

Consolidated Financial Statements. A consolidated balance sheet and profit and loss account of a holding company and its subsidiaries is required when a company, incorporated in South Africa, which is not the wholly owned subsidiary of another company, has one or more subsidiary companies at year end. In certain cases group accounts may be prepared in other forms, e.g., by submitting audited financial statements of the subsidiary or subsidiaries in addition to those of the holding company. Where no consolidated accounts are prepared, the directors must report the reason therefor, and the auditor in his report must state whether or not he concurs with the directors' statement.

In a holding company's unconsolidated balance sheet, shares in and amounts due from subsidiary companies must be shown separately with a breakdown between shares and indebtedness. Amounts written off the carrying value of such shares or reasonable provisions against losses of subsidiaries need not be disclosed, provided that the method of arriving at the value of the shares is disclosed.

Even though consolidated accounts are presented, the holding company must also prepare and present its own balance sheet and profit and loss account excluding those of its subsidiaries.

Pooling of Interests

The "pooling of interests" concept is not recognized in South Africa.

Inventories

It is not necessary to disclose the basis of inventory valuation in the accounts, although more and more companies are doing so.

Fixed Assets and Investments

The basis on which the fixed assets and investments are recorded must be disclosed on the balance sheet, as well as the quoted market value of investments.

Interest on borrowed money which is used to finance the construction of a plant for a new company may be capitalized. Debt discount for funds used for the same purpose may also be capitalized.

The Companies Act permits, when shares have been issued to finance plant construction, and provided proper authorization has been made in company articles or by special resolution, that interest be computed on the amount of paid-up share capital and charged as part of the plant construction cost.

Revaluation of Fixed Assets

There is no regulation prohibiting the revaluation of fixed assets. Such revaluation is usually on the basis of an appraisal and this fact must be stated on the financial statements. It is not unusual to add the date of the appraisal and to state whether it was made by a sworn appraiser. The credit arising on revaluation would be shown in a capital reserve section (not distributable). There is no tax payable on the increment in net asset value and depreciation on the revalued portion is not an allowable tax deduction.

Intangible Assets

Write-offs or write-downs of intangible assets may be charged against "reserves" with full disclosure, but the preferred method is to charge them against the profit and loss account.

Liabilities

Each secured liability must be specified as well as the assets which secure such liabilities.

Long-term Leases

It is not a normal procedure to disclose commitments under long-term leases unless such leases are not entered into in the ordinary course of business.

Treasury Shares or Debentures

Companies may not deal in their own shares. They may, however, re-acquire their own debentures, and any resultant profit is usually credited to capital surplus.

Reserves and Provisions

There is an important difference in terminology between the United States and South Africa in regard to reserves and provisions. In South Africa amounts set aside out of profits are either provisions or reserves.

A provision is an amount written off or retained to provide for depreciation, renewals or diminution in value of assets or retained by way of providing for any known liability where the exact amount cannot be determined with reasonable accuracy.

An amount set aside for purposes other than the above is a reserve. Reserves are divided into revenue reserves and capital reserves. A capital reserve does not include any amount regarded as free for distribution through the profit and loss account, and a revenue reserve is any reserve other than a capital reserve. The aggregate amounts respectively of capital reserves, revenue reserves and provisions for known liabilities are required to be stated in the balance sheet under separate headings.

When any amount retained to provide for depreciation, renewals or diminution in value or for any known liability is in excess of that which the directors and auditors believe necessary, the excess is treated as a revenue reserve and not as a provision. If, contrary to the opinion of the directors, the auditors consider that an amount should be treated as a reserve, they are required to report specifically on that subject to the shareholders.

A deficit in the profit and loss account may first be applied against revenue reserves and then against capital reserves. If neither type of reserves exist, the deficit should be deducted from capital. Some auditors believe that a reserve for increased cost of replacement of assets should be considered as a capital reserve—not available for dividends.

Secret Reserves

"Secret reserves" are not permitted except in the case of banks and insurance companies.

Share Premium Account

When a company issues shares at a premium, the amount of such premium will be transferred to a "share premium account"; this account may be charged with the fixed amount of "bonus shares" (stock dividends) issued to shareholders, with preliminary expenses, expenses, commissions or discounts on any issue of shares or debentures, or with premiums payable on redemption of any preference shares or debentures of the company.

Statement of Profit and Loss

Depreciation and Depletion. Except for mining undertakings, companies in South Africa follow the usual United States practice of charging periodic income with the cost of fixed assets through amortization, depreciation or depletion. In the case of mining companies, the initial capital expenditure is not amortized and, therefore, the replacement of fixed assets is charged to income. For tax purposes, however, this expenditure is amortized over the life of the mine.

The "declining-balance" method is the most common depreciation method being used. By a recent change in tax practice the "straight-line" method has also been authorized. It is an exception where depreciation is provided on the cost of buildings acquired for investment purposes; however, it is a fairly general practice to provide for depreciation of buildings in industrial or commercial use.

Stock Dividends. Stock dividends are usually accounted for by the issuing company on the basis of the par value of shares distributed.

Tax-effect Accounting

It is a generally accepted practice to provide for the tax effect when different depreciation methods are used for book and tax purposes.

REQUIREMENTS FOR PUBLIC
SALE OF SECURITIES

The Companies Act requires that a copy of every prospectus proposed to be issued by a company will be filed for registration with the Registrar of Companies. If the prospectus states that the whole or a portion of the shares or debentures offered for subscription has been underwritten, a copy of the underwriting contract and certain other documents will also be filed with the Registrar.

The contents and requirements for preparation of a prospectus or offer to sell securities are included in the sixth schedule to the Companies Act, and must include the following (summarized):

1. Material and relevant particulars of the company and its subsidiaries concerning all share capital, and options thereon, any premium to be paid on shares to be issued, loans, working capital, history and prospects, agreements, directors' and vendors' interests, expenses of the issue and the purpose thereof; also the time of opening of subscription lists and the closing thereof

2. An auditor's report covering dividend information on all types of shares issued during previous five years, and indicating when no dividends were paid, information as to any write up of fixed assets within three years, balance sheet at the closing date and profit and loss account covering preceding five years, with such adjustments considered necessary.

The adjustments made and the reasons therefor must be indicated to the Registrar of Companies and to the Stock Exchange committee, but need not otherwise be published.

Where the prospectus covers a holding company and its subsidiaries, the financial statements should include the latest statement of assets and liabilities of the holding company and its subsidiaries either on a combined or an individual basis. The profit and loss accounts for the preceding five years of the holding company and its subsidiaries either on a combined or an individual basis should be included. If the proceeds of the issue are to be used to purchase a business or acquire another corporate body and that body will become a subsidiary, it is necessary to submit a report by accountants who must be named in the prospectus, giving similar information in respect of such business or corporate body.

There must also be a directors' report showing any material change in the assets or liabilities of the company or any of its subsidiaries which may have taken place between the date as of which the financial statements of the company or its subsidiaries were presented and the date of the prospectus.

REQUIREMENTS FOR LISTING OF SECURITIES ON THE STOCK EXCHANGE

The rules and regulations of the Johannesburg Stock Exchange, the only exchange in South Africa, set forth the minimum standards of disclosure and the requirements for publication of the information in prospectuses by companies seeking to have their shares listed for trading. Applicants must meet certain preliminary requirements, as follows:

1. The company must name a member of the stock exchange to act as its sponsor in all liaison work with the Committee of the Stock Exchange.
2. A listing fee must be paid.
3. The company must submit the memorandum and articles of association for examination. The Committee insists that the articles conform to its requirements and indicate control of issue of stock securities, preemptive rights, absence of transfer restrictions, reasonable borrowing power of the board, remuneration of directors and reporting on subsidiaries. (A company will not be listed where certain shares confer special privileges of management and control.)
4. If the securities have already been issued publicly, a definite proportion must still be held by the public. This rule has been interpreted to mean holding by at least 200 persons and it is required to assure marketability of the shares.
5. A list of shareholders certified by the company's auditor must also be submitted.

The main document that must be prepared in connection with the application for listing is the "Advertised Statement" which may take the form of a prospectus, provided all the necessary information is included in full. It must be published in a Johannesburg newspaper and one other national daily newspaper.

The ending balance sheet must mark a period which ended within twelve months prior to the date of application. The auditor must also report on material changes in the accounts between the date of the last balance sheet and the application date; he must state that debtors' and creditors' accounts do not include any nontrade amounts; he must report on the adequacy of the bad debt provision; he must make a statement that the directors have certified that adequate provision has been made for obsolete, damaged or defective goods; he must make a statement on the basis of valuation of supplies, raw materials and work-in-progress; and he must make a statement as to the elimination of inter-company accounts in consolidation.

In addition, the "Supporting Statement," "General Undertaking" and "Statutory Declaration" must be presented. The supporting statement is signed by the directors and covers certain additional information. The general undertaking is a resolution by the board to supply all information required by the Committee of the Stock Exchange and to furnish such additional information on a continuing basis as is required. The statutory declaration is sworn to by the chairman and the secretary and also affirms certain facts. There are also numerous other documents which must be submitted plus special requirements in connection with amalgamations and the protection of minority interests in such undertakings.

AUSTRALIA

FORMS OF BUSINESS ORGANIZATION

The incorporation of companies in Australia is governed by the laws of the several states and federally administered territories comprising the Commonwealth of Australia. The previously differing state laws and federal ordinances have recently been superseded by new acts and ordinances based on a *pro forma* Uniform Companies Act adopted with certain local modifications by each of the various states and territories.

A company organized under the Act in one state must register in any other state in which it wishes to do business. The Uniform Companies Act provides for three main types of companies: public company, proprietary (or private) company and exempt proprietary company.

An individual may carry on business in his own legal name as a sole proprietorship, but if he wishes to use a different business name he must comply with certain formal registration requirements. Partnerships may be formed under the laws of the different states and resemble the general partnership found under British and United States laws.

The Public Company

This form closely resembles the publicly held United States corporation. The liability of its members is limited to the uncalled amount (if any), on their shareholdings. The public company may be formed by not less than five persons and is, in essence, a company in which public ownership is or may become substantial. These companies must add to their names the word "Limited" or its abbreviation "Ltd."

Shares issued by all types of limited companies must have a nominal value and may be issued at par or at a premium, but may not be issued at a discount without court approval. Bearer shares are not permitted. Shareholders need not be Australian citizens or residents. Financial statements, accompanied by the directors' statement, the secretary's declaration and a report of the auditors must be presented to the annual meeting of shareholders, and must be of a date not more than six months prior to such meeting.

Copies of these statements and reports, the contents of which are prescribed by the Companies Act, must be delivered to the Registrar of Companies of the state under the laws of which the company is incorporated or registered.

All types of limited companies must have a memorandum, which is a printed document, containing the name of the company, its objects, particulars of its authorized capital, full names, addresses and occupations of the original subscribers and the number of shares each subscriber agrees to take of the capital. Each company is also required to have articles of association which set out the regulations for the management of the company, or, in the event that articles of association have not been prepared, the provisions of articles set out in a Schedule to the Companies Act apply.

The management of a company is vested in the directors, who are elected by the shareholders. The actions of the directors are regulated by the provisions of the Companies Act and the memorandum and articles of association of the company.

The Companies Act provides that every company will have one or more secretaries, each of whom will be a natural person and one of whom will be a resident of the state in which the company is incorporated. The secretary is appointed by the directors, and, in practice, is a full-time employee and frequently is responsible for the financial records as well as the statutory records of the company.

Under the Income Tax Assessment Act, each company must have a "public officer" who represents the company on income tax matters and is responsible for the company's observance of its obligations under the income tax legislation. The secretary of a company is frequently the "public officer."

The Proprietary (or Private) Company

This form of corporate organization is most commonly used by foreign investors and corresponds to the American closely held corporation. A proprietary company is one which, by its constitution, restricts the right to transfer its shares, limits the number of shareholders to fifty (exclusive of employees and former employees) and prohibits invitations to the public to subscribe for its shares or debentures or to deposit money with this company. Its name must be followed by the words "Proprietary Limited" or the abbreviations "Pty. Ltd." This company may be formed by not less than two incorporators, except that if it is a wholly owned subsidiary of a public company it need have only one member.

Proprietary companies are subject to the same requirements for the sub-

4

mission to shareholders and filing of the audited financial statements as are public companies.

The Exempt Proprietary Company

This type of company is normally available for use only by family businesses and small groups of individuals. An exempt proprietary company is a proprietary company in which no share is deemed to be owned by a public company. With the annual consent of all its members, they may dispense with the requirement for appointment of an auditor. This company is permitted to make loans to its directors, the practice of which is prohibited to the public and proprietary companies. The exempt proprietary company is also exempted from filing its annual financial statements with the Registrar of Companies.

Branch or Subsidiary of Foreign Corporation

When a foreign corporation conducts business in Australia through a branch, that corporation must register within one month after it establishes a place of business or commences to carry on business within the state. Registration formalities include: (a) the presentation to the state of certified copies of the corporation's certificate of incorporation, by-laws, particulars of directors, to the Registrar of Companies, (b) payment of the prescribed registration fees, which are related to the total authorized capital of the foreign corporation, and (c) the appointment of an agent. Once the requirements have been satisfied, a certificate is issued stating that the foreign corporation has been registered as a foreign company under the appropriate state Companies Act, and the foreign corporation gains the same rights, powers and privileges as a company incorporated in that state. A copy of the foreign corporation's annual accounts or financial statements must be presented to the local Registrar of Companies, accompanied by an affidavit by the company agent.

When the foreign corporation conducts business in Australia by forming an Australian subsidiary company, the normal formalities relating to the incorporation of a company in Australia apply, and there are no special requirements which apply to the foreign corporation.

Other Forms of Business Organization

Partnerships. The unlimited liability of partners, of which there may be no more than twenty, for the debts of the partnership is joint and several. However, a form of limited partnership is permitted in some

5

states provided at least one of its partners has unlimited liability.

The firm's name may include the name "Company" or the initials "Co." or "Coy." If the name consists of a different name or differs from the legal names of its partners, the partnership must be registered under a Business Names Act with the local Registrar of Companies, in those states in which it proposes to do business.

No-liability Company. Only companies formed for mining purposes are permitted to be incorporated as no-liability companies. These companies must add to their names the words "No Liability" or the initials "N. L."

The distinguishing characteristic of a "No-Liability" company is that the shareholder, having subscribed to shares and paid in the required initial percentage, is not liable for the unpaid balance, nor for any other debts or liabilities of the company. However, if a call is made on the shareholder for an additional payment on his subscription, and if he does not wish to comply, he must forfeit his shares. They are then sold at auction, and any excess of selling price over the amount of calls due plus expenses of sale is returned to the shareholder upon the surrender of his shares. The Companies Act requires disclosure in the annual return of the details of calls made, sales of forfeited shares, forfeited shares unsold, etc.

Dividends are payable on shares even though subscriptions are not fully paid, provided the subscriber has met all calls for payments on his shares at the dividend date.

Company Limited by Guarantee. This company is formed on the basis that the liability of its members is limited by the memorandum of association to such amount as the members may respectively undertake to contribute to the assets of the company in the event of its liquidation.

Business Records

Section 161 of the Uniform Companies Act states that:

> ... every company and the directors and managers thereof shall cause to be kept in the English language such accounting and other records as will sufficiently explain the transactions and financial position of the company and enable true and fair profit and loss accounts and balance sheets and any documents required to be attached thereto to be prepared from time to time, and shall cause these records to be kept in such manner as to enable them to be conveniently and properly audited.

Other books required to be kept, in addition to accounting records, are: minute books, register of members, register of directors, managers and secretaries, register of charges (mortgage or any agreement to execute a mortgage on demand or otherwise), register of shareholdings of directors and register of debenture holders. The Act sets out in detail the information to be included in each. The Act prescribes that records should be kept not less than seven years, at the registered office of the company, and be available for inspection by directors at all times.

TAX AGENTS

Any person or firm who charges, directly or indirectly, any fee for preparing or assisting in the preparation of an income tax return must be registered by the Tax Agents' Board. Registration is granted by the Board to any person of good repute who is a member of a recognized body of accountants or who can otherwise satisfy the Board as to his competence to prepare income tax returns and to transact business on behalf of taxpayers in income tax matters. Generally, this means that an applicant for registration must submit references from his employer or other third parties, testifying to his experience in the preparation of income tax returns and other related matters.

Every income tax return includes a questionnaire which must be signed by either the public officer or, if the return is prepared by a tax agent, by such tax agent.

THE ACCOUNTING PROFESSION

During the early development of Australia, professional accounting was carried out by men who had been trained in Great Britain, and this accounts for the influence of United Kingdom accounting practices on the profession in Australia.

The first organization of accountants in Australia was formed in Adelaide in 1885, and, during the following years, similar bodies were constituted in the other capital cities.

The development of the profession of public accountants has been guided by The Institute of Chartered Accountants in Australia and, to a lesser extent, by The Australian Society of Accountants. These organizations have their own by-laws and codes of ethics, conduct their own examinations, produce their own publications and bulletins, and are continually engaged in improving the status of the profession and on research into new accounting techniques.

In addition to these two organizations, The Australasian Institute of Cost Accountants has been constituted to further the interests and status of cost accountants.

The Institute of Chartered Accountants in Australia

The Institute was formed and granted a Royal Charter in 1928, and was the successor to The Australasian Corporation of Public Accountants, founded in 1907.

At June 30, 1963, membership totaled 4,548, of whom 2,537 were in public practice as Fellows or Associates. The other members consisted of 729 Associates-not-in-Practice, who are on the staffs of practicing members, and 1,282 members who are engaged outside the profession, largely in commerce and industry, and are classified as Members-on-the-Separate-List.

The designation, "Chartered Accountant" may be used after the name of any member of the Institute in public practice or by any member who is employed by a chartered accountant. The plural, "Chartered Accountants," after a firm's name signifies that all partners in that firm are chartered accountants. Members-on-the-Separate-List cannot use the designation "Chartered Accountant"; however, they may use the initials, "F.C.A." or "A.C.A.," according to their status, or describe themselves individually as "Fellow (or Associate) of the Institute of Chartered Accountants in Australia."

The Chartered Institute is the only body of accountants in the British Commonwealth outside the British Isles, to operate under a Royal Charter. To be admitted as a member of the Institute, it is necessary:

1. To be twenty-one years of age and a resident (not necessarily a citizen) of the Commonwealth
2. To submit evidence of good character
3. To have completed the examinations of the Institute
4. To have obtained the required experience in the service of a chartered accountant.

Exemptions from the latter two requirements may be granted to members of the United Kingdom of Chartered Accountants, and each case is dealt with on its merits by the Council of the Institute.

Eligibility for the examinations of the Institute is based on university entrance requirements, and the required practical experience is five years within the last eight years preceding the application for admission, or, in the case of university graduates, three years within the last five years. Exemption from part of the examinations is granted to university graduates and to those who have passed the full examinations of certain approved accountancy examining bodies.

The examinations of the Institute are of a high standard and include the following subjects:

Intermediate
>Accounting
>
>Auditing
>
>Commercial law
>
>Company law
>
>Banking and bills of exchange
>
>The law relating to bankruptcy, liquidations and receiverships
>
>Miscellaneous law (including partnership, insurance, arbitration, and executorship).

Final
>Advanced accounting
>
>Auditing and business investigations
>
>Professional practice (ethics)
>
>Federal income tax law and practice.

The work of the chartered accountant in Australia is similar to that of the chartered accountant in the United Kingdom, and, accordingly, he engages in certain activities such as company secretarial and share registrar work, which are not customary in the United States.

The Australian Society of Accountants

The Society was formed in 1952, as a result of a merger between the old established Commonwealth Institute of Accountants and The Federal Institute of Accountants, and later The Australian Association of Accountants.

At June 30, 1963, membership totaled approximately 25,000 of whom only a small number were in public practice. Some of the members are also members of The Institute of Chartered Accountants in Australia. Those members in public practice provide services similar to chartered accountants.

Members of the Society are classified as Fellows or Associates and may use the initials "F.A.S.A." or "A.A.S.A." after their names. They may also describe themselves individually as "Fellow (or Associate) of The Australian Society of Accountants."

The Society is active in raising the standard and status of the commercial accountant and conducts examinations similar to those of The Institute of Chartered Accountants in Australia. Eligibility for the examinations of the Society is based on satisfactory completion of English and mathematics at high school level. Experience in public accounting is not a requirement for membership in the Society.

Ethics

The Institute of Chartered Accountants in Australia and The Australian Society of Accountants have strict rules of conduct covering such subjects as inconsistent business practice, acceptance of commissions, contingent fees, advertising, etc. In addition, members must not permit their names to be used on the certificates of estimated future profits often found in prospectuses or other published documents.

The professional ethics of The Institute of Chartered Accountants in Australia are not formally promulgated by the Institute in codified form, but members are expected to comply with the spirit of ethical professional conduct. From time to time, the Council of the Institute issues pronouncements on particular matters of general importance, and members are expected to obtain guidance or seek specific rulings from the Council as appropriate.

The concept of independence is recognized by the profession particularly in reference to appointments to act for public companies, shares in which are quoted on stock exchanges. Although there have been no specific pronouncements by the major institutes precluding an auditor from holding shares in a client company, office regulations of many accounting firms prohibit or severely curtail dealings by its members in shares of clients.

Appointment of Auditors

The Uniform Companies Act provides that companies will, at each annual general meeting, appoint a person or persons or a firm of registered auditors to be the auditor or auditors of the company until the next annual general meeting, except that if all the members of an exempt proprietary company so agree, and it is so recorded in the minutes of the company, an auditor need not be appointed.

The Companies Act also provides that any reports required by the Act are to be prepared only by a "registered company auditor" (see below) and that he will not consent to be appointed as such if: (a) he is indebted to the company or to a corporation that is deemed to be related to that company as affiliate, in an amount exceeding five hundred pounds, or (b) he is an officer of the company; a partner, employer or employee of an officer of the company; or a partner or employee of an employee of an officer of the company or affiliate, except where the company in question is an exempt proprietary company.

An accounting firm may be appointed as auditor of a company provided all partners in that firm, resident in Australia, are registered company auditors in the state in which the company is incorporated. A person or firm may not be appointed as auditor unless consent to act as such has been previously given in writing.

The appointment of the first auditors is usually made by the directors of the company, and the auditors so appointed retire at the first annual general meeting. Thereafter, the appointment is made by shareholders at the annual general meeting, and no person or firm, other than the retiring auditor, is eligible for reappointment unless specific notice regarding such appointment has been given to shareholders seven days prior to the date of the meeting. A casual vacancy in the position of auditor between annual meetings may be filled by the directors.

Registered or Licensed Company Auditor

The Companies Act of each state provides for the appointment of a Companies Auditors Board. A function of the Board is to effect and control the registration or licensing of company auditors and liquidators. In some states, however, the Board is established and registration effected under Public Accountants Registration Acts which were enacted prior to the introduction of the Uniform Companies Act.

Registration as a Company Auditor. Any person may register as a company auditor in a state, if, in addition to presenting proof of general good conduct and character to the Companies Auditors Board, he meets any of the following requirements:

1. Was licensed or registered as a company auditor under a prior Act

2. Is a member of The Institute of Chartered Accountants in Australia or The Australian Society of Accountants or of any other organization established outside Australia prescribed by the rules of the Board

3. Is a registered company auditor in any state or territory of the Commonwealth

4. Holds a degree from any university in the Commonwealth and has passed examinations in subjects representing a course of study in accountancy or auditing of three years' duration, and in commercial law (including company law) of two years' duration

5. Holds the certificate in accountancy of a prescribed university or institute of technology or technical college.

6. Has satisfied the Board that he has a thorough knowledge of accounts and auditing and of the provisions of the Companies Act and of such other subjects as are prescribed.

A separate application to each board is required to register as a liquidator, and in these instances the boards require evidence of the applicant's experience in liquidation work and procedures.

Registrations of both company auditors and liquidators are renewable annually. Registration as a company auditor may be obtained by a nonresident of Australia who is a member of The Institute of Chartered Accountants or The Australian Society of Accountants.

The Board may impose disciplinary action, including cancellation of registration, on any registered company auditor found to have been guilty of discreditable conduct.

AUDITING STANDARDS

Standards of auditing in Australia are generally patterned after British practice. Much has been done, especially by The Institute of Chartered Accountants in Australia, toward defining auditing standards and revising auditing procedures so as to eliminate extensive detailed tests of transactions. There is no official single statement of auditing standards in Australia, as such, but the Institute's "Statement on General Principles of Professional Auditing Practice (1960)" covers many of the same points as the pamphlet "Auditing Standards and Procedures" of the American Institute.

General Standards

The profession has reached a high level of technical education and training, and continuing progress is being made through the research work carried out by the Institute and the Society. The concept of independence in Australia has been described in the section, Ethics (p. 10).

Standards of Field Work

In the past few years, greater emphasis has been placed on the necessity for making a proper evaluation of internal control, and this is now a generally accepted auditing requirement. Various research publications have been issued by the professional organizations on this subject.

Written audit programs are being used; bank accounts are directly confirmed and so are receivables, although positive confirmations are not generally used. The observation of physical inventories is becoming general practice with many firms.

Standards of Reporting

The text of Australian auditors' reports follow the requirements set forth in the Companies Act, which establishes that the auditor will state in his report whether, in his opinion:

1. The balance sheet and profit and loss account are properly drawn up in accordance with the provisions of the Act and so as to give a true and fair view of the state of the company's affairs.
2. The accounting and other records (including registers) examined by him are properly kept in accordance with the provisions of the Act.

and the Act continues by saying that every auditor will state in his report:

1. If he has not obtained all the information and explanations that he required
2. If, in his opinion, proper accounting and other records have not been kept by the company
3. If, in his opinion, the returns submitted from branches not visited by the auditor are inadequate
4. If, in his opinion, according to the best of his information and the explanations given to him and as shown by the accounting and

13

other records of the company, the profit and loss account and the balance sheet are not in agreement with the company's accounting and other records or are not properly drawn up so as to give a true and fair view of the state of the company's affairs as at the end of the period of accounting

5. If, in his opinion, according to the best of his information and the explanations given to him, the accounting and other records, the balance sheet and the profit and loss account do not give the information required by the Act.

The Companies Act, in referring to the subject of the financial statements of holding companies and their subsidiaries, states that:

> If the auditor's report on the balance sheet or profit and loss account of a subsidiary company is qualified in any way, the separate balance sheet of the subsidiary company or the consolidated balance sheet of the holding company (as the case may be) shall contain particulars of the manner in which the report is qualified.

There is no reference in the auditor's report to adherence to generally accepted accounting principles, nor to generally accepted auditing standards in the scope section of the report.

Consistency. The old Companies Acts of several states included a requirement that the auditors should express an opinion as to whether or not the profit and loss account was properly drawn up so as to exhibit a true and correct view of the results of the business for the year. In addition, it has been a generally accepted principle that any inconsistencies which materially affect the profit for the year require special disclosure.

Under the Uniform Companies Act, auditors are required to state that the accounts give a true and fair view of the profit of the company. This requirement has tended to place more emphasis on consistency in the application of accounting principles and, in addition, the act requires the directors to disclose in their report to stockholders any changes in such principles which have materially affected results of the annual operations.

Materiality. This principle is generally understood and observed in Australia. The recent Companies Act contains several references to "materiality."

DIRECTORS' REPORT

The Uniform Companies Act requires that the directors submit financial statements to the annual meeting of stockholders as at the close of the fiscal year, with a report thereon signed on behalf of the directors by two directors, or, in the case of a proprietory company having one director only, by that director. The director's report must state that in their or his opinion: (a) The profit and loss account is drawn up so as to give a true and fair view of the results of the business of the company for the period covered by the account; and (b) the balance sheet is drawn up so as to exhibit a true and fair view of the state of affairs of the company as at the end of that period.

The financial statements presented to the shareholders must also be accompanied by a statutory declaration of the secretary of the company verifying, to the best of his knowledge and belief, the correctness of said statements. These two statements together with the auditor's opinion are often shown on a page attached to the financial statements and are headed, respectively: Statement by the Directors, Declaration by the Secretary and Report of the Auditors to the Members.

The Companies Act also requires that the directors' report should state whether the results of annual operations were materially affected by items of an abnormal nature, including the following:

1. Changes in accounting principles
2. Any transfers to or from reserves or provisions
3. Writing off of substantial amounts of bad debts
4. Any substantial increase or decrease in the value of trading stock (inventory) owing to a change in the basis of valuation of the whole or any part of it
5. Any item of an unusual nature or value which appears in the accounts
6. Any absence from the accounts of any material items usually included therein.

The directors' report must fully disclose any stock options issued during the period covered by the profit and loss statement.

ACCOUNTING PRINCIPLES AND PRACTICES

Form and Content of Financial Statements

There are no statutory or other requirements as to the form of financial statements, which, in general, resembles British practice. In 1963, The Institute of Chartered Accountants in Australia issued certain recommendations along the lines of those issued in 1942, by The Institute of Chartered Accountants in England and Wales. In most cases, the balance sheet shows assets on the right side; the liabilities section on the left side usually begins with the capital accounts. The use of general headings for a balance sheet, such as "liabilities" and "assets" is not recommended by the Institute, which instead suggests the grouping of various items under appropriate headings. The minimum contents of the balance sheet and income statement are prescribed by the recent Uniform Companies Act which lists, in detailed schedules, the required disclosures, as to (A) the balance sheet, and (B) the income statement.

Statement Presentation

A   *Balance sheet*
1. Summary of authorized and issued capital by classes of shares. The capital must be clearly described by means of a note to the balance sheet
2. The amount of the share premium account
3. Particulars of any redeemed debentures which the company has power to reissue
4. Under separate headings, so far as they are not written off:

   a. The preliminary organization expenses
   b. Any expenses incurred in connection with any issue of shares or debentures
   c. Any sums paid by way of commission in respect of any shares or debentures
   d. Any sums allowed by way of discount in respect of any debentures
   e. The amount of the discount allowed on any issue of shares at a discount
   f. The amount of goodwill and of any patents and trademarks.
5. The reserves, provisions, liabilities, fixed assets and current assets classified separately under headings appropriate to the company's business, showing separately the tax provision

and stating the method used to arrive at the amount of assets under each heading, but where the amount of any class is not material it may be included under the same heading as some other class.

6. Under separate headings, stating the method used to arrive at the amount of investments under each heading:
   a. Investments in government, municipal and other public debentures, stocks or bonds
   b. Investments in subsidiaries
   c. Investments in securities of other companies (not subsidiaries) traded on any prescribed exchange
   d. Investments in any other companies.
7. The aggregate quoted market value of investments must be shown under separate headings:
   a. Amounts owed by subsidiaries to parent company
   b. Trade receivables
   c. Amount of any loans outstanding made to a director of the company or of an affiliate of the company, or made to another company in which a director of the company or of an affiliate company owns a controlling interest
   d. Other receivables.
8. Balance of profit and loss account
9. Debentures, showing separately amounts that are redeemable later than twelve months after the date of the balance sheet
10. Liabilities (other than debentures, bank loans and overdrafts) secured by any charge on the assets whether registered or not, showing separately the portion payable later than twelve months after the date of the balance sheet
11. Bank loans and overdrafts
12. Unsecured loans payable, showing separately the portion payable later than twelve months after the date of the balance sheet
13. Amounts owed to subsidiaries by parent companies
14. Amounts payable to trade customers
15. Other payables
16. Under separate headings (to be stated by way of note if not otherwise shown):
    a. Unsecured contingent liabilities
    b. Contingent liabilities secured by the company's assets
    c. Where practicable, the aggregate amount, if it is material, of contracts for capital expenditures, so far as that amount has not been provided for.
17. Dividends in arrears on preferred shares.

Formerly, many Australian companies netted such items as bad debt allowances, allowances for depreciation, amortization, etc., directly against the related asset. If portions of an asset (inventory, fixed assets) were valued on different bases, it was not considered necessary to indicate the amount attributable to each basis. As a result of the rule indicated as 5, p. 16, netting of reserves and allowances is not permitted, and both the basis and the related amounts of the assets must be shown.

Interest and Service Charges on Installment Receivables. In the case of installment sales or loans of finance companies, the Companies Act requires that unearned interest or service charges included in the receivables account must be shown as a separate deduction from the total receivables outstanding.

Premium on Share Capital. Premium on the issue of shares in cash or other consideration is generally shown within the "reserves" group in the shareholders' funds section of the balance sheet.

Conversion of Foreign Exchange. The Companies Act requires that the financial statements must express amounts in Australian currency only, and explain the basis of any conversion made into Australian currency.

  B   *Income statement*
1. The net balance of profit and loss on the company's trading
2. Income from investments in subsidiaries of the company
3. Income from other investments distinguishing between income received from any shares and debentures which are traded on prescribed stock exchanges and income received from other sources
4. Amounts charged for depreciation or amortization of investments, goodwill and fixed assets
5. The amount of interest on the company's debentures and loans of fixed term
6. Any profit or loss arising from the sale or revaluation of fixed assets or intangibles if brought into account in determining the company's profit or loss
7. The amount, if material, set aside or proposed to be set aside for, or withdrawn from reserves
8. The amount, if material, set aside to provisions other than provisions for depreciation, renewals or diminution in value of assets or, as the case may be, the amount, if material, withdrawn from such provisions and not applied for the purposes thereof

9. The amounts provided for redemption of share capital and for redemption of loans
10. Provision made for payment of income tax in respect of the period of accounting
11. The aggregate amount of dividends paid and the aggregate amount of the dividend proposed to be paid
12. The total amount paid to the directors as remuneration for their services. Salaries, bonuses and commissions paid by way of salary to directors who are engaged in full time employment of the company or any subsidiary of the company need not be included in this amount
13. The total amount paid to the auditors as remuneration for their services as auditors.

The income statement which is usually designated as "profit and loss account" generally includes the analysis of the profit and loss appropriation account (earned surplus). The Companies Act does not require the disclosure of sales and costs of sales in the income statement and this information is not, therefore, generally included.

Comparative Financial Statements. A new requirement of the Uniform Companies Act is that every balance sheet and profit and loss account must be in comparative form showing the amounts applicable to the immediately preceding period.

Consolidated Financial Statements. Financial statements of holding companies must be accompanied by separate statements for each subsidiary or by consolidated statements of the holding company and all its subsidiaries eliminating all intercompany transactions. The form of such statements must be consistent with the profit and loss account and balance sheet of the holding company and must be accompanied by the auditors' report thereon.

Pooling of Interests

Accounting for acquisitions on a "pooling of interests" basis is not permitted.

Inventories

The Lifo method for inventory pricing is not commonly used for financial accounting purposes.

Fixed Assets

It is not uncommon for companies, especially wholly owned Australian subsidiaries of foreign corporations, to revalue fixed assets and shares held in subsidiary and associated companies, and to capitalize a resulting upward revaluation reserve by an issue of bonus shares. Such a bonus issue is virtually free of Australian income tax in the hands of resident shareholders.

Goodwill

Purchased goodwill and goodwill arising on the acquisition of other companies is often carried forward indefinitely as an "intangible asset." Any writeoff or writedown of intangible assets of this nature is recorded as an appropriation of profit, and not as a charge to income.

Deferred Charges

Preliminary expense and costs of raising capital classified as "intangible assets" are frequently written off as an appropriation.

Statement of Income

Depreciation. Depreciation of buildings, which do not form a portion of the integral part of a plant or comprise structural improvements for agricultural purposes, is not an allowable deduction for tax purposes and accordingly is not commonly provided for financial accounting purposes. There are many Australian companies which do not provide for depreciation of buildings, other than to the very minor extent to which depreciation of these assets is allowable for tax purposes.

Depreciation on the revaluation increment of fixed assets is not deductible for tax purposes.

A few larger public companies make appropriations of profits for the excess of depreciation calculated on the replacement value of fixed assets over depreciation calculated on the cost or lesser valuation at which the assets are recorded in the books.

Tax-effect Accounting. Deferred and prepaid tax accounting is not common, except in the case of companies engaged in mining and entitled to special tax concessions.

Stock Dividends. Stock dividends are frequently accounted for on the basis of the par or nominal value of the shares issued.

REQUIREMENTS FOR PUBLIC SALE
OF SECURITIES—THE PROSPECTUS

The Companies Act prohibits the public sale of shares and debentures if not accompanied by a prospectus. The Act describes in detail the rules to be observed in issuing a prospectus. A copy of the prospectus must first be filed with the Registrar of Companies.

The prospectus must include a report by a registered company auditor, who need not be the company's regular auditor, with respect to: (a) profits and losses and assets and liabilities of the company and of any guarantor company referred to in the prospectus; and (b) the rates of dividends, if any, paid by the company for each class of shares in the last five years preceding the date of the prospectus.

A report by an investigating accountant (who must also be a registered company auditor) engaged by the underwriters may also be included in the prospectus. The profit and loss accounts must cover each of the five years preceding the last date to which the accounts of the company were prepared. The statements of assets and liabilities must be that of the last date mentioned, which date shall in no case be more than nine months before the issue date of the prospectus, or twelve months if authorized by the Crown Law Officer. The same information required of the issuing company must also be furnished about any business to be acquired directly or indirectly with the proceeds, or any part of the proceeds, of the issue of the shares or debentures. If the issuing company or any of the guarantor companies have subsidiaries, the information referred to above must be submitted in addition, either for each group of subsidiaries, or individually for each subsidiary, or combined with the statements of the holding companies. If the proceeds of the issue, or any part of them, are to be applied to the acquisition of shares of another corporation, the reports mentioned according to the Companies Act, Fifth Schedule, Part II will:

2(a). Indicate how the profits or losses of the other corporation dealt with by the report would, in respect of the shares to be acquired, have concerned members of the company and what allowance would have been required to be made in relation to assets and liabilities so dealt with, for holders of other shares if the company had at all material times held the shares to be acquired; and (b). Where the other corporation has subsidiaries, deal with the profits or losses and the assets and liabilities of the corporation and its subsidiaries in the manner provided in relation to the company and its subsidiaries.

The Companies Act also requires a report by the directors as to whether since the date of the latest financial statements and up to a date not earlier than fourteen days before the issue of the prospectus:

1. The business of the company has in their opinion been satisfactorily maintained.
2. There have in their opinion arisen any circumstances adversely affecting the company's trading or the value of its assets.
3. The current assets appear in the books at values which are believed to be realizable in the ordinary course of business.
4. There are any contingent liabilities by reason of any guarantees given by the company or any of its subsidiaries.
5. There are any changes in published reserves or any unusual factors affecting the profit of the company and its subsidiaries.

The state of Victoria has passed (1963) a Companies Public Borrowings Act, which introduces certain additional requirements for prospectuses used in connection with offerings of mortgage debentures or debentures. Under certain circumstances, there must be financial statements presented to the Registrar as of the end of six months after the close of the fiscal year, and the financial statements must be reported upon by the auditors. Similar changes are expected to be brought into force in the other states and territories some time in the future.

REQUIREMENTS FOR LISTING OF SECURITIES ON THE STOCK EXCHANGE

Any company which desires to sell its shares or debentures to the public must issue a prospectus, and if it desires its shares or debentures to be listed on a stock exchange must also conform to the "Official Listing Requirements" of the appropriate stock exchange. Substantial uniformity in the rules of all stock exchanges has been achieved through the Australian Associated Stock Exchanges, to which the various stock exchanges of the country belong. Financial statements of publicly held companies must be filed with the corresponding stock exchanges together with the auditors' reports.

INDIA | 22

FORMS OF BUSINESS ORGANIZATION

Business in India may adopt any of the forms of organization generally found in other countries: the sole proprietorship, the partnership, the private and the public companies and branches of companies incorporated abroad. Many government-owned enterprises operate as limited companies. Company legislation is fundamentally based on British law. The Companies Act of 1956 is comprehensive and deals with problems which are peculiar to India, among them the "managing agency" system.

The managing agency is an organization peculiar to India. It may be an individual, firm or body corporate (as defined by the Act, the term "body corporate" includes domestic as well as foreign corporations, while the term "company" refers only to Indian companies), which is appointed, in addition to the Board of Directors, to manage the whole or substantially the whole affairs of a company, providing it with a wide range of financial and technical services. In other cases, a firm or body corporate may be appointed as "secretaries and treasurers" to manage a company partially or wholly, under the supervision of the company's Board of Directors, and generally would have less power than the managing agents. Managing agents, but not the secretaries and treasurers, may be empowered to appoint a limited number of directors of the managed company.

There are specific regulations that apply to banks, insurance companies, cooperative societies and electric utilities.

Foreign investors, with the approval of the Indian government, may organize an Indian company or participate in an existing one, or may open a foreign branch. In the case of a new enterprise, the prospective investors must first obtain approval for the project in accordance with the requirements established by the Industries (Development and Regulation) Act of 1951, as amended.

Companies—General

Companies may be limited by guarantee, or limited by shares, or they may be unlimited companies.

A company having the liability of its members limited by the Memorandum and Articles of Association to such amounts as the members may respectively undertake to contribute in the event of liquidation, is a company limited by guarantee.

Companies limited by shares are those in which the liability of the members is limited by the Memorandum and Articles of Association to the amount of the shares subscribed, and may be private or public, depending on the limitations on the number of shareholders and on the sale of its capital, as explained later on. In the case of companies limited by shares or by guarantee, the name of the company must end with the word "Limited" or with the abbreviation "Ltd," except where the central government permits otherwise.

All companies must submit to the registrar of the corresponding state copies of the Memorandum and Articles of Association, and copies of the agreement, if any, which the company proposes to enter into with any individual, firm or body corporate to be appointed as its managing agent or with any firm or body corporate to be appointed as its secretaries and treasurers.

The capital may be represented by common and preferred shares, called "equity shares" and "preference shares," respectively. A company may issue shares at a discount only under certain conditions including: (a) the shares must be of a class already issued and (b) the amount of the discount (not to exceed 10 per cent) must be authorized by a resolution passed at a general stockholders meeting and be approved by the court. The central government, however, may permit a higher rate in certain cases.

The Board of Directors must appoint the auditors within one month of the date of registration of the company, failing which, the company in a general meeting may make the first appointment. The same or other auditors must be appointed at every annual general meeting thereafter. If this requirement is not fulfilled, the central government may appoint a person to fill the vacancy. When a company changes its auditor, the new auditor is required to inform the registrar within thirty days as to whether or not he accepts the appointment.

The remuneration of the auditors is fixed by the authority appointing them, that is, the Board of Directors or the shareholders or the central government as the case may be. The shareholders of some companies at the annual general meeting authorize the directors to fix the remuneration of the auditors.

Within forty-two days from the annual general meeting, the company must file with the registrar its annual return containing the particulars specified in Schedule V of the Companies Act, and signed by two directors, or by a director and the managing agent, or the secretary and treasurer, if any. The return must be accompanied by the financial statements, the board's report and the auditor's report, and by statements signed by the same two persons, indicating, among others, that:

1. The return states the facts as they stood on the date of the annual general meeting.
2. Since the date of the last return all issues and transfers of shares and debentures have been properly recorded.
3. In the case of a private company, no invitations to the public for subscription of shares or debentures have been made.
4. Where its members are more than fifty, they are represented by employees or former employee members.

In the case of a private company, copies of the balance sheet must be filed separately from the copies of the profit and loss account, since the law establishes that no person other than a member of the company concerned will be entitled to inspect or obtain copies of the profit and loss account of private companies.

For public companies, a shareholders' meeting must be held within a period not less than one month and not more than six months from the date of commencement of business, which is called the "statutory meeting." A "statutory report" must be delivered to every shareholder not later than twenty-one days before the date of the meeting, containing, among other information, the status of the capital issued and paid; an abstract of receipts and disbursements up to a date within seven days of the date of the report; the names and addresses of the directors, the auditors, managing agents, secretaries and treasurers.

Annual general meetings must be held in every year. The first annual general meeting may be held at any time within eighteen months of incorporation and also within nine months of the close of the first financial period. Subsequent meetings must be held within fifteen months of each other and also within six months of the close of the financial year.

The Companies Act prohibits under certain prescribed circumstances any company from making loans, or giving any guarantee, or providing any security in connection with a loan made by or to any other person, to a director of the company or to its holding company or any of the director's relatives without the previous approval of the central government. Excepted from this prohibition are private companies (unless a subsidiary of a public company) and a banking company.

5

Any director of a company who is concerned or has an interest directly or indirectly in any contract or arrangement entered or to be entered into by that company, must disclose the nature of his interests at a meeting of the Board of Directors.

As to contracts in which a director has an interest, the following formalities are generally required:

1. Permission by the Board of Directors
2. An entry in the "Register of Contracts."

Private Companies

The number of members of a private company is limited to fifty (excluding employees and former employees who became members while in the employment of the company). The by-laws must restrict the rights of members to transfer their shares and prohibit any invitation to the public to subscribe for any shares or debentures of the company. Apart from these restrictions, the Companies Act requires that to retain the privileges of a private company, the shareholdings in its paid-up capital, by one or more bodies corporate, shall not exceed 25 per cent. There are certain exceptions to this rule, the more important of which are as follows:

1. If the entire share capital is held by one or more foreign bodies corporate, or
2. If the entire share capital is held by a single (Indian) private company and one nominee, or
3. If each of the companies holding shares is itself a private company with no body corporate members, provided the total number of shareholders of all the above companies is not more than fifty.

Private companies other than subsidiaries of public companies enjoy certain privileges and fewer formalities are required than those applicable to public companies. The distinctions between private and public companies in India are similar to arrangements in the United Kingdom. A private company may be formed by not less than two persons, and it must have at least two directors.

Public Companies

A public company is one which does not have the limitations of a private company and may be formed by seven or more persons and must have at least three directors. The Act permits the company to fix the term of appointment of up to one-third of the total number of its directors, subject to the other provisions of the Act. The remaining two-thirds must be persons who, in order of seniority, will retire by rotation at each annual general meeting.

The Act establishes the overall managerial remuneration payable to the directors, managing director, managing agent, secretaries and treasurers, and managers of public companies at 11 per cent of its net profits (as computed under the statute), exclusive of the fees paid to directors for attendance at board meetings. A minimum remuneration up to fifty thousand rupees may be allowed by the government in any loss year or whenever profits are inadequate. The central government may authorize, subject to certain conditions, an increase of this minimum where satisfactory evidence is furnished that the amount is insufficient for the effective management of the business.

There are smaller limits of remuneration for each of the categories of management personnel within the over-all limit of 11 per cent. In the case of directors, additional remuneration may be sanctioned by a special resolution of the company in respect of nonmanagerial services, e.g., that of solicitor.

Branch of a Foreign Corporation

The foreign company must first obtain approval of the central government and file with the Registrar of Joint Stock Companies at New Delhi and the Registrar of the State where its principal office will be located, duly legalized copies of the certificate of incorporation and by-laws, a complete list of its directors and the name and address of one or more persons resident in the country who have been authorized to represent the company. Copies of the annual financial statements of the head office as well as of the branch must be submitted to the registrar together with the reports required of public companies in accordance with the Act, but the central government may waive this requirement or modify it upon request of the foreign branch. Such waivers have been granted in very few cases. Foreign companies with major business activities confined to India are, however, permitted to file the annual financial statements (of their head office) recast in the "Indian" form (as given in Schedule VI of the Companies Act) instead of their Indian branch accounts. Several provisions of the Act do not relate to branches of foreign companies, and the Act is far less stringent with regard to such branches.

7

Partnerships

The Act provides that a partnership which is organized for the purpose of profits and has more than twenty partners must register as a company under the Act. If the partnership is in the banking business it must register if the number of partners exceeds ten.

Business Records

The Act states that every company must keep proper accounting records in respect to: (1) all sums of money received and expended, (2) all sales and purchases, including inventory records, and (3) the assets and liabilities; and keep also minute books, shareholders' registers, etc. The books must be maintained adequately in order to give a true and fair view of the affairs of the company and must be kept for a period of not less than eight years; however, for income tax purposes, the period of assessment can be extended up to seventeen years in certain circumstances.

THE ACCOUNTING PROFESSION

The Chartered Accountant

The chartered accountant in India is the equivalent of the United States CPA. The Companies Act establishes that every company must appoint auditors and that only chartered accountants within the meaning of the Chartered Accountant Act of 1949 can qualify for such appointment. The Companies Act specifically disqualifies the following persons as auditors:

A body corporate

An officer or employee of the company

A partner or any person in the employment of an officer or employee of the company

A person indebted to the company or guaranteeing or securing others' indebtedness to the company in excess of one thousand rupees

A director or member of a private company or a partner of a firm which is the managing agent or the secretaries and treasurers of the company

A director or the holder of shares exceeding 5 per cent in nominal value of the subscribed capital of any body corporate which is the managing agent, or the secretaries and treasurers of the company

Anyone who has been disqualified on the basis of any of the above circumstances, as auditor of a company or body corporate, which is that company's subsidiary or holding company.

The Chartered Accountants Act of 1949, provides for the registration of all accountants who have passed the required examinations which consist of three parts: preliminary, intermediate and final; and who have completed the apprenticeship period, either as an articled clerk or as an audit clerk, of four and eight years, respectively.

To be admitted to the preliminary examination the applicant must have passed the intermediate examinations at any of the prescribed universities or an examination recognized by the central government as an equivalent. To take the intermediate examination, the candidate must be a university graduate, hold the National Diploma in Commerce Examination held by the All India Council for Technical Education, or have passed the preliminary examination and, in addition, he must be serving the last thirty months of his articled service or the last sixty months of his audit service and have obtained a certificate from the head of the coaching organization (described later). The final examination may be taken not less than eleven months after passing the intermediate examination and the candidate must be serving his last twelve months as an articled or audit clerk and have obtained a certificate from the head of the coaching organization.

The professional coaching course offered by the Institute of Chartered Accountants has been patterned after the correspondence courses used in other countries and especially those in the United States. The entire program presently consists of about sixty test papers, including the following subjects: accounting, cost accounting, statistics, income tax auditing, company law and economics. Attempts to consolidate the courses offered at the universities and the Institute's course have not as yet been successful.

The preliminary paper covers English, bookkeeping, elements of economics and modern administration, arithmetic and commercial geography. The intermediate paper covers accounting, statistics, cost accounting, auditing, commercial law and general commercial knowledge. The final examination is divided into two parts comprising papers on advanced accounting, auditing, taxation, cost accounting, management accounting, law and economics. The passing grade in the examination is 40 per cent in any one paper, with an average of 50 per cent for all papers.

To be an articled clerk, the individual must be sixteen years of age and be either a graduate or hold the National Diploma of Commerce or have passed the preliminary examination of the Institute of Chartered Accountants. He must register as a student for the course given by the Institute. He may pay to his principal a sum not exceeding two thousand rupees, which amount must be refunded to him in installments or at the completion of clerkship. The rules applicable to audit clerks are similar to these, except that the period of their service (for practical training) is double that of the articled clerks and no premium is charged. The chartered accountants' regulations state that only associates and fellows of the Institute who are in practice may take articled clerks. A fellow in practice may take two articled clerks, but if he has been in practice for at least seven years, he may take three; recently the number of articled clerks allowed to a fellow after fifteen years of practice has been increased to four. An associate in continuous practice for at least three years may take one articled clerk.

The whole system of articleship and training is currently being reviewed by the Council of the Institute of Chartered Accountants of India. It is possible that the number of years of apprenticeship will be reduced.

Functions of the Chartered Accountant. The chartered accountant examines and reports upon financial statements of business enterprises. Under the Companies Act of 1956, every company formed under its provisions must appoint an auditor who is a member of the Institute of Chartered Accountants of India.

The chartered accountant advises clients on tax matters, prepares returns, and represents clients before the tax authorities. He provides management services of various kinds for his clients and undertakes special investigations for specific purposes on behalf of managements or for government departments. He may act as liquidator of a company which has failed. He may do the work of the secretary of a company, act as registrar and transfer agent of its shares and debentures, and establish valuations for shares, especially of private companies for estate duty, for sale, and other purposes.

The Institute of Chartered Accountants

The Institute was organized in 1949 by the Chartered Accountants Act of that year, and the Chartered Accountants Regulations subsequently issued. Previously, only persons holding certificates issued by the government in accordance with the regulations of the Indian Accounting Board of 1932 were authorized to make audits of public companies. The 1949 Act gave complete autonomy to the profession and placed its entire regulation and supervision in the hands of the Institute, which was made an accrediting body as well as a professional society. The central government made, however, two reservations: It would have representation in the Council of the Institute, which was created under the Act to manage the affairs of the Institute and exercise control over it, and would keep also for itself the final approval of any regulations of the Council. The Council is composed of twenty-four fellow chartered accountants and six other persons nominated by the central government.

The Institute is formed by two classes of members: associates and fellows, referred to as Associate Chartered Accountants (A.C.A.) and Fellow Chartered Accountants (F.C.A.). Both are entitled to vote in the elections of the Council, but only fellows may be elected. A fellow is a member who has been in public practice for at least five years.

The membership of the Institute is about 6,500 chartered accountants. *The Chartered Accountant* is the monthly journal published by the Institute. Membership in the Chartered Institutes in the United Kingdom will in certain circumstances confer the right of election to membership in the Institute of Chartered Accountants in India, since the Indian qualification is recognized in the United Kingdom, and members of the Institute may practice in the United Kingdom after observing certain formalities laid down by the Board of Trade.

The Chartered Accountants' Act of 1949 provides that unless similar reciprocity is granted to members of the Indian Institute, to practice in another country, members of institutes in that country may not become members of the Indian Institute or practice in India.

Code of Ethics

The Institute of Chartered Accountants has recently issued a code of conduct and the Chartered Accountants Act of 1949 also cites various acts or omissions as "professional misconduct" which may provoke an inquiry by the disciplinary committee and the Council of the Institute. The reports of the committee, findings of the Council and judgments of the high courts are published in the Institute's journal under the section "Disciplinary Matters."

Some of the more important acts mentioned in the Act (above) as constituting professional misconduct are (condensed):

Payment of commission or brokerage to the laity, or acceptance of part of profits of the professional work of a lawyer, auctioneer, broker or any other of the laity

Securing professional business in an unethical manner, or by solicitation or improper advertising

Accepting appointment as auditor, previously held by another chartered accountant, without first communicating with the latter in writing

Accepting professional fees which are contingent upon the results of his employment

Engaging in any business or occupation not compatible with the profession of chartered accountant, except that of director of a company of which neither he nor any of his partners is the auditor

Permitting a person not a member of the Institute or a member not being his partner to sign on his behalf or behalf of his firm any report upon financial statements.

The Companies Act provides for the imposition of a maximum fine of one thousand rupees upon any auditor who, either in his report or in any document signed by him, willfully defaults his duties as established by the Act in Section 227 on Powers and Duties of Auditors (see Standards of Reporting) and Section 229 on Signature of Audit Report.

Institute of Cost and Works Accountants

The Institute was organized as a company in 1944 by a group of industrial accountants. Later, by the Cost and Works Accountants Act of 1959, the company was replaced by the Institute as it stands at present. It has its own correspondence course and examinations, which necessarily only partially overlap with those of the Institute of Chartered Accountants.

AUDITING STANDARDS

The British influence on the Indian accounting profession is predominant. The Indian profession as such has not issued any pronouncements on auditing standards, but the Institute of Chartered Accountants has issued (1962) its second edition of "A Guide to Company Audit" which takes into consideration the 1960 amendments to the Companies Act of 1956, and discusses in some detail satisfactory auditing procedures.

General Standards

The profession in India, through its requirements for membership in the Institute and its technical assistance offered to members, prompted the same type of general standards as to training and proficiency and due care on the part of the auditor, which are recognized in the United Kingdom.

Independence. The need for independence in mental attitude is recognized by the Companies Act in its list of matters which disqualify a person for appointment as an auditor. It is not considered improper for an auditor to have a financial interest (not representing a substantial interest) in a company upon which he reports.

Standards of Field Work

The standards of field work as to planning and supervision, obtaining competent evidential matter, and study and evaluation of internal control are similar to those of the United Kingdom. It is not usual to confirm accounts receivable or to observe physical inventory-taking, although this is sometimes done when considered desirable.

Standards of Reporting

The requirements of reporting have been established by the Companies Act, which states that the auditor must make a report to the members of the company on every balance sheet and profit and loss account and on every other document annexed thereto. This report will state whether in his opinion and to the best of his information and according to the explanations given to him, the said accounts give a true and fair view of the state of affairs of the company at the end of the financial year and of its profit or loss for the period then ended and comply with the requirements set forth in Parts I and II of Schedule VI of the Act, which relate to the form and content of the balance sheet and of the profit and loss account.

The auditor's report must also state: (a) whether he has obtained all the information and explanations which to the best of his knowledge and belief were necessary for the purposes of his audit; (b) whether in his opinion, proper books of account as required by law have been kept by the company so far as appears from his examination of those books, and proper returns adequate for the purposes of his audit have been received from branches not visited by him; (c) whether the report on the accounts of any branch office audited under Section 228 by a person other than the company's auditor has been forwarded to him as required by that Section and how he has dealt with the same in preparing the auditor's report; (d) whether the company's balance sheet and profit and loss account dealt with by the report are in agreement with the books of account and returns.

Where certain of the matters referred to above are reported in the negative or with a qualification, the auditor's report will state the reason for such negative statement or qualification.

REPORT OF BOARD OF DIRECTORS

The Companies Act specifies the contents of the report of the Board of Directors which should be a part of the annual return, as follows: (1) the state of the company's affairs; (2) the amounts, if any, which it proposes to carry to any reserves in the balance sheet; (3) the amount of dividends recommended to be paid.

The directors must include comments on any material changes that took place during the period if they consider that such comments will not be harmful to the business of the company or its subsidiaries. These comments would refer to changes in the following: (a) the nature of the company's business or of its subsidiaries, (b) the industry or trade in which the company operates, and (c) any material changes and com-

mitments affecting the financial position of the company which have occurred between the date of the balance sheet and the date of the report.

The report should contain adequate explanations regarding every
reservation, qualification or adverse remark contained in the auditor's
report.

A copy of the balance sheet, together with the profit and loss account,
the auditors' report, and every other document required by law to be
attached to the balance sheet, must be sent to every holder of shares or
debentures not less than twenty-one days before the date of the
annual general meeting or, in the case of private nonsubsidiary companies, the notice period specified in the company's articles.

ACCOUNTING PRINCIPLES AND PRACTICES

Form and Content of Financial Statements

The Companies Act prescribes the form and contents of the balance
sheet and the profit and loss account. The principle of extensive disclosure is always present in the rules of statement presentation set
forth in Schedule VI of the Act, which applies to all companies ex-
cepting insurance companies, banks and electric utilities which are
governed by special acts. The central government may exempt any
company from compliance with any of these requirements if the exemption is necessary in the "public interest"; very few companies have been
so exempted.

Statement Presentation

The balance sheet presentation is the usual type followed by British
companies showing capital and liabilities on the left side and fixed assets,
investments and current assets, in that order, on the right side. Footnotes will be added to the balance sheet disclosing claims against the
company, uncalled liabilities, fixed dividends in arrears, estimated
amount of unexecuted contracts and other amounts for which the company is contingently liable.

Comparative Financial Statements. The Companies Act states that the balance sheet and the profit and loss statement must show the comparable figures for the preceding period.

Consolidated Financial Statements. Consolidated financial statements are not generally prepared, but the Companies Act requires that the balance sheet of the holding company must be accompanied by the financial statements, the boards' report and the auditors' report of each of its subsidiaries, all prepared in accordance with the requirements of the Act. Also, a statement must be attached showing the extent of the parent's interest in each subsidiary and the profits or losses not included in the parent's accounts. The lapse of time between the balance sheet dates of the holding company and the subsidiaries cannot exceed six months. When the financial years do not coincide, the following information must be shown in respect of each subsidiary:

1. Whether during that lapse of time there has been any change in the holding company's interest in the subsidiary
2. Whether during the same period any material changes have occurred in respect of fixed assets, investments or loans of the subsidiary.

Current Assets, Loans and Advances

Current assets include: interest accrued on investments, stores and spare parts, loose tools, stock-in-trade, works in progress, sundry debtors (secured, unsecured and doubtful; the provision for bad debts must be deducted and any excess provision shown as reserve or surplus) and cash and bank balances (current, call and deposit accounts must be segregated). Loans and advances must be broken down as to: advances and loans to subsidiaries, bills of exchange, advances receivable in cash or in kind or for value to be received (taxes, insurance, etc.), balances on current account with managing agents or secretaries and treasurers.

If, in the opinion of the directors, any of the current assets do not have a value on realization in the ordinary course of business equal to the book value, the fact should be stated.

Investments

These must be properly segregated and the basis of valuation described. Additions to and deductions from investments must be disclosed. In the case of investment in shares, a list of investments should be attached to the balance sheet showing the names of the managing agents or secretaries and treasurers of such companies, if any, and also stating the total investment in companies in the same group.

Fixed Assets

The following captions must be shown separately: goodwill, land, buildings, leaseholds, railway sidings, plant and machinery, furniture and fixtures, development of property, patents, trademarks and designs, livestock and vehicles. Fixed assets must be stated at cost (except as stated in the following paragraph); current additions and deductions must be shown as well as the accrued depreciation. It is established that when the original cost (at the promulgation of the Act) could not be ascertained without unreasonable expense and delay, the valuation shown by the books less the accumulated depreciation could be used, and the proceeds of any subsequent sales shown as a deduction.

Restatement of fixed assets are permitted, and the credit is recorded in a capital reserve account. Depreciation on the restatement is not allowed for tax purposes. Any restatements of fixed assets must be disclosed in the financial statements for the succeeding five years.

Deferred Charges

These include—to the extent not written off—preliminary expenses, commissions, discounts and other share and debenture issue expenses, interest paid during construction, unadjusted development expenditures, and other items.

Liabilities and Capital

The following captions must be shown separately:

Share capital, describing the amounts authorized, issued and called, for each class of shares.

Reserves and surplus, including premium account and profits on issue of shares. Current additions and deductions must be shown for each account. A debit balance in the profit and loss account, if any, must be deducted from the uncommitted reserves. The act provides that when preference shares are redeemed, the amount equivalent to their par value must be transferred to the capital redemption reserve fund out of profit and loss account or uncommitted reserves.

Capital and revenue reserves have to be shown separately. A capital reserve is defined as one not available for distribution through the profit and loss account.

Secured loans, including accrued interest. Amounts payable for debentures, loans and advances from banks, subsidiaries, directors, managing agents, etc., must be shown separately and the nature of the security must be specified in each case.

Unsecured loans, including accrued interest have the same disclosure requirements as secured loans.

Current Liabilities and Provisions

Current liabilities comprise acceptances, sundry creditors, amounts payable to subsidiaries, advance payments received, unclaimed dividends and others. Provisions include tax provisions, proposed dividends, employees' pensions, insurance, etc. Provision for contingencies is also to be included in current liabilities.

Provisions vs. Reserves

The difference between a reserve and a provision has a special significance under the Companies Act: (a) The expression "provision" means any amount written off or retained by way of providing for depreciation, renewals or diminution in value of assets, or retained by way of providing *for any known liability* of which the amount cannot be determined with substantial accuracy; (b) the expression "reserve" relates to any appropriations of profit, which is not a specific provision for a known liability.

Statement of Profit and Loss

The Act states that the profit and loss account must disclose every material item, including receipts and expenses in respect of nonrecurring transactions of an exceptional nature, as well as any material effect of changes in the bases of accounting. The following, among other items, must always be disclosed:

1. The turnover (i.e., the aggregate amount of net sales)
2. Commission paid to sole or other selling agents
3. Brokerage and discount on sales, other than the usual trade discount

4. In the case of manufacturing concerns, the purchases of raw materials and the opening and closing inventories of goods produced
5. In the case of other concerns, the gross income derived from the different operations
6. In the case of all concerns having work in progress, the amounts for which work has been completed at the beginning and at the end of the accounting period
7. The amounts provided for depreciation, renewals or dimunition in value of fixed assets
8. The amount of interest on the company's debentures and other fixed loans, showing separately any interest paid to managing agent, managing director, secretaries and treasurers
9. Income tax provision
10. The amounts provided for repayment of shares and debentures
11. The aggregate, if material, of amounts set or proposed to be set aside to reserves but not including provisions made to meet any specific liability, contingency or commitment known at the date of the balance sheet
12. The aggregate, if material, of any amounts drawn from such reserves
13. Provisions for specific liabilities, contingencies or commitments and the amounts withdrawn from such provisions as are no longer required
14. Expenses in connection with stores and spare parts: power and fuel; rent; repairs; salaries, wages and bonuses, contributions to provident and other funds; workmen and staff welfare expenses; insurance; taxes other than on income; and miscellaneous expenses
15. Income from other sources, such as trade investments; other investments and interest must be segregated
16. Detailed information of payments made to various categories of managerial personnel, i.e., directors, managing agents, managers, secretaries and treasurers.
17. Payments to auditors as for professional services, expenses or any other capacity, separately.

Depreciation

The Companies Act requires a company to provide a minimum amount of depreciation in the accounts before any dividends can be declared. This minimum can be computed either by applying rates allowable for tax purposes to the book value of each depreciable asset or by reference to the number of years for which depreciation allowances are given for tax purposes before a specific residual value is reached.

REQUIREMENTS FOR PUBLIC SALE OF SECURITIES

The Prospectus

Public sale of shares or debentures must be accompanied by a prospectus. The contents of the prospectus are listed in Schedule II of the Act, and include a report prepared by the auditors of the company in respect to:

1. Profits and losses for each of the five annual periods preceding the issue of the prospectus, after making suitable and appropriate adjustments for nonrecurring or exceptional items. If the company has subsidiaries, in addition to this information, similar information individually as to each subsidiary or with the combined profits and losses of the subsidiaries.
2. Assets and liabilities as of the last day to which the accounts were prepared. In the case of subsidiaries, the report must be presented in any of the forms referred to above.
3. Dividends paid by the company for each class of share during the five preceding years. If no dividends were paid, this fact should be stated.

If the proceeds of the sale of shares or debentures are to be used in the acquisition of another company, a profit and loss statement for the five preceding years and a balance sheet of the company to be acquired, of a date not prior to four months before the date of the prospectus, must be annexed. If the prospective acquisition is that of a body corporate, in addition to the mentioned information, the report must include a statement showing the effect of the acquisition on the shareholders' equity. If the body corporate has subsidiary companies, the same information referred to in (1) and (2) above must be submitted.

A statement of the auditor's consent as expert must be made a part of the prospectus.

REQUIREMENTS FOR LISTING SECURITIES ON THE STOCK EXCHANGE

A company which wishes to list securities for trading on the Calcutta Stock Exchange, which at the same time are being offered for sale to the public, must fulfill the following conditions:

The subscription list inviting applications for the securities offered for sale must have been kept open for at least three days.

The Prospectus will have been advertised in the newspapers.

At least 49 per cent of the total issue, excluding the portion issued to the parent company and foreign collaborators, must have been offered to the public.

The Memorandum and Articles of Association of the company must contain certain provisions prescribed by the Exchange.

The company must execute a Listing Agreement.

The Listing Agreement must be accompanied by a number of documents, of which the following are of interest to accountants:

The prospectus

Directors' reports and balance sheets for the last five years.

JAPAN 23

23

FORMS OF BUSINESS ORGANIZATION

The basic statutory law governing the organization of business enterprises is the Commercial Code of Japan, as amended. The types of business organization permissible under the provisions of this code are the single entrepreneur or merchant, partnerships and stock corporations. With the exception of the single entrepreneur, all other business organizations are classified as "Kaisha" or Company, which is defined as an association for the purpose of engaging in commercial activities.

A kaisha can be a partnership of which there are three variations, or a Kabushiki Kaisha which is the most common form of business organization for large and organized businesses, and closely resembles a United States corporation. Corporations are identified by an abbreviated designation such as K.K. (abbreviation of Kabushiki Kaisha); & Co., Ltd. or Co., Inc. after the company name.

Kabushiki Kaisha (Stock Corporation)

The formation of a corporation requires at least seven promoters who prepare, sign, have notarized and register the articles of incorporation. There is no stipulation in the Commercial Code as to the qualifications of the promoters or their nationalities.

Included among the provisions of the Commercial Code dealing with corporations are the following:

1. The number of shares to be issued at the time of incorporation must not be less than one-fourth of the total shares authorized.

2. Registration of incorporation must be made within two weeks of the promotors having underwritten all the shares issued or within two weeks after the completion of the general organization meeting of promoters and the share subscribers in cases where the promoters have not subscribed for all the shares.

3. The directors and the statutory examiner (Kansa Yaku) must be elected at the general organization meeting mentioned above, and at subsequent general meetings of shareholders. At least three directors must be elected. The maximum term of a director is two years except that the first term following incorporation is limited to one year. However, there is no specific limitation on re-election.

The Commercial Code also prescribes such corporate matters as duties of directors, Board of Directors, its meetings, minutes of such meetings, appointment of a representative director, duties of the statutory examiner, issuance of shares and debentures, keeping of records and accounts, alteration of articles of incorporation, reorganization, dissolution and liquidation.

The following matters related to corporations in Japan are of interest:

Directors and Officers. There is no distinction between directors and officers in the sense United States corporations use the terms. In most cases, directors are at the same time officers active in company affairs, although there are some exceptions.

Gakumen Kabu (Stock). In predominant cases, stock has a par value, most common par value being fifty yen. However, after World War II the Commercial Code provided for five-hundred yen par value stock for companies newly organized and issuing par value stock. Dividends are commonly expressed as a percentage of par value. No-par value stock may also be issued.

Shihonkin (Capital). Shihonkin (referring to stated or paid-in capital) is the common word used in describing the size of a corporation in Japan. Capital increase is frequently made through a combination of new issues, stock splits, and stock dividends with additional capital paid in by subscribers of new issues or transferred from capital surplus and retained earnings.

Often, capital stock increases are made by offering subscription rights to existing stockholders at par value; or at less than par value if the company has available revaluation surplus which may be transferred to capital in the amount of the difference between par and the offering price. (See also under "fixed asset revaluation.")

The word Shihonkin is used often in establishing criteria for certain requirements or privileges or as a basis of comparison. Growth of corporations is expressed as an increase in stated capital as well as in sales volume or in profits.

Shasai (Debentures). The Commercial Code provides that debentures cannot be issued in an amount in excess of the combined total of the

4

stated capital and reserves (reserves in this case means the remainder of the equity accounts); new debentures cannot be issued until the subscription payment for prior debentures is completed.

The Code also provides for serial debentures and convertible debentures, the latter being relatively new in Japan.

Partnerships

The Commercial Code provides for two, and the Yugen Kaisha (limited partnership) Code provide for a third type of partnership organization.

Gomei Kaisha, a general or unlimited partnership, is created after the charter (partnership agreement) is drawn up and is registered in a local registration office; it is a juridical person. The partnership is dissolved by charter provision, agreement by all company members (partners), a merger, decrease in the number of members to one, bankruptcy and by court order. The Codes also prescribe the liquidation procedures.

Goshi Kaisha is a combined limited and unlimited partnership consisting of partners in both categories. As the word "Goshi" (meaning joint capital) indicates, this form of partnership permits a capital contribution by inactive partners whose liability and authority would be limited. Under certain circumstances where limited partners no longer exist, a Goshi Kaisha can become a Gomei Kaisha through a simple procedure.

The Yugen Kaisha (limited company) is governed by the limited company or the Yugen Kaisha Law. It is a limited partnership having the characteristics of a corporation. The number of members is limited to fifty persons, each with a share representing his investment. Directors are chosen, usually but not necessarily, from among the members. Public offering of shares is not authorized. The law provides for mergers and change of organization into a corporation. This form of business organization is not very common.

Other forms of partnerships, similar to United States partnerships, are governed by the Civil Code of Japan (Articles 667-688, Section 12, "Partnerships").

Branches and Subsidiaries of Foreign Enterprises

Branches of foreign enterprises are subject to the same provisions of the Commercial Code as are companies formed in Japan. A foreign company which intends to engage in commercial transactions on a continual basis must appoint a representative in Japan and establish an office there.

A subsidiary can be established as a domestic corporation (Kabushiki Kaisha), which was discussed earlier.

Business Records

The Commercial Code of Japan requires that every business maintain its books of account and periodically prepare an inventory of assets and a balance sheet. The books of account and important documents must be kept for ten years.

KANSA YAKU (STATUTORY EXAMINER)

The Commercial Code provides that a statutory examiner (Kansa Yaku) who is elected by the shareholders will examine and report upon financial statements which the directors propose to submit to a general meeting of shareholders. The Code prescribes the right of the examiner to review or make copies of books and records of account, request a report on accounting from directors or, when necessary, investigate affairs of the company and the state of its property.

There is no legal requirement that the statutory examiner be a professional accountant or auditor. There are a few instances where the statutory examiner is a professional auditor who conducts an audit of the financial statements. In most cases, the statutory examiner does not have an audit staff. His function as an auditor is not comparable to that of an internal auditor nor to an independent auditor.

ZEIRISHI (TAX AGENTS)

Under the Tax Agent Law (Zeirishi Ho), the main functions of a ZEIRISHI are those of representing clients in tax matters, preparation of tax returns, and providing advice on tax matters. The principal requirement is to pass the Tax Agent Examination or to have qualifications evaluated by and to register with the Ministry of Finance. Tax agents are not allowed to engage in audits. Both lawyers and CPAs may engage in tax practice after registration.

THE ACCOUNTING PROFESSION

The origin of the public accounting profession is said to date back to 1907, although no legal basis existed until 1927, when the former Public Accountant Law (Keirishi Ho) was promulgated. This law was repealed in 1948, when the present CPA Law was enacted. Under the former law, the title of public accountant (Keirishi) was granted to anyone graduating from a college or professional school with a major in accounting. The practice of a public accountant consisted primarily of services to small businesses in bookkeeping, preparation of financial statements, and tax work after special registration. The audit of corporations by independent public accountants, in general, was rare until the enactment of the Securities Exchange Law and Certified Public Accountant Law in 1948.

The Securities and Exchange Law and related Ministry of Finance ordinances require corporations of above a certain size, whose shares are listed or publicly held, to present prescribed financial statements together with an audit report prepared by an independent certified public accountant.

The present law established a CPA system comparable to that of the United States, setting forth qualifications, examination requirements, duties, and penal provisions. Public accountants registered under the former law were allowed to reregister and to continue their practice as registered public accountants (Keirishi).

Another group of professional accountants is the foreign CPAs, who will be discussed later.

In order to practice within one of the above groups, the accountant must register with the Ministry of Finance; registration must be renewed every three years.

Forms of Practice

Although there are many instances where one CPA is engaged by another CPA, or assistants are engaged by a CPA, there is no legal provision for public accounting to be practiced by a partnership of CPAs or an association of individual CPAs. This is also true of registered public accountants.

The Japanese public accounting profession recognizes this problem, particularly in connection with the audit of large companies, and an effort is being made to seek a change in legislation providing for the organization of accounting firms in partnership form.

Konin Kaikeishi (Certified Public Accountant)

Qualifications. Other than the usual exclusion of minors, adjudicated incompetents, persons with certain criminal records, and those whose licenses have been suspended or revoked, the basic qualifications are the passing of the three separate CPA examinations. These examinations are conducted by the CPA Examination Committee consisting of professors and businessmen appointed by the Minister of Finance.

Preliminary Examination. This examination covers the Japanese language, mathematics and the writing of an essay on a given subject in social science. College graduates and those who have fulfilled certain minimum requirements are exempted from the preliminary examination.

Intermediate Examination. Only those who have passed the preliminary examination or those who have been exempted may apply for the intermediate examination which covers accounting theory, accounting practice, cost accounting, auditing, the Commercial Code, economics and business management. The purpose of the intermediate examination is to measure the applicant's knowledge of the above subjects which are necessary to perform duties as a junior CPA (Kaikeishi Ho). The status of a junior CPA is similar to non-CPA assistants engaged by CPAs in the United States, except that certain formal recognition is given and the title (Kaikeshi Ho) is registered. College professors, assistant professors and holders of doctorate degrees are exempted from the intermediate examination in their fields of specialization.

Final Examination. The purpose of the final examination is to measure the applicant's capability to apply specialized knowledge, and includes advanced accounting, auditing practice, financial analysis and tax accounting. In order to be admitted to the final examination, the applicant must be or have the qualification of a junior CPA with one year's practice under a CPA or other organizations designated by the Ministry of Finance, and two additional years of practice, after having obtained junior CPA status under a CPA. The law accepts certain general accounting experience, specifically defined, in lieu of practice under a CPA. The final examination is held twice a year.

Gaikoku Konin Kaikeishi (Foreign CPA)

Article 16-2 of the CPA Law provides for registration as a foreign CPA. A person who has met requirements in a foreign country corresponding to the Japanese CPA qualifications and has sufficient knowledge of Japanese laws and ordinances relating to accounting (as determined by an oral examination) may apply to the Ministry of Finance for approval to practice as a foreign CPA. He must then register with the Ministry of Finance and may then use the title, "Foreign CPA." At the latest examination in 1962, about half of the applicants were successful.

Kaikeishi Ho (Junior CPA)

Junior CPA (Kaikeisha Ho) is sometimes referred to as an "assistant accountant," but the Japanese Institute of CPAs uses the term "junior CPA."

Those who have passed the intermediate CPA examination or have equivalent qualifications can register with the Ministry of Finance and practice public accounting as junior CPAs. In practice, most junior CPAs are engaged by CPAs. However, there are some independent practitioners.

Keirishi (Registered Public Accountant)

Those who practiced public accounting under the old law (repealed in 1948), were permitted to reregister as registered public accountants and to continue practice except for the audit and certification of financial statements under the requirements of the Securities and Exchange Law.

9

Konin Kaikeishi Shinsa Kai (CPA Examination Committee)

The Committee is an adjunct organization under the Ministry of Finance organized to investigate and study matters of importance relating to the CPA system, its administration and examinations. The members consist of not more than ten persons appointed by the Minister of Finance from among officials of the government offices concerned and professors. The term of a Committee member is two years. The Committee has fifteen subcommittee members who conduct CPA examinations each year.

Professional Accounting Organization

The Japanese Institute of CPAs, organized in 1949, is the only CPA organization in Japan. As of December 1963, the Institute had ten regional chapters, ten standing committees and approximately 1,700 members and 700 associate members. The Institute publishes a periodical, *The Certified Public Accountant,* operates a research and training center, conducts or sponsors research, cooperates with the Ministry of Finance in developing sound audit procedures and accounting principles and represents Japanese CPAs in international relations as well as internally as a professional organization. Junior CPAs may become associate members of the Institute.

The Institute promulgated for its members the standard audit engagement contract format and provisions, and fee schedules. The model contract was developed jointly with the Japan Federation of Business Organizations (Kei Dan Ren), which is a federation of trade associations and large businesses.

Other professional organizations are as follows:

The Association of Foreign Certified Public Accountants in Japan

Japan Registered Public Accountants Association

The Japan Federation of Tax Agents Association. Both the national federation and regional associations are established under the Tax Agent Law. Regional associations are established on the basis of one for each National Tax Bureau district.

Code of Ethics

The Japanese Institute of CPAs published, in 1950, *Rules of Professional Ethics,* which included the following (condensed):

A member will not engage in any business or occupation, concurrently with that of CPA, which is incompatible or inconsistent therewith.

A member will not sign a report purporting to express his opinion on financial statements unless such statements have been examined by him, a member or employee of his firm, or a member of the Institute.

A member will not solicit clients, will not compete against other members on the amount of fee, nor render service for a fee based upon the results of such work.

A member will not injure the practice of other members, nor make offer of employment to an employee of another member without first obtaining permission of the latter.

Summary of Legal and Professional Requirements Affecting the Accounting Profession and Practice

Legal	Administering Body
Commercial Code	Ministry of Justice
Civil Code	Ministry of Justice, Court
CPA Law	Ministry of Finance
Finance Ministry Regulations relating to CPA Law	,, ,, ,,
Securities and Exchange Law	,, ,, ,,
Ministry of Finance Regulations relating to preparation of financial statements for reporting under the Securities and Exchange Law	,, ,, ,,
Ministry of Finance Regulations relating to the examination and certification of financial statements under the Securities and Exchange Law	,, ,, ,,
Regulations concerning balance sheets and profit and loss statements of Kabushiki Kaisha	Ministry of Justice
Tax Laws	Ministry of Finance
Administrative laws and regulations relating to specific industries	,, ,, ,, and other Ministries

Professional	*Administering Body*
Business Accounting Principles (generally accepted accounting principles)—Kigyo Kaikei Gensoku	Business Accounting Council (Kigyo Kaikei Shingi Kai) Appointed by Minister of Finance
Working Rules for Preparing Financial Statements—Zaimu Sho Hyo Iunsoku	" " " " "
Audit Standards	" " " " "
Working Rules for Conduct of Audits	" " " " "
Reporting Standards	" " " " "
Rules of Conduct	Japanese Institute of CPAs
Audit Engagement Contract Standards	" " " "
Audit Fee Schedule	" " " "
Series of Bulletins on Auditing	" " " "

AUDITING STANDARDS

Audit of large corporate businesses by independent auditors did not become common practice until the enactment of the Securities and Exchange Law and the CPA Law in 1948. Prior to that time auditing was limited to internal auditing and to the audit of governmental and institutional organizations.

The Securities and Exchange Law and related Ministry of Finance regulations require corporations of above a certain size, whose shares are offered to or held by the public, to submit periodically a comprehensive report of business to the Ministry of Finance. This report, called Yuka Shoken Hokokusho (Securities Report), must include financial statements which have been audited by an independent CPA. In addition, the Ministry of Finance requires submission of an audit report by the CPA which includes the auditor's opinion on the financial statements and a summary of audit work done in a fairly detailed format prescribed. These constitute legal requirements for auditing and reporting standards.

The Business Accounting Council under the Ministry of Finance published, as interim reports, *Audit Standards, Working Rules for Conduct of Audits* and *Reporting Standards.* The interim reports state in part that "these standards and rules are a summarization of principles developed among various auditing practices and considered fair and reasonable, and while they bind no one legally, they are the standards every professional auditor should abide by." Thus, these standards and rules might be considered as codified generally accepted auditing and reporting standards.

The Committee on Auditing Procedure of the Japanese Institute of CPAs has also published a series of *Notes* covering subjects such as retirement pay, depreciation, audit reports, etc.

Auditing and Reporting Standards Established by the Business Accounting Council

Auditing Standards. The general standards section of the interim report sets forth in general terms, auditors' qualifications, independence, confidential nature of work, exercise of professional care, determination of scope and method of audit, materiality, consistency and adherence to the business accounting principles. (Comparable to generally accepted accounting principles—discussed later).

The "working rules for conduct of an audit" section defines terms identifying types of specific audit work such as testing, observation, confirmation, etc., and prescribes the entire audit work from general preliminary examination to audit procedures for specific statement items. A review is to be made of internal controls, using an internal control questionnaire for reliance thereon in determining the scope and methods of audit. This section of the report prescribes a "normal audit procedure" to be followed. Generally, the audit statements as indicated above are similar to those in the United States. Some exceptions noted are as follows:

1. Confirmation of bank balances is required for checking accounts. For deposits supported by a bank passbook or a certificate of deposit, examination of these is considered sufficient.

2. Accounts receivable are confirmed when it is considered necessary.

3. Observation of physical inventory taking is required when it is considered necessary.

4. Confirmation of accounts payable and loans payable is required when it is considered necessary.

Reporting standards. The section of the Council's interim report pertaining to the audit report is called, "the working rules for preparing the audit report" and contains essentially the following requirements:

1. The report should contain the outline of the work the auditor has performed and his opinion on the financial statements. It should be dated, signed and sealed with the CPA's name.

2. The audit report must include the following information:

   a. Summary of the scope of the audit
   b. Whether the audit was conducted in accordance with the generally accepted standards
   c. Whether the normal auditing procedures and other procedures determined to be necessary under the circumstances were employed.

3. This report should contain an expression of opinion on the financial statements taken as a whole.

4. In order to render such an opinion, the following must be stated:

   a. Whether the company's accounting principles and practices are in conformity with the business accounting principles
   b. Whether the above principles and procedures are applied consistently
   c. Whether the company's financial statements conform to the format and rules contained in the working rules for preparing financial statements (published by the Business Accounting Council for commerce and industry or those specifically established by the government ministries involved for regulated industries).

5. The auditor must render an opinion if he determines that the financial statements fairly represent the company's position at balance-sheet date and the results of operations for the period.

6. The auditor must state the effect on the financial statements of the following:

   a. When normal audit procedures, while practicable and rational, were omitted with respect to a significant item in the financial statements
   b. When a significant item in the financial statements was treated contrary to business accounting principles

    c. When the company's accounting principles and procedures were changed, resulting in a material effect upon the net income of the period—"except that if the change was made for justifiably achieving the leveling of periodic income or financial stability of the enterprise, such changes need not be cited." (In the Ministry of Finance Regulation on the audit certification of financial statements, which is discussed later, the above exception from the requirement to render a qualified opinion is further restricted to businesses with seasonal fluctuations and only when applied consistently each period.) Similar exception is afforded to certain accounting treatments based on tax laws which may not be acceptable under the business accounting principles

    d. When significant items of financial information are not disclosed as provided in the working rules for preparing financial statements.

7. If, by including the exceptions in the audit report, the opinion rendered becomes meaningless, the auditor must withhold his opinion and make a statement to that effect with his reasons.

8. Material events subsequent to the balance sheet date, such as a merger, acquisition, etc., having a significant effect on the business must be disclosed in the audit report.

While reporting upon the larger companies in Japan tends to follow the above rules, reports by individual CPAs upon medium-sized and smaller companies rarely include any qualifications as to scope of work performed, disagreement with accounting principles applied, or notations of inconsistent treatment.

Audit and Reporting Standards Established by the Ministry of Finance and Regulation for Audit Certification of Financial Statements for the Securities and Exchange Purposes

The above regulation states that the audit must be conducted in accordance with the audit practice generally recognized as fair and reasonable, "which shall be the audit standards and working rules contained in the interim report by the Business Accounting Council." (As discussed previously.)

With respect to the reporting standards, the regulation prescribes the report format which includes an itemized check-list type record of audit work performed. Any significant item which is not in conformity with generally accepted accounting principles or which reflects deviation from consistency must be so noted with reasons and its effects on the financial statements.

Some of the provisions noted are as follows:

1. In evaluating for conformity with generally accepted accounting principles, accounting treatment of provisions for depreciation, bad debts and retirement allowance, treatment of deferred items, determination of costs of goods manufactured, recording of sales and other transactions and adjustments, "it must be remembered that the tax laws alone should not be regarded as the basis."

2. The following instances may be regarded as being in conformity with accounting principles generally considered fair and reasonable:

   a. Items of loss or expense allowed under the tax law though they may not necessarily be in conformity with the accounting principles generally considered fair and reasonable.

   b. Accounting treatment which is an established and rational method in a given industry.

3. Significant deviation from the format of financial statements prescribed in the Ministry of Finance regulations must be so noted and differences shown.

4. If expression of an opinion becomes impossible due to severe limitation on the conduct of the audit or incomplete records, the CPA must indicate that he is withholding his opinion giving reasons therefor in his report.

5. The requirement for disclosure of inconsistent treatment may be waived if justifiable reason can be adduced. Among the limited number of specific situations stated in the law are:

   a. In the case of a company whose business is seasonal, changes made in accounting treatment to adjust seasonal profit fluctuation between the first half and the second half of the year, when applied consistently each period, are considered justifiable. (Note: In Japan, most companies use a six-month period as an accounting period.)

   b. Valuation of inventories and marketable securities at market (when lower than cost) where cost has been used consistently in the past (i.e., a switch from cost to lower of cost or market).

   c. Depreciation over a relatively short period of assets that have become obsolete.

   d. Deviations from past standards on items that are difficult to determine exactly (e.g., repairs vs. capital expenditures; amount of bad debt writeoff).

   e. Deviations from previous years allowed by tax laws.

An example of an unqualified report of a Japanese CPA for securities and exchange purposes is shown below:

Auditor's Report

To the President,
    XYZ Company.

Date:
Auditor:
    Name:
    Address:

. . . .
(signature)

1. Scope of Audit: I have examined the financial statements (balance sheet, income statement, surplus statement, statement of appropriation of surplus and schedules), consisting of a part of the registration statement for the period December 1, 19... through May 31, 19..., in relation to the required audit under the Article 193-2 of the Securities Exchange Law.

My examination was made in accordance with the generally accepted auditing standards, and accordingly included normal auditing procedures and such other auditing procedures as I considered necessary in the circumstances.

2. Auditor's Opinion: In my opinion, based upon my examination, the accounting principles and procedures of the company are in conformity with generally accepted accounting principles, and were applied on a basis consistent with that of the preceding business year, and the presentations of the financial statements are in conformity with the forms illustrated by the Regulations.

Therefore, in my opinion, the financial statements fairly present the financial position of XYZ Company as of May 31, 19.., and the results of their operations for the period then ended.

3. Independence: I have no material interests in the company.

Independence. In connection with the requirement to be "independent," engagement as a CPA for certification of financial statements for the Securities and Exchange Law purposes is prohibited under the following circumstances:

1. Where the CPA or his spouse was an officer of, or its equivalent,

17

or in a position of responsibility in financial affairs in the company within the past year

2. Where the CPA was an employee or had a material interest in the company within the one year. Material interest is defined in the Ministry of Finance's ordinance relating to audit certification of financial statements. Included in the definition are stock holdings and debenture holdings of over certain amounts, creditor-debtor relationship, business relationships and other indications of substantial interest

3. Where the CPA, within the past two years, was closely associated with the company as a public servant (local or national government official), through duties of his office.

There is a requirement that a statement by the CPA regarding his relationship with the company being audited, in the light of these restrictions, must be included in the audit report submitted to the Ministry of Finance.

ACCOUNTING PRINCIPLES AND PRACTICES

The accounting principles and practices in Japan do not differ materially from those in the United States. The business accounting principles and the working rules for preparing financial statements, published by the Business Accounting Council, may be regarded, in the absence of legal compulsion, as equivalent to generally accepted accounting principles and procedures. However, this does not necessarily mean that these principles and rules were developed out of general practice over a period of time. Business accounting principles were established to improve Japanese accounting practices of presentation of financial statements of business enterprises in order to protect investors and thus aid in the development of Japanese industries. These principles resulted from the studies and writings by appointed government officials, professors and practitioners.

Today, the business accounting principles and the working rules for preparing financial statements, published by the Business Accounting Council, are regarded as "the accounting principle and practice generally accepted as fair and reasonable," and are incorporated to some extent into the laws and regulations which affect business accounting and financial reporting.

The Commercial Code of Japan has recently been revised to include, as legal requirements, more of the accounting principles and financial reporting standards reflected in the "Business Accounting Principle." With a relatively centralized authority in and around the Ministry of Finance, it may be presumed that increasingly effective steps will be taken to eliminate differences among the Commercial Code and other legal and administrative requirements, tax laws and generally accepted accounting principles.

Form and Content of Financial Statements

General principles or postulates contained in business accounting principles include the principles of disclosure, clarity, consistency, conservatism and basic uniformity as to source and correctness among statements prepared for various purposes, i.e., shareholders, creditors, tax, etc. The concept of materiality is stated in various disclosure or classification requirements.

Business accounting principles include the concept of matching revenues with cost, accrual basis accounting, operating income as distinguished from nonoperating, realization basis, elimination of intracompany profits, etc. Accounting for installment sales and recognizing income or loss in long-term construction projects is essentially similar to the United States practices.

Statement Presentation

1. Under the working rules for preparing financial statements, financial statements are generally considered to consist of:

   Income (loss) statement

   Statement of cost of goods manufactured (if applicable)

   Statement of surplus

   Statement of appropriation of earned surplus

   Balance sheet

   Schedules supporting financial statements.

2. Under the Securities and Exchange Law and related rules, financial statements and supporting schedules required for submission are:

Balance sheet

Profit and loss statement

Statement of surplus or deficit

Statement of appropriation of surplus

Schedule of securities held

Schedule of tangible fixed assets

Schedule of intangible fixed assets

Schedule of securities of affiliated companies held

Schedule of capital contribution to affiliated companies

Schedule of loans to affiliated companies

Schedule of debentures

Schedule of long-term loans

Schedule of loans from affiliated companies

Schedule of capital

Schedule of capital surplus

Schedule of profit reserve and voluntary reserve

Schedule of depreciation

Schedule of allowances.

Generally, the form of statement presentation as indicated by both of the above pronouncements is similar to that customary in the United States. Most Japanese companies adopt a fiscal year beginning April 1, as does the government, and report on a semiannual basis. Others report annually and some on a calendar-year basis.

Consolidated Financial Statements. Preparation of consolidated financial statements is unusual in Japan. There is no requirement that financial statements of parent companies be supplemented either with individual statements of the subsidiaries or with information comparing parent company's investment with underlying net assets, or parent company's dividend and interest income from subsidiaries for the period with the related net income of such subsidiaries.

Assets

Current Assets. The "one-year rule" for current assets is incorporated in business accounting principles.

Marketable securities held for a temporary period may be shown at cost value. No mention is made of the cost basis, lower of cost or market or writeup from cost in the business accounting principles, and most companies record them at cost.

Inventories are stated by most companies at cost, following the provisions of the Commercial Code, even though recording them "at lower of cost or market" is "a generally accepted accounting principle."

Fixed Asset Revaluation. Because of severe currency inflation experienced in the period immediately following World War II, the government enacted a "Fixed Assets Revaluation Law" in 1950 (as amended in 1952 and 1953), for an across-the-board revaluation of assets using stipulated adjustment factors. In the books of the companies, a credit entry was made to fixed asset revaluation reserve under the capital surplus section, with a debit to the asset account. A fixed asset revaluation tax of generally under 6 per cent was levied on the amount of the writeup; depreciation thereafter was based on the revalued assets. In general, most of the assets as valued under the "Fixed Assets Revaluation Law" have now been fully depreciated.

In connection with the revaluation, additional laws were enacted to provide for buildup of stated capital by transfer of portions of the revaluation reserve with or without public offering of new shares. Also, a special law was passed to extend similar revaluation to small companies.

Other than the special asset revaluation, business accounting principles stipulate cost basis for all fixed assets.

Intangible Assets and Deferred Charges. Intangible assets must be amortized on a fixed basis, and shown net after deduction of amortization on the balance sheet. Detailed schedules showing accumulated amortization are required.

A recent revision of the Commercial Code specifies amortization for various classes of intangibles and deferred charges. Some of the more important are:

Goodwill, organization expense and research and development cost within five years

Debenture issue expense within three years, or over the life of the debentures, whichever is shorter

Stock issue expense within three years.

Losses of unusually large magnitude, such as those due to natural disasters or war, incurred on fixed assets or other assets required for business operation (loss of capital nature), when larger than earned surplus and when special statutes are enacted, can be deferred and amortized by charge against earned surplus in future periods. This treatment is limited to cases where writeoff against future-generated earned surplus is feasible within a reasonable period of time. In practice, the use of this procedure is rare.

Included in the deferred charges classification is the so-called "construction interest" which is paid to stockholders until the company's operation produces profits. To encourage investment, the Commercial Code in Article 291 provides for payment of such special interest to stockholders when, due to the nature of business, a corporation does not commence its business until two years or more after its incorporation. This interest covers a specific period prior to the commencement of business and at a certain rate. Inclusion of this provision in the charter of incorporation requires the approval of a court. The law further provides that such costs may be carried on the asset side of the balance sheet and amortized.

Liabilities

Provision for Retirement Allowance. Japanese companies normally have two bases for computing retirement allowances. Broadly speaking, one basis is for those retiring voluntarily, and the second is for those retiring at retirement age or at the request of the company. For tax purposes, the company may only deduct 50 per cent of the total liability computed on what is called the voluntary basis. Many companies accrue liability only for this tax-deductible portion; this may vary significantly from the liability computed on the involuntary basis. Under the reporting standards in Japan, this probably does not require qualification of the CPA's opinion.

Affiliated Company Loans. Loans to and from affiliated companies are to be shown separately from those with nonaffiliated companies.

Overdue Liabilities. Overdue liabilities must be disclosed.

Capital

Financial statement presentation of capital items is somewhat rigidly prescribed by the Commercial Code, the Securities and Exchange Law and other regulations. Clear distinction is made among capital stock items, capital surplus items and earned surplus items. If the loss for the period exceeds the amount of earned surplus, the excess may be charged to capital surplus. Approval of shareholders is generally required. Disclosure by footnote on the balance sheet is required in this case.

Treasury Stock. The Commercial Code prohibits acquisitions of a company's own shares except in certain limited cases, usually for temporary holding and disposition, and requires the stock to be separately listed under "other current assets." The Business Accounting Council recommends treatment of treasury stock as a reduction in capital and gains or losses from treasury stock transactions as capital surplus increase or decrease (either cost or face value).

Legal and Other Reserves of Corporations. The Commercial Code provides that a company must transfer an amount equal to at least 10 per cent of dividends paid to a legal reserve until the amount so transferred reaches one-fourth of the stated capital of the company. This is referred to as a "profit" (earned surplus) reserve. In addition, certain specified capital surplus items, consisting of:

Premium on stock issues

Credits arising from amalgamations and mergers

Credits arising from reduction of capital

are included in the legal reserve required by the Commercial Code and are referred to as "capital reserve" (Shihon Jumbikin).

The profit (earned surplus) reserve is shown on the balance sheet as a separate item under retained earnings. The capital reserve portion of the legal reserve is shown separately under the capital surplus section.

Surplus

"Surplus," as an all-inclusive concept, is defined as the excess of net worth over the legal capital.

Capital Surplus. This caption, in addition to the items classified as the capital portion of the legal reserve (above), includes such items as: increases in surplus resulting from acquisitions of subsidiaries, mergers, etc.; contributions from government or others for capital expenditures; contributions resulting from forgiveness of debt; excess of insurance proceeds over book amount of insured property (originally from fluctuation in monetary value); and gains on disposal of treasury stock.

Earned Surplus. Represents accumulated unappropriated profits and losses from operations.

Kakaku Hendo Jumbikin (Price Fluctuation Reserve). A special tax law prescribes the procedure for deducting provisions for losses due to price declines in inventories and marketable securities. The Business Accounting Council's published opinion regards this reserve as earmarked earned surplus rather than an asset valuation account.

Intracompany Sales and Profit. Under business accounting principles, it is expected that elimination be made of corresponding purchase and sale and of intracompany profit from the inventory at the end of the period. On the other hand, if elimination of purchases and sales is not practicable, it is considered acceptable to eliminate only profit from the end of period inventory.

Income and Surplus Statement

Directors' Bonuses. Directors' bonuses are treated as appropriations of surplus.

Depreciation. Methods used are generally similar to those in the United States. Declining-balance methods are often used in Japan. The basis of an asset is the cost or revalued amount, the latter being the amount arrived at under special legislation, "Fixed Assets Revaluation Law." Depreciation is deductible for tax purposes at specified rates only to the extent recorded in the books. Few companies record depreciation in excess of the amounts deductible for tax purposes. Accelerated depreciation is provided in special instances.

Nonoperating Items. Nonoperating income and expense are separated from operating income and expense, but unusual bad debt losses are included in nonoperating expense. Special discounts, such as those resulting from early payment in lieu of notes on sales or purchase are included in the nonoperating section. Ordinary allowance, trade discount, returns, etc., are offset against sales or purchases. Corrections of prior year's income and expense are shown in the surplus statement.

Tax-effect Accounting. Financial accounting in Japan tends to follow the rules laid down in tax law and regulations, and accordingly there are seldom differences between book and taxable income which might require allocation of income tax charges between years. Under the revised

Commercial Code, income tax is now considered an expense in the period for which income is presented. Prior to this revision, income tax was considered an appropriation of earnings.

REQUIREMENTS FOR PUBLIC OFFERING AND LISTING

Registration, Periodic Reporting and Prospectus

The Securities and Exchange Law and the related Ministry of Finance regulations require submission by corporations publicly offering their shares of stock or debentures (generally those making offerings of capital of over 50 million yen) of a registration statement including a prospectus and subsequent periodic reports called Yuka Shoken Hokokusho for each accounting period.

The registration statements should include: (1) general information, (2) history, major lines of businesses, and major facilities, (3) information on current operations, (4) financial information, and (5) information on the new issues.

The annual reports or semiannual reports should disclose: (1) general information, (2) major lines of businesses and major facilities, (3) information on current operations, and (4) financial information.

The financial information should include: (1) a balance sheet, (2) an income statement, (3) a surplus statement, (4) a statement on the distribution and appropriation of earned surplus, and (5) schedules showing details of major items on the balance sheet and income statement.

The law requires that this financial information be accompanied with an audit report by a certified public accountant independent of the registrant.

In addition, under regulations effective July 1, 1963, all issues of stock to nonresidents, except for those sold on stock exchanges, must be approved by the Ministry of International Trade and Industry. The company must also file a registration statement (Yuka Shoken Todokeidesho) with the Ministry of Finance.

Listing Requirement on Japanese Stock Exchanges

General. Up to the latter part of 1961, there were three major stock exchanges in Japan: Tokyo, Osaka and Nagoya, in their order of importance. Since then, so-called "second market" sections (Dai Ni Shijo) were opened in each exchange permitting the listing and trading of over-the-counter issues which did not qualify for listing on the principal exchanges.

Stock exchanges are maintained and operated by member securities companies (corporations) under the Securities and Exchange Law administered by the Ministry of Finance.

Listing Requirements for the First Market Section.

> Paid-up capital: 1 million yen or over
> Shareholders: 3,000 or over

Distribution of Shares. After the public offering, the number of shares owned by those who hold blocks of less than 5,000 shares of 50 yen par value must be at least 20 per cent of the total shares issued or 5 million shares representing 10 per cent or more of the total shares issued.

Trading Record. Monthly average number of shares traded for the last six months:

1. In case of listing on one exchange: 200,000 and over
2. in case of listing on two exchanges: 200,000 and over in one exchange or total of 250,000 and over in two exchanges
3. in case of listing on three exchanges: 200,000 and over in one exchange or total of 300,000 and over in three exchanges.

Number of Years of Operation. Three or more years continuously.

Dividend Rate. Ten per cent and over per share on par value for the last three six-month periods or two years if the accounting period is a full year with a good prospect of this percentage being maintained.

Delisting or Transfer. Stocks listed in the second market section may be transferred to the first market section when the latter's requirements are met. Reversal of this transfer or delisting can be made by the Stock Exchange with some probational periods.

Listing Requirements for The Second Market Section.

> Paid-up capital: Over 1 million yen
> Shareholders: Over two hundred and fifty after public offering (judgment to be made by the Exchange authorities).

Distribution of Shares. After public offering, the number of 'floating shares" must be 400,000 or more and these must represent 5 per cent or more of the total shares issued. When 5 per cent of the total shares issued exceeds 5 million shares, the minimum for floating shares is 5 million shares. "Floating shares" are defined as shares owned in blocks of less than 5,000 shares at par value of 50 yen per share. For other par values, the following formula applies:

$$5000 \text{ shares } \times \frac{50}{\text{par value}}$$

A minimum of 200,000 shares plus 2.5 per cent of total shares must be publicly offered at the time of listing.

Number of Years of Operation. Two years since incorporation.

Dividends. At least 10 per cent per share on par value of capital stock for the last three six-month accounting periods or two years if the accounting period is a full year. Also there must be a reasonable prospect for dividend payment in the current and subsequent periods. (Some exceptions).

Review and approval of listing applications are required by both the Stock Exchange Board of Governors and the Minister of Finance. It takes approximately two months for this to be completed.

NEW ZEALAND   24

FORMS OF BUSINESS ORGANIZATION

The principal forms of business organization are incorporated companies, partnerships and sole traders. Almost all industrial and commercial enterprises are established as incorporated companies with limited liability.

Regulations governing the formation and operation of incorporated companies are contained in the Companies Act 1955, which, in many respects, follows the United Kingdom Companies Act 1948.

No company, association or partnership of more than twenty-five persons may carry on business unless it is registered as a company under the Act. A company may be "limited by shares," "limited by guarantee" or be "unlimited."

The Public Company

Companies which have raised capital by offering shares to the general public are referred to as "public" companies, although this designation is not used in the Companies Act 1955. Public companies most closely resemble the usual United States corporation, and when "limited by shares," the liability of shareholders is limited to the amount unpaid, if any, on their subscriptions to capital stock.

Companies may be duly incorporated by registering with the Registrar of Companies:

1. A Memorandum of Association which is, in effect, its charter outlining its objects and powers, detailing its share capital and stating that its liability is limited (if such is the case); and
2. Articles of Association which set out the rights and restrictions that govern the relationship between members.

These must be signed by all subscribers detailing the number of shares taken by each. The Registrar of Companies, having approved the proposed name of the company (which must conclude with the word "limited" when that is the case), then issues a certificate that the company is registered and that it may commence business.

A company must have at least seven members at all times.

The Companies Act 1955, provides that every company shall appoint an auditor or auditors who shall make a report to the members on the financial statements examined by them and presented to the company in general meeting. The appointment of auditors is discussed in more detail later.

Each year, public companies are required to file with the Registrar of Companies an annual return including information to the date of its annual general meeting, which reads as follows:

1. Address of registered office
2. Location of registrar of members (which may be other than at the registered office)
3. Summary of share capital and debentures
4. Amount of registered indebtedness, i.e., mortgages and other charges given over the property of the company
5. Particulars of directors and secretary
6. List of members, their holdings and changes therein since the last return.

A certified copy of the relevant annual accounts together with the auditors' report thereon and the directors' report must accompany the annual return.

Copies of the company's accounts must also be filed with the Commissioner of Inland Revenue.

Finance Emergency Regulations

The Minister of Finance, as a result of the Finance Emergency Regulations 1940 (No. 2), must consent to the registration of any company with a capital exceeding £10,000 or to the issue of capital or sale of securities exceeding £10,000 in any one year. Any prospectus so issued shall contain a statement that his consent has been obtained or is not required, as the case may be. However, by a "general consent" as of June 28, 1962, prior application is not necessary for any such "issues of capital" except where:

1. An overseas company desires to commence business in New Zealand.

2. A New Zealand registered company proposes to issue securities overseas or to make an "issue of capital" overseas.

It is necessary for prospectuses, etc., issued by companies for circulation overseas to include the notice of disclaimer where the issue requires consent.

These restrictions are subject, at any time, to possible change in government policy.

Private Companies

Companies which are incorporated under Part VIII of the Companies Act as private companies are, on one hand, free from many reporting and other requirements, while, on the other hand, they are not permitted to offer their shares for public subscription. The requirements for the Memorandum of Association and the Articles of Association are the same as for a "public company," previously described.

Private companies are usually formed to obtain the advantages of limited liability for family businesses, small closely held businesses and for subsidiaries of other corporations. This is the more convenient form of incorporation for a subsidiary.

A private company need have only two members, but membership is restricted to twenty-five, except where employees are also members in which case the limit is fifty. The capital must be fully subscribed, that is, all shares must be allotted to members even though they need not be paid up. There need be only one director.

A private company may, in its articles of association, make provisions, giving privileges or imposing restrictions on its members with or without creating classes of members. For instance, the articles may restrict the transfer of shares, attach preferred voting to certain shares, and appoint some or all directors for "life."

A private company which is not a subsidiary of a public company may dispense with the requirement of being audited provided it has not borrowed monies from the public. This is done by the members passing a *unanimous* resolution annually that no auditor be appointed.

A private company may issue debentures or obtain monies from the public on deposit on the basis of a prospectus issued for such purposes. It may not issue a prospectus inviting subscriptions for shares capital.

Unless private companies have obtained loans from the public on the basis of a prospectus inviting subscription, they are not required to file copies of their annual accounts, directors' reports and auditors' reports with their annual returns to the Registrar of Companies.

5

Partnerships

The usual general partnership with unlimited liability of partners as recognized under British and American law is also found in New Zealand.

Special partnerships may also be formed to transact business, other than banking and insurance. They may have different classes of partners, some with limited liability. These special partnerships must be registered in the Supreme Court.

Subsidiary or Branch of a Foreign Corporation

A foreign corporation may form a New Zealand subsidiary to conduct operations in that country, usually as a private company for reasons given above. Such a subsidiary is subject to the provisions of the Company Act 1955.

Foreign companies establishing a branch for the purpose of doing business in New Zealand shall register as an "overseas company" defined in the Companies Act 1955. The information required on registration includes the names and addresses of one or more persons resident in New Zealand or of a company incorporated in New Zealand authorized to accept, on behalf of the overseas company, service of process and any notices required to be served on the company.

Every overseas company shall on all places of business, bill heads, letter paper and notices state the name of the company, the country in which it is incorporated and the fact that it is limited (if that is the case).

Every overseas company shall annually file such accounts as would be required if it had been incorporated in New Zealand with the Registrar of Companies. These accounts are those for the company or group as a whole and are not confined to those of its New Zealand business and assets. Full compliance with this provision is not required for companies incorporated in the United Kingdom and Australia on a reciprocal basis.

Overseas insurance companies must also comply with other pertinent legislation.

Business Records

The Companies Act 1955, states that every New Zealand company must keep "full, true and complete accounts of the affairs and transactions of the company." If accounting records are maintained outside New Zealand, returns must be sent to New Zealand at least every six months and retained there to show with reasonable accuracy the financial position of the company. These returns must enable the company's annual accounts to be prepared in accordance with the Act.

All New Zealand businesses, be they companies, partnerships, or individuals, are required to file copies of their accounts with the Taxes Division of the Inland Revenue Department. The contents of accounts and other requirements of the Income Tax Acts do not necessarily follow those of the Companies Act 1955.

THE ACCOUNTING PROFESSION

The accounting profession in New Zealand has been regulated since the formation of the New Zealand Society of Accountants, by Act of Parliament in 1908. The Society is the recognized body of accountants and its stated objectives are to promote the interests of accounting and to control and regulate the profession in New Zealand.

The Act of 1908, and subsequent legislation defined the terms "public accountant" and "registered accountant" and restricted the use of these terms to members of the Society. By legislation in 1963, the term "accountant" is protected in relation to public practice. This legislation also provided for a fidelity fund to protect the public against defalcations by practitioners.

Unlike other countries of the British Commonwealth the term "chartered accountant" is not used.

Public Accountants

Members of the Society in public practice are designated as "public accountants" and may either be associates (A.P.A.N.Z.) or fellows (F.P.A.N.Z.).

A public accountant in New Zealand is defined by legislation as a person who, "being a member of the New Zealand Society of Accountants, proves to the satisfaction of the Council that he is carrying on or is about to carry on the public practice of accountancy in New Zealand by placing

7

his services at the disposal of the community for remuneration, but not entirely at the disposal of any one individual, firm or corporation and by maintaining an office or place at which his services may be engaged, and who is available at all times to undertake work on behalf of the public."

Registered Accountants

Members of the Society who are not in public practice or who are resident outside of New Zealand are designated "registered accountants" and may be either associates (A.R.A.N.Z.) or fellows (F.R.A.N.Z.). The rights and duties of associates and fellows are the same, and fellowship status is a matter of standing and years of service. Individual application is required for a change to this status.

The registered accountant is of equal stature to the accountant in public practice.

Functions of Accountants

In addition to auditing the accounts of companies, the keeping of financial records, the preparation of annual accounts and the filing of returns, accountants may also: perform secretarial work; act as tax consultants; prepare tax returns; accept appointments as trustees; act in liquidations; provide assistance in the field of financial management; install accounting systems, cost and budgetary controls; and act as agents for insurance companies and building societies. Accountants may also act as directors where this function does not interfere with their independence.

The New Zealand Society of Accountants

Qualifications for Membership. Membership is available to persons who have passed the Society's professional examinations and have satisfied its Council that they are of good character and reputation; are not engaged in any business or occupation inconsistent with the integrity of the profession; and (since 1958) have completed five years' practical accounting experience. This experience must have been gained in the office of an approved undertaking—a public accountant, a government department, a bank, an insurance company, an approved local body or

8

other approved commercial or industrial undertaking. The period is reduced to three years for university graduates.

Membership is also available to members of certain accounting bodies
in the United Kingdom, Australia and Canada, upon taking up permanent residence in New Zealand.

A prescribed academic level of education and training was established
as early as 1911. The Society has always encouraged students to take
the courses required for a Bachelor of Commerce degree in addition to
the courses required to meet the professional requirements, and, to this
end, cross-credits between most professional and degree subjects are
allowed.

The latest examination syllabus for the professional course which will
take most students four or five years to complete is as follows:

Accounting I

Accounting II

Commercial Law I

Commercial Law II

Economics

Cost and Management Accounting

Advanced Financial Accounting

Taxation, Trustee Law and Accounts

Auditing.

The membership of the Society as at November 30th, 1963, included:

Public Accountants—fellows and associates (i.e., members
in public practice)   2,049

Registered Accountants—fellows and associates (i.e., members not in public practice)   5,414
                                                            _____
                                                             7,463
                                                            ======

Activities of the Society. The Society has its own publication, the *Accountants' Journal,* which is published monthly and contains articles on
a wide range of technical subjects including taxation, practitioners,
secretarial and student sections. It also includes pronouncements of the
Society and of overseas accounting organizations.

The Society holds conventions every five years to hear papers on
technical subjects. Its first residential summer school was held in 1964

to hear papers and to discuss and study these in small groups. These meetings and discussions have exerted a strong influence on the establishment and acceptance of accounting principles and auditing standards. Research lectures have been given from time to time on various accounting topics.

In 1946, the Society issued its "Recommendations on Accounting Principles" which generally followed the pronouncements of the Institute of Chartered Accountants in England and Wales. These recommendations have been withdrawn for revision.

There are branches or subbranches of the Society in eighteen towns and cities throughout New Zealand.

Ethics. The Society has adopted a written code of ethics which is strictly enforced. This code includes the following:

1. A member may not accept an engagement where the amount of remuneration is contingent upon the member's findings or results thereof.
2. A member may not prepare or certify as correct any statement which he knows to be false, incorrect or misleading.
3. Unaudited statements must be so indicated.
4. A member may not offer employment to an employee of a fellow member without prior consultation with the fellow member.
5. A client must be informed of any business connections, interests or affiliations which might influence a member's judgment.
6. A member may not encroach upon the business of another member. If a member is approached by a client of another member to give services or advice of a special nature, he shall inform the other member of the circumstances.
7. A member may not solicit professional work.
8. A member may not have any association with an enterprise or activity of a questionable character which could bring the member, Society or the profession into disrepute.

The New Zealand Society of Accountants Rule (1958) No. 60 covers the manner and under whose name or names a member may practice. The effect of this rule is to prohibit overseas firms of accountants from practicing under their own names in New Zealand, unless they were established in the country prior to the effective date of the rule.

Other Organizations of Accountants

There are also in New Zealand the Incorporated Institute of Accountants which is open to all qualified members of the New Zealand Society of Accountants, and the recently formed Practising Accountants Association which comprises nonqualified practitioners.

Appointment of Auditors

The Companies Act 1955, provides that every company shall have an auditor who shall (with some exceptions) be a member of the New Zealand Society of Accountants. The auditor holds office from the conclusion of one annual general meeting to the conclusion of the next; a retiring auditor may be reappointed without any resolution being passed.

If no auditor is appointed or reappointed at an annual general meeting, the Registrar of Companies may appoint one.

The following are not qualified for appointment as the auditor of a company:

1. An officer or servant of the company
2. A person who is a partner of or in the employment of an officer or servant of the company (This does not apply to private companies)
3. A body corporate
4. Any person who is disqualified to be auditor of any other company in a group—be it a subsidiary or a holding company.

AUDITING STANDARDS

General Standards

Although there have been no formal pronouncements on auditing standards, the Society has published articles on this subject from time to time in its monthly journal. Public accountants of New Zealand have always realized the importance of maintaining high auditing standards. The general standards and standards of field work compare favorably with those of the other countries of the British Commonwealth and in the United States.

Independence. Although the Code of Ethics states that a client must be informed of any business connections, interests or affiliations which might influence the judgment of a member of the Society, the public accountant is free to hold shares in a company being audited, so long as this does not, in his opinion, affect his independence or professional judgment. Auditors of private companies sometimes do accountancy work for their clients.

The Companies Act prohibits the appointment as auditor of: (a) An officer or servant of the company, or (b) except in the case of private companies, a person who is a partner of or in the employment of an officer or servant of the company.

Accordingly, a public accountant may not act as a director of a public company being audited by his firm or by one of his partners. In the case of a private company, one partner of a firm may be a director or officer while his partner, being a public accountant, may properly be the auditor of the company.

Standards of Field Work

There is no statute which defines auditing procedures in New Zealand, nor are there any other requirements similar to those of the United States Securities and Exchange Commission. Auditing procedures existing in New Zealand include the following:

1. Confirmation of receivables is generally performed on a negative basis, although a number of firms use a combination of the positive and negative forms of confirmation.
2. Except for the practice of the larger firms, it is not customary for the public accountant to witness physical inventories, although he would spend a sufficient amount of time to assure himself that the client's procedures were adequate and he would extensively review the pricing of the inventory. With respect to inventories, the auditor relies to a considerable extent on representations of management.
3. There is no requirement that a public accountant review the system of internal accounting controls, although this might be done as part of normal audit procedure.
4. Checks are not normally returned by banks. Since the passing of the Cheques Act in 1960, it has not been necessary for checks to be endorsed when they are deposited in the account of the payee.
5. Direct confirmation of bank balances is not requested in all instances by the auditor. Some auditors would review the certificate of balance issued by the bank to the client.

Standards of Reporting

There is a statutory duty under the Companies Act for the auditor to make a report to the shareholders setting out information required under the Act's Section 166, Auditors' Report.

One form of auditors' unqualified report, which complies with the requirements of the Companies Act 1955, is as follows:

> We have obtained all the information and explanations that we have required. In our opinion proper books of account have been kept by the company so far as appears from our examination of those books. In our opinion, according to the best of our information and the explanations given to us and as shown by the said books, the balance sheet and the profit and loss accounts are properly drawn up so as to give respectively a true and fair view of the state of the company's affairs as at .... (date) .... and the results of its business for the year ended on that date.
>
> According to such information and explanations the accounts, the balance sheet, and the profit and loss account give the information required by the Companies Act of 1955 in the manner so required.

Penalties are provided in the Act for issuing, circulating or publishing any balance sheet without a copy of the profit and loss account or auditor's report attached thereto.

The Department of Inland Revenue does not require certified financial statements.

Public accountants in New Zealand believe that while their primary legal responsibility is to the stockholders who appoint them, they have a moral obligation to banks, lending institutions, creditors and other third parties.

Consistency. The Act states that any change in the basis of accounting which distorts the accounts must be disclosed.

Materiality. The New Zealand public accountant has the same concept of materiality and its effect on his work and on his opinion relating to the financial statements as a CPA in the United States.

Disclosure of Subsequent Events. Although footnotes are widely used, subsequent events having a material effect on the financial statements would not normally be disclosed in a footnote, although practice is moving in the direction of such disclosure. However, this information would probably be given in the directors' report.

13

DIRECTORS' REPORT

A directors' report must be attached to the balance sheet submitted to the annual general meeting of shareholders. This report must include the following: (a) the state of the company's affairs, (b) the recommended dividend, (c) the proposed transfers to reserve accounts, and (d) any changes or proposed changes in the nature of the company's or its subsidiaries' business.

It is permissible to include in the Directors' Report information required by statute to be given in the accounts. If this procedure is adopted it is an offense to issue a balance sheet unless the Directors' Report is attached.

ACCOUNTING PRINCIPLES AND PRACTICES

The accounting rules and practices in New Zealand are based mainly on the Companies Act 1955. The eighth schedule of this Act lists the requirements which must be followed in the preparation of financial statements. As previously indicated, the Society has issued (1946) "Recommendations on Accounting Principles," which have been withdrawn pending review.

Form and Content of Financial Statements

Statement Presentation. The general arrangement of the balance sheet in New Zealand is similar to that customary in the United Kingdom—capital and liabilities on the left side and assets on the right side. There is still a preference for the order of items used by the United States public utility company, i.e., fixed assets and shareholders' equity at the head of the asset and liability sides, respectively; the "account" form is used more than the "statement" form.

Under the Act the balance sheet of a company must give a "true and fair view" of the state of affairs of a company at the end of its financial year.

Comparative Financial Statements. The Act requires that comparative figures be presented for the immediately preceding period.

Consolidated Financial Statements. The preparation of consolidated financial statements is covered in the Act under the section dealing with accounts of holding and subsidiary companies. As a general rule, group or consolidated accounts covering a holding company and its subsidiary companies and consisting of a consolidated balance sheet and a consolidated profit and loss account are required to be prepared.

In certain cases group accounts may be presented in a form other than as a completely consolidated balance sheet and profit and loss account.

A subsidiary may be excluded from the consolidated accounts in the following cases:

1. When it is impracticable or of no real value to members of the company in view of the insignificant amounts involved
2. When it would involve expense and delay out of proportion to the value to members of the company
3. When it would be misleading
4. When it would be harmful to the business of the holding company or any of its subsidiaries
5. When the business of the subsidiary is so different from that of the holding company that they cannot be regarded as a single undertaking.

If either of the last two of these cases is invoked, the consent of the Governor-General by Order in Council is required. When the assets and liabilities of any one subsidiary are not brought into the consolidation, the holding company's investment in the subsidiary and any loans or advances to the subsidiary must appear as separate items.

Pooling of Interests

The term "pooling of interests" has no accounting significance in New Zealand.

Current Assets

In general, current assets must be classified under headings appropriate to the company's business. If the directors of the company are of the opinion that the realizable value or current value of current assets in the ordinary course of business is less than their balance sheet value, the directors must make appropriate disclosure on the balance sheet or in a statement or report annexed thereto.

Inventories. The basis of valuation of inventories is not required to be stated in the accounts. Although undisclosed inventory reserves are not uncommon, there is a growing trend to eliminate this practice.

Investments. Investments not held for sale or for conversion into cash may be shown at market value or at cost less provision for decline in value.

Fixed Assets. Companies are required to indicate on their balance sheets the basis of valuation of all fixed assets.

For each group of fixed assets, it is necessary to disclose the total original cost or valuation plus additions less deletions, and the total depreciation provided to date. (The Act expressly provides that the book value at the commencement of the Act may be treated as if it were a valuation of the assets made at that date.)

The cost of fixed assets constructed by or for the account of a company does not usually include indirect costs or costs of financing.

Revaluation of fixed assets is permitted under the Act and such write-ups are not taxed.

Deferred Charges. Preliminary expenses, share or debenture issue expenses, commissions paid in respect of shares or debentures, discounts allowed on issue of debentures and discounts allowed on issue of shares must all be stated under separate headings until written off.

Bond discount and expense are usually written off in the year incurred.

Intangibles. Write-offs or write-downs of intangible assets may be charged to reserve accounts provided full disclosure is made.

Liabilities

Secured liabilities must be disclosed, but the assets which secure the liabilities need not be disclosed. The net aggregate amount recommended for dividends must be shown separately.

Liabilities in Foreign Currency. Indebtedness in foreign currency is usually stated in local currency at exchange rates prevailing at balance sheet date, and the basis of conversion stated. Normal fluctuations in exchange rates are charged or credited to income. There must be disclosed (usually by footnotes) assets in foreign currencies subject to exchange restrictions.

Debentures. In New Zealand, the term "debenture" is applied to both secured and unsecured borrowings. Debentures of the company held by a nominee or in trust for the company and the amount at which they are recorded must be stated. The balance sheet must also state the details of any redeemed debentures which the company has the power to reissue.

Contingent Liabilities. There should be footnote disclosure of any contingent liabilities, including the amount of any potential liability that may arise from assets pledged for the purpose of guaranteeing the liabilities of others. The aggregate amount or estimated amount of contracts for capital expenditures for a material amount not otherwise provided for must also be shown. Material commitments under long-term leases are not required to be disclosed.

Reserves and Provisions. There is an important difference in terminology between the United States and New Zealand in regard to reserves and provisions.

As provided in the Companies Act 1955, in New Zealand a provision is generally an amount charged against profits or other surpluses to meet: (a) specific requirements where the accounts cannot be estimated closely, and (b) specific commitments, known contingencies and diminution in values of assets existing as of the date of the balance sheet where the amounts involved cannot be determined with substantial accuracy.

Reserves are amounts appropriated from profits or other surpluses other than to meet known liabilities, contingencies, commitments or diminution in value of assets. In other words, the intentions of directors in creating provisions and reserves are paramount in determining their classification. Provisions when their existence is no longer justified may require reclassification as reserves.

Reserves would be included with other "Shareholders' funds" while provisions would be shown with "Current liabilities" usually under appropriate headings.

Reserves are further divided into capital reserves and revenue reserves. Capital reserves are those which are generally not regarded as being available for distribution by way of dividends to shareholders.

Capital reserves created by the upward revaluation of fixed assets or by the issuance of shares at a premium may be utilized to issue bonus (stock dividend) shares. Such bonus shares and those shares issued from pre-1957 revenue reserves (subject to certain restrictions) are free of income tax (as dividends) in the hands of the recipients.

The accounts must set out details of capital and revenue reserves (and any movements therein) and of provisions.

17

Secret Reserves. Provisions for depreciation, renewals or diminution in the value of assets need not be stated under separate headings. However, where any such provision, created after September 1, 1955, is in excess of that which, in the opinion of the directors, is reasonably necessary for the purpose, then such excess shall be treated as a reserve and so disclosed.

Capital

Share Capital. The following information must be set forth either on the balance sheet or as a footnote thereto:

1. Issued and paid-up capital
2. Amount and earliest date of redemption of any redeemable preference shares
3. Any option on unissued shares—number, description and amount of shares affected
4. Any share capital on which interest has been paid out of capital and the rate of interest
5. Fixed cumulative dividends in arrears.

Share Premium Account. This account corresponds to the paid-in surplus account in the United States. It must be shown separately as a capital reserve and may be utilized to write off preliminary expenses, commissions paid, discount allowed on issue of shares or debentures, or premiums paid in redemption of redeemable preference shares or debentures.

Any shares issued to acquire any other business or assets should be fairly valued by the directors and the surplus credited to the Share Premium Account. In acquiring a subsidiary company, such valuation may be the book value of such subsidiary's shareholders' funds.

The acquisition cost may be capitalized by the issue of bonus shares (stock dividends) which would not be taxable in the hands of the recipients.

Profit and Loss Account

The trend is toward the statement form of profit and loss account. Sales and cost of sales are usually shown by private companies but seldom appear in the accounts of public companies. It is not unusual for the chairman of a public company to disclose sales in his address at the annual meeting.

The profit and loss account must give a "true and fair view" of the profit or loss of the company for the financial year and must disclose any material change in the basis of accounting. Items to be shown separately are:

1. Income from investments distinguishing between:
   a. Government and other public stock
   b. Investments in companies
   c. Other investments.
2. Provision for normal depreciation or diminution in value of fixed assets—if no provision is made, it must be stated
3. Provision for New Zealand taxation on income derived during the financial year
4. Transfers to or from provisions other than for 2 above
5. Transfers or proposed transfers to or from reserves
6. Extraneous, nonrecurring and exceptional transactions unless immaterial
7. Directors' remuneration excluding salaries paid to full time salaried directors
8. Auditor's remuneration unless fixed by the Company in general meeting
9. Interest paid on the company's debentures or fixed loans
10. Amount provided for redemption of share capital and loans
11. Dividends paid on all share capital during the year. It is usual, however, to make a provision for any proposed final dividend being recommended by the directors.

Depreciation. Most concerns, as a matter of expediency, follow the rates and procedures established for tax purposes. In general, buildings are depreciated on a straight line basis while other assets are usually depreciated on a declining balance basis. Depreciation on an amount representing upward revaluation of fixed assets is not an allowable deduction for tax purposes.

Stock Dividends. Stock dividends (bonus shares) are accounted for by the issuing company on the basis of the paid-up value of the shares, without consideration being given to market or fair value thereof.

Directors' Emoluments. In New Zealand, only that portion of directors' emoluments which is classed as directors' fees need be shown in the accounts. If a director is also a full-time employee of the company, his salary need not be disclosed. *(cont. at top of p. 22)*

(Cont. from Line 5, top of p. 22)

or (b) otherwise by circumstances of an exceptional or nonrecurrent nature; or (c) by any change in the basis of accounting.

REQUIREMENTS FOR PUBLIC SALE OF SECURITIES

The Companies Act 1955, and Companies Amendment Acts of 1960 and 1963, contain regulations and requirements governing: (a) public issues of shares, debentures, unsecured deposits and unsecured notes by way of prospectus or any document deemed to be a prospectus under the Act, and (b) take-over offers.

Prospectus Issues

The following is a brief summary of the principal matters to be specified in a prospectus as set out in the Fourth Schedule of the Companies Act 1955:

1. Description of share capital and relative voting rights
2. Details of directors and particulars of any interest they have in the promotion of the company or in any property to be acquired
3. The minimum amount to be raised by the issue before shares are allotted
4. Particulars of any property to be acquired out of the proceeds of the issue and the source of any other funds required
5. The amount of any preliminary expenses, commission on sale of shares or promotional fee to be paid
6. A report by the auditors on the profits and losses and rates of dividend paid for each of the preceding five financial years and on the assets and liabilities at the last balance date. Where the company is a holding company, group figures are to be given.
7. A report by a qualified accountant on any business or company to be acquired out of the issue, showing the profits and losses for each of the preceding five financial years and the assets and liabilities at the last balance-sheet date.

A public company making an issue of shares or debentures to existing members, whether or not the "rights" are transferable to nonmembers, is relieved from complying with the foregoing, but it must file particulars of the offer with the Registrar of Companies.

While a private company is prohibited from offering its shares to the public, it may invite the public to deposit money or lend money to it, provided the Act's requirements regarding prospectuses are observed.

Take-over Offers

The following is a brief summary of the matters to be included in statements to be issued by the company making the offer ("offeror") and the company receiving it ("offeree") as required by the First and Second Schedules of the Companies Amendment Act 1963. The regulations do not apply to private companies where all offerees agree in writing to waive the Act's requirements, or where offers are made to not more than six members of a company.

1. Statement by offeror—matters to be specified in every offer:
   a. If offer is conditional, the minimum acceptance required, and the latest date on which the offeror can declare the offer to become unconditional
   b. Consideration, method and period of payment
   c. Details of shares of offeree already held by offeror directly or indirectly.
2. Additional matters to be specified when securities are offered as consideration:
   a. Description of company and its business, country of incorporation and details of directors
   b. Statement of the profit and loss of the company for each of the preceding five financial years and the rates of dividends paid. The issued and paid-up capital, changes in capital structure over the period and the sources of any increase in capital
   c. The paid-up value of the securities offered and whether they will be uniform in all respects with securities previously issued. If not uniform, details of differences and limitations are to be disclosed
   d. Whether Stock Exchange Listing of the securities offered will be applied for
   e. Details of latest sale prices of the securities immediately prior to the offer, rate of dividend and dividend yield for both offeror and offeree's securities where possible. Details of the

(Cont. on Line 6, p 22)

(Cont. at top of p. 20)

(cont. from p. 19);-

Extraordinary Charges and Credits. The eighth schedule of the Companies Act 1955, provides that there will be shown in the Profit and Loss Account either by way of note or otherwise, any material respects by which any items shown in the profit and loss account are affected:

(a) by transactions of a sort not usually undertaken by the company;

(cont. from p. 21) highest and lowest sale prices during each of the three years preceding the offer with explanations of variations due to alterations in capital

f. Details of any material change in indebtedness since the last balance date and where the offer is made more than six months after the last balance date an estimate of the current trend of profit or loss

g. A copy of the latest accounts and balance sheet and directors' report is to be attached.

REQUIREMENTS FOR LISTING OF SECURITIES ON THE STOCK EXCHANGE

The New Zealand Stock Exchange has certain listing requirements, but does not require any accounting information other than that required under the Companies Act 1955. It requires that there exist a sufficiently wide-spread public holding to ensure a free market for the shares, and that the Exchange and the stockholders be advised promptly as to dividend declarations, proposed changes in capital structure, changes in directors and similar information. The Exchange strongly recommends that all shareholders receive printed copies of the chairman's annual address to shareholders, and that semi-annual reports be issued to them.

THE PHILIPPINES

25

THE PHILIPPINES **25**

FORMS OF BUSINESS ORGANIZATION

The forms of business organization in the Philippines are similar to those found in the United States—the single proprietorship, the partnership and the corporation. Philippine business law is generally modeled after that prevailing in the United States, although there are some aspects which were derived from Spanish law.

A foreign partnership may do business in the Philippines by filing with the office of the Philippine Securities and Exchange Commission, three copies of its partnership agreement, certified by a Philippine consul and by complying with certain other formalities. A foreign corporation may not do business in the Philippines until it has obtained a license from the Securities and Exchange Commission. Such license is granted upon filing various documents.

Corporations

A corporation may be organized by no less than five or more than fifteen persons, the majority of whom must be residents of the Philippines. The notarized articles of incorporation must be filed with the Philippine Securities and Exchange Commission, which publishes, at the company's expense, information on the firm's assets and liabilities in a newspaper of general circulation, and issues a certificate of incorporation to the corporation. The articles of incorporation include the usual information as to name, purpose, location and duration (which normally may not exceed fifty years; amendments of articles are allowed to extend life not more than fifty years at a time); names and addresses of incorporators; number, names and addresses of directors; number of shares and amount of capital stock (for no-par stock, only the number of shares into which the capital stock is divided need be stated); names and addresses of subscribers and amounts of their subscriptions, as well as payments made on subscriptions.

An affidavit by the treasurer of the company must accompany the articles of incorporation showing that at least 20 per cent of the authorized capital stock has been subscribed and at least 25 per cent of the subscription price has been paid into the corporation.

A code of by-laws must also be adopted and filed with the Securities and Exchange Commission within thirty days after filing the articles of incorporation. In practice, the thirty-day period usually runs from the date of issue of the certificate of incorporation.

Control of the corporation is exercised by a Board of Directors elected by the members or stockholders; such directors of a stock corporation must own at least one share, and at least two directors of all corporations organized under the Philippine Corporation Law must be residents of the Philippines.

All corporations, as well as general partnerships with a capital of 3,000 pesos or more, must register with the Securities and Exchange Commission. All businesses must register with the Bureau of Internal Revenue. Registration of business names in certain instances are made with the Bureau of Commerce, renewable usually every five years as stated in the certificate of registration.

Partnerships

The Civil Code of the Philippines governs the formation of partnerships and the obligations and rights of partners, including limited partners. It is similar to the United States Uniform Partnership Act and the Uniform Limited Partnership Act.

Two or more persons may form a general partnership, and every contract of partnership having a capital of 3,000 pesos or more must appear in a public instrument recorded in the office of the Securities and Exchange Commission.

Limited partnerships are formed by two or more persons with one or more general partners (with unlimited liability) and one or more limited partners, whose liability is limited to the amount of capital paid in. While the code is silent on the information to be contained in a general partnership agreement, it does provide that a limited partnership agreement should contain, among other items: (a) kind of business, duration and location of principal place of business; (b) names and residence of each limited and general partner, specifying his category; (c) contributions and compensation of each limited partner (contribution may not be in services).

The notarized certificate containing this information must be recorded in the office of the Securities and Exchange Commission.

4

Business Records

All merchants are required by the Code of Commerce to keep a "book of inventories and balances," a journal, a ledger and copies of correspondence, as well as certain other records.

Corporations are required under the Corporation Law to keep a record of all business transactions, minute books for meetings of directors and stockholders, and a stock and transfer book.

A regulation of the Bureau of Internal Revenue, approved by the Department of Finance, requires that journals, ledgers, invoices, receipts, and the like are to be submitted to the Bureau for approval and registration before they may be used.

THE ACCOUNTING PROFESSION

In the early nineteen hundreds, a few British accountants commenced limited accounting practices in Manila. The activities of these and their successors grew until accountancy was recognized as a profession in March 1923, with the passage of Act No. 3105. This Act also created a Board of Accountancy, which was given the power, among others, to issue the certificate of "Certified Public Accountant." Provision was made in the Act, and in subsequent amendments, for issuance of the certificate, without examination, to public accountants (including foreigners) who had been in practice in the Philippines for stated periods of time, (which, at the latest, constitute continuous practice for a period of one year before 1926).

Certified Public Accountants

Requirements for the Certificate. The applicant must be a Filipino citizen (or a subject or citizen of a foreign country granting reciprocal privileges, by law, to Filipinos with respect to the practice of accountancy), of good moral character and at least twenty-one years of age. He must be a high school graduate and holder of a four-year degree of Bachelor of Science in Commerce or an equivalent degree, covering at

5

least 120 unit-hours of accounting and auditing, economics, banking and finance, commercial law, management, mathematics, statistics, business and government, and English and Spanish. It is required that the courses in accounting and auditing be taught by a reputable certified public accountant. Since 1954, there has been no specific experience requirement; prior to that time, three years' experience in professional accounting could be substituted for a somewhat lesser educational requirement of three years' study in accounting and commercial subjects.

After approval of his application, the applicant must take the scheduled examination given by the Board of Accountancy. The examination covers theory of accounts, commercial law, auditing theory and practice, and practical accounting. Having passed this examination, he takes the "oath of the profession" administered by the Board, which issues him a certificate of registration as "Certified Public Accountant." Each CPA practicing his profession must pay an annual professional license fee to the national government.

Functions. The law mentions, but does not define what is meant by the practice of the profession of certified public accountant. Section 63 of the Rules and Regulations (which is also designated as Rule 16 of the Code of Ethics) of the Board of Accountancy states that a person shall be deemed to be so engaged if he (condensed):

1. Indicates to the public that he is qualified to render professional services as an accountant
2. Maintains a regular office for the transaction of business as a certified public accountant
3. Performs services for a client involving an audit or verification of financial transactions
4. Prepares or signs reports of audits of financial statements to be used for publication or governmental purposes
5. Prepares or signs a statement tending to reflect the results of an examination of financial records to be used for the purpose of obtaining credit.

The report of an independent certified public accountant on financial statements is required in a number of instances. Stock corporations, with an authorized or paid-up capital of 50,000 pesos or more, are required to file copies of annual certified financial statements with the Securities and Exchange Commission. Branches of foreign corporations are required to file certified financial statements annually, both for the branch itself and for the company as a whole. The Internal Revenue Code provides that corporations, partnerships or persons whose gross quarterly sales, earnings, receipts or output exceed 25,000 pesos must file certified financial statements with their tax returns. The return itself need not be signed by a CPA.

Other government regulatory bodies, such as the Central Bank and the Public Service Commission, which exercise jurisdiction over banks and public utilities, respectively, also require audited financial statements for varied purposes.

The Government Regulatory Body

The Board of Accountancy. This Board, established by Act 3105 of March 1923, regulates the practice of accountancy in the Philippines. It is composed of a chairman and two members, appointed by the President of the Philippines. The Board is composed of certified public accountants of recognized standing, academically and morally qualified, and who have been in practice for at least ten years.

There have been a total of about 8,500 CPAs registered with the Board since 1923, of whom about 7,500 were registered since 1945. The present number of active registrants is not available.

The Board has the authority to promulgate rules and standards for the practice of the profession and to issue CPA certificates to those who have qualified. It has the power to suspend or revoke CPA licenses of persons found guilty of unprofessional conduct or for some other sufficient cause. There have been relatively few cases decided under these provisions.

While Section 64 of the Revised Rules and Regulations of the Board of Accountancy (1954) permits the practice of accountancy by a corporation, the Philippine Institute of Certified Public Accountants does not favor the corporate form of organization for such practice. There is at least one firm in the Philippines which does practice as a corporation.

Ethics. The Board of Accountancy, under its authority to ". . . set professional standards for the practice of their profession" promulgated a Code of Ethics in 1954. The principal areas covered may be summarized as follows:

1. The CPA must be loyal in his relations both to the public and to his client; he must conduct himself in a manner creditable to his profession.
2. He must not share fees with the laity, nor accept fees nor commissions from business turned over to others as an incident to services to a client.
3. He must not render any report or statements which are not based

on work done by him personally or by his staff under his supervision.

4. He must not be compensated on a contingent-fee basis.
5. He must not divulge the private affairs of his clients.
6. He must not wilfully make false, incomplete or misleading reports.
7. He must not advertise his services.
8. He must not permit his name to be used in connection with earnings forecasts, in a manner to suggest that he can vouch for their accuracy.
9. He must not certify financial statements of any enterprise in which he is a director, officer or salaried employee, or a stockholder having more than 10 per cent interest in the capital paid in or which he is committed to acquire, without disclosing such relationship or interest in his report. (See also discussion under the topic "Auditing Standards.")

Rule 16 of the Code defines the acts, which, if performed, cause an individual to be deemed to be engaged in the practice of the profession of CPA (summarized under the subtopic "Certified Public Accountants"). If a person, not a CPA, performs any of the enumerated acts, he is liable for the unauthorized practice of accountancy under the rule.

The Professional Organization

The Philippine Institute of Certified Public Accountants. In 1929, a group of CPAs organized an association called the Philippine Institute of Certified Public Accountants. This organization was largely successful in protecting the CPA certificate and in promoting the accounting profession in general, but little attention was given to developing standards of performance in the profession itself. World War II caused suspension of its activities. After the war, the Institute was revived and incorporated, and its name became the Philippine Institute of Accountants. Although the certificate of CPA is a prerequisite to membership, it was felt that the omission of "certified public" from the name would emphasize that its purpose was no longer primarily protective, but was to improve the professional standing of its members. In November 1961, the original name, Philippine Institute of Certified Public Accountants (PICPA), was adopted to avoid confusion of the Institute's initials (PIA) with other associations bearing the same initials and to make known that its members are certified public accountants. There are presently about 2,800 members of the Institute.

The PICPA does not concentrate its activities in Manila and its sub-

8

urbs alone. It has given active support and encouragement to the establishment of provincial chapters in order to serve members in the other geographic areas as well. As of the end of 1962, thirteen chapters had been organized and all are actively engaged in implementing the Institute's program in the provinces.

The Institute also encourages the formation of junior Philippine Institutes of Accountants in colleges and universities in order to make accounting students aware, at an early date, of the need for professional unity. These organizations have recently organized into a national federation.

Various services are rendered by the PICPA to its members. In addition to annual conventions, monthly membership meetings are held where speakers in accounting and allied fields, such as banking, finance and economics, are invited. The Institute also publishes an excellent quarterly magazine and a monthly news bulletin which contains, among other things, tax rulings and decisions and commercial law digests. It also publishes reprints of new laws, opinions, rules of government entities and other materials of interest to members.

On the improvement of technical standards, the Institute's activities include the issuance of bulletins on audit standards and procedures. Since 1949, the Institute has released the following bulletins:

No. 1—"Audit Procedures for Import Quota Applications"

No. 2—"Audit Fees"

No. 3—"Reports and Certifications by the Independent Certified Public Accountant"

No. 4—"Audit Procedures for Cash"

No. 5—"Audit Procedures for Accounts Receivable"

No. 6—"Audit Procedures for Inventories"

No. 7—"Audit Procedures for Investments"

No. 8—"Audit Procedures for Property, Plant and Equipment"

No. 9—"Audit Procedures for Liabilities"

No. 10—"Audit Procedures for Capital Stock and Surplus"

No. 11—"Audit Procedures for Income and Expenses"

AUDITING STANDARDS

The Philippine Institute of Certified Public Accountants, through its committee on auditing standards and procedures, issued a "Statement of Auditing Standards" in 1949, which followed that issued by the American Institute of Accountants (now AICPA) in 1947. The statement includes the following headings:

General Standards:

Training and proficiency of the auditor

Independence in his mental attitude and approach

Due care in the performance of his work.

Standards of Field Work:

Adequate planning of the field work and proper instruction and supervision of assistants, if any

Proper study and evaluation of the client's existing internal control as a basis for reliance thereon by the auditor

Competence of evidential matter.

Standards of Reporting:

Adherence to generally accepted accounting principles

Observance of consistency in the application of generally accepted accounting principles, except where conditions warrant otherwise

Adequacy of informative disclosures either in the report or certificate, or in the financial statements.

The "Statement of Auditing Standards" recommends the confirmation of accounts receivable, and supervision or observation of physical inventory-taking.

The Code of Ethics promulgated by the Board of Accountancy has been previously discussed. The Institute has also published a Code of Ethics which differs in minor respects from that of the Board, but which essentially covers the same ground and does not differ in principle.

Independence

In preparing the present "Statement of Auditing Standards," the committee took into consideration practices common in the Philippines, which differ in some aspects from those in the United States. For example, as to independence, in both countries the auditor is prohibited from engaging in any other business which would compromise his independence or objectivity. In the Philippines (based on Section 60 of the Rules and Regulations of the Board of Accountancy), it is generally not considered an impairment of independence to be an officer or director of the company, or to own more than 10 per cent of its outstanding stock, provided that in these instances he fully discloses his position in his report.

The PICPA, however, discourages practitioners from assuming the dual role of auditor and officer or director of the same company, and under the law requiring certified financial statements to accompany income tax returns (as supplemented by subsequent rulings of the Bureau of Internal Revenue), he is prevented from certifying the financial statements of the company reported upon under the following situations, even if disclosed:

1. Where a member of his family, consisting of his spouse, descendants, ascendants, and brothers and sisters living in the family home and dependent upon him for support, owns more than 10 per cent of the capital paid or committed to be acquired
2. Where the company is controlled and/or owned by his family consisting of his spouse, descendants, ascendants, and brothers and sisters living in the family home and dependent upon him for support
3. Where an immediate member of his family (spouse or child living with him) is either president, manager or director of the company
4. If he keeps the books of accounts as an independent certified public accountant and then certifies the financial statements drawn from the books kept by him.

Standards of Reporting

Bulletin No. 3 of the PICPA is entitled "Reports and Certifications of the Independent Certified Public Accountant." This is an amplification of the recommendation contained in "Auditing Standards" (1949) that the short form report suggested by the AICPA be adopted. The bulletin deals with qualifications, denial of opinion, procedures when statements are prepared without audit but typed on the auditor's stationery, suggestions for reports to certain government agencies, and suggested forms of report under various conditions. In signing the standard report upon an examination of financial statements, the Philippine CPA implies that the examination was made in accordance with the auditing standards laid down by the Institute, and that in his opinion the statements fairly present the financial position and results of operations for the period, in conformity with generally accepted accounting principles applied on a consistent basis.

The Institute's committee on accounting and auditing procedures is presently undertaking a revision of the "Statement of Auditing Standards" to include a fourth standard of reporting similar to that issued by the AICPA, which latter standard states that:

> The report shall either contain an expression of opinion regarding the financial statements, taken as a whole, or an assertion to the effect that an opinion cannot be expressed. When an over-all opinion cannot be expressed, the reasons therefor should be clearly stated. In all cases where an auditor's name is associated with financial statements the report should contain a clear-cut indication of the character of the auditor's examination, if any, and the degree of responsibility he is taking.

The revision is also expected to up-date the PICPA's "Statement of Auditing Standards" in certain other respects.

ACCOUNTING PRINCIPLES AND PRACTICES

During the period of establishment and initial growth of the public accounting profession in the Philippines, the country was an American possession. American accounting textbooks were used in teaching, and a number of Filipinos studied accounting in American universities. Many of the larger companies in the Philippines were subsidiaries or branches of American companies, and their accounting reflected United States accounting principles. Further, Title II (Income Tax) of the Philippine Internal Revenue Code was originally patterned after the United States law. For these reasons, the "generally accepted accounting principles" recognized in the Philippines are similar to those recognized in the United States.

12

The Philippine Government, through the Board of Accountancy, has not issued any pronouncements of accounting principles to be followed, nor has the Securities and Exchange Commission issued any regulatory bulletins regarding accounting matters. Government organizations indirectly aid the PICPA in that they require compliance with the Institute's standards in reports submitted to them. The Institute's own pronouncements are embodied in its bulletins on audit standards and procedures enumerated under the subtopic "The Professional Organization."

The Institute endeavors to promote adherence to generally accepted accounting principles through its publications and technical meetings, but lacks the facilities to aggressively police compliance on the part of all its members. It, of course, has no power to discipline practicing accountants—CPAs or non-CPAs—who are not members of the Institute.

Form and Content of Financial Statements

The form of financial statements follows that type which is common in the United States. The rules of disclosure are similar.

Consolidated Financial Statements. The tax laws do not contain provisions for filing consolidated returns. But such statements are common for financial purposes (see section on requirements for listing on the Stock Exchange, *infra*).

Inventories

Inventory pricing methods are similar to those used in the United States. The Bureau of Internal Revenue has not issued any ruling approving or disapproving the Lifo method, but has indicated informally that it is not acceptable; it is seldom used in practice. A change in inventory pricing methods is permitted provided a valid reason exists and prior permission is obtained from the Bureau of Internal Revenue.

Statement of Income

Provision for Bad Debts. An estimated provision for bad or doubtful accounts is not a permissible deduction for income tax purposes, but the accounts charged off are deductible. However, book entries need not follow the tax rule, and many companies make the usual provision for doubtful accounts in the books.

Depreciation. The straight-line method of computing the allowance for depreciation of plant and property is the most common method in use. The Bureau of Internal Revenue has recently ruled that the declining-balance and the sum-of-the-years' digits methods are acceptable in proper instances, and there are no pronouncements of the Institute prohibiting their use.

Tax-effect Accounting. It is permissible for a business enterprise to use a different method of providing depreciation for financial reporting purposes from that used in computing taxable income. However, this is not generally permitted by the Bureau of Internal Revenue and good reasons for doing so must be adduced. It is therefore rather uncommon and the problem of "tax-effect accounting" seldom arises.

Contingency and Other Reserves. As a general rule, provisions for losses not actually incurred are not allowable tax deductions.

REQUIREMENTS FOR PUBLIC SALE OF SECURITIES

Securities must be registered with the Securities and Exchange Commission before they are offered to the public for sale. This is done by filing a sworn registration statement with the SEC. Among the information called for in the registration statement are: the names and addresses of the directors, executive, financial and accounting officers, and underwriters; the general character of the business to be transacted by the issuer; a statement of the capitalization of the issuer; a copy of the security being registered and of any circular, prospectus or communication to be used for the public offering of the security; the specific purposes for which security is offered; the remuneration paid or to be paid to directors and officers; the amount of issue of the security being offered; the price at which the security will be sold; a detailed statement showing the items of cash, property, intangible assets and other considerations for which securities have been or are to be issued in payment; the amount of cash or of capital stock which may be paid as promotion fee, etc.

The SEC requires that the registration statement be accompanied by the applicant's balance sheet as of a date not more than ninety days prior to the date of filing such application, together with the related income statement. Both statements must be accompanied by an independent certified public accountant's report. A long-form report is usually preferred.

REQUIREMENTS FOR LISTING SECURITIES ON THE STOCK EXCHANGE

The procedure for listing on the Manila Stock Exchange (the only security exchange presently operating in the Philippines), consists of filing a listing agreement and listing application, forms for which are available at said stock exchange. Among the things to which the issuer agrees with the MSE in the listing agreement are: to publish annually and submit to the stockholders, at least fifteen days before the annual meeting of the corporation, a consolidated balance sheet at the end of the year, a consolidated income statement and analysis of consolidated surplus for the year; or a similar set of financial statements of the applicant as a separate entity and of each subsidiary owned or controlled, if any. These statements have to be certified by a certified public accountant.

Among the information called for in the listing application forms are: the number of shares to be listed; distribution of capital stock among shareholders; nature of applicant's business; authority granting the issuance of securities; purpose of the issue and uses of proceeds therefrom; history of applicant corporation; tabulated list of subsidiaries stating date and place of incorporation; nature of business and composition of capital stock issues; amount of and other information on mortgage and other indebtedness; description of property owned (including those owned by subsidiaries); policy on depreciation; dividends paid or declared; names and addresses of directors, transfer agents and registrars; names of officers; etc. Additional information is required of corporations which own or operate mines.

The listing application forms must be accompanied by certain papers, among which are the registration and licensing order of the Securities and Exchange Commission of the securities to be listed and the applicant's latest balance sheet and related income statement, duly certified by an independent certified public accountant. A listing fee, the amount of which is based on authorized capital, is also paid.

Two copies of the listing application forms are filed with the Securities and Exchange Commission.

If the Manila Stock Exchange approves the listing, it sends notice to the SEC of such approval. Listing thereof becomes effective ten days after it is noted by the Commission or within such shorter time as it may determine.

APPENDIX

ILLUSTRATIVE BALANCE SHEETS,
STATEMENTS of INCOME and SURPLUS
COUNTRIES in CERTAIN WORLD AREAS

Exhibit 1(a)

ILLUSTRATIVE BALANCE SHEET of a UNITED STATES COMPANY

BALANCE SHEET at December 31, 19___

ASSETS:

Current assets:
Cash . . . . . .
Marketable securities, at cost (at market quotations $. . . . . .) . . . . . .
Accounts receivable, trade . . . . . .
Accounts receivable, other . . . . . .
Notes receivable . . . . . .
. . . . . .
Less, Allowance for doubtful notes and accounts . . . .

Inventories, at the lower of first-in, first-out cost or market:
Raw materials . . . . . .
Work in process . . . . . .
Finished goods . . . .

Prepaid expenses . . . .
Total current assets . . . . . .

Investments (at cost) and long-term receivables . . . . . .

Property, plant and equipment, at cost:
Land . . . . . .
Buildings, machinery and equipment . . . . . .
Less, Allowance for depreciation . . . .
Construction work in progress . . . .

Goodwill, patents, trademarks, etc., at cost . . . . . .
Less, Allowance for amortization . . . .

Deferred charges:
Unamortized debt discount and expense . . . . . .
Other . . . .

Total . . . . . .

LIABILITIES:

Current liabilities:
Accounts payable, trade . . . . . .
Notes payable to banks . . . . . .
Long-term debt, portion due within one year . . . . . .
Accrued expenses . . . . . .
Federal income taxes . . . . . .
Other current liabilities . . . .

Total current liabilities . . . . . .

Long-term debt, portion due after one year:
First mortgage, 4% bonds, due 1972 . . . . . .
Debentures, 4½%, due serially to 1975 . . . .

Other long-term liabilities and accruals:
Deferred compensation, less applicable income taxes . . . . . .
Deferred taxes on income . . . . . .
Deferred investment tax credit . . . .

CAPITAL:

Capital stock:
Common, authorized 1,000,000 shares, no par value; issued and outstanding 750,000 shares, stated at . . . . . .
Preferred, $4 cumulative preferred, par value $100 per share; authorized, issued and outstanding 150,000 shares . . . .

Surplus:
Premium on capital stock . . . . . .
Appropriated for increased replacement cost of facilities . . . . . .
Earned surplus . . . .

Total . . . . . .

Exhibit 1(b)

ILLUSTRATIVE
STATEMENT OF INCOME and EARNED SURPLUS
of a UNITED STATES COMPANY
year ended December 31, 19___

Net sales . . . . . .

Cost of goods sold . . . . . .

Gross profit on sales . . . . . .

Selling, administrative and general expenses . . . .

Other income:
Interest and dividends . . . . . .

Royalties . . . .

. . . . . .

Other deductions:
Interest on funded debt . . . . . .

Other interest . . . . . .

Amortization of debt discount, expense . . . .

Income before federal taxes on
income . . . . . .

Federal taxes on income:
Currently payable . . . . . .

Deferred . . . .

Net income . . . . . .

Earned surplus, balance January 1, 19___ . . . . . .

. . . . . .

Deduct:
Dividends:
On common stock, $7 per share . . . . . .

On preferred stock, $4 per share . . . . . .

Appropriations for increased replacement cost of facilities . . . .

Earned surplus, balance December 31, 19___ . . . . . .

Depreciation included in costs and expenses above amounted to $. . . . . .

BALANCE GENERAL – DICIEMBRE 31, 19___ (Balance Sheet at December 31, 19___)

ACTIVO (Assets)	
DISPONIBILIDADES (Current assets):	
CAJA (Cash on hand)	......
BANCOS (Cash in bank)	....
CRÉDITOS (Receivables):	
POR VENTAS (From sales)	......
DEUDORES COMUNES (Accounts receivable)	......
OBLIGACIONES A COBRAR (Notes receivable)	......
DEUDORES HIPOTECARIOS (Mortgages receivable)	......
DEUDORES MOROSOS (Doubtful accounts)	......
MENOS (Less):	
PROVISIÓN PARA DEUDORES INCOBRABLES (Provision for doubtful accounts)	....
BIENES DE CAMBIO (Inventories):	
MATERIAS PRIMAS (Raw materials)	......
PRODUCTOS EN CURSO DE ELABORACIÓN (Work in process)	......
PRODUCTOS ELABORADOS (Finished goods)	....
INVERSIONES (Investments):	
VALORES MOBILIARIOS (Securities):	
CON COTIZACIÓN (Listed)	......
SIN COTIZACIÓN (Not listed)	....
BIENES DE USO (Fixed assets):	
TIERRAS Y MEJORAS (Land and improvements)	......
EDIFICIOS, MAQUINARIAS, INSTALACIONES (Buildings, machinery, installations)	......
HERRAMIENTAS, MOLDES Y MATRICES (Tools, molds and dies)	......
CONSTRUCCIONES, OBRAS ENCURSO (Construction work in progress)	......
MENOS (Less):	
AMORTIZACIONES ANTERIORES (Prior years' depreciation)	......
AMORTIZACIONES DEL EJERCICIO (Depreciation for the year)	....
BIENES INMATERIALES (Intangible assets):	
MARCAS DE FÁBRICA O DE COMERCIO (Trademarks)	......
PATENTES DE INVENCIÓN (Patents)	......
CONCESIONES (Concessions)	......
LLAVE DEL NEGOCIO (Goodwill)	....
CARGOS DIFERIDOS (Deferred charges):	
GASTOS ADELANTADOS (Prepaid expenses)	......
GASTOS DE ORGANIZACIÓN (Organization expenses)	......
DESCUENTOS POR COLOCACION DE DEBENTURES (Debenture discount expense)	....
TOTAL DEL ACTIVO (Total assets)	......

PASIVO (Liabilities)	
DEUDAS (Payables):	
COMERCIALES (Trade)	......
PROVEEDORES (Vendors)	......
OBLIGACIONES A PAGAR (Notes payable)	......
DEUDAS COMERCIALES DIVERSAS (Sundry payables)	......
ADELANTOS EN CUENTA CORRIENTE (Bank overdrafts)	......
PROVISIONES (Accrued liabilities):	
PROVISIÓN PARA IMPUESTOS (Accrual for taxes)	......
PROVISIÓN PARA CARGAS SOCIALES (Accrual social charges)	......
PREVISIONES (Liability reserves):	
PREVISIÓN LEY 11.729 (Reserve for dismissal indemnities)	......
PREVISIÓN POR RESPONSABILIDADES HACIA TERCEROS (Liabilities to third parties)	....
UTILIDADES DIFERIDAS Y A REALIZAR EN EJERCICIOS FUTUROS (Deferred income):	
RENTAS ANTICIPADAS (Unearned rents)	......
BENEFICIOS A REALIZAR EJERCICIOS FUTUROS (Unearned income)	....
FINANCIERAS (Financial):	
ACREEDORES HIPOTECARIOS (Liability on mortgages)	......
DEBENTURES (Debentures)	......
CAPITAL, RESERVAS Y RESULTADOS (Capital, Reserves and Results)	
CAPITAL SUSCRIPTO (Subscribed capital)	
ACCIONES EN CIRCULACIÓN (Shares in circulation)	......
ACCIONES EN CARTERA (ART. 343 CODIGO DE COMERCIO) (Stocks reacquired; Art. 343 Commercial Code)	......
DIVIDENDOS EN ACCIONES A DISTRIBUIR (Undistributed stock dividend)	....
RESERVAS (Reserves):	
LEGAL (Legal)	......
PARA RENOVACIÓN BIENES DE USO (For renewal of fixed assets)	......
PRIMAS DE EMISIÓN (Premiums on issue of shares)	......
PARA DIVIDENDOS FUTUROS (For future dividends)	......
OTRAS RESERVAS (Other reserves)	....
UTILIDADES (O PERDIDAS): (Profit or loss):	
SALDO DEL EJERCICIO ANTERIOR (Balance at beginning of year)	......
SALDO DEL EJERCICIO (Earnings for the year)	......
MENOS (Less):	
DIVIDENDO PROVISIONAL (Provisional dividend)	....
TOTAL DEL PASIVO (Total liabilities)	......

CUENTAS DE ORDEN (Memorandum Accounts)

DOCUMENTOS DESCONTADOS (Notes discounted)
FIANZAS OTORGADAS (Guarantees)
DEPOSITOS DE ACCIONES EN GARANTÍA—DIRECTORES (Shares deposited by directors as guarantee)
ACCIONES DE LA SOCIEDAD RECIBIDAS EN CUSTODIA (Company shares received in custody)
MERCADERÍAS RECIBIDAS EN CONSIGNACION (Merchandise received on consignment)
DIVIDENDOS ACUMULATIVOS EN PAGO DE ACCIONES PREPERIDAS (Unpaid cumulative dividends on preferred shares)

Exhibit 2(b)

ILLUSTRATIVE
INCOME STATEMENT of an ARGENTINE COMPANY

CUADRO DEMONSTRATIVO DE GANANCIAS Y PÉRDIDAS
(Profit and Loss Statement)

VENTAS NETAS DE MERCADERIAS O PRODUCTOS
(Net sales of merchandise or products) ....

MENOS (Less):
COSTO DE LAS MERCADERÍAS O PRODUCTOS
VENDIDOS (Cost of merchandise or products sold) ......
MÁS (O MENOS) (Add or deduct):
DIFERENCIA ENTRE INVENTARIOS FINAL E
INICIAL (Difference between opening and closing
inventories) ......

MENOS (Less):
SUELDOS (Salaries) ......
RETRIBUCIONES DE DIRECTORES Y GERENTES
(Directors' and managers' remunerations) ......
CARGAS SOCIALES (Social security charges) ......
AMORTIZACIONES (Amortizations) ......
HONORARIOS (Fees) ......
IMPUESTOS (Taxes) ......
INTERESES Y DESCUENTOS (Interest and discounts) ......
COMISIONES (Commissions) ......
PROPOGANDA (Advertising) ......
GASTOS DE OFICINA (Office expenses) ......

MÁS (O MENOS) (Add or deduct):
DIVIDENDOS (Dividends) ......
RENTA DE TÍTULOS (Bond interest) ......
ALQUILERES (Rents) ......
RECUPERO DE DEUDORES (Bad debts recovered) ......
VENTA DE INMUEBLES (Sale of real estate, net) ......
VENTA DE VALORES MOBILIARIOS (Sale of securi-
ties, net) ....

GANANCIA (O PÉRDIDA) DEL EJERCICIO
(Profit [or loss] for the period) ......

Exhibit 3(a)

ILLUSTRATIVE BALANCE SHEET of a BRAZILIAN (INDUSTRIAL) COMPANY

BALANÇO GERAL EM 31 DE DEZEMBRO DE 19___
(Balance Sheet at December 31, 19___)

ATIVO (Assets)

IMOBILIZADO (Fixed assets):
  TERRENOS E EDIFÍCIOS (Land and buildings)   . . . . . .
  EQUIPAMENTOS E INSTALAÇÕES INDUSTRIAIS
    (Plant equipment)   . . . . . .
  MÓVEIS E UTENSÍLIOS (Office equipment and fixtures) . . . . . .
  VEÍCULOS (Vehicles)   . . . . . .

      SUBTOTAL (Subtotal)   . . . . . .

REAVALIAÇÃO DO ATIVO (Revaluation of assets)   . . . . . .
OBRAS EM ANDAMENTO (Construction in progress)   . . . .

REALIZÁVEL A LONGO PRAZO (Long-term receivable):
  DEPÓSITOS E CAUÇÕES (Guarantee deposits)   . . . . . .
  EMPRÉSTIMOS COMPULSÓRIOS (Compulsory loans)   . . . . . .
  INVESTIMENTOS (Investments)   . . . .

REALIZÁVEL A CURTO PRAZO (Short-term receivable):
  DUPLICATAS A RECEBER (Trade notes receivable)   . . . . . .

    MENOS (Less):
      DUPLICATAS DESCONTADAS (Trade notes dis-
      counted)   . . . .

  CONTAS A RECEBER (Accounts receivable)   . . . . . .
  MATERIAIS EM ESTOQUE (Operating supplies)   . . . . . .
  MATÉRIAS PRIMAS (Raw material)   . . . . . .
  PRODUTOS EM ELABORAÇÃO (Work in process)   . . . . . .
  PRODUTOS ACABADOS (Finished products)   . . . .

DISPONÍVEL (Funds available):
  CAIXA (Cash on hand)   . . . . . .
  BANCOS (Cash in banks)   . . . .

PENDENTE (Pending accounts):
  DESPESAS DIFERIDAS (Deferred charges)   . . . . . .
  PAGAMENTOS ANTECIPADOS (Advanced payments)   . . . .
  CONTAS DE COMPENSAÇÃO (Contra accounts)   . . . .

      TOTAL DO ATIVO (Total assets)   . . . . . .

PASSIVO (Liabilities and Net Worth)

NÃO EXIGÍVEL (Net worth):
  CAPITAL (Capital)   . . . . . .
  RESERVA LEGAL (Legal reserve)   . . . . . .
  RESERVA PARA DEVEDORES DUVIDOSOS (Reserve for
    doubtful accounts)   . . . . . .
  LUCROS SUSPENSOS (Undistributed profits)   . . . . . .
  FUNDO PARA DEPRECIAÇÃO (Reserve for depreciation) . . . .

EXIGÍVEL A LONGO PRAZO (Long-term liabilities):
  BANCO DO BRASIL — C/FINANCIAMENTO (Bank of Brazil,
    financing account)   . . . . . .
  BNDE — C/FINANCIAMENTO (National Development Bank,
    financing account)   . . . .

EXIGÍVEL A CURTO PRAZO (Short-term liabilities):
  FORNECEDORES (Suppliers)   . . . . . .
  CONTAS A PAGAR (Accounts payable)   . . . . . .
  SALÁRIOS E ORDENADOS A PAGAR (Salaries and wages
    payable)   . . . . . .
  IMPÓSTO DE RENDA NA FONTE (Withholding tax)   . . . . . .
  DIVIDENDOS (Dividends)   . . . .

PENDENTE (Pending accounts):
  CRÉDITOS DIFERIDOS (Deferred credits)   . . . . . .
  CONTAS DE COMPENSAÇÃO (Contra accounts)   . . . . . .

      TOTAL DO PASSIVO (Total liabilities and net worth) . . . . . .

Exhibit 3(b)

ILLUSTRATIVE INCOME STATEMENT of a BRAZILIAN COMPANY

DEMOSTRAÇÃO DA CONTA DE LUCROS E PERDAS
EM 31 DE DEZEMBRO DE 19___
(Profit and Loss Statement at December 31, 19___)

DÉBITO (Debits)		CRÉDITO (Credits)	
DESPESAS GERAIS DO EXERCÍCIO (General expenses for the period)	. . . . . .	SALDO DOS EXERCÍCIOS ANTERIORES (Balance of previous years)	. . . . . .
IMPOSTOS (Taxes)	. . . . . .		
JUROS E DESCONTOS (Interests and discounts)	. . . . . .	PRODUTO DAS OPERAÇÕES SOCIAIS (Result of current year's operations)	. . . . . .
DEPRECIAÇÃO DO ATIVO FIXO (Depreciation of fixed assets)	. . . . . .		
RESERVA PARA DEVEDORES DUVIDOSOS (Reserve for doubtful accounts)	. . . . . .	JUROS E DESCONTOS (Interests and discounts earned)	. . . . . .
RESERVAS E PROVISÕES (Provisions and reserves [for contingencies])	. . . . . .	OUTRAS RECEITAS (Other income)	. . . . . .
RESERVA LEGAL (Legal reserve)	. . . . . .		
SALDO EM 31 DE DEZEMBRO DE 19___ (Balance as of December 31, 19___*)	. . . . . .		
	. . . . . .		. . . . . .

*Current year end.

NOTE: This form of statement used either by trade and/or industrial corporations contains the minimum required by the corporation law for publication purpose only.

ILLUSTRATIVE BALANCE SHEET of a FRENCH COMPANY

Exhibit 4(a)

BILAN AU 31 DECEMBRE 19____ (Balance Sheet at December 31, 19____)

	MONTANTS BRUTS Gross (Book Value)	AMORTISSEMENTS (Depreciation)	MONTANTS NETS Net (Book Value)

ACTIF (Assets)

FRAIS D'ETABLISSEMENT (Organization expense)

IMMOBILISATIONS (Fixed assets):
TERRAINS (Land)
CONSTRUCTIONS (Building)
MATÉRIEL ET OUTILLAGE (Machinery and equipment)
MATÉRIEL ET MOBILIER DE BUREAU (Office plant and furniture)
MATÉRIEL DE TRANSPORTS (Vehicles)
AGENCEMENTS ET INSTALLATIONS (Fittings)
IMMOBILISATIONS INCORPORELLES (Goodwill, patents, etc.)
IMMOBILISATIONS EN COURS (Building or plant in process)

AUTRES VALEURS IMMOBILISEES (Other noncurrent assets:
TITRES DE PARTICIPATION (Investments)
PRÊTS Á PLUS D'UN AN (Loans receivable after one year)
DÉPÔTS ET CAUTIONNEMENTS (Miscellaneous deposits)

VALEURS D'EXPLOITATION (Inventories):
MATIÈRES PREMIÈRES (Raw materials)
PRODUITS FINIS (Finished goods)
TRAVAUX EN COURS (Work in process)
EMBALLAGES COMMERCIAUX (Packing)

VALEURS REALISABLES ET DISPONIBLES (Current assets):
CLIENTS (Accounts receivable)
DÉBITEURS DIVERS (Sundry debtors)
COMPTE DE RÉGULARISATION (Charges paid in advance)
TITRES DE PLACEMENT (Marketable securities)
PRÊTS Á MOINS D'UN AN (Loans receivable within one year)
EFFETS À RECEVOIR (Notes receivable)
BANQUES (Bank account)
CHÈQUES POSTAUX (Postal check account)
CAISSE (Cash)

RESULTATS:
DÉFICIT DE L'EXERCICE (Loss for the period)

TOTAL DE L'ACTIF (Total assets)

PASSIF (Liabilities)

CAPITAUX PROPRES ET RESERVES (Capital and reserves):
CAPITAL SOCIAL (Capital)
PRIMES D'ÉMISSION (Premium on issue of shares)
RÉSERVE LÉGALE (Legal reserve)
RÉSERVE DE RENOUVELLEMENT DES STOCKS (Reserve on stocks)
RÉSERVE SPÉCIALE DE REEVALUATION (Special revaluation reserve)
RÉSERVES GÉNÉRALES (General reserves)
PLUS-VALUES À RÉINVESTIR (Reserve on capital gains)

REPORT À NOUVEAU (Profits or losses brought forward)

SITUATION NETTE AVANT RÉSULTATS (Net worth before income)

PROVISIONS (Provisions):
PROVISIONS POUR PERTES ET CHARGES (Provisions for losses and charges)
PROVISIONS POUR RISQUES DIVERS (Provisions for contingencies)

DETTES A LONG ET MOYEN TERME (Long- and medium-term debt):
EMPRUNTS À LONG ET MOYEN TERME (Long- and medium-term loan)

DETTES A COURT TERME (Current liabilities):
FOURNISSEURS (Accounts payable)
CRÉDITEURS DIVERS (Sundry creditors)
COMPTES DE RÉGULARISATION PASSIF (Accrued expenses)
EMPRUNTS À MOINS D'UN AN (Short-term loan)
EFFETS À PAYER (Notes payable)
BANQUES (Bank overdraft)

RESULTATS:
BÉNÉFICES DE L'EXERCICE (Profit for the period)

TOTAL DU PASSIF (Total liabilities)

Exhibit 4(b)

ILLUSTRATIVE INCOME STATEMENT of a FRENCH COMPANY

EXPLOITATION GENERALE
(Trading account)

	MONTANT BRUT Gross (Book Value)	PROVISION POUR DEPRECIATION (Depreciation)	MONTANT NET Net (Book Value)		MONTANT BRUT Gross (Book Value)	PROVISION POUR DEPRECIATION (Depreciation)	MONTANT NET Net (Book Value)
STOCK AU DÉBUT DE L'EXERCICE (Stock as at January 1, 19—)				STOCK EN FIN D'EXERCICE (Stock as at December 31, 19—)			
ACHATS DE MATIÈRES ET MARCHANDISES (Purchases of raw materials and goods)				VENTES DE MARCHANDISES ET PRODUITS FINIS (Sales of products and goods)			
FRAIS DE PERSONNEL (Salaries, wages, social and fiscal charges on salaries)				SUBVENTIONS D'EXPLOITATION RECUES (Subsidies)			
IMPÔTS ET TAXES (Taxes)				VENTES DE DÉCHETS ET D'EMBALLAGES RÉCUPÉRABLES (Sales of scrap, etc.)			
TRAVAUX, FOURNITURES ET SERVICES EXTÉRIEURS (Supplies and services)				RISTOURNES, RABAIS ET REMISES OBTENUS (Discounts and allowances)			
TRANSPORTS ET DÉPLACEMENTS (Transport and travel)				PRODUITS FINANCIERS (Interest, etc.)			
FRAIS DIVERS DE GESTION (Administrative expenses)				TRAVAUX FAITS PAR L'ENTREPRISE POUR ELLE-MÊME (Self-constructed assets)			
FRAIS FINANCIERS (Bank charges and interest)				TRAVAUX ET CHARGES NON IMPUTABLES À L'EXPLOITATION DE L'EXERCICE (Charges concerning later years)			
DOTATION DE L'EXERCICE AUX AMORTISSEMENTS (Depreciation for the year)							
DOTATION DE L'EXERCICE AUX PROVISIONS (Provisions for the year)							
SOLDE CRÉDITEUR (Trading profits carried forward)				SOLDE DÉBITEUR (Trading losses carried forward)			

ILLUSTRATIVE BALANCE SHEET of a GERMAN COMPANY (AKTIENGESELLSCHAFT)

Exhibit 5(a)

BILANZ ZUM 31. DEZEMBER 19___ (Balance Sheet at December 31, 19___)

STAND AM JAHRESANFANG (Balance as of Jan. 1, 19__)	ZUGANG (Additions)	ABGANG (Retirements)	ABSCHREIBUNG (Depreciation)	STAND AM JAHRESENDE (Balance as of Dec. 31, 19__)

AKTIVA (Assets)

I. AUSSTEHENDE EINLAGEN AUF DAS GRUNDKAPITAL (Outstanding payments on subscribed share capital)

II. ANLAGEVERMÖGEN (Fixed assets and investments)
BEBAUTE GRUNDSTÜCKE (Buildings, including land)
  a. GESCHÄFTS- UND WOHNGEBÄUDE (Office buildings and dwelling houses, including land)
  b. FABRIKGEBÄUDE UND ANDERE BAULICHKEITEN (Factory and other buildings, including land)
UNBEBAUTE GRUNDSTÜCKE (Land not built upon)
MASCHINEN UND MASCHINELLE ANLAGEN (Machinery and heavy equipment)
WERKZEUGE, BETRIEBS- UND GESCHÄFTSAUSSTATTUNG (Tools, factory and office equipment)
KONZESSIONEN, PATENTE, LIZENZEN, MARKEN- UND ÄHNLICHE RECHTE (Franchises, patents, licenses, trademarks and similar rights)
BETEILIGUNGEN (Trade investments)
ANDERE WERTPAPIERE DES ANLAGEVERMÖGENS (Other securities held as long-term investments)
IM BAU BEFINDLICHE ANLAGEN (Plant under construction)
ANZAHLUNGEN AUF DAS ANLAGEVERMÖGEN (Advance payments on account of fixed assets)

III. UMLAUFVERMÖGEN (Revolving assets)
ROH-, HILFS- UND BETRIEBSSTOFFE (Raw materials and supplies)
HALBFABRIKATE (Semifinished products)
FERTIGE ERZEUGNISSE, WAREN (Finished goods, including merchandise)
WERTPAPIERE DES UMLAUFVERMÖGENS (Marketable securities)
EIGENE AKTIEN UND AKTIEN EINER HERRSCHENDEN GESELLSCHAFT (IM NENNBETRAG VON DM..) (Treasury shares, and shares in a controlling company (nominal DM..)
HYPOTHEKEN, GRUND- UND RENTENSCHULDEN (Mortgages and other land charges)
VON DER GESELLSCHAFT GELEISTETE ANZAHLUNGEN (Advances to suppliers)
FORDERUNGEN AUF GRUND VON WARENLIEFERUNGEN UND LEISTUNGEN (Accounts receivable, trade)
FORDERUNGEN AN KONZERNUNTERNEHMEN (Receivables from associated companies)
FORDERUNGEN GEMÄSS § 80 AKTIENGESETZ (Receivables from managers)
FORDERUNGEN AN AUFSICHTSRATSMITGLIEDER, SOWEIT SIE NICHT AUS GESCHÄFTEN ENTSTANDEN SIND, DIE DER BETRIEB DER GESELLSCHAFT GEWÖHNLICH MIT SICH BRINGT (Receivables from directors other than trade accounts subject to the usual trade terms)
WECHSEL (Notes receivable)
SCHECKS (Checks)
KASSENBESTAND, BUNDESBANK- UND POSTSCHECKGUTHABEN (Cash in hand, in federal bank and in postal check accounts)
ANDERE BANKGUTHABEN (Cash at other banks)
SONSTIGE FORDERUNGEN (Other receivables)

IV. POSTEN, DIE DER RECHNUNGSABGRENZUNG DIENEN (Deferred charges and prepaid expenses)

V. REINVERLUST (Net loss)
VORTRAG (Loss [Profit] c/f from preceding year)
VERLUST (GEWINN) DES GESCHÄFTSJAHRES (Loss [Profit] for the year)

PASSIVA (Liabilities and shareholders' equity)

I. GRUNDKAPITAL (Share capital [state separately each class of shares])

II. RÜCKLAGEN (Reserves)
GESETZLICHE RÜCKLAGE (Legal reserve)
ANDERE RÜCKLAGEN (Free reserves)

III. WERTBERICHTIGUNGEN ZU POSTEN DES ANLAGEVERMÖGENS (Adjustment to fixed assets)

IV. RÜCKSTELLUNGEN (Reserves for estimated liabilities and accrued expenses)

V. VERBINDLICHKEITEN (Liabilities)
ANLEIHEN (Loans [indicate whether secured])
HYPOTHEKEN, GRUND- UND RENTENSCHULDEN (Mortgages and other liabilities secured by real estate)
ANZAHLUNGEN VON KUNDEN (Customers' prepayments)
VERBINDLICHKEITEN AUF GRUND VON WARENLIEFERUNGEN UND LEISTUNGEN (Liabilities to suppliers)
VERBINDLICHKEITEN GEGENÜBER KONZERNUNTERNEHMEN (Liabilities to associated companies)
VERBINDLICHKEITEN AUS DER ANNAHME VON GEZOGENEN WECHSELN UND DER AUSSTELLUNG EIGENER WECHSEL (Notes payable)
VERBINDLICHKEITEN GEGENÜBER BANKEN (Liabilities to banks)
SONSTIGE VERBINDLICHKEITEN (Other liabilities)

VI. POSTEN, DIE DER RECHNUNGSABGRENZUNG DIENEN (Deferred income)

VII. REINGEWINN (Net profit)
VORTRAG (Profit [Loss] b/f from preceding year)
GEWINN (VERLUST) DES GESCHÄFTSJAHRES (Profit [Loss] of current year)

BILANZVERMERKE (Notes):
EVENTUALVERBINDLICHKEITEN AUS BÜRGSCHAFTEN USW (Contingent liabilities in regard to guarantees, etc.)
LASTENAUSGLEICH-VERMÖGENSABGABE (1) (Levy under the law on the equalization of burdens incidental to war and its aftermath)
  a. GEGENWARTSWERT (Capital value)
  b. VIERTELJAHRESBETRAG (Amount of quarterly instalments)

NOTE (1): This is merely an informative disclosure. According to German law, debts under the Equalization of Burdens Levy need not be capitalized as a liability.

Exhibit 5(b)

ILLUSTRATIVE INCOME STATEMENT of a GERMAN COMPANY (AKTIENGESELLSCHAFT)

GEWINN- UND VERLUSTRECHNUNG FÜR DIE ZEIT VOM ...... BIS ...... (Profit and Loss Account for the Period from ...... to ......)

UMSATZERLÖSE (Net sales) ......

ERHÖHUNG ODER VERMINDERUNG DES BESTANDES AN FERTIGEN UND HALBERTIGEN ERZEUGNISSEN (Increase or decrease of finished and semifinished products) ....

ANDERE AKTIVIERTE EIGENLEISTUNGEN (Other manufacturing expenses) ......

GESAMTLEISTUNG (Total output) ......

AUFWENDUNGEN FÜR ROH-, HILFS- UND BETRIEBSSTOFFE, FÜR DIESEN GLEICHZUSETZENDE FREMDLEISTUNGEN UND FÜR BEZOGENE WAREN (Raw materials and supplies, contracted services and purchased goods consumed in manufacturing and sales) ......

ROHERTRAG/ROHAUFWAND (Gross profit [loss]) ......

ERTRÄGE AUS GEWINNABFÜHRUNGSVERTRÄGEN (Income from profit transfer agreements) ......

ERTRÄGE AUS BETEILIGUNGEN (Income from trade investments) ......

ENTRÄGE AUS ANDEREN WERTPAPIEREN DES ANLAGEVERMÖGENS (Income from other securities held as long-term investments) ......

SONSTIGE ZINSEN UND ÄHNLICHE ERTRÄGE (Other interest and similar income) ......

ERTRÄGE AUS DEM ABGANG VON GEGENSTÄNDEN DES ANLAGEVERMÖGENS UND ZUSCHREIBUNGEN ZU GEGENSTÄNDEN DES ANLAGEVERMÖGENS (Income from the retirement and from the appraisal of fixed assets) ......

ERTRÄGE AUS DER AUFLÖSUNG VON WERTBERICHTIGUNGEN (Income from the cancellation of allowances) ......

ERTRÄGE AUS DER AUFLÖSUNG VON RÜCKTELLUNGEN (Income from the cancellation of overstated reserves for estimated liabilities and accrued expenses) ......

SONSTIGE ERTRÄGE (Other income) ......

ERTRÄGE AUS VERLUSTÜBERNAHMEVERTRÄGEN (Income from loss transfer agreements) ....
......

LÖHNE UND GEHÄLTER (Wages and salaries) ......

SOZIALE ABGABEN (Social taxes [or statutory social contributions]) ......

SOZIALE AUFWENDUNGEN, SOWEIT SIE NICHT UNTER ANDEREN POSTEN AUSZUWEISEN SIND (Fringe benefits not included elsewhere) ......

ABSCHREIBUNGEN UND WERTBERICHTIGUNGEN AUF DIE IN § 131 ABS.I A II NR 1 BIS 5 BEZEICHNETEN GEGENSTÄNDE DES ANLAGEVERMÖGENS (Depreciation and amortization of fixed assets including patents) ......

ABSCHREIBUNGEN UND WERTBERICHTIGUNGEN AUF DIE IN § 131 ABS.I A II NR 6 UND 7 BEZEICHNETEN GEGENSTÄNDE DES ANLAGEVERMÖGENS (Amounts written off investments) ......

ABSCHREIBUNGEN UND WERTBERICHTIGUNGEN AUF DIE IN § 131 ABS.I A III NR 4 BIS 16 BEZEICHNETEN GEGENSTÄNDE DES UMLAUFVERMÖGENS (Allowances for and amounts written off current assets other than inventories) ......

VERLUSTE AUS DEM ABGANG VON GEGENSTÄNDEN DES ANLAGEVERMÖGENS (Losses on the retirement of fixed assets and investments) ......

ZINSEN UND ÄHNLICHE AUFWENDUNGEN (Interest and similar expense) ......

STEUERN (Taxes)
  a. VOM EINKOMMEN, VOM ERTRAG UND VOM VERMÖGEN (On income and net assets) ......
  b. SONSTIGE (Other) ....

LASTENAUSGLEICH-VERMÖGENSABGABE (Equalization of burdens levy) ......

AUFWENDUNGEN AUS VERLUSTÜBERNAHME-VERTRÄGEN (Losses arising from loss transfer agreements) ......

SONSTIGE AUFWENDUNGEN (Other expenses) ......

AUF GRUND EINES GEWINNABFÜHRUNGSVERTRAGES ABGEFÜHRTE GEWINNE (Profits transferred to parent company under profit transfer agreements) ....

JAHRESÜBERSCHUSS/JAHRESFEHLBETRAG (Profit or loss for the period) ......

GEWINNVORTRAG/VERLUSTVORTRAG AUS DEM VORJAHR (Profit or loss brought forward from the preceding year) ......
......

ENTNAHMEN AUS RÜCKLAGEN (Release of reserves)
  1. AUS DER GESETZLICHEN RÜCKLAGE (Release of legal reserve) ......
  2. AUS EINER FREIEN RÜCKLAGE (Release of free reserves) ....

EINSTELLUNGEN IN RÜCKLAGEN (Amounts appropriated to reserves)
  a. IN DIE GESETZLICHE RÜCKLAGE (Appropriated to legal reserve) ....
  b. IN FREIE RÜCKLAGEN (Appropriated to free reserves) ....

REINGEWINN/REINVERLUST (Accumulated net profit or loss) ......

Exhibit 6(a)

ILLUSTRATIVE
BALANCE SHEET of an ITALIAN COMPANY

BILANCIO AL 31 DICEMBRE 19____
(Balance Sheet at December 31, 19____)

ATTIVO (Assets)			PASSIVO (Liabilities)		
IMMOBILIZZAZIONI (Fixed assets):			CAPITALE SOCIALE (Capital)		......
IMMOBILI (Land and buildings)	......				
IMPIANTI E MACCHINARIO (Plant and machinery)	......		RISERVE (Reserves):		
MOBILI (Furniture)	......	......	LEGALE (Legal reserve)	......	
			STRAORDINARIA FACOLTATIVA (Extraordinary reserve)	......	......
TITOLI (Investments):					
PARTECIPAZIONI (Equity investments)	......		FONDO AMMORTAMENTO DELLE IMMOBILIZZAZIONI (Depreciation reserve)		......
TITOLI A REDDITO FISSO (Fixed income securities)	......	......			
			DEBITI A SCADENZA DIFFERITA (Long-term debt)		......
MERCI (Inventories)		......	DEBITI CORRENTI (Current liabilities):		
			VERSO FORNITORI (Suppliers)	......	
CASSA (Cash on hand)		......	VERSO BANCHE (Banks)	......	
			VERSO SOCIETA COLLEGIATE (Associated companies)	......	......
CREDITI (Accounts receivable):	......				
VERSO CLIENTI (Customers)	......		RISCONTI E PARTITE VARIE (Advance payments and miscellaneous liabilities)		......
VERSO BANCHE (Banks)	......				
VERSO SOCIETA COLLEGATE (Associated companies)	......	......	UTILE DA RIPARTIRE (Profits for distribution):		
			AVANZO UTILI INDIVISI ESERCIZI PREC. (Retained earnings of previous years)	......	
RISCONTI E PARTITE VARIE (Prepaid expenses and miscellaneous)		......	UTILE DELL'ESERCIZIO (Current year's profits)	......	......
CAUZIONI DEGLI ADMINISTRATORI (Directors' bonds)		......	CAUZIONI DEGLI AMMINISTRATORI (Directors' bonds)		......
ALTRI CONTI D'ORDINE (Contra accounts)		......	ALTRI CONTI D'ORDINE (Contra accounts)		......
		......			......

Exhibit 6(b)

ILLUSTRATIVE
INCOME STATEMENT of an ITALIAN COMPANY
CONTO PERDITE E PROFITTI
(Statement of Profit and Loss)

COSTI (Cost)				RICAVI (Income)	
RIMANENZE INIZIALI (Opening balances):				RICAVI VENDITE (Sales)	. . . . . .
MERCI (Inventories)	. . . . . .				
DIVERSE: SALDO ATTIVO RISCONTI (Miscellaneous: Advance payments)	. . . . . .	. . . . . .		REDDITI IMMOBILIARI (Income from real property)	. . . . . .
ACQUISTI (Purchases)	. . . . . .				
COSTI ED ONERI VARI DI LAVORO (Labor costs and related expenses)	. . . . . .			PROVENTI FINANZIARI (Income on investments):	
				DIVIDENDI SU PARTECIPAZIONI E CEDOLE (Dividends and interest)	. . . . . .
COSTI DIVERSI DI ESERCIZIO (Miscellaneous operating costs)	. . . . . .				
ONERI TRIBUTARI (Taxes)	. . . . . .			PROVENTI DIVERSI (Miscellaneous income)	. . . . . .
ONERI FINANZIARI (Financial expenses):					
INTERESSI (Interest)	. . . . . .				
QUOTA AMMORTAMENTO COSTO E DISAGGIO EMISSIONE MUTUI OBBLIGAZIONARI E IPOTECARI (Amortization and discount expenses on debenture and mortgage loan issues)	. . . . . .	. . . . . .	. . . . . .		
AMMORTAMENTO DELLE IMMOBILIZZAZIONI (Depreciation on fixed assets)		. . . . . .			
MENO, RIMANENZE FINALI (Less, Closing balances):					
MERCI (Inventories)	. . . . . .				
DIVERSE: SALDO ATTIVO RISCONTI (Miscellaneous: Advanced payments)	. . . . . .	. . . . . .			
		. . . . . .			
UTILE DELL'ESERCIZIO (Net profit for the year)		. . . . . .			
		. . . . . .			. . . . . .

Exhibit 7(a)

ILLUSTRATIVE
BALANCE SHEET of a NETHERLANDS COMPANY
BALANS PER 31 DECEMBER
Balance Sheet as at December 31

DUURZAME PRODUCTIEMIDDELEN NA AFSCHRIJVINGEN (Land, buildings, plant and machinery less depreciation) ......

IMMATERIELE ACTIVA (Intangible assets) ......

DEELNEMINGEN IN ANDERE ONDERNEMINGEN EN VORDERINGEN DAAROP (Investments in and amounts due from associated companies) ......

OVERIGE VASTGELEDGE MIDDELEN (Other long-term assets) ......

VOORRADEN [Inventories (stocks)] ......

VORDERINGEN (Accounts receivable, prepaid expenses) ......

LIQUIDE MIDDELEN (Cash in hand and at banks, short-term investments) ......

......

EIGEN VERMOGEN (Capital and reserves):

    AANDELEN KAPITAAL (Share capital) ......

    AGIO RESERVE (Paid-in surplus) ......

    VERMOGENSVERSCHILLEN DOOR HERWAARDERING (Differences in net worth due to revaluations) ......

    WINSTRESERVE (Retained earnings) ....

SCHULDEN OP LANGE TERMIJN (Long-term liabilities) ......

VOORZIENINGEN (Provisions, taxation equalization reserve) ......

SCHULDEN OP KORTE TERMIJN (Current liabilities) ......

TE VERDELEN WINST (Profit available for distribution) ......

......

Exhibit 7(b)

ILLUSTRATIVE

INCOME STATEMENT of a NETHERLANDS COMPANY
WINST-EN VERLIESREKENING OVER HET BOEKJAAR
(Profit and Loss Account for the Year)

OMZET (Sales) ......

KOSTPRIJS VAN DE OMZET (Cost of sales) ......

WAARIN BEGREPEN: (Including):
 AFSCHRIJVINGEN (Depreciation) ......
 OVERIGE KOSTEN (Other costs) ....

BEDRIJFSRESULTAAT (Operating income) ......

OVERIGE BATEN (Other income)

DEELNEMINGEN }
BELEGGINGEN } (Investments) ......
INKOMEN (Income) ......
KOERSWINSTEN (Exchange profits) ....

ONTVANGEN RESP. BEREKENDE INTREST
 (Interest received) ......
DIVERSEN (Sundry) ....

OVERIGE LASTEN (Other charges)

BETAALDE INTREST (Interest paid) ......
DIVERSEN (Sundry) ....

WINST VÓÓR AFTREK VAN BELASTING
 (Profit before taxes) ......

VOORZIENING VÓÓR BELASTING OVER DE
 WINST (Provision for taxes on profit) ......

WINST (Profit) ......

VOORSTEL TOT WINSTBESTEMMING (Proposed appropriation) ......

Exhibit 8(a)

ILLUSTRATIVE
BALANCE SHEET of a SWEDISH COMPANY
BALANSRÄKNING DEN 31 DECEMBER 19——
(Balance Sheet at December 31, 19——)

TILLGÅNGAR (Assets)

OMSÄTTNINGSTILLGÅNGAR (Current assets)
KASSA, BANK OCH REMISSOR PÅ VÄG (Cash, bank and remittances in transit) ......
FRÄMMANDE VÄXLAR (-VARU) FRÅN UTOMSTÅENDE [Bills receivable (-trade) from 3rd parties] ......
FRÄMMANDE VÄXLAR (-VARU) FRÅN DOTTERBOLAG [Bills receivable (-trade) from subsidiaries] ......
VARUFORDRINGAR (Trade debtors) ......
ÖVRIGA FORDRINGAR (Sundry debtors) ......
FORDRINGAR HOS DOTTERBOLAG (Receivables from subsidiaries) ......
FORDRINGAR HOS STYRELSELEDAMÖTER M.FL. (Receivables from members of the board, etc.) ......
OBLIGATIONER OCH ANDRA VÄRDEPAPPER (Bonds and other securities) ......
AKTIER OCH ANDELAR I UTOMSTÅENDE BOLAG (SPEC.) (Shares and parts in nonassociated companies [spec.]) ......
VARULAGER (Stock) ....

SPÄRRADE LIKVIDA TILLGÅNGAR (Blocked liquid assets) ......

ANLÄGGNINGSTILLGÅNGAR (Fixed assets)
FRÄMMANDE VÄXLAR (FÖRLAGSVÄXLAR) FRÅN UTOMSTÅENDE [Bills (long-term) from 3rd parties] ......
FRÄMMANDE VÄXLAR (FÖRLAGSVÄXLAR) FRÅN DOTTERBOLAG [Bills (long-term) from subsidiaries] ......
AKTIER OCH ANDELAR I UTOMSTÅENDE FÖRETAG (SPEC.) (Shares and parts in nonassociated companies [spec.]) ......
AKTIER OCH ANDELAR I DOTTERBOLAG (SPEC.) (Shares and parts in subsidiaries [spec.]) ......
ANDRA VÄRDEPAPPER OCH FORDRINGAR (Sundry securities and debts) ......
FORDRINGAR HOS DOTTERBOLAG (Long-term claims on subsidiaries) ......
MASKINER OCH INVENTARIER (Machinery and equipment) ......
FABRIKSFASTIGHETER, KONTORSFASTIGHETER, ETC., (SPEC.) (Factory buildings, office buildings, etc., [spec.]) ......
ORGANISATIONSKOSTNADER (Organization costs) ......
PATENT, LICENSER, VARUMÄRKEN, ETC., (Patents, licenses, trademarks, etc.) ......
AFFÄRSVÄRDE (Goodwill) ....

FORDRINGAR PÅ GRUND AV AKTIETECKNING (Claims due to subscribed shares) ......
......

SKULDER OCH EGET KAPITAL (Liabilities and capital)

KORTFRISTIGA SKULDER (Short-term liabilities)
EGNA ACCEPTER TILL UTOMSTÅENDE (Acceptances to 3rd parties) ......
EGNA ACCEPTER TILL DOTTERBOLAG (Acceptances to subsidiaries) ......
SKULDER TILL DOTTERBOLAG (Liabilities to subsidiaries) ......
LEVERANTÖRSKULDER (Liabilities to suppliers) ......
ÖVRIGA KORTFRISTIGA SKULDER (Sundry short-term liabilities) ......

SKATTESKULDER (Taxes payable)

LÅNGFRISTIGA SKULDER (Long-term liabilities)
SKULDER TILL DOTTERBOLAG (Liabilities to subsidiaries) ......
ÖVRIGA LÅNGFRISTIGA SKULDER (INTECKNINGSLÅN, BANKLÅN, ETC.) (Sundry long-term liabilities, mortgages, bank loans, etc.) ......
PENSIONSFONDER (SPEC.) (Pension funds [spec.]) ......
OBLIGATIONSLÅN (Loans of bonds) ......
FÖRLAGSLÅN (Loans of debentures) ......

*VÄRDEMINSKNINGSKONTO (Depreciation reserve) ......
*LAGERREGLERINGSKONTO (Inventory reserve) ......
INVESTERINGSFONDER (Investment funds) ......

EGET KAPITAL (Capital)
AKTIEKAPITAL (Share capital) ......
RESERVFOND (Reserve fund) ......
SKULDREGLERINGSFOND (Debt adjustment fund) ......
DISPOSITIONSFOND OCH ANDRA FRIA FONDER (Fund at disposal and other funds) ......
BALANSERADE VINSTMEDEL (Balanced profits) ......
ÅRETS VINST ELLER FÖRLUST (VID FÖRLUST •/. -TECKEN) [Profit or loss of the year (at loss •/. -mark)] ......
......

STÄLLDA PANTER: (SPEC). (Assets pledged: [spec.]) ......
ANSVARSFÖRBINDELSER: (SPEC.) (Contingent liabilities: [spec.]) ......
VINSTDISPOSITION ENL. BESLUT Å BOLAGSSTÄMMA DEN ...... (Distribution of profit according to resolution of the meeting of the shareholders as per ......) ......

*Generally these reserves are deducted from the related asset.

Exhibit 8(b)

**ILLUSTRATIVE
INCOME STATEMENT OF A SWEDISH COMPANY**

VINST- OCH FÖRLUSTRÄKNING FÖR ÅR 19⎯
(Profit and Loss Account for the Year 19⎯)

INTÄKTER (Income):

RÖRELSEN (Gross operating profit) . . . . . .

UTDELNING FRÅN DOTTERBOLAG (Dividends from subsidiaries) . . . . . .

UTDELNING FRÅN ANDRA BOLAG (Other dividends) . . . . . .

RÄNTOR FRÅN DOTTERBOLAG (Interest from subsidiaries) . . . . . .

ÖVRIGA RÄNTOR (Other interests) . . . . . .

VINST Å FÖRSÅLDA FASTIGHETER (Gain from sales of estate) . . . . . .

VINST Å FÖRSÅLDA MASKINER OCH INVENTARIER (Gain from sales of machinery and equipment) . . . . . .

VINST Å FÖRSÅLDA AKTIER (Gain from sales of shares) . . . . . .

. . . . . .

KOSTNADER (Expenditure):

FÖRVALTNINGSKOSTNADER (General administrative costs) . . . . . .

RÄNTOR TILL DOTTERBOLAG (Interest to subsidiaries) . . . . . .

RÄNTOR TILL PENSIONSSTIFTELSER (Interest to pension funds) . . . . . .

ÖVRIGA RÄNTOR (Other interests) . . . . . .

SKATTER (Taxes) . . . . . .

AVSKRIVNINGAR (Depreciation):
  BYGGNADER (Buildings) . . . . . .
  MASKINER OCH INVENTARIER (Machinery and equipment) . . . . . .
  AKTIER (Shares) . . . . . .

AVSÄTTNING TILL PENSIONSSTIFTELSER (Pension funds) . . . . . .

AVSÄTTNING TILL INVESTERINGSFOND FÖR RÖRELSE (Business investment reserve) . . . . . .

. . . . . .

VINST FÖR ÅRET (Net profit of the year) . . . . . .

Exhibit 9(a)

ILLUSTRATIVE
BALANCE SHEET of a UNITED KINGDOM COMPANY
BALANCE SHEET, 31st DECEMBER, 19___

Preceding Year		Authorized £	Issued and Fully Paid £	Preceding Year		Cost or Valuation £	Accumulated Depreciation £	£
......	SHARE CAPITAL	......	......	......	FIXED ASSETS	......	......	......
......	CAPITAL RESERVES		......	......	TRADE INVESTMENTS			....
......	REVENUE RESERVES		......	......	CURRENT ASSETS			....
	Total Capital and Reserves		......	......	EXPENDITURE CARRIED FORWARD			......
	FUTURE TAXATION (See D. 1.)		......					
......	LOAN CAPITAL		......					
......	CURRENT LIABILITIES AND PROVISIONS		......		.... } Directors			
£			£	£				£ ......

Necessary notes to financial statements would appear on a separate page. The notes would describe the bases of determining the carrying values of items such as fixed assets and inventories, and would also show details supporting the more significant captions in the financial statements to the extent that this information is not presented on the face of the statements.

Exhibit 9(b)

ILLUSTRATIVE
INCOME STATEMENT of a UNITED KINGDOM COMPANY

PROFIT and LOSS ACCOUNT for the year ended 31st DECEMBER, 19——

Preceding Year £		£	£	£
......	TRADING PROFIT BEFORE TAXATION			......
	(Note)			
	After Charging			
......	Emoluments of directors	......		
......	Pension paid to former director	......		
	Compensation paid to director and former director	......		
......			......	
......	Depreciation		......	
......	Interest on loan capital (gross)		......	
......	Auditor's remuneration and expenses		......	
	And Crediting			
......	Investment income		......	
	Less			
......	UNITED KINGDOM TAXATION ON THE PROFIT FOR THE YEAR			......
......	TRADING PROFIT AFTER TAXATION			......
......	EXCEPTIONAL OR NONRECURRENT ITEMS			......
......	NET PROFIT AVAILABLE FOR APPROPRIATION			......
......	PROFIT UNAPPROPRIATED, BEGINNING OF YEAR			......
......	AMOUNTS TRANSFERRED TO RESERVES			......
......	DIVIDENDS PAID OR PROPOSED (NET OF TAX)			......
......				......
......	PROFIT UNAPPROPRIATED, END OF YEAR			......

NOTE: The information set out in the box is required to be stated separately under the 8th Schedule of the Companies Act, 1948; however, auditors' remuneration need not be disclosed if it is approved in the Annual General Meeting.

Exhibit 10(b)

ILLUSTRATIVE
PROFIT AND LOSS ACCOUNT of a SOUTH AFRICAN COMPANY
for the year ended 31 December, 19—

Operating profits		. . . . . .
Add:		
Income from trade investments	. . . . . .	
Surplus on disposal of fixed assets	. . . . . .	. . . . . .
Deduct:		
Depreciation	. . . . . .	
Provision for replacement and renewal of machinery	. . . . . .	
Directors' emoluments	. . . . . .	. . . . . .
Trading profit		. . . . . .
Add:		
Dividends received	. . . . . .	
Interest received	. . . . . .	. . . . . .
		. . . . . .
Deduct, Interest paid:		
On fixed loans	. . . . . .	
On other borrowed monies	. . . . . .	. . . . . .
Profit before taxation		. . . . . .
Taxation for the current year		. . . . . .
Net profit after taxation		. . . . . .
Add, Unappropriated profits, beginning of year		. . . . . .
		. . . . . .
Deduct, Transfers to reserves:		
Capital reserve	. . . . . .	
Revenue reserves:		
General reserve	. . . . . .	
Contingency reserve	. . . . . .	
Machinery replacement reserve	. . . . . .	. . . . . .
		. . . . . .
Dividends:		
On preference shares	. . . . . .	
On ordinary shares:		
Paid	. . . . . .	
Proposed	. . . . . .	. . . . . .
Unappropriated profits carried forward to next year		. . . . . .

Exhibit 10(a)

ILLUSTRATIVE
BALANCE SHEET of a SOUTH AFRICAN COMPANY
BALANCE SHEET at 31 December, 19___

Share capital:
Authorized and issued:
    100,000 shares, 5% cumulative preference shares R 2 each ......

    1,000,000 ordinary shares of 50 cents each ....

Capital reserves:
Share premium account ......

Capital reserve account ....

Revenue reserves:
General reserve ......

Contingency reserve ......

Machinery replacement and renewal reserve ......

Unappropriated profit ....

    Total capital and reserves ......

Long-term loans:
Secured by first mortgage bonds on freehold property ......

Current liabilities:

Trade and other creditors ......

Accrued expenses ......

Short-term loans ......

Taxation ......

Dividend (interim) declared and payable on ordinary shares ......

Proposed final dividend on ordinary shares ....

    Total ......

Fixed assets:
Land, buildings, machinery and equipment, at cost ......
    Less, Accumulated depreciation ....

Investments in other companies:
Quoted shares at cost (at market quotations, R......),
    less amounts written off ......
Other shares at cost, less amounts written off ......
Loans and current accounts ....

Current assets:
Stocks and stores on hand ......
Debtors and prepayments ......
Cash on deposit and at bank ....

    Total ......

Details of balance sheet items, movement in reserves, directors' remuneration, and other required disclosures are given in attached notes to financial statements.